CONTENTS

THE CRAFTWORKER'S YEAR BOOK

Revised Edition

ISBN 1 902874 05 6

WRITE ANGLE PRESS
16 Holm Oak Drive
Madeley
Crewe CW3 9HR
ENGLAND

Telephone: +44 (0)1782 750986
E-mail: charles.wallin@btclick.com

Printed in Great Britain by
Crewe Colour Printers Ltd

FOREWORD

Welcome to the Silver Jubilee edition of The Craftworker's Year Book. First off, our thanks must go to all the readers and advertisers who have supported the title over the last 25 years and also to Stephen and Jean Lance at Lance Publications for coming up with the idea in the first place and seeing the book through its early years.

SILVER JUBILEE 25 YEARS Edition

Our aim at Write Angle Press this year, as in all others, has been to both improve and expand the range of information that we are able to provide.

There are a few items worth noting. The special article (overleaf) from the Crafts Council is also the result of an anniversary - it's 10 years since the last survey of this type in British crafts - and is included not least because it throws up some interesting findings and comments that we're sure will provoke a variety of responses.

On a far more workaday note, in our second section we're now showing the months in which each organiser is active, meaning that you can more easily cross-reference back to the diary.

Aside from that, with an enthusiastic response from suppliers, we have been able to more than double the size of that section of the book while this year's edition also sees the most detailed information that we've so far gathered together on both courses and publications.

Many of the changes and improvements that we've made over the years have been the direct result of comments from readers and we continue to invite your correspondence at any time. Our contact details are on the opposite page. Of course we don't adopt every suggestion - we've always resisted the idea of including what we think is unreliable footfall data for craft fairs, for instance - but generally speaking if we think an idea really adds to the book's usefulness and we have the resources to incorporate it, we will.

To those both new to the craft world and already well established in it, we wish you inspiration and success in equal measure throughout 2005. We look forward to serving the craft community for another 25 years and we'll endeavour to take you all along with us on the next leg of this trip.

Making it in the 21st Century

a socio-economic survey of crafts activity in England and Wales, 2002-2003

by Louise Taylor, Director of the Crafts Council

For the Crafts Council, 2004 was a dynamic year that saw the launch of a number of new initiatives and attractions. Among these major developments were the opening of the inaugural COLLECT, the international art fair for contemporary objects, and the online launch of the Crafts Council's visual database Photostore, enabling worldwide access to over 50,000 images of contemporary craft objects.

But perhaps one of the most significant areas of activity for 2004 was the release of the results of the Crafts Council's socio-economic survey of craft activity, *Making it in the 21st Century*, which is the first report released on the craft sector for 10 years.

Making it in the 21st Century was prepared in partnership with Arts Council England and the Arts Council of Wales. The Crafts Council used the National Register of Makers as well as approaching guilds and societies to survey over 2,000 makers using a detailed questionnaire. The findings of the survey reflect an exceptional dynamism and commitment amongst makers and reveal a real passion for the crafts, balanced with a keen entrepreneurial spirit.

Presented at a seminar at the Royal College of Art in April, the report highlighted some truly significant findings about the crafts sector, which is now estimated to be worth over £800 million - double the estimated value of the sector in 1994. The survey looked at all aspects of craft from textiles, ceramics and jewellery to lettering and fashion accessories. By analysing who works in craft, where they work and how they work, the report aims to give direction and support to this vibrant and burgeoning element of our society and economy.

Interestingly, self-employed female entrepreneurs emerged as the driving force behind the sector. Crafts have become the only art form with more women practitioners than men, with 67% of makers being female.

Other stereotypes of craft were overturned: surprisingly craft is no longer restricted to rural areas, with significant activity taking place in cities. It is also attracting a younger, more professional following with more makers setting up businesses in their 20s and nearly two-thirds having trained on full-time art/design courses. Encouragingly, survival rates for businesses have risen with 58% of makers in business for at least a decade and nearly 30% of enterprises trading for more than 20 years - a surprising statistic given the uncertainty of the country's economy.

But perhaps one of the most significant findings was related to lifestyle satisfaction. Despite comparatively low financial returns, a staggering 94% of those questioned reported job and

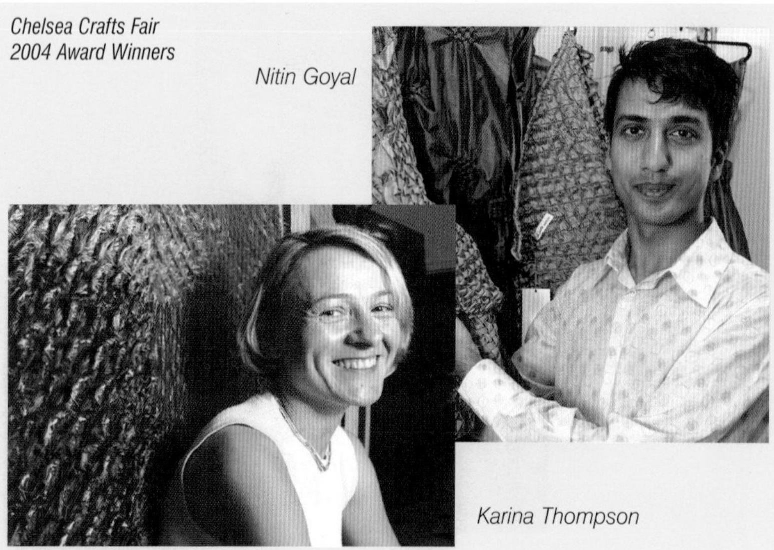

Chelsea Crafts Fair 2004 Award Winners

Nitin Goyal

Karina Thompson

lifestyle satisfaction. This is particularly revealing at a time when there is so much social pressure to follow a fast-track career path. Perhaps today's overworked society is beginning to see the benefits of a more balanced, fulfilled lifestyle in favour of high financial reward? Certainly, a large part of this satisfaction comes from the realisation of individual creative potential and the 'buzz' that this can generate.

What is also interesting is that craft businesses are revealed as model businesses: they are smaller, have sustained growth and flexibility and are family friendly – all the things that business consultants are being asked to deliver. *Making it in the 21st Century* clearly illustrates the crucial role of the crafts in the country's mixed economy, with public money invested in the sector contributing significantly to cultural and commercial enterprises.

This is an invaluable report for the Crafts Council that will inform the organisation's ongoing strategy to provide the best economic and creative support for the future of the crafts. No other survey looks at individual design businesses or artists with such a level of scrutiny, a fact that we have to celebrate.

This report and survey could serve as a 'model' for those who work in other creative industries. Speaking at the launch seminar, the then Minister of State for the Arts, Estelle Morris MP, spoke at length about this, commenting about the importance of crafts and its heritage and the position of the sector within the creative industries: "I think if you play it right your time has come," she said.

Over the last few years, we have noticed a surge in interest in the handmade, the distinctive, the 'one-off' - the fascination of buying into individuality that somehow fits in a greater desire for a designer-lifestyle. The Crafts Council has been responding to this demand with events like COLLECT and Chelsea Crafts Fair and through the launch of Photostore Online, enabling more universal access to contemporary craft and the commissioning process.

Such initiatives have, without doubt, contributed to the economic boom in the craft industry.

Kamini Chauhan

Anna Lorenz

Chelsea Crafts Fair 2004 Award Winners

Photos by John Chase

There is an increasing sophistication of craft makers and buyers, which has resulted in the old-fashioned image of craft finally being dispelled, highlighting the importance of craft as a dynamic art form.

As Sir Christopher Frayling, Chair of Arts Council England, commented so pertinently: "This report puts a big dent in some of the stereotypes surrounding the crafts in the 21st century; it reveals that the crafts are deeply embedded in the contemporary creative industries, that craftspeople are becoming increasingly entrepreneurial, and that on the whole the crafts aren't rural. It is a fascinating and timely document".

A full copy of the report has now been published and a summary can be accessed via the Crafts Council's website at: www.craftscouncil.org.uk

CRAFT SHOWS, FAIRS, FESTIVALS AND EXHIBITIONS

Details of around 1500 events are listed in this diary section and while no effort is spared in the accurate preparation of this listing, mistakes can occur and details may be subject to change. We accept information submitted to us in good faith and we cannot accept any liability for loss, financial or otherwise, that may occur as a result of any error or omission in this work. **We strongly recommend that readers contemplating a visit to any events listed here contact the organiser before starting out to be sure that both date and venue remain unchanged.** The organisers' full details are contained in the next section.

Jan 1 — **CRAFTS AT THE FORUM/The Forum, Norwich, Norfolk**
Norfolk Events

Jan 8-9 — **BLAKEMERE CRAFT FAIR**
Blakemere Craft Centre, Chester Road, Sandiway, Northwich, Cheshire
Blakemere Craft Centre

Jan 9-12 — **CUMBREX 2005/Belsfield/Burnside Hotels, Bowness-on-Winderemere, Cumbria** (trade only event)
Northern Exhibitions

Jan 12-17 — **COLLECT – INTERNATIONAL ART FAIR FOR CONTEMPORARY OBJECTS/Victoria & Albert Museum, London**
Crafts Council

Jan 15 — **CIRENCESTER CRAFTSMAN'S MARKET**
Corn Hall, Market Place, Cirencester, Glos
Cirencester Craftsman's Market

Jan 15 — **CRAFTS AT THE FORUM/The Forum, Norwich, Norfolk**
Norfolk Events

Jan 15-16 — **BLAKEMERE CRAFT FAIR**
Blakemere Craft Centre, Chester Road, Sandiway, Northwich, Cheshire
Blakemere Craft Centre

Jan 15-Feb 27 — **GET FRESH 2 – EMERGING SOUTH WEST MAKERS**
Devon Guild of Craftsmen, Riverside Mill, Bovey Tracey, Devon
Devon Guild of Craftsmen

Jan 16-19 — **YORKSHIRE & EAST COAST GIFTS TRADE FAIR**
Southlands Hotel, West Street, Scarborough, North Yorks
Northern Exhibitions

Jan 20-23 — **STITCH & CREATIVE CRAFTS SHOW**
Sandown Park Exhibition Centre, Esher, Surrey
Nationwide Exhibitions (UK) Ltd

Jan 21-23 — **CHILFORD HALLS HOME DESIGN & INTERIORS EXHIBITION**
Linton, Cambs
Buckingham Events

Jan 21-23 **LONDON MODEL ENGINEERING EXHIBITION/Alexandra Palace, Alexandra Palace Way, Wood Green, London N22**
Meridienne Exhibitions Ltd

Jan 22-23 **BLAKEMERE CRAFT FAIR**
Blakemere Craft Centre, Chester Road, Sandiway, Northwich, Cheshire
Blakemere Craft Centre

Jan 23-26 **SCOTLAND'S INTERNATIONAL TRADE FAIR/SECC, Glasgow** (trade event)
Trade Fairs (Scotland) Ltd

Jan 23-26 **WALES SPRING FAIR/North Wales Conference Centre, The Promenade, Llandudno, Conwy** (trade event)
Wales Craft Council

Jan 28-30 **WOBURN ABBEY HOME DESIGN & INTERIORS EXHIBITION**
Woburn, Beds
Buckingham Events

Jan 29-30 **BLAKEMERE CRAFT FAIR/Blakemere Craft Centre, Chester Road, Sandiway, Northwich, Cheshire**
Blakemere Craft Centre

Jan 30 **KINVER CRAFT SHOW**
Community Centre, A449/A458, Kinver, nr Stourbridge
Central Promotions

Jan 30 **TEDDY BEAR & DOLL FAIR/North Stafford Hotel, Station Road, Stoke-on-Trent, Staffs**
Cherish Events

Feb 4-6 **STITCH & CREATIVE CRAFTS SHOW**
G-MEX Centre, Manchester
Nationwide Exhibitions (UK) Ltd

Feb 5 **CIRENCESTER CRAFTSMAN'S MARKET**
Corn Hall, Market Place, Cirencester, Glos
Cirencester Craftsman's Market

Feb 5 **CRAFTS AT THE FORUM**
The Forum, Norwich, Norfolk
Norfolk Events

Feb 5-6 **CRAFT FAIR/Victoria Halls, Hartley Wintney, Hants**
Arts & Craft Fairs

Feb 5-6 **BLAKEMERE CRAFT FAIR**
Blakemere Craft Centre, Chester Road, Sandiway, Northwich, Cheshire
Blakemere Craft Centre

Feb 5-6 **CRAFT FAIR/Market House, Hawes, Wensleydale, North Yorks**
Wensleydale Craft Fairs

Feb 6	**CRAFT FAIR** **BAE Marconi Club, Gardiners Way, Gardiners Lane South, Basildon, Essex** Hallmark Craft Fairs
Feb 6	**MILLENNIUM CRAFTS & GIFTS/Community Centre, Lyndhurst, Hants** Millennium Crafts & Gifts
Feb 6	**CRAFT FAIR/Belbroughton Recreation Centre, Belbroughton, Worcs** Shirecrafts
Feb 11-13	**CREATIVE STITCHES & HOBBYCRAFTS** **Brighton Centre, Brighton, East Sussex** ICHF
Feb 12	**DOLLS HOUSE & MINIATURES + CRAFTS/Somerset Hall, High Street, Portishead, North Somerset** Dolls House, Miniatures & Crafts
Feb 12-13	**BLAKEMERE CRAFT FAIR** **Blakemere Craft Centre, Chester Road, Sandiway, Northwich, Cheshire** Blakemere Craft Centre
Feb 12-13	**PRE ST VALENTINE'S WEEKEND AT PLANT INFORMATION HOUSE** **Dobbies Garden World, Nuneaton Road, B4111 Mancetter, nr Atherstone, Warks** Shirecrafts
Feb 12-13	**CRAFTS AT FORT PURBROOK** **Fort Purbrook, Portsdown Hill, Cosham, Hants** Woodland Crafts
Feb 12-13	**ARTS & CRAFT FAIR** **St William College, York, North Yorks (Viking Festival Week)** Yorkshire Craft Fairs
Feb 13	**ARTS & CRAFT FAYRE/Hartington Village Hall, Hartington, Derbys** Biddulph Arts & Craft Fayres
Feb 14	**OUTDOOR STALLS AT VALENTINE LAMP LIGHTING** **Catherine Street + Catherine Hill, Frome, Somerset** Frome Town Centre Promotions Group
Feb 15-17	**CRAFT HOBBY & STITCH TRADE SHOW/NEC, Birmingham** ICHF
Feb 18-20	**COTSWOLD CREATIVE CRAFTS SHOW/Centaur Centre, Cheltenham, Glos** Nationwide Exhibitions (UK) Ltd
Feb 19	**CIRENCESTER CRAFTSMAN'S MARKET/Corn Hall, Market Place, Cirencester, Glos** Cirencester Craftsman's Market
Feb 19	**CRAFTS AT THE FORUM/The Forum, Norwich, Norfolk** Norfolk Events

Feb 19-20	**BLAKEMERE CRAFT FAIR** **Blakemere Craft Centre, Chester Road, Sandiway, Northwich, Cheshire** Blakemere Craft Centre
Feb 19-20	**CRAFT FAYRE/North Stafford Hotel, Station Road, Stoke-on-Trent, Staffs** Cheshire Fayre
Feb 19-20	**CRAFT FAIR/Woodgreen, Godmanchester, Cambs** Kingfisher Promotions
Feb 20	**CRAFT FAIR/Shrigley Hall Hotel, Pott Shrigley, Macclesfield, Cheshire** Creative Crafts Association
Feb 20	**EAST MIDLANDS DOLL FAIR/Kelham Hall, Kelham, Newark, Notts** East Midlands Doll Fairs
Feb 20	**CRAFT FAIR/Blackwater Leisure Centre, Park Drive, Maldon, Essex** Hallmark Craft Fairs
Feb 20	**MILLENNIUM CRAFTS & GIFTS/Community Centre, Lyndhurst, Hants** Millennium Crafts & Gifts
Feb 20	**REDESMERE CRAFTS/Siddington Village Hall, A34, nr Macclesfield, Cheshire** Redesmere Crafts Association
Feb 20	**GOODYEAR PAVILION CRAFT FAIR** **Goodyear Pavilion, Stafford Road, Oxley, Wolverhampton** Shirecrafts
Feb 20	**ARTS & CRAFT FAIR/Bankfield Hotel, Bingley, West Yorks** Yorkshire Craft Fairs
Feb 22-27	**MAURTRAID CRAFTSHOW/The Centre MK in Middleton Hall, Milton Keynes Shopping Centre, Bucks** Maurtraid Craftshows
Feb 25-27	**YOU CAN MAKE IT: CRAFT SUPPLIES SHOW/Thorpe Park, nr Chertsey, Surrey** ETES Ltd
Feb 26	**CITY OF WELLS SPRING CRAFT FAIR/Town Hall, Market Square, Wells, Somerset** West Country Craft Fairs
Feb 26-27	**BRENTWOOD CRAFT & GIFT SHOW/Brentwood Centre, Doddinghurst Road, Brentwood, Essex** Aztec Events
Feb 26-27	**BLAKEMERE CRAFT FAIR/Blakemere Craft Centre, Chester Road, Sandiway, Northwich, Cheshire** Blakemere Craft Centre

Feb 26-27 **STAFFORD CRAFT SHOW/County Showground, A518 Uttoxeter Road, Stafford**
Central Promotions

Feb 26-27 **SHIRECRAFTS CRAFT WEEKEND/venue tba**
Shirecrafts

Feb 27 **CRAFT FAIR/Floral Hall, The Promenade, Southport**
Creative Crafts Association

Feb 27 **TYNESIDE DOLLS' HOUSE & MINIATURES FAIR/Lancastrian Suite, Federation Brewery, Dunston, Gateshead, Tyne & Wear**
Dolly Domain Fairs

Feb 27 **ART, CRAFT & GIFT FAIR/Village Hall, Woburn, Beds**
Falcon Fairs

Feb 27 **LAUDERDALE HOUSE ARTS & CRAFTS**
Lauderdale House, Waterlow Park, Highgate Hill, London N6
Lauderdale Arts & Crafts

Mar 1 **MILLENNIUM CRAFTS & GIFTS/Community Centre, Lyndhurst, Hants**
Millennium Crafts & Gifts

Mar 3-6 **CREATIVE STITCHES/SECC, Glasgow**
ICHF

Mar 4-6 **CRAFT FAIR/Rivendell Garden Centre, Mill Lane, Widnes, Cheshire**
Creative Crafts Association

Mar 5 **CIRENCESTER CRAFTSMAN'S MARKET**
Corn Hall, Market Place, Cirencester, Glos
Cirencester Craftsman's Market

Mar 5 **ART, CRAFT & GIFT FAIR/Town Hall, Brackley, Northants**
Falcon Fairs

Mar 5 **CRAFTS FOR MOTHER'S DAY/Commemoration Hall, Huntingdon, Cambs**
Huntingdon Craft Market

Mar 5 **ARTS & CRAFT FAIR/Town Hall, Stokesley, nr Middlesbrough**
Yorkshire Craft Fairs

Mar 5-6 **BLAKEMERE CRAFT FAIR/Blakemere Craft Centre, Chester Road, Sandiway, Northwich, Cheshire**
Blakemere Craft Centre

Mar 5-6 **CRAFT & GARDEN FAIR AT CANFORD PARK**
Magna Road, Canford Magna, nr Wimborne, Dorset
Craft Carnival

Mar 5-6 **MINIATURA/National Exhibition Centre, Birmingham**
Miniatura

information
inspiration
ideas
for craftspeople
Every month you will find the most up to date information on how and where to sell your work. Future issues will contain sections on:
Craft Fair Organisers,
Craft Supplies,
Craft Galleries,
Crafts on the Web,
and Courses & Workshops.
Plus when you subscribe you will be able to access all the latest information about shows and suppliers from our website 24 hours a day, 7 days a week.
To see the latest issue, order a single copy or subscribe go to:
www.craftsman-magazine.com
PO Box5, Driffield
East Yorkshire
YO25 8JD
Tel: 01377 255213
Fax: 01377 255730

Mar 5-6 **MOTHERS DAY WEEKEND OF CRAFTS (MARQUEE)**
Ullesthorpe Garden Centre, Lutterworth, Leics
Shirecrafts

Mar 5-6 **CRAFT FAIR/Market House, Hawes, Wensleydale, North Yorks**
Wensleydale Craft Fairs

Mar 6 **CRAFT FAIR/Rushden & Diamonds FC Sports Centre, Nene Park, Irthlingborough, Northants**
DK Fairs

Mar 6 **ART, CRAFT & GIFT FAIR/Village Hall, Denham, Bucks**
Falcon Fairs

Mar 6 **CRAFT FAIR/Clwyd Theatre Cymru, Mold, Flintshire**
Gwynedd & Clwyd Association of Craftworkers

Mar 6 **CRAFT & GIFT EVENT/Balmer Lawn Hotel, Brockenhurst, Hants**
IGF Marketing

Mar 11-13 **HAGLEY HALL HOME DESIGN & INTERIORS EXHIBITION/Stourbridge, West Midlands**
Buckingham Events

Mar 11-13 **INSPIRATIONAL HOME & GARDEN EXHIBITION**
Hanbury Hall, Droitwich, Worcs
South West Events Ltd

Mar 11-Apr 24 **BIG HAND LITTLE HAND EXHIBITION – HIGHLIGHTING EDUCATIONAL WORK/Devon Guild of Craftsmen, Riverside Mill, Bovey Tracey, Devon**
Devon Guild of Craftsmen

Mar 12-13 **BLAKEMERE CRAFT FAIR**
Blakemere Craft Centre, Chester Road, Sandiway, Northwich, Cheshire
Blakemere Craft Centre

Mar 12-13 **CRAFT FAIR/The Maltings, Ely, Cambs**
Kingfisher Promotions

Mar 12-13 **CONTEMPORARY TEXTILES FAIR/Landmark Arts Centre, Ferry Road, Teddington, Middx** (preview Mar 11)
Landmark Arts Centre

Mar 12-13 **QUALITY CRAFT & GIFT FAIR/Sun Pavilion, Valley Gardens, Harrogate, North Yorks**
Quality Fairs

Mar 12-13 **SHIRECRAFTS MARQUEE EVENT**
Dobbies Garden Centre, Clifton, Lancs
Shirecrafts

Mar 12-13 **ARTS & CRAFT FAIR/St William College, York, North Yorks**
Yorkshire Craft Fairs

Mar 13 **ARTS & CRAFT FAYRE/Hartington Village Hall, Hartington, Derbys**
Biddulph Arts & Craft Fayres

Mar 13 **TEDDY BEAR & DOLL FAIR/Middleton Hall, nr Tamworth, Staffs**
Cherish Events

Mar 13 **CRAFT FAIR/Dunkenhalgh Hotel, Clayton le Moors, Accrington, Lancs**
Creative Crafts Association

Mar 13 **FAIRFIELD SPRING CRAFT & GIFT FAIR/Fairfield Halls, Park Lane, Croydon, Surrey**
Fairfield (Croydon) Ltd

Mar 13 **CRAFT FAIR/Thurrock Civic Hall, Blackshots Lane, Grays, Essex**
Hallmark Craft Fairs

Mar 13 **CRAFT STALLS AT ST PATRICK'S DAY EVENT/Luton Town Centre, Luton, Beds**
Luton Borough Council

Mar 13 **MILLENNIUM CRAFTS & GIFTS/Community Centre, Lyndhurst, Hants**
Millennium Crafts & Gifts

Mar 13 **NEWBURY DOLLS HOUSE & MINIATURES FAIR/Newbury Racecourse, Berks** (provisional date)
Warners Dolls House & Miniatures Fairs

Mar 13 **7th ANNUAL SPRING CRAFT FAIR/Royal Shakespeare Theatre, Stratford-upon-Avon, Warks**
West Country Craft Fairs

Mar 16-20 **COUNTRY LIVING MAGAZINE SPRING FAIR/Business Design Centre, Upper Street, Islington, London**
Upper Street Events

Mar 17-20 **SEWING FOR PLEASURE/NEC, Birmingham**
ICHF

Mar 17-20 **RURAL CRAFTS ASSOCIATION AT SPRING HOUSE INTERIOR & GARDEN SHOW/Dublin, Republic of Ireland**
Rural Crafts Association

Mar 18-20 **CRAFT & DESIGN SHOW/Spectrum Leisure Centre, Guildford, Surrey**
Craft in Focus

Mar 18-20 **INSPIRATIONAL HOME & GARDEN EXHIBITION/Powderham Castle, Kenton, nr Exeter, Devon**
South West Events Ltd

Mar 19 **CIRENCESTER CRAFTSMAN'S MARKET/Corn Hall, Market Place, Cirencester, Glos**
Cirencester Craftsman's Market

Mar 19 **ART, CRAFT & GIFT FAIR/Town Hall, Towcester, Northants**
Falcon Fairs

Mar 19 **HARROGATE LACE EVENT 2005/Pavilions, Great Yorkshire Showground, Wetherby Road, Harrogate, North Yorks**
John & Jennifer Ford

Mar 19 **SALISBURY SPRING CRAFT FAIR/Guildhall, Market Place, Salisbury, Wilts**
Kevin Murphy Craft Fairs

Mar 19 **ARTS & CRAFT FAIR/The Milton Rooms, Malton, North Yorks**
Yorkshire Craft Fairs

Mar 19-20 **SPRING ART, CRAFT & GIFT SHOW/Bournemouth International Centre, Exeter Road, Bournemouth, Dorset**
BIC Exhibitions

Mar 19-20 **BLAKEMERE CRAFT FAIR/Blakemere Craft Centre, Chester Road, Sandiway, Northwich, Cheshire**
Blakemere Craft Centre

Mar 19-20 **CRAFT FAIR/Haydock Park Racecourse, St Helens, Merseyside**
Creative Crafts Association

Mar 19-20 **CRAFTS AT SPRING SHOW/East of England Showground, Peterborough, Cambs**
East of England Showground

Mar 19-20 **SPRING CRAFT FAIR/Hylands House, Hylands Park, Chelmsford, Essex**
Guild of Essex Craftsmen

Mar 19-20 **SHIRECRAFTS MARQUEE EVENT AT DOBBIES AIR AMBULANCE WEEKEND Dobbies Garden World, Nuneaton Road, B4111 Mancetter, nr Atherstone, Warks**
Shirecrafts

Mar 20 **BEWDLEY CRAFT SHOW/Ramada (Heath) Hotel, Habberley Road, Bewdley, Worcs**
Central Promotions

Mar 20 **ART, CRAFT & GIFT FAIR/Village Hall, Woburn, Beds**
Falcon Fairs

Mar 20 **YEOVIL SPRING CRAFT FAIR/Westland Leisure Complex, Westbourne Close, Yeovil, Somerset**
Kevin Murphy Craft Fairs

Mar 20 **ARTS & CRAFT FAIR/Bankfield Hotel, Bingley, West Yorks**
Yorkshire Craft Fairs

Mar 21-27 **CRAFTS AT THE FORUM/The Forum, Norwich, Norfolk**
Norfolk Events

Mar 24 **MILLENNIUM CRAFTS & GIFTS/Community Centre, Lyndhurst, Hants**
Millennium Crafts & Gifts

Mar 24-28 **GOSPORT & FAREHAM FOLK FESTIVAL**
Ferneham Halls, Osborn Road, Fareham, Hants
Hampshire Music & Arts Festivals

Mar 24-29 **SHIRECRAFTS EASTER MARQUEE WEEK**
Evesham Country Park, Evesham By-Pass A46, Worcs
Shirecrafts

Mar 25 **NATIONAL WILDLIFE CARVING & SCULPTURE EXHIBITION 2005/Courtyard Gallery, Pensthorpe, Fakenham, Norfolk**
Pensthorpe

Mar 25-26 **WESTON-SUPER-MARE EASTER CRAFT FAIR/Winter Gardens Pavilion, Royal Parade, Weston-super-Mare, North Somerset**
Kevin Murphy Craft Fairs

Mar 25-28 **CRAFT FAIR/Hawes Market Hall, Hawes, North Yorks**
Cosy Crafts

Mar 25-28 **COTTAGE CRAFT FESTIVAL/Norfolk Showground, Dereham Road, New Costessey, Norwich, Norfolk**
Country Cottage Crafts

Mar 25-28 **EDEN CRAFTS MARQUEE AT SELBY GAME FAIR/Carlton Towers, Carlton, nr Goole**
Eden Crafts

Mar 25-28 **CRAFT FAIR/Town Hall, Lloyd Street, Llandudno, Conwy**
Event~Reality

Mar 25-28 **SELBY GAME FAIR/Carlton Towers, Carlton, nr Selby**
Exhibition Management (main event organiser)

Mar 25-28 **LIVE CRAFT SHOW/Harewood House, Leeds, West Yorks**
HD Events Ltd

Mar 25-28 **WELLS & MID-SOMERSET 12th ANNUAL EASTER CRAFT FESTIVAL/Town Hall, Market Square, Wells, Somerset**
West Country Craft Fairs

Mar 25-28 **YORKRAFT CRAFT EVENT/Hill's Institute, Malton Gate, Thornton Dale, North Yorks**
Yorkraft

Mar 26 **LEEDS DOLL & TEDDY FAIR/Pudsey Civic Hall, Dawson's Corner, Pudsey, Leeds**
Dolly Domain Fairs

Mar 26 **LLANIDLOES CRAFT FAIR/Community Centre, Llanidloes, Powys**
Llanidloes Arts & Crafts Fairs

Mar 26-27 **BLAKEMERE CRAFT FAIR**
Blakemere Craft Centre, Chester Road, Sandiway, Northwich, Cheshire
Blakemere Craft Centre

Mar 26-28 **3 SHIRES CRAFT GUILD/Memorial Hall, Upton-on-Severn, Worcs**
3 Shires Craft Guild

Mar 26-28 **ARTS & CRAFT FAYRE/Hartington Village Hall, Hartington, Derbys**
Biddulph Arts & Craft Fayres

Mar 26-28 **EASTER COUNTRY SHOPPING FAIR**
Tenants Hall, Tatton Park, nr Knutsford, Cheshire
Countrywide Events

Mar 26-28 **EASTER CRAFT & GARDEN FAIR AT SOMERLEY/nr Ringwood, Hants**
Craft Carnival

Mar 26-28 **EASTER CRAFT FAIR/Woodgreen, Godmanchester, Cambs**
Kingfisher Promotions

Mar 26-28 **EASTER CRAFT & COUNTRY SHOW**
St Mary's Recreation Ground, Lesley Close, Bourne Road, Bexley, Kent
Oakleigh Craft Fairs

Mar 26-28 **HAMPSHIRE SPRING GARDEN & CRAFT SHOW**
Broadlands, Romsey, Hants
RVT Events

Mar 26-28 **CRAFTS AT FORT PURBROOK**
Fort Purbrook, Portsdown Hill, Cosham, Hants
Woodland Crafts

Mar 26-28 **EASTER CRAFT FESTIVAL/St William College, York, North Yorks**
Yorkshire Craft Fairs

Mar 27 **LAUDERDALE HOUSE ARTS & CRAFTS**
Lauderdale House, Waterlow Park, Highgate Hill, London N6
Lauderdale Arts & Crafts

Mar 27 **SPRING/EASTER CRAFT FAIR**
Pavilion Theatre, Marine Parade, Worthing, West Sussex
Worthing Theatres

Mar 27-28 **EASTER CRAFT FAYRE/Buxton Pavilion, Buxton, Derbys**
Cheshire Fayre

Mar 27-28 **COXWOLD CRAFT FAIR/Village Hall, Coxwold, North Yorks**
Coxwold Craft Fairs

Mar 27-28 **CRAFT & GIFT MARQUEE AT MIDLAND FESTIVAL OF TRANSPORT**
Weston Park, Shropshire
Craft People 2000

Mar 27-28	**THRUMPTON HALL EASTER CRAFT & GARDEN SHOW** **Thrumpton Hall, Thrumpton, Notts** Fables Events Ltd
Mar 27-28	**PLANT & CRAFT FAIR/Cheltenham Racecourse, Glos** Hobby Horse Events Ltd
Mar 27-28	**EASTER CRAFT & GIFT EVENT** **Brockenhurst College, Brockenhurst, Hants** IGF Marketing
Mar 27-28	**WEYMOUTH EASTER CRAFT FAIR** **Pavilion Complex, The Esplanade, Weymouth, Dorset** Kevin Murphy Craft Fairs
Mar 27-28	**MILLENNIUM CRAFTS & GIFTS/Community Centre, Lyndhurst, Hants** Millennium Crafts & Gifts
Mar 27-28	**CRAFT & GIFT FAIR/Reebok Stadium, Horwich, nr Bolton, Lancs** North West Craft & Gift Fairs
Mar 27-28	**QUALITY CRAFT & GIFT FAIR/Normanby Hall, Normanby, North Lincs** Quality Fairs
Mar 27-28	**REDESMERE CRAFTS** **Siddington Village Hall, A34, nr Macclesfield, Cheshire** Redesmere Crafts Association
Mar 27-28	**EASTER CRAFT FESTIVAL/Duncombe Park, Helmsley, North Yorks** Yorkshire Craft Fairs
Mar 28	**ART, CRAFT & GIFT FAIR/Village Hall, Woburn, Beds** Falcon Fairs
Mar 28	**CRAFT & GIFT FAIR/Evron Centre, Filey, North Yorks** Hardy Fairs Ltd
Mar 28	**EASTER EGGSTRAVAGANZA & CRAFT FAIR/The Argory, Derrycaw Road, Moy, Co Tyrone** National Trust - The Argory
Mar 28-29	**EASTER CRAFT FAIR/Sandwell Park Farm, Sandwell Valley Country Park, Salters Lane, West Bromwich, West Midlands** Sandwell Valley Craft Fairs
Mar 30-31	**CRAFT FAIR/Electric Mountain, Llanberis, Caernarfon** Event~Reality
Mar 30-Apr 2	**CRAFT & GARDEN FAIR AT KINGSTON LACY/nr Wimborne, Dorset** Craft Carnival
Mar 31-Apr 1	**CRAFT FAIR/Market House, Hawes, Wensleydale, North Yorks** Wensleydale Craft Fairs

Mar 31-Apr 3 **STITCH 2005/National Hall, Olympia, London**
Creative Exhibitions Ltd

Apr date tba **CRAFT MARQUEE AT SPRING GARDENING SHOW**
Capel Manor College, Bullsmoor Lane, Enfield, Middx
Fig Fairs

Apr 1-3 **STOWE SCHOOL HOME DESIGN & INTERIORS EXHIBITION**
Buckingham, Bucks
Buckingham Events

Apr 2 **CIRENCESTER CRAFTSMAN'S MARKET**
Corn Hall, Market Place, Cirencester, Glos
Cirencester Craftsman's Market

Apr 2 **ARTS & CRAFT FAIR/Town Hall, Stokesley, nr Middlesbrough**
Yorkshire Craft Fairs

Apr 2-3 **CRAFT FAIR/Victoria Halls, Hartley Wintney, Hants**
Arts & Craft Fairs

Apr 2-3 **BLAKEMERE CRAFT FAIR**
Blakemere Craft Centre, Chester Road, Sandiway, Northwich, Cheshire
Blakemere Craft Centre

Apr 2-3 **ESSEX CRAFT FAIR**
Cliffs Pavilion Theatre, Station Road, Westcliff-on-Sea, Essex
Hallmark Craft Fairs

Apr 2-3 **MODEL ACTIV 05/Warwickshire Exhibition Centre, Fosse Way, Junction A425/B4455, nr Leamington Spa, Warks**
Meridienne Exhibitions Ltd

Apr 2-3 **CRAFT SHOW/New Hall School, Boreham, nr Chelmsford, Essex**
(provisional dates)
Penny Farthing Craft Fairs

Apr 2-3 **QUALITY CRAFT & GIFT FAIR/Cannon Hall, Cawthorne, South Yorks**
Quality Fairs

Apr 2-3 **DOBBIES GARDEN CENTRE CRAFT SHOW/Dobbies Garden Centre, Gailey Island, Junction A5/A449 Stafford Road, Gailey, Staffs**
Shirecrafts

Apr 2-3 **CRAFTS AT LANCING COLLEGE/Lancing, West Sussex**
Woodland Crafts

Apr 3 **TELFORD CRAFT SHOW/Moat House Hotel, M54 J5, Telford Town Centre, Shropshire** (provisional date)
Central Promotions

Apr 3 **COXWOLD CRAFT FAIR/Village Hall, Coxwold, North Yorks**
Coxwold Craft Fairs

Apr 3-5 **BRITISH CRAFT TRADE FAIR/Great Yorkshire Showground, Wetherby Road, Harrogate, North Yorks**
PSM Ltd

Apr 5 **MILLENNIUM CRAFTS & GIFTS/Community Centre, Lyndhurst, Hants**
Millennium Crafts & Gifts

Apr 5-7 **CRAFT FAIR/Electric Mountain, Llanberis, Caernarfon**
Event~Reality

Apr 6 **CARMARTHENSHIRE CRAFTS/St Peters Hall, Nott Square, Carmarthen**
Carmarthenshire Crafts

Apr 7-9 **CRAFT STANDS AT GRAND NATIONAL MEETING/Aintree Racecourse, Aintree, Liverpool**
Aintree Racecourse Co Ltd

Apr 7-9 **STITCH & CREATIVE CRAFTS SHOW/Kings Hall, Belfast**
Nationwide Exhibitions (UK) Ltd

Apr 8-10 **WESTONBIRT SCHOOL HOME DESIGN & INTERIORS EXHIBITION Tetbury, Glos**
Buckingham Events

Apr 9 **3 SHIRES CRAFT GUILD/St John's Hall, Churchdown, Glos**
3 Shires Craft Guild

Apr 9 **FOCUS CRAFT GROUP/Town Hall, Inverurie, Aberdeenshire**
Festival of Crafts Unique to Scotland (FOCUS)

Apr 9 **CRAFT SHOW/Assembly Hall, Station Road, Chingford, London E4**
Oakleigh Craft Fairs

Apr 9 **ARTS & CRAFT FAIR/The Milton Rooms, Malton, North Yorks**
Yorkshire Craft Fairs

Apr 9-10 **BLAKEMERE CRAFT FAIR/Blakemere Craft Centre, Chester Road, Sandiway, Northwich, Cheshire**
Blakemere Craft Centre

Apr 9-10 **BRITISH MADE CRAFTS AT GATESHEAD FLOWER SHOW/Central Nursery Complex, Lobbley Hill, Gateshead, Tyne & Wear**
Gateshead Metropolitan Council

Apr 9-10 **CRAFTS AT GARDENERS' WEEKEND/Lamport Hall, Lamport, Northants**
Hobby Horse Events Ltd

Apr 9-10 **CRAFT SHOW/The Grange Barn, Coggeshall, Essex**
K.C. Craft Shows

Apr 9-10 **SHIRECRAFTS MARQUEE EVENT/St Peters Garden Centre, Norton, Worcs**
Shirecrafts

Apr 10 **TEDDY BEAR & DOLL FAIR/Buxton Pavilion, Buxton, Derbys**
Cherish Events

Apr 10 **MILLENNIUM CRAFTS & GIFTS/Community Centre, Lyndhurst, Hants**
Millennium Crafts & Gifts

Apr 10 **REDESMERE CRAFTS/Siddington Village Hall, A34, nr Macclesfield, Cheshire**
Redesmere Crafts Association

Apr 10 **HOVE DOLLS HOUSE & MINIATURES FAIR/Town Hall, Norton Road, Hove, East Sussex**
Warners Dolls House & Miniatures Fairs

Apr 10 **SPRING CRAFT FAIR**
Royal Shakespeare Theatre, Stratford-upon-Avon, Warks
West Country Craft Fairs

Apr 10 **ARTS & CRAFT FAIR/Bankfield Hotel, Bingley, West Yorks**
Yorkshire Craft Fairs

Apr 14 **CRAFT FAIR/Market House, Hawes, Wensleydale, North Yorks**
Wensleydale Craft Fairs

April 14-17 **MAURTRAID CRAFTSHOW/The Centre MK in Middleton Hall, Milton Keynes Shopping Centre, Bucks**
Maurtraid Craftshows

Apr 14-17 **COUNTRY LIVING MAGAZINE SPRING FAIR SCOTLAND/Royal Highland Centre, Ingliston, Edinburgh**
Upper Street Events

Apr 15-16 **BRITISH CRAFTS SPRING**
Chiswick Town Hall, Heathfield Terrace, London W4
British Crafts

Apr 15-17 **CRAFT SPACES AT SUFFOLK SPRING GARDEN SHOW**
Suffolk Showground, Bucklesham Road, Ipswich, Suffolk
Aztec Events

Apr 15-17 **CRAFT & DESIGN SHOW**
University of Kent Sports Centre, Canterbury, Kent
Craft in Focus

Apr 15-17 **FASHION, CRAFT & DESIGN**
Secretts Garden Centre, Milford, Godalming, Surrey
Rural Crafts Association

Apr 16 **CIRENCESTER CRAFTSMAN'S MARKET**
Corn Hall, Market Place, Cirencester, Glos
Cirencester Craftsman's Market

Apr 16 **ART, CRAFT & GIFT FAIR/Town Hall, Towcester, Northants**
Falcon Fairs

Apr 16-17 **BLAKEMERE CRAFT FAIR**
Blakemere Craft Centre, Chester Road, Sandiway, Northwich, Cheshire
Blakemere Craft Centre

Apr 16-17 **YORK HOMES, GARDENS & GIFT SHOW**
Knavesmire Suite, York Racecourse
Doug Moore

Apr 16-17 **CRAFT MARQUEE AT DUNDEE SPRING GARDEN SHOW**
Dundee Ice Arena, Dundee
Dundee City Council

Apr 16-17 **CRAFTS AT GARDENERS' WEEKEND/Coughton Court, Studley, Warks**
Hobby Horse Events Ltd

Apr 16-17 **WOODEX 05/Warwickshire Exhibition Centre, Fosse Way, Junction A425/B4455, nr Leamington Spa, Warks**
Meridienne Exhibitions Ltd

Apr 16-17 **SHIRECRAFTS MARQUEE WEEKEND/Worcester Garden Centre, A38 Droitwich Road, Worcester**
Shirecrafts

Apr 16-17 **CRAFTS IN THE BARN AT SPRING GARDEN FESTIVAL/Michelham Priory, Upper Dicker, Hailsham, East Sussex**
Sussex Past

Apr 16-17 **ARTS & CRAFT FAIR/St William College, York, North Yorks**
Yorkshire Craft Fairs

Apr 17 **ARTS & CRAFT FAYRE/Hartington Village Hall, Hartington, Derbys**
Biddulph Arts & Craft Fayres

Apr 17 **ART, CRAFT & GIFT FAIR/Village Hall, Woburn, Beds**
Falcon Fairs

Apr 17 **CRAFT FAIR/Hinchingbrooke House, Huntingdon, Cambs**
Kingfisher Promotions

Apr 17 **LAUDERDALE HOUSE ARTS & CRAFTS**
Lauderdale House, Waterlow Park, Highgate Hill, London N6
Lauderdale Arts & Crafts

Apr 17 **BEARS & DOLLS/National Exhibition Centre, Birmingham**
Miniatura

Apr 17 **CRAFT & GIFT FAIR/Wilmslow Leisure Centre, Wilmslow, Cheshire**
North West Craft & Gift Fairs

Apr 17 **CRAFT SHOW/Red Lion, Great North Road, Hatfield, Herts**
Oakleigh Craft Fairs

Blakemere
Shopping Experience

Apr 17 **QUALITY CRAFT & GIFT FAIR**
Sun Pavilion, Valley Gardens, Harrogate, North Yorks
Quality Fairs

Apr 18 **COXWOLD CRAFT FAIR/Village Hall, Coxwold, North Yorks**
Coxwold Craft Fairs

Apr 19 **MILLENNIUM CRAFTS & GIFTS/Community Centre, Lyndhurst, Hants**
Millennium Crafts & Gifts

Apr 19-21 **CRAFT FAIR/Town Hall, Lloyd Street, Llandudno, Conwy**
Event~Reality

Apr 21-22 **CRAFT FAIR/Market House, Hawes, Wensleydale, North Yorks**
Wensleydale Craft Fairs

Apr 21-24 **TEXTILE SHOWCASE 2005/Royal Jersey Exhibition Hall, La Route de la Trinité, Trinity, Jersey**
Art in the Frame Foundation

Apr 21-24 **STITCH & CREATIVE CRAFTS SHOW/Royal Bath & West Showground, Shepton Mallet, Somerset**
Nationwide Exhibitions (UK) Ltd

Apr 22-24 **CRAFT SPACES AT NEWARK & NOTTS GARDEN SHOW/Newark & Notts Showground, Winthorpe, Newark, Notts**
Aztec Events

Apr 22-24 **GOODWOOD HOUSE HOME DESIGN & INTERIORS EXHIBITION**
Chichester, West Sussex
Buckingham Events

Apr 22-24 **COTTAGE CRAFT FESTIVAL/Suffolk Showground, Bucklesham Road, Ipswich, Suffolk**
Country Cottage Crafts

Apr 22-24 **CRAFTS AREA AT NATIONAL MOTORHOME SHOW/East of England Showground, Peterborough, Cambs** (provisional dates)
Warners Exhibitions

Apr 23 **ART, CRAFT & GIFT FAIR/Town Hall, Brackley, Northants**
Falcon Fairs

Apr 23 **CRAFT STALLS AT ST GEORGE'S DAY EVENT**
Luton Town Centre, Luton, Beds
Luton Borough Council

Apr 23 **CRAFTS AT THE FORUM/The Forum, Norwich, Norfolk**
Norfolk Events

Apr 23 **ARTS & CRAFT FAIR/Crescent Hotel, Ilkley, West Yorks**
Yorkshire Craft Fairs

Apr 23-24	**BLAKEMERE CRAFT FAIR** **Blakemere Craft Centre, Chester Road, Sandiway, Northwich, Cheshire** Blakemere Craft Centre
Apr 23-24	**CRAFTS & GIFTS AT NESS GARDEN FESTIVAL/Ness, Wirral, Cheshire** Cheshire Fayre
Apr 23-24	**CRAFT MARQUEE AT HATTON COUNTRY WORLD** **A4177 Hatton, between Warwick and Solihull, Warks** Cottage Industries
Apr 23-24	**ART & COUNTRY SHOPPING FAIR** **Tenants Hall, Tatton Park, nr Knutsford, Cheshire** Countrywide Events
Apr 23-24	**CRAFT FAIR/Lowther Pavilion, Lytham, Lancs** Creative Crafts Association
Apr 23-24	**EDEN CRAFTS MARQUEE AT ERIDGE GAME FAIR** **Eridge Park, Tunbridge Wells, Kent** Eden Crafts
Apr 23-24	**ERIDGE GAME FAIR/Eridge Park, Tunbridge Wells, Kent** Exhibition Management (main event organiser)
Apr 23-24	**EAST ANGLIAN GAME & COUNTRY FAIR/Royal Norfolk Showground, Dereham Road, New Costessey, Norwich, Norfolk** Grand Promotion Events Ltd
Apr 23-24	**CRAFT MARQUEE AT WEALD OF KENT GARDEN SHOW/The Hop Farm Country Park, Paddock Wood, Kent** WMH Leisure
Apr 24	**ART, CRAFT & GIFT FAIR/Village Hall, Denham, Bucks** Falcon Fairs
Apr 24	**CRAFT FAIR/Mill Hall, Bellingham Lane, Rayleigh, Essex** Hallmark Craft Fairs
Apr 24	**MILLENNIUM CRAFTS & GIFTS/Community Centre, Lyndhurst, Hants** Millennium Crafts & Gifts
Apr 24	**REDESMERE CRAFTS** **Siddington Village Hall, A34, nr Macclesfield, Cheshire** Redesmere Crafts Association
Apr 24	**KENT DOLLS HOUSE & MINIATURES FAIR/Ramada Hotel & Resort, Hollingbourne, nr Maidstone, Kent** Warners Dolls House & Miniatures Fairs
Apr 24-26	**SELECT 2005 (showcase of British manufactured products)/Westpoint Exhibition Centre, Exeter, Devon** Hale Events Ltd

Apr 25 **COXWOLD CRAFT FAIR/Village Hall, Coxwold, North Yorks**
Coxwold Craft Fairs

Apr 28-May 1 **BRITISH MADE CRAFTS AT HARROGATE SPRING FLOWER SHOW Great Yorkshire Showground, Wetherby Road, Harrogate, North Yorks**
North of England Enterprises Ltd

Apr 30 **DOWNTON CUCKOO FAIR/The Village Greens, Downton, Salisbury, Wilts**
Downton Cuckoo Fair Ltd

Apr 30 **FOCUS CRAFT GROUP/Town Hall, Banchory, Aberdeenshire**
Festival of Crafts Unique to Scotland (FOCUS)

Apr 30-May 1 **ARTS & CRAFT FAYRE/Hartington Village Hall, Hartington, Derbys**
Biddulph Arts & Craft Fayres

Apr 30-May 2 **CRAFT SPACES AT SOUTHEND GARDEN SHOW/Garon Park, Southend-on-Sea, Essex**
Aztec Events

Apr 30-May 2 **CRAFT MARQUEE AT ANNUAL BATH SPRING FLOWER SHOW Royal Victoria Park, Bath**
Bath & NE Somerset Council

Apr 30-May 2 **BLAKEMERE CRAFT FAIR/Blakemere Craft Centre, Chester Road, Sandiway, Northwich, Cheshire**
Blakemere Craft Centre

Apr 30-May 2 **CRAFT FAIR/Hawes Market Hall, Hawes, North Yorks**
Cosy Crafts

Apr 30-May 2 **CRAFT FAIR/Town Hall, Lloyd Street, Llandudno, Conwy**
Event~Reality

Apr 30-May 2 **COUNTRYSIDE & CRAFTS COME TO TOWN/Morden Hall Park, Morden, Surrey**
Four Seasons Craft Fayres Ltd

Apr 30-May 2 **LIVE CRAFT SHOW/Chiltern Open Air Museum, Chalfont St Giles, Bucks**
HD Events Ltd

Apr 30-May 2 **CRAFTS AT GARDENERS' WEEKEND/Audley End House, Saffron Walden, Essex**
Hobby Horse Events Ltd

Apr 30-May 2 **WEALD OF KENT CRAFT SHOW/Penshurst Place, nr Tonbridge, Kent**
ICHF

Apr 30-May 2 **CANALWAY CAVALCADE/Little Venice, Paddington, London W2/W9**
IWA Festivals

Apr 30-May 2 **SANDRINGHAM CRAFT SHOW/Sandringham, Norfolk**
Living Heritage Craft Shows

Apr 30-May 2 **LLANDUDNO TRANSPORT FESTIVAL/Bodafon Fields, Llandudno, Conwy**
Llandudno Transport Festival

Apr 30-May 2 **CRAFT & GIFT MARQUEE AT MEOLS HALL GARDEN & LEISURE SHOW Meols Hall, Southport**
North West Craft & Gift Fairs

Apr 30-May 2 **CHADWELL HEATH MAY SHOW CRAFT MARQUEE/High Road (A118), Chadwell Heath, Essex**
Oakleigh Craft Fairs

Apr 30-May 2 **SHIRECRAFT BANK HOLIDAY MARQUEE/Dobbies Garden World, Nuneaton Road, B4111 Mancetter, nr Atherstone, Warks**
Shirecrafts

Apr 30-May 2 **CRAFT MARQUEE AT TONBRIDGE GARDEN & HOME SHOW Town Centre Park, rear of High Street, Tonbridge, Kent**
Susan Adams Business Services Ltd

Apr 30-May 2 **RUSHDEN CAVALCADE & COUNTRY SHOW CRAFT MARQUEE/Lancaster Farm, nr Higham Ferrers, Northants**
T.C.T.C.

Apr 30-May 2 **CRAFT MARQUEE AT MAY DAY FAIR/St Fagans, Cardiff**
Wales Craft Council

Apr 30-May 2 **CRAFT MARQUEE AT FAVERSHAM GARDEN SHOW/Farming World, Faversham, Kent**
WMH Leisure

Apr 30-May 2 **YORKRAFT CRAFT EVENT/Hill's Institute, Malton Gate, Thornton Dale, North Yorks**
Yorkraft

Apr 30-May 2 **MAY BANK HOLIDAY ARTS & CRAFT FAIR/St William College, York, North Yorks**
Yorkshire Craft Fairs

May 1 **MARQUEE AT STEAM & VINTAGE SHOW/Monmouth Showground (formerly held at Speech House in Forest of Dean)**
Border Counties Vintage Club Ltd

May 1 **ARTS & CRAFT FAIR/Crown Hotel, Harrogate, North Yorks**
Yorkshire Craft Fairs

May 1-2 **STAFFORD CRAFT SHOW/County Showground, A518 Uttoxeter Road, Stafford**
Central Promotions

May 1-2 **CRAFTS & GIFTS AT SIGNAL 1 SHOW Trentham Gardens, Stoke-on-Trent, Staffs**
Cheshire Fayre

May 1-2 **COXWOLD CRAFT FAIR/Village Hall, Coxwold, North Yorks**
Coxwold Craft Fairs

May 1-2 **CRAFTS & GIFT AT TRUCKFEST/Show Buildings, East of England Showground, Peterborough, Cambs**
Craft Lincs

May 1-2 **CRAFT & GIFT MARQUEE AT WORLD'S NO 1 KIT CAR SHOW/NAC, Stoneleigh, Warks**
Craft People 2000

May 1-2 **CRAFT STANDS AT MAGNIFICENT MOTORS/Western Lawns, Seafront, Eastbourne, East Sussex**
Eastbourne Borough Council

May 1-2 **EDEN CRAFTS MARQUEE AT SOUTH OF ENGLAND SPRING SHOW South of England Showground, Ardingly, West Sussex**
Eden Crafts

May 1-2 **CRAFT SHOW/Layer Marney Tower, nr Colchester, Essex**
K.C. Craft Shows

May 1-2 **CRAFTS FESTIVAL/Lamport Hall, Lamport, Northants**
Kingfisher Promotions

May 1-2 **MARQUEE AT LEICESTERSHIRE COUNTY SHOW/Dishley Grange Farm, Loughborough, Leics**
Leicestershire Agricultural Society Ltd

May 1-2 **CRAFT, GIFT & FOOD MARQUEE AT MAGNIFICENT MOTORS Western Lawns, Seafront, Eastbourne, East Sussex**
Sovereign Fairs

May 1-2 **CELTIC WEEKEND/Michelham Priory, Upper Dicker, Hailsham, East Sussex** (only crafts relevant to Iron Age)
Sussex Past

May 1-3 **CLUN GREENMAN FESTIVAL/The Castle Meadow, Clun Castle, Clun, Shropshire**
Clun Greenman Festival

May 1-Sept 30 **CRAFTS SALE/Monymusk Arts Centre, Monymusk, by Inverurie, Aberdeenshire**
Monymusk Arts Trust

May 2 **MARQUEE AT THE HIGHLAND FLING/Graves Park, Hemsworth Road, Sheffield**
Allott Agency

May 2 **CRAFTS AT BURNLEY MAY DAY FESTIVAL/Towneley Park, Todmorden Road, Burnley, Lancs**
Burnley May Day Festival

May 2 **CRAFT & GIFT FAIR/Evron Centre, Filey, North Yorks**
Hardy Fairs Ltd

May 2 **FESTIVAL OF ARTS & CRAFTS/Lauderdale House, Waterlow Park, Highgate Hill, London N6**
Lauderdale Arts & Crafts

May 2 **BRITISH CRAFTS AT NORTH SOMERSET SHOW/Bathing Pond Field, Wraxall (B3130), nr Bristol**
North Somerset Show (main event organiser)

May 2 **RURAL CRAFTS ASSOCIATION AT NORTH SOMERSET SHOW/Bathing Pond Field, Wraxall (B3130), nr Bristol**
Rural Crafts Association

May 2-4 **CRAFT MARQUEE AT CITY OF NOTTINGHAM STEAM FAIR Wollaton Park, Nottingham**
Kingfisher Craft Marquee Management

May 4-7 **LIVING CRAFTS/Hatfield House, Hatfield, Herts**
Living Crafts Ltd

May 5 **CARMARTHENSHIRE CRAFTS/St Peters Hall, Nott Square, Carmarthen**
Carmarthenshire Crafts

May 5-8 **HEART OF ENGLAND CRAFTWORKERS MARQUEE AT MITSUBISHI MOTORS BADMINTON HORSE TRIALS/Badminton Village, Glos**
Heart of England Craftworkers Ltd

May 5-8 **RURAL CRAFTS ASSOCIATION AT MITSUBISHI MOTORS BADMINTON HORSE TRIALS/Badminton Village, Glos**
Rural Crafts Association

May 6-8 **CRAFT SPACES AT DORSET GARDEN SHOW Canford Park Arena, Poole, Dorset**
Aztec Events

May 6-8 **BLENHEIM PALACE HOME DESIGN & INTERIORS EXHIBITION Woodstock, Oxon**
Buckingham Events

May 6-8 **CERAMIC ART LONDON 2005/Royal College of Art, London**
Ceramic Art London

May 6-8 **CRAFT MARQUEE AT TEESSIDE GARDEN & WOOD FESTIVAL Preston Park, Yarm, Tees Valley**
Doug Moore

May 7 **CIRENCESTER CRAFTSMAN'S MARKET Corn Hall, Market Place, Cirencester, Glos**
Cirencester Craftsman's Market

May 7 **SPRING CRAFT MARKET/Commemoration Hall, Huntingdon, Cambs**
Huntingdon Craft Market

May 7	**ARTS & CRAFT FAIR/Town Hall, Stokesley, nr Middlesbrough** Yorkshire Craft Fairs
May 7-8	**BLAKEMERE CRAFT FAIR/Blakemere Craft Centre, Chester Road, Sandiway, Northwich, Cheshire** Blakemere Craft Centre
May 7-8	**CRAFT & GIFT MARQUEE AT NEWARK & NOTTS COUNTY SHOW** **Newark Showground, Notts** Craft People 2000
May 7-8	**TEESDALE GAMEFAIR** **Witton Castle, Witton-le-Wear, nr Bishop Auckland, Co Durham** Exhibition Management
May 7-8	**MARQUEE WEEKEND OF CRAFTS** **Ullesthorpe Garden Centre, Lutterworth, Leics** Shirecrafts
May 8	**MILLENNIUM CRAFTS & GIFTS/Community Centre, Lyndhurst, Hants** Millennium Crafts & Gifts
May 8	**CRAFT MARQUEE AT SANDWELL'S HISTORIC VEHICLE SHOW** **Sandwell Showground, Sandwell Valley Country Park, Salters Lane, West Bromwich, West Midlands** Sandwell Valley Craft Fairs
May 8	**CRAFT MARQUEE AT SOUTH SUFFOLK AGRICULTURAL SHOW** **Ampton Racecourse, Ingham, nr Bury St Edmunds, Suffolk** South Suffolk Agricultural Show
May 8	**COWPIE COUNTRY SHOW/Betchworth, nr Dorking, Surrey** Surrey Federation of Young Farmers Clubs
May 8	**9th ANNUAL MAY CRAFT FAIR** **Royal Shakespeare Theatre, Stratford-upon-Avon, Warks** West Country Craft Fairs
May 10	**MILLENNIUM CRAFTS & GIFTS/Community Centre, Lyndhurst, Hants** Millennium Crafts & Gifts
May 12– June 12	**BLUE...WHERE THE SKY MEETS THE SEA & THE SHORE** **The Harbour Gallery, Le Boulevard, St Aubin, Jersey** Art in the Frame Foundation
May 13-15	**CRAFT SPACES AT NORFOLK GARDEN SHOW** **Norfolk Showground, Dereham Road, New Costessey, Norwich, Norfolk** Aztec Events
May 13-15	**CRAFT FAIR/Stapeley Water Gardens, Nantwich, Cheshire** Creative Crafts Association
May 13-15	**LIVE CRAFT SHOW/Osbourn House, Isle of Wight** HD Events Ltd

May 13-15 **OPEN AIR EXHIBITION AT SOUTHERN MOTORCARAVAN SHOW**
Newbury Showground, Hermitage, Thatcham, Berks
Warners Exhibitions

May 13-15 **CRAFT MARQUEE AT YORKSHIRE GARDEN SHOW**
Lotherton Hall, Towton Road, nr Leeds, West Yorks
Yorkshire Garden Show

May 14 **3 SHIRES CRAFT GUILD/Bredon Village Hall, Bredon, Glos**
3 Shires Craft Guild

May 14 **ART, CRAFT & GIFT FAIR/Town Hall, Brackley, Northants**
Falcon Fairs

May 14 **ARTS & CRAFT FAIR/The Milton Rooms, Malton, North Yorks**
Yorkshire Craft Fairs

May 14-15 **MOIRA CANAL FESTIVAL**
Moira Furnace, Furnace Lane, Moira, nr Burton-on-Trent
Ashby Canal Trust

May 14-15 **BLAKEMERE CRAFT FAIR**
Blakemere Craft Centre, Chester Road, Sandiway, Northwich, Cheshire
Blakemere Craft Centre

May 14-15 **SHIBDEN HALL CRAFT FAIR**
Shibden Hall, Listers Road, Halifax, West Yorks
Calderdale MBC

May 14-15 **CRAFT MARQUEE AT NEWARK/Newark & Nottingham County Showground, Newark, Notts**
Cottage Industries

May 14-15 **CRAFTS AT GARDENERS' WEEKEND/Weston Park, nr Shifnal, Staffs**
Hobby Horse Events Ltd

May 14-15 **CRAFT MARQUEE AT BRONTE VINTAGE GATHERING**
Howarth Road, Cullingworth, Bradford, West Yorks
Kingfisher Craft Marquee Management

May 14-15 **SPRING FAIR/Sutton House, Homerton High Street, London E9**
National Trust - Sutton House

May 14-15 **RURAL CRAFTS ASSOCIATION AT CHATSWORTH INTERNATIONAL HORSE TRIALS/Chatsworth House, Baslow, Derbys**
Rural Crafts Association

May 14-15 **SPRING CRAFT FAIR/Saltram House, Plymouth, Devon**
Saltram House

May 15 **COXWOLD CRAFT FAIR/Village Hall, Coxwold, North Yorks**
Coxwold Craft Fairs

May 15 **ART, CRAFT & GIFT FAIR/Village Hall, Woburn, Beds**
Falcon Fairs

May 15 **CRAFT FAIR/Sportcentre, Brentwood School, Middleton Hall Lane, Brentwood, Essex**
Hallmark Craft Fairs

May 15 **QUALITY CRAFT & GIFT FAIR**
Sun Pavilion, Valley Gardens, Harrogate, North Yorks
Quality Fairs

May 15 **WEST COUNTRY EMBROIDERERS FESTIVAL**
Wincanton Racecourse, Somerset
West of England Events

May 17-19 **CRAFT FAIR/Town Hall, Lloyd Street, Llandudno, Conwy**
Event~Reality

May 19 **CRAFT FAIR/Market House, Hawes, Wensleydale, North Yorks**
Wensleydale Craft Fairs

May 19-21 **BEAUTY, HEALTH & LIFESTYLE MARQUEE AT DEVON COUNTY SHOW**
Westpoint, Clyst St Mary, Exeter, Devon
BHLR Ltd

May 19-21 **EDEN CRAFTS MARQUEE AT DEVON COUNTY SHOW**
Westpoint, Clyst St Mary, Exeter, Devon
Eden Crafts

May 19-21 **WEST COUNTRY CRAFTS MARQUEE AT DEVON COUNTY SHOW**
Westpoint, Clyst St Mary, Exeter, Devon
Enterprise Tamar Ltd

May 19-21 **RURAL CRAFTS ASSOCIATION AT DEVON COUNTY SHOW**
Westpoint, Clyst St Mary, Exeter, Devon
Rural Crafts Association

May 20-22 **CRAFT SPACES AT ESSEX GARDEN SHOW**
Brentwood Centre, Doddinghurst Road, Brentwood, Essex
Aztec Events

May 20-22 **ELTON HALL HOME DESIGN & INTERIORS EXHIBITION**
Peterborough, Cambs
Buckingham Events

May 20-22 **MOTOR CARAVAN JAMBOREE & LEISURE SHOW**
Kent County Showground, Detling, nr Maidstone, Kent
Motor Caravan Jamboree

May 21 **CIRENCESTER CRAFTSMAN'S MARKET**
Corn Hall, Market Place, Cirencester, Glos
Cirencester Craftsman's Market

May 21 **CRAFTS AT BRISTOL DOWNS ON ORGAN DONATION AWARENESS DAY**
Bristol Downs, Bristol
Cottage Industries

May 21 **CRAFT MARQUEE AT DALRY SHOW/Lynnholm Farm, Dalry, Ayrshire**
Dalry Farmers' Society

May 21 **ART, CRAFT & GIFT FAIR/Town Hall, Towcester, Northants**
Falcon Fairs

May 21 **MOULTON VILLAGE FESTIVAL CRAFT MARKET**
Public Gardens, Church Street, Moulton, Northants
Moulton Village Festival

May 21 **CRAFTS AT THE FORUM/The Forum, Norwich, Norfolk**
Norfolk Events

May 21 **CRAFT MARQUEE AT OTLEY SHOW**
Showground, Bridge End, Otley, West Yorks
Wharfedale Agricultural Society

May 21-22 **BLAKEMERE CRAFT FAIR**
Blakemere Craft Centre, Chester Road, Sandiway, Northwich, Cheshire
Blakemere Craft Centre

May 21-22 **CRAFT FAIR/Sandon Hall, Sandon, Staffs**
Creative Crafts Association

May 21-22 **CRAFTS AT ROYAL WELSH SMALLHOLDERS & GARDEN FESTIVAL**
Royal Welsh Showground, Llanelwedd, Builth Wells, Powys
Royal Welsh Agricultural Society Ltd

May 21-22 **CRAFT MARQUEE AT HERTS GARDEN SHOW**
Knebworth House, Stevenage, Herts
WMH Leisure

May 22 **TEDDY BEAR & DOLL FAIR/Clwyd Theatr, Mold, Flintshire, North Wales**
Cherish Events

May 22 **COXWOLD CRAFT FAIR/Village Hall, Coxwold, North Yorks**
Coxwold Craft Fairs

May 22 **TYNESIDE DOLLS & TEDDY FAIR**
Lancastrian Suite, Federation Brewery, Dunston, Gateshead, Tyne & Wear
Dolly Domain Fairs

May 22 **ART, CRAFT & GIFT FAIR/Village Hall, Denham, Bucks**
Falcon Fairs

May 22 **MILLENNIUM CRAFTS & GIFTS/Community Centre, Lyndhurst, Hants**
Millennium Crafts & Gifts

May 22 **WEYMOUTH & SOUTH DORSET SPRING CRAFT MARKET**
Weymouth Pavilion, Esplanade, Weymouth, Dorset
West Country Craft Fairs

May 26-27 **CRAFT FAIR/Market House, Hawes, Wensleydale, North Yorks**
Wensleydale Craft Fairs

May 27-28 **MARQUEE AT BALLYMENA SHOW**
Ballymena Showground, Ballymena, Co Antrim
County Antrim Agricultural Association

May 27-30 **ARTISAN SHOWCASE 2005 (part of THE COUNTRY FAYRE)/Royal Jersey Exhibition Hall, La Route de la Trinité, Trinity, Jersey**
Art in the Frame Foundation

May 27-30 **THE CRAFT & DESIGN EXPERIENCE/Fawley Court, Marlow Road, Henley-on-Thames, Oxon**
CDE Ltd

May 27-30 **CRAFT & GIFT MARQUEE AT CARAVAN CLUB NATIONAL RALLY**
Burghley House, Stamford, Lincs
Craft People 2000

May 28 **CRAFT & GIFT FAIR**
Leconfield Hall, Market Square, Petworth, West Sussex
Craft Developments

May 28 **FOCUS CRAFT GROUP/Town Hall, Stonehaven, Aberdeenshire**
Festival of Crafts Unique to Scotland (FOCUS)

May 28-29 **CRAFTS & GIFTS AT ARLEY HALL COUNTRY FAIR**
Arley Hall, nr Knutsford, Cheshire
Cheshire Fayre

May 28-29 **EDEN CRAFTS MARQUEE AT HERTS COUNTY SHOW**
Herts County Showground, Dunstable Road, Redbourn, Herts
Eden Crafts

May 28-30 **ARTS & CRAFT FAYRE/Hartington Village Hall, Hartington, Derbys**
Biddulph Arts & Craft Fayres

May 28-30 **BLAKEMERE CRAFT FAIR**
Blakemere Craft Centre, Chester Road, Sandiway, Northwich, Cheshire
Blakemere Craft Centre

May 28-30 **CRAFTS & GIFTS AT SPRING GARDEN FESTIVAL**
Bodelwyddan Castle, St Asaph, Denbighshire
Cheshire Fayre

May 28-30 **CRAFT FAIR/Hawes Market Hall, Hawes, North Yorks**
Cosy Crafts

May 28-30 **SPRING CRAFT & GARDEN SHOW AT CHETTLE**
Chettle House, Chettle, nr Blandford, Dorset
Craft Carnival

May 28-30 **CRAFT FAIR/Gawsworth Hall, Gawsworth, Macclesfield, Cheshire**
Creative Crafts Association

May 28-30 **CRAFT FAIR/Town Hall, Lloyd Street, Llandudno, Conwy**
Event~Reality

May 28-30 **CRAFT MARQUEE AT TOM ROLT VINTAGE RALLY**
Tywyn Show Field, Tywyn, Gwynedd
Ffeiriau Arbennig

May 28-30 **COUNTRY CRAFT FAYRE/Aldenham Country Park, Elstree, Herts**
Four Seasons Craft Fayres Ltd

May 28-30 **LIVE CRAFT SHOW/Mapledurham, nr Reading**
HD Events Ltd

May 28-30 **COUNTRY CRAFTS WEEKEND/Shugborough, Milford, Staffs**
Hobby Horse Events Ltd

May 28-30 **CRAFTS AT GARDENERS' WEEKEND**
Harewood House, Leeds, West Yorks
Hobby Horse Events Ltd

May 28-30 **ESSEX CRAFT SHOW/Blake Hall, Ongar, Essex**
Living Heritage Craft Shows

May 28-30 **OXFORDSHIRE CRAFT SHOW/Blenheim Palace, Woodstock, Oxon**
Living Heritage Craft Shows

May 28-30 **SPRING BANK HOLIDAY CRAFT & COUNTRY STEAM RALLY**
Hook Road Arena, Hook Road, nr Epsom, Surrey
Oakleigh Craft Fairs

May 28-30 **SELWOOD STEAM & VINTAGE SHOW/Southwick, nr Trowbridge, Wilts**
Selwood Steam & Vintage Vehicle Preservation Society

May 28-30 **ASPIRE FESTIVAL/Vaynol Estate, Bangor, Gwynedd** (provisional dates)
Vaynol Enterprises Ltd

May 28-30 **CRAFT MARQUEE AT KENT GARDEN SHOW**
County Showground, Detling, nr Maidstone, Kent
WMH Leisure

May 28-30 **CRAFTS AT FORT PURBROOK**
Fort Purbrook, Portsdown Hill, Cosham, Hants
Woodland Crafts

May 28-30 **YORKRAFT CRAFT EVENT**
Hill's Institute, Malton Gate, Thornton Dale, North Yorks
Yorkraft

May 28-30 **SPRING BANK HOLIDAY ARTS & CRAFT FAIR**
St William College, York, North Yorks
Yorkshire Craft Fairs

May 28-31 **CRAFT FAIR/The Green, Beaumaris, Ynys Môn**
Gwynedd & Clwyd Association of Craftworkers

May 29 **BT COUNTRY FAIR/Florence Court, Enniskillen, Co Fermanagh**
National Trust - Florence Court

May 29 **ARTS & CRAFT FAIR/Crown Hotel, Harrogate, North Yorks**
Yorkshire Craft Fairs

May 29-30 **MARQUEE AT SHEFFIELD MAYFEST/Hillsborough Park, Penistone Road, Sheffield**
Allott Agency

May 29-30 **CRAFTS AT VINTAGE STEAM & TRACTOR RALLY**
Horncastle Road (B1183), Carrington, nr Boston, Lincs
Carrington Rally

May 29-30 **CRAFTS AT BIRMINGHAM BANK HOLIDAY WEEKEND**
Cannon Hill Park, Birmingham
Cottage Industries

May 29-30 **COXWOLD CRAFT FAIR/Village Hall, Coxwold, North Yorks**
Coxwold Craft Fairs

May 29-30 **BRITISH CRAFTS AT STEAM & WOODLAND FAIR**
Eastnor Castle, Ledbury, Herefordshire
Eastnor Castle

May 29-30 **SPRING GARDEN FAIR & FLOWER FESTIVAL**
Finchcocks, Goudhurst, Kent
Finchcocks

May 29-30 **FRAMLINGHAM SPORTS CLUB CRAFT FAIR**
(marquee in) Grounds of Framlingham Castle, Framlingham, Suffolk
Framlingham Sports Club

May 29-30 **WEYMOUTH BANK HOLIDAY CRAFT FAIR**
Pavilion Complex, The Esplanade, Weymouth, Dorset
Kevin Murphy Craft Fairs

May 29-30 **CRAFT FAIR/The Maltings, Ely, Cambs**
Kingfisher Promotions

May 29-30 **LAMPORT STEAM & COUNTRY FESTIVAL**
Lamport Hall, Lamport, Northants
Lamport Enterprises Ltd

May 29-30 **MABE STEAM-UP & SHINDIG/Carnsew Farm, Antron Hill, Mabe, Penryn, Cornwall**
Mabe Shindig

May 29-30 **MILLENNIUM CRAFTS & GIFTS/Community Centre, Lyndhurst, Hants**
Millennium Crafts & Gifts

May 30 **CRAFT & GIFT FAIR/Evron Centre, Filey, North Yorks**
Hardy Fairs Ltd

May 30 **CRAFT STALLS AT LUTON INTERNATIONAL CARNIVAL**
Luton Town Centre, Luton, Beds
Luton Borough Council

May 30 **CRAFT MARQUEE AT NORTHUMBERLAND COUNTY SHOW/Tynedale Park, Corbridge, Northumberland**
Northumberland County Show

May 30 **CRAFTS AT ROTHBURY STREET FAIR**
Rothbury High Street & Village Greens, Northumberland
Rothbury Street Fair

May 30 **RURAL CRAFTS ASSOCIATION AT SURREY COUNTY SHOW**
Stoke Park, London Road, Guildford, Surrey
Rural Crafts Association

May 30 **CRAFT COURTYARD AT SHERBORNE CASTLE COUNTRY FAIR**
Sherborne Castle, Dorset
Sherborne Castle Country Fair

June 1-2 **BEAUTY, HEALTH & LIFESTYLE MARQUEE AT SUFFOLK COUNTY SHOW**
Suffolk County Showground, Bucklesham Road, Ipswich, Suffolk
BHLR Ltd

June 1-2 **CRAFTS AT STAFFORDSHIRE COUNTY SHOW**
County Showground, Stafford, Staffs
Cheshire Fayre

June 1-2 **RURAL CRAFTS ASSOCIATION AT SUFFOLK COUNTY SHOW**
Suffolk County Showground, Bucklesham Road, Ipswich, Suffolk
Rural Crafts Association

June 1-4 **HEART OF ENGLAND CRAFTWORKERS MARQUEE AT ROYAL BATH & WEST SHOW/Bath & West Showground, Shepton Mallet, Somerset**
Heart of England Craftworkers Ltd

June 1-4 **RURAL CRAFTS ASSOCIATION AT ROYAL BATH & WEST SHOW**
Bath & West Showground, Shepton Mallet, Somerset
Rural Crafts Association

June 2 **CARMARTHENSHIRE CRAFTS/St Peters Hall, Nott Square, Carmarthen**
Carmarthenshire Crafts

June 3-4 **NORTH ANTRIM AGRICULTURAL SHOW**
Ballymoney Showgrounds, North Road, Ballymoney, Co Antrim
North Antrim Agricultural Association Ltd

June 3-5 **CRAFT SPACES AT EAST OF ENGLAND GARDEN SHOW**
Woodgreen Animal Shelter, Godmanchester, Huntingdon, Cambs
Aztec Events

June 3-5 **INGATESTONE HALL HOME DESIGN & INTERIORS EXHIBITION**
Chelmsford, Essex
Buckingham Events

June 3-5	**THE CONTEMPORARY CRAFT FAIR 2005** **Mill Marsh Park, Bovey Tracey, Devon** Crafts at Bovey Tracey
June 3-5	**WOODFEST WALES/St Asaph, Denbighshire** Event~Reality
June 3-5	**LIVE CRAFT SHOW/Loseley Park, Compton, Guildford, Surrey** HD Events Ltd
June 4	**BRITISH MADE CRAFTS AT CAMPSIE SHOW** **Bogton Farm, Torrance, by Glasgow** Blaircraft
June 4	**CIRENCESTER CRAFTSMAN'S MARKET** **Corn Hall, Market Place, Cirencester, Glos** Cirencester Craftsman's Market
June 4	**CRAFTS AT THE FORUM/The Forum, Norwich, Norfolk** Norfolk Events
June 4	**ARTS & CRAFT FAIR/Town Hall, Stokesley, nr Middlesbrough** Yorkshire Craft Fairs
June 4-5	**BLAKEMERE CRAFT FAIR** **Blakemere Craft Centre, Chester Road, Sandiway, Northwich, Cheshire** Blakemere Craft Centre
June 4-5	**CRAFT MARQUEE AT WOLVERHAMPTON STEAM RALLY** **West Park, Park Road West, Wolverhampton** Cottage Industries
June 4-5	**CRAFT & GIFTS MARQUEE AT YORKSHIRE TRUCKING SPECTACULAR** **Driffield Showground, Driffield, East Yorks** Craft Lincs
June 4-5	**CRAFT & GIFT MARQUEE AT LEIGHTON BUZZARD BY-PASS RALLY** **A5 By-Pass, Leighton Buzzard, Beds** Craft People 2000
June 4-5	**DEEPING AGRICULTURAL SHOW & COUNTRY FAYRE** **Market Deeping, nr Peterborough** Deeping Agricultural Show & Country Fayre
June 4-5	**CRAFT MARQUEE AT KIRKLEATHAM GARDEN SHOW** **Kirkleatham Hall, Redcar** Doug Moore
June 4-5	**ARTS & CRAFTS SECTION AT BEWL GARDEN SHOW** **Bewl Water, off A21, Lamberhurst, Tunbridge Wells, Kent** Kent & Sussex Border Lions

June 4-5 **CRAFT STANDS AT MID SHROPSHIRE VINTAGE CLUB CHARITY VINTAGE VEHICLE RALLY/West Midlands Agricultural Showground, Berwick Road, Shrewsbury**
Mid Shropshire Vintage Club Ltd

June 4-5 **GARDENING & FOOD FAIR 2005**
Courtyard Gallery, Pensthorpe, Fakenham, Norfolk
Pensthorpe

June 5 **CRAFT STALLS AT CARRICK LOWLAND GATHERING**
Victory Park, Girvan, Ayrshire
Carrick Lowland Gathering

June 5 **COXWOLD CRAFT FAIR/Village Hall, Coxwold, North Yorks**
Coxwold Craft Fairs

June 5 **CRAFTS AT KENILWORTH SHOW**
Hurst Farm, Crackley Lane, Kenilworth, Warks
Kenilworth & District Agricultural Society

June 5 **LAUDERDALE HOUSE ARTS & CRAFTS**
Lauderdale House, Waterlow Park, Highgate Hill, London N6
Lauderdale Arts & Crafts

June 5 **QUALITY CRAFT & GIFT FAIR/Cannon Hall, Cawthorne, South Yorks**
Quality Fairs

June 5 **YORK DOLLS HOUSE & MINIATURES FAIR/York Racecourse, York**
Warners Dolls House & Miniatures Fairs

June 6-9 **CRAFT FAIR/Electric Mountain, Llanberis, Caernarfon**
Event~Reality

June 9 **CRAFT FAIR/Market House, Hawes, Wensleydale, North Yorks**
Wensleydale Craft Fairs

June 9-11 **BEAUTY, HEALTH & LIFESTYLE MARQUEE AT ROYAL CORNWALL SHOW**
Royal Cornwall Showground, Wadebridge, Cornwall
BHLR Ltd

June 9-11 **MIDSUMMER MADNESS/Bridgend Town Centre, South Wales**
Bridgend Festivals

June 9-11 **CRAFTMAKER EVENTS AT SOUTH OF ENGLAND SHOW**
South of England Showground, Ardingly, West Sussex
Craftmaker Events

June 9-11 **EDEN CRAFTS MARQUEE AT ROYAL CORNWALL SHOW**
Royal Cornwall Showground, Wadebridge, Cornwall
Eden Crafts

June 9-11 **CORNISH CRAFTS MARQUEE AT ROYAL CORNWALL SHOW**
Royal Cornwall Showground, Wadebridge, Cornwall
Enterprise Tamar Ltd

June 9-11 **HEART OF ENGLAND CRAFTWORKERS MARQUEE AT SOUTH OF ENGLAND SHOW/South of England Showground, Ardingly, West Sussex**
Heart of England Craftworkers Ltd

June 9-11 **RURAL CRAFTS ASSOCIATION AT ROYAL CORNWALL SHOW**
Royal Cornwall Showground, Wadebridge, Cornwall
Rural Crafts Association

June 9-11 **RURAL CRAFTS ASSOCIATION AT SOUTH OF ENGLAND SHOW**
South of England Showground, Ardingly, West Sussex
Rural Crafts Association

June 9-12 **RURAL CRAFTS ASSOCIATION AT GUARDIAN COLLECTIONS BRAMHAM HORSE TRIALS/Bramham Park, Wetherby, West Yorks**
Rural Crafts Association

June 9-12 **WELSH CRAFTS AT BLENHEIM PALACE FLOWER SHOW**
Blenheim Palace, Woodstock, Oxon (dates to be confirmed)
Wales Craft Council

June 10-12 **CRAFT STALLS AT WIMBORNE FOLK FESTIVAL**
Town Square/High Street/Corn Market etc, Wimborne Minster, Dorset
Wimborne Folk Festival

June 11 **CRAFT & COLLECTABLES/Woodford Community Centre, Woodford, Stockport, Cheshire** (supporting Francis House Hospice)
Craft & Collectables

June 11 **ART, CRAFT & GIFT FAIR/Town Hall, Brackley, Northants**
Falcon Fairs

June 11 **CRAFTS AT HONLEY SHOW/Farnley Tyas, nr Huddersfield, West Yorks**
Honley Agricultural Show Ltd

June 11 **CRAFT MARQUEE AT LORD MAYOR'S GALA**
East Park, Holderness Road, Hull, East Yorks
Kingston upon Hull City Council

June 11 **MITCHAM CARNIVAL**
Three Kings Piece, Commonside West, Mitcham, Surrey
Mitcham Carnival

June 11 **ARTS & CRAFT FAIR/The Milton Rooms, Malton, North Yorks**
Yorkshire Craft Fairs

June 11-12 **CRAFT STANDS AT BELPER STEAM & VINTAGE EVENT**
Eyes Meadow, Duffield, Derbys
Belper Steam & Vintage Event

June 11-12 **BLAKEMERE CRAFT FAIR**
Blakemere Craft Centre, Chester Road, Sandiway, Northwich, Cheshire
Blakemere Craft Centre

June 11-12 **BUGLAWTON HALL SCHOOL VINTAGE FAIR**
Buglawton Hall School, Buxton Road, Buglawton, Congleton, Cheshire
Buglawton Hall School Vintage Fair

June 11-12 **CRAFT FAYRE/Buxton Pavilion, Buxton, Derbys**
Cheshire Fayre

June 11-12 **IRISH COUNTRY LIFESTYLE FESTIVAL/Shanes Castle, Antrim, Co Antrim**
Country Lifestyle Exhibitions Ltd

June 11-12 **CRAFT & GIFT MARQUEE AT WHITWELL STEAM FAYRE**
St Paul's Warden, Beds
Craft People 2000

June 11-12 **GREEN DAYS CRAFT FAIR/Acton Green (opp Turnham Green Station), Chiswick, London W4**
Green Days Craft Fair

June 11-12 **CRAFT & GARDEN SHOW**
Cressing Temple Barns, Cressing (B1018), nr Braintree, Essex
Hallmark Craft Fairs

June 11-12 **CRAFT MARQUEE AT HMS SULTAN SUMMER SHOW**
Polo Fields, HMS Sultan, Gosport, Hants
HMS Sultan Summer Show

June 11-12 **MINIATURA/SECC, Glasgow**
Miniatura

June 11-12 **CRAFT & GIFT FAIR/Bodelwyddan Castle, St Asaph, Denbighshire**
North West Craft & Gift Fairs

June 11-12 **FOOD & CRAFT SHOW/Mersea Island Vineyards, Mersea Island, nr Colchester, Essex** (provisional dates)
Penny Farthing Craft Fairs

June 11-12 **CRAFTS AT EVESHAM COUNTRY PARK/Evesham By-Pass A46, Worcs**
Shirecrafts

June 11-18 **CRAFT STANDS AT HASTINGS DIRECT INTERNATIONAL TENNIS**
International Lawn Tennis Centre, College Road, Eastbourne, East Sussex
Eastbourne Borough Council

June 12 **COXWOLD CRAFT FAIR/Village Hall, Coxwold, North Yorks**
Coxwold Craft Fairs

June 12 **MILLENNIUM CRAFTS & GIFTS/Community Centre, Lyndhurst, Hants**
Millennium Crafts & Gifts

June 12 **ARTS & CRAFT FAIR/Crown Hotel, Harrogate, North Yorks**
Yorkshire Craft Fairs

June 14 **MILLENNIUM CRAFTS & GIFTS/Community Centre, Lyndhurst, Hants**
Millennium Crafts & Gifts

June 14-17 **QUALITY CRAFT & GIFT FAIR/Guildhall, York, North Yorks**
Quality Fairs

June 16 **CRAFT FAIR/Market House, Hawes, Wensleydale, North Yorks**
Wensleydale Craft Fairs

June 16-19 **CRAFTS AT BEVERLEY & EAST RIDING FOLK FESTIVAL**
Beverley, East Yorks
Beverley & East Riding Folk Festival

June 17-19 **CRAFT SPACES AT SOUTH EAST ESSEX GARDEN SHOW**
Barleylands Farm, Barleylands, Billericay, Essex
Aztec Events

June 17-19 **HIGHCLERE CASTLE HOME DESIGN & INTERIORS EXHIBITION**
Newbury, Berks
Buckingham Events

June 17-19 **CRAFT & GIFTS MARQUEE AT EAST OF ENGLAND SHOW**
East of England Showground, Peterborough, Cambs
Craft Lincs

June 17-19 **CRAFT FAIR**
Burnside Garden Centre, New Lane, Thornton Cleveleys, Lancs
Creative Crafts Association

June 17-19 **CRAFTS AT EAST OF ENGLAND COUNTRY SHOW**
East of England Showground, Peterborough, Cambs
East of England Showground (main event organiser)

June 17-19 **EDEN CRAFTS MARQUEE AT EAST OF ENGLAND SHOW**
East of England Showground, Peterborough, Cambs
Eden Crafts

June 17-19 **EDEN CRAFTS MARQUEE AT THREE COUNTIES SHOW**
Three Counties Showground, Malvern, Worcs
Eden Crafts

June 17-19 **GLOBAL FUSION – FAIRLY TRADED GLOBAL CRAFTS**
Pestalozzi International Village, Sedlescombe, East Sussex
Global Fusion

June 17-19 **LIVE CRAFT SHOW/Berkeley Castle, Glos**
HD Events Ltd

June 17-19 **MIDDLEWICH FOLK & BOAT FESTIVAL/Middlewich, Cheshire**
Middlewich Folk & Boat Festival

June 17-19 **RURAL CRAFTS ASSOCIATION AT EAST OF ENGLAND SHOW**
East of England Showground, Peterborough, Cambs
Rural Crafts Association

June 17-19 **RURAL CRAFTS ASSOCIATION AT URBAN ESCAPES 2005**
Lee Valley Showground, M25 J26
Rural Crafts Association

June 18 **3 SHIRES CRAFT GUILD/St Michael's Church Hall, Bishops Cleeve, Glos**
3 Shires Craft Guild

June 18 **HILLY FIELDS SUMMER FAIR**
Hilly Fields Park, Hilly Fields Crescent, London SE4
Brockley Society

June 18 **CIRENCESTER CRAFTSMAN'S MARKET**
Corn Hall, Market Place, Cirencester, Glos
Cirencester Craftsman's Market

June 18 **ART, CRAFT & GIFT FAIR/Town Hall, Towcester, Northants**
Falcon Fairs

June 18 **FOCUS CRAFT GROUP AT OLDMELDRUM SPORTS**
Oldmeldrum, Inverurie, Aberdeenshire
Festival of Crafts Unique to Scotland (FOCUS)

June 18 **CRAFTS AT THE FORUM/The Forum, Norwich, Norfolk**
Norfolk Events

June 18 **OVINGHAM GOOSE FAIR/Village Green, Ovingham, Northumberland**
Ovingham Goose Fair

June 18 **PORTCHESTER GALA**
Portchester Castle, Castle Street, Portchester, nr Fareham, Hants
Portchester Gala

June 18 **ARTS & CRAFT FAIR/Crescent Hotel, Ilkley, West Yorks**
Yorkshire Craft Fairs

June 18-19 **BLAKEMERE CRAFT FAIR**
Blakemere Craft Centre, Chester Road, Sandiway, Northwich, Cheshire
Blakemere Craft Centre

June 18-19 **CRAFT MARQUEE AT HATTON COUNTRY WORLD**
A4177 Hatton, between Warwick and Solihull, Warks
Cottage Industries

June 18-19 **CRAFT & GIFT MARQUEE AT STAPLEFORD STEAM**
Stapleford, nr Melton Mowbray, Leics
Craft People 2000

June 18-19 **MIDSUMMER ART FAIR**
Landmark Arts Centre, Ferry Road, Teddington, Middx (preview June 17)
Landmark Arts Centre

June 18-19 **CRAFT & COUNTRY SHOW**
High Elms Country Park, Shire Lane, Farnborough, nr Bromley, Kent
Oakleigh Craft Fairs

June 18-19 **WELSH GAME FAIR/Llandeilo, Carmarthenshire**
Welsh Game Fair

June 18-19 **CRAFT MARKET**
Whiteley Village Outlet Shopping, Whiteley, Fareham, Hants
Woodland Crafts

June 19 **COXWOLD CRAFT FAIR/Village Hall, Coxwold, North Yorks**
Coxwold Craft Fairs

June 19 **EASTON FESTIVAL/Easton Farm Park, Easton, Woodbridge, Suffolk**
Easton Festival

June 19 **ART, CRAFT & GIFT FAIR/Village Hall, Woburn, Beds**
Falcon Fairs

June 19 **CRAFT MARQUEE AT CLUMBER SHOW/Clumber Park, Worksop, Notts**
National Trust - Clumber Park

June 19 **QUALITY CRAFT & GIFT FAIR**
Sun Pavilion, Valley Gardens, Harrogate, North Yorks
Quality Fairs

June 19 **WEST OF ENGLAND BEAD FAIR/Wincanton Racecourse, Somerset**
West of England Events

June 19 **WHITSTABLE COMMUNITY CENTRE FUN DAY**
Tankerton Slopes, Marine Parade, Whitstable, Kent
Whitstable Festivals & Events Ltd

June 19 **ARTS & CRAFT AT GUISBOROUGH TOWN FAIR**
Guisborough Hall, Guisborough
Yorkshire Craft Fairs

June 21-22 **CHESHIRE COUNTY SHOW**
County Showground, Tabley, Knutsford, Cheshire
Cheshire Agricultural Society

June 21-23 **CRAFT FAIR/Town Hall, Lloyd Street, Llandudno, Conwy**
Event~Reality

June 22-23 **BEAUTY, HEALTH & LIFESTYLE MARQUEE AT LINCOLNSHIRE SHOW**
Lincolnshire Showground, Grange-de-Lings, Lincoln
BHLR Ltd

June 22-23 **CRAFT & GIFTS MARQUEE AT LINCOLNSHIRE SHOW**
Lincolnshire Showground, Grange-de-Lings, Lincoln
Craft Lincs

June 22-23 **EDEN CRAFTS MARQUEE AT LINCOLNSHIRE SHOW**
Lincolnshire Showground, Grange-de-Lings, Lincoln
Eden Crafts

June 22-23	**HEART OF ENGLAND CRAFTWORKERS MARQUEE AT LINCOLNSHIRE SHOW/Lincolnshire Showground, Grange-de-Lings, Lincoln** Heart of England Craftworkers Ltd
June 22-23	**RURAL CRAFTS ASSOCIATION AT LINCOLNSHIRE SHOW Lincolnshire Showground, Grange-de-Lings, Lincs** Rural Crafts Association
June 23	**CRAFT FAIR/Market House, Hawes, Wensleydale, North Yorks** Wensleydale Craft Fairs
June 23-26	**BEAUTY, HEALTH & LIFESTYLE MARQUEE AT ROYAL HIGHLAND SHOW Royal Highland Centre, Ingliston, Edinburgh** BHLR Ltd
June 23-26	**HANDCRAFTS COMPETITION & EXHIBITION AT ROYAL HIGHLAND SHOW/Royal Highland Centre, Ingliston, Edinburgh** Royal Highland Show (main event organiser)
June 23-26	**RURAL CRAFTS ASSOCIATION AT ROYAL HIGHLAND SHOW Royal Highland Centre, Ingliston, Edinburgh** Rural Crafts Association
June 24-26	**ENTERTAIN ALFRESCO/Penshurst Place, nr Tonbridge, Kent** ICHF
June 25	**FOCUS CRAFT GROUP/Town Hall, Banchory, Aberdeenshire** Festival of Crafts Unique to Scotland (FOCUS)
June 25	**THE PARTY IN THE PARK CRAFT SHOW Gosfield School, Gosfield, Halstead, Essex** K.C. Craft Shows
June 25	**MIDSUMMER CRAFT FAIR/Town Hall, Market Square, Wells, Somerset** West Country Craft Fairs
June 25-26	**CRAFT FAIR/Victoria Halls, Hartley Wintney, Hants** Arts & Craft Fairs
June 25-26	**BLAKEMERE CRAFT FAIR/Blakemere Craft Centre, Chester Road, Sandiway, Northwich, Cheshire** Blakemere Craft Centre
June 25-26	**CRAFT FAIR/Hawes Market Hall, Hawes, North Yorks** Cosy Crafts
June 25-26	**CRAFT & GARDEN FAIR AT SIR HAROLD HILLIER GARDENS nr Romsey, Hants** Craft Carnival
June 25-26	**CRAFT & GIFTS MARQUEE AT SHROPSHIRE & WEST MIDLANDS AGRICULTURAL SHOW/Showground, Berwick Road, Shrewsbury, Shropshire** Craft Lincs

June 25-26 **CRAFT & GIFT MARQUEE AT BEDFORD INTERNATIONAL KITE FESTIVAL/Russell Park, Bedford**
Craft People 2000

June 25-26 **STEAM & VINTAGE 100 ENGINE RALLY**
Astle Park, Chelford, nr Macclesfield, Cheshire
Five Counties Vintage Organisation Ltd

June 25-26 **CRAFT & GIFT MARQUEE AT BASC COUNTRY FAIR/Bodelwyddan Castle, St Asaph, Denbighshire**
North West Craft & Gift Fairs

June 25-26 **CRAFT WEEKEND AT DOBBIES OF GAILEY/Dobbies Garden Centre, Gailey Island, Junction A5/A449 Stafford Road, Gailey, Staffs**
Shirecrafts

June 25-26 **SHROPSHIRE & WEST MIDLANDS AGRICULTURAL SHOW**
Showground, Berwick Road, Shrewsbury, Shropshire
Shropshire & West Midlands Agricultural Society (main event organiser)

June 25-26 **ARTS & CRAFTS MARQUEE AT SOUTHAMPTON BALLOON & FLOWER FESTIVAL/Southampton Common, Southampton, Hants**
Southampton City Council

June 25-26 **CRAFT MARQUEE AT FIRE ENGINE & HISTORIC VEHICLE RALLY**
Preston Hall Museum & Park, Yarm Road, Stockton-on-Tees
Stockton-on-Tees Council

June 25-26 **CRAFTS AT BRIGHTON RACECOURSE**
Freshfield Road, Brighton, East Sussex
Woodland Crafts

June 26 **MARQUEE AT SHEFFIELD FESTIVAL OF TRANSPORT**
Graves Park, Hemsworth Road, Sheffield
Allott Agency

June 26 **ARTS & CRAFT FAYRE/Hartington Village Hall, Hartington, Derbys**
Biddulph Arts & Craft Fayres

June 26 **MARQUEE AT CASTLE POINT SHOW/Waterside Farm Showground, Somnes Avenue, Canvey Island, Essex**
Castle Point Borough Council

June 26 **COXWOLD CRAFT FAIR/Village Hall, Coxwold, North Yorks**
Coxwold Craft Fairs

June 26 **CRAFT MARQUEE AT DERBYSHIRE COUNTY SHOW**
The Showground, Borrowash Road, Elvaston, Derbys
Derbyshire Agricultural & Horticultural Society Ltd

June 26 **FOCUS CRAFT GROUP/Victoria Hall, Ballater, Aberdeenshire**
Festival of Crafts Unique to Scotland (FOCUS)

June 26 **HORBURY SHOW**
Carr Lodge Park, Wakefield Road, Horbury, Wakefield, West Yorks
Rotary Club of Horbury & Ossett Phoenix

June 29-30 **BEAUTY, HEALTH & LIFESTYLE MARQUEE AT ROYAL NORFOLK SHOW**
Royal Norfolk Showground, Dereham Road, New Costessey, Norwich, Norfolk
BHLR Ltd

June 29-30 **RURAL CRAFTS ASSOCIATION AT ROYAL NORFOLK SHOW**
Norfolk Showground, Dereham Road, New Costessey, Norwich, Norfolk
Rural Crafts Association

June 30 **MALTON SHOW/Scampston Park, Scampston, Malton, North Yorks**
Malton Agricultural Society

July date tba **CRAFT STANDS AT SKATE FESTIVAL**
Prince William Parade, Eastern Seafront, Eastbourne, East Sussex
Eastbourne Borough Council

July date tba **CRAFT MARQUEE AT SUMMER GARDENING SHOW**
Capel Manor College, Bullsmoor Lane, Enfield, Middx
Fig Fairs

July date tba **MAURTRAID CRAFTSHOW/venue tbc**
Mautraid Craftshows

July date tba **CRAFT & GIFT MARQUEE AT EASTBOURNE MOTORSHOW**
Sussex Downs College + Park College, Kings Drive, Eastbourne, East Sussex
Sovereign Fairs

July date tba **CRAFT, GIFT & FOOD MARQUEE AT THE ARGUS BRIGHTON MOTOR SHOW/Brighton Racecourse, East Sussex**
Sovereign Fairs

July date tba **LAMBETH COUNTRY SHOW/Brockwell Park, Herne Hill, London SE24**
Ubique Leisure Ltd

July 1-2 **MARQUEE AT HOLLOWELL STEAM & HEAVY HORSE SHOW**
Hollowell Rally Field, off A5199, north of Northampton
Hollowell Steam & Heavy Horse Show

July 1-3 **CRAFT FAIR/Bents Garden Centre, Glazebury, nr Warrington, Cheshire**
Creative Crafts Association

July 1-3 **LIVE CRAFT SHOW/Audley End House, Saffron Walden, Essex**
HD Events Ltd

July 1-9 **RURAL CRAFTS ASSOCIATION AT GUILDFORD FESTIVAL**
Guildford High Street, Guildford, Surrey
Rural Crafts Association

July 2	**3 SHIRES CRAFT GUILD/Abbey Parish Hall, Tewkesbury, Glos** 3 Shires Craft Guild
July 2	**CIRENCESTER CRAFTSMAN'S MARKET** **Corn Hall, Market Place, Cirencester, Glos** Cirencester Craftsman's Market
July 2	**CRAFT MARQUEE AT DOUNE & DUNBLANE SHOW** **Keir Mains, Dunblane, Perthshire** Doune & Dunblane Agricultural Society
July 2	**CRAFT MARQUEE AT MACHEN AGRICULTURAL SHOW** **Mill Farm, Machen, Caerphilly** Machen Agricultural Show
July 2	**CRAFTS AT THE FORUM/The Forum, Norwich, Norfolk** Norfolk Events
July 2-3	**BLAKEMERE CRAFT FAIR/Blakemere Craft Centre, Chester Road, Sandiway, Northwich, Cheshire** Blakemere Craft Centre
July 2-3	**COTTAGE INDUSTRIES CRAFT MARQUEE AT RAF WADDINGTON AIR SHOW/RAF Waddington Airbase, Lincoln** Cottage Industries
July 2-3	**CRAFT & GIFTS MARQUEE AT RAF WADDINGTON AIRSHOW** **RAF Waddington Airbase, Lincoln** Craft Lincs
July 2-3	**CRAFTS & GIFTS AT TRUCKWEST SOUTHWEST** **Show Buildings, Royal Bath & West Showground, Shepton Mallet, Somerset** Craft Lincs
July 2-3	**CRAFT MARQUEE AT GREAT YORKSHIRE STEAM FAIR** **Duncombe Park, Helmsley, North Yorks** Kingfisher Craft Marquee Management
July 2-3	**LANCHESTER SHOW/Newhouses Farm, Lanchester, Co Durham** Lanchester Agricultural Society
July 2-3	**CRAFT VILLAGE AT BEXLEY SHOW** **Danson Park, Danson Road, Bexleyheath, Kent** Oakleigh Craft Fairs
July 2-Sept 11	**DEVON GUILD OF CRAFTSMEN SUMMER EXHIBITION** **Devon Guild of Craftsmen, Riverside Mill, Bovey Tracey, Devon** Devon Guild of Craftsmen
July 3	**COXWOLD CRAFT FAIR/Village Hall, Coxwold, North Yorks** Coxwold Craft Fairs

July 3 **EAST MIDLANDS DOLL FAIR/Kelham Hall, Kelham, Newark, Notts**
East Midlands Doll Fairs

July 3 **CRAFT FAIR/The Maltings, Ely, Cambs**
Kingfisher Promotions

July 3 **MILLENNIUM CRAFTS & GIFTS/Community Centre, Lyndhurst, Hants**
Millennium Crafts & Gifts

July 3-6 **EDEN CRAFTS MARQUEE AT THE ROYAL SHOW/NAC, Stoneleigh, Warks**
Eden Crafts

July 3-6 **RURAL CRAFTS ASSOCIATION AT THE ROYAL SHOW**
NAC, Stoneleigh, Warks
Rural Crafts Association

July 5-10 **CRAFT MARQUEE AT INTERNATIONAL EISTEDDFOD**
Llangollen, Denbighshire
Wales Craft Council

July 7 **CARMARTHENSHIRE CRAFTS/St Peters Hall, Nott Square, Carmarthen**
Carmarthenshire Crafts

July 7 **CRAFT FAIR/Market House, Hawes, Wensleydale, North Yorks**
Wensleydale Craft Fairs

July 9 **FOCUS CRAFT GROUP/Town Hall, Inverurie, Aberdeenshire**
Festival of Crafts Unique to Scotland (FOCUS)

July 9 **FORRES HIGHLAND GAMES/Grant Park, Victoria Road, Forres, Moray**
Forres Highland Games

July 9 **LICHFIELD MEDIEVAL MARKET/Lichfield Cathedral Close, Lichfield, Staffs**
Lichfield Medieval Market

July 9 **NEWTON CARNIVAL/Parish Grounds, Newton, Alfreton, Derbys**
Newton Carnival Team

July 9 **CRAFT TENT AT TENDRING HUNDRED SHOW**
Lawford House Park, nr Manningtree, Essex
Tendring Hundred Show

July 9 **ARTS & CRAFT FAIR/The Milton Rooms, Malton, North Yorks**
Yorkshire Craft Fairs

July 9-10 **BLAKEMERE CRAFT FAIR**
Blakemere Craft Centre, Chester Road, Sandiway, Northwich, Cheshire
Blakemere Craft Centre

July 9-10 **BRIDGEND SHOW/Pencoed College, Pencoed, Bridgend**
Bridgend Festivals

July 9-10 **CRAFTS AT SALISBURY SHOW/Hudson's Field (A345), Salisbury, Wilts**
Burlyn Events Ltd

July 9-10 **CRAFT FAYRE/Sizergh Castle, nr Kendal, Cumbria**
Cheshire Fayre

July 9-10 **CRAFT FAIR/Hawes Market Hall, Hawes, North Yorks**
Cosy Crafts

July 9-10 **CRAFT MARQUEE AT WOLVERHAMPTON CITY SHOW**
West Park, Park Road West, Wolverhampton
Cottage Industries

July 9-10 **CRAFT & GIFT MARQUEE AT BEDFORDSHIRE'S COUNTRY SHOW**
Old Warden, nr Biggleswade, Beds
Craft People 2000

July 9-10 **32nd HISTORIC VEHICLE GATHERING**
Powderham Castle, Kenton, nr Exeter, Devon
Historic Vehicle Gathering

July 9-10 **CRAFTS AT GARDENERS' WEEKEND/Shugborough, Milford, Staffs**
Hobby Horse Events Ltd

July 9-10 **CRAFTS AT SCOTTISH TRANSPORT EXTRAVAGANZA**
Glamis Castle, Glamis, by Forfar, Angus
Strathmore Vintage Vehicle Club Ltd

July 9-10 **WIRRAL SHOW CRAFT MARQUEE/Harrison Drive, New Brighton, Wirral**
Wirral Show Craft Marquee

July 9-10 **QUEEN ELIZABETH COUNTRY PARK SHOW**
Queen Elizabeth Country Park, nr Petersfield, Hants
Woodland Crafts

July 10 **ARTS & CRAFT FAYRE/Hartington Village Hall, Hartington, Derbys**
Biddulph Arts & Craft Fayres

July 10 **COXWOLD CRAFT FAIR/Village Hall, Coxwold, North Yorks**
Coxwold Craft Fairs

July 10 **TYNESIDE DOLLS' HOUSE & MINIATURES FAIR**
Lancastrian Suite, Federation Brewery, Dunston, Gateshead, Tyne & Wear
Dolly Domain Fairs

July 10 **LAUDERDALE HOUSE ARTS & CRAFTS**
Lauderdale House, Waterlow Park, Highgate Hill, London N6
Lauderdale Arts & Crafts

July 10 **CRAFT MARQUEE AT ALTON SHOW**
Froyle Park, Upper Froyle, Alton, Hants
North East Hants Agricultural Association

July 10 **WEYMOUTH & SOUTH DORSET SUMMER CRAFT FAIR**
Weymouth Pavilion, Esplanade, Weymouth, Dorset
West Country Craft Fairs

July 10	**CRAFT MARQUEE AT WILMSLOW SHOW** **Wilmslow High School, Wilmslow, Cheshire** Wilmslow Show
July 10	**CRAFT FAIR AT CASTLE ASHBY COUNTRY FAIR** **Horton Road, Brafield-on-the-Green, Northants** Yardley Hastings Society
July 11	**STITHIANS SHOW/The Showground, Stithians, nr Truro, Cornwall** Stithians Agricultural Association
July 12	**MILLENNIUM CRAFTS & GIFTS/Community Centre, Lyndhurst, Hants** Millennium Crafts & Gifts
July 12-14	**BEAUTY, HEALTH & LIFESTYLE MARQUEE AT GREAT YORKSHIRE SHOW** **Great Yorkshire Showground, Wetherby Road, Harrogate, North Yorks** BHLR Ltd
July 12-14	**CRAFT FAIR/Town Hall, Lloyd Street, Llandudno, Conwy** Event~Reality
July 12-14	**DESIGNER & CRAFTS MARQUEE AT GREAT YORKSHIRE SHOW** **Great Yorkshire Showground, Wetherby Road, Harrogate, North Yorks** Exhibition Management
July 12-14	**HEART OF ENGLAND CRAFTWORKERS MARQUEE AT GREAT YORKSHIRE SHOW/Great Yorkshire Showground, Wetherby Road, Harrogate, North Yorks** Heart of England Craftworkers Ltd
July 12-14	**RURAL CRAFTS ASSOCIATION AT GREAT YORKSHIRE SHOW** **Great Yorkshire Showground, Wetherby Road, Harrogate, North Yorks** Rural Crafts Association
July 14	**CRAFT FAIR/Market House, Hawes, Wensleydale, North Yorks** Wensleydale Craft Fairs
July 14-17	**CRAFT & GIFT MARQUEE AT LAND ROVER ENTHUSIAST EVENT** **Billing Aquadrome, Northampton** Craft People 2000
July 15	**CRAFT & GIFT FAIR/Evron Centre, Filey, North Yorks** Hardy Fairs Ltd
July 15-17	**BEAUTY, HEALTH & LIFESTYLE MARQUEE AT KENT COUNTY SHOW** **Kent County Showground, Detling, nr Maidstone, Kent** BHLR Ltd
July 15-17	**CRAFT FAIR/High Legh Garden Centre, Knutsford, Cheshire** Creative Crafts Association
July 15-17	**EDEN CRAFTS MARQUEE AT KENT COUNTY SHOW** **Kent County Showground, Detling, nr Maidstone, Kent** Eden Crafts

July 15-17	**CRAFT MARQUEE AT GREAT BOCONNOC STEAM FAIR** **Boconnoc Estate, Middle Taphouse, Liskeard, Cornwall** Liskeard Steam & Vintage Club
July 15-17	**RURAL CRAFTS ASSOCIATION AT KENT COUNTY SHOW** **Kent County Showground, Detling, nr Maidstone, Kent** Rural Crafts Association
July 15-17	**OPEN AIR EXHIBITION AT MIDSUMMER MUSIC & LEISURE SHOW** **Lincolnshire Showground, Grange-de-Lings, Lincoln** Warners Exhibitions
July 15-17	**CRAFTS AT WEETING STEAM RALLY & COUNTRY SHOW** **Weeting, Brandon, Suffolk** Weeting Steam Rally & Country Show
July 16	**CRAFTS AT CASTLEWELLAN & DISTRICT AGRICULTURAL SHOW** **Forest Park, Castlewellan, Co Down** Castlewellan & District Agricultural Show
July 16	**CIRENCESTER CRAFTSMAN'S MARKET/Corn Hall, Market Place, Cirencester, Glos** Cirencester Craftsman's Market
July 16	**CRAFTS AT CUMBERLAND COUNTY SHOW** **Rickerby Park, Carlisle, Cumbria** Cumberland Agricultural Society
July 16	**CRAFTS AT THE FORUM/The Forum, Norwich, Norfolk** Norfolk Events
July 16-17	**BLAKEMERE CRAFT FAIR** **Blakemere Craft Centre, Chester Road, Sandiway, Northwich, Cheshire** Blakemere Craft Centre
July 16-17	**CRAFT FAIR/Hawes Market Hall, Hawes, North Yorks** Cosy Crafts
July 16-17	**MADE IN LANCASHIRE MARQUEE AT GREAT ECCLESTON AGRICULTURAL SHOW/The Showground, Great Eccleston, Preston, Lancs** Great Eccleston & District Agricultural Society
July 16-17	**HEART OF ENGLAND CRAFTWORKERS MARQUEE AT HOLKHAM COUNTRY SHOW/Holkham Park, Wells-next-the-Sea, Norfolk** Heart of England Craftworkers Ltd
July 16-17	**CRAFTS AT CHILTERN SHOW/Great Missenden, Bucks** HD Events Ltd
July 16-17	**CRAFT VILLAGE AT DAGENHAM TOWN SHOW** **Central Park, Raynham Road North, Dagenham, Essex** Oakleigh Craft Fairs

July 16-17 **CRAFT FAIR AT ROYAL INTERNATIONAL AIR TATTOO**
RAF Fairford, Fairford, Glos
Royal International Air Tattoo

July 16-17 **RURAL CRAFTS ASSOCIATION AT HOLKHAM COUNTRY FAIR**
Holkham Park, Wells-next-the-Sea, Norfolk
Rural Crafts Association

July 16-17 **CRAFT WEEKEND AT DOBBIES OF GAILEY**
Dobbies Garden Centre, Gailey Island, Junction A5/A449 Stafford Road, Gailey, Staffs
Shirecrafts

July 16-17 **SHIRECRAFTS MARQUEE AT WOODLANDS**
Woodlands Nurseries, Ashby Road, Stapleton, Leics
Shirecrafts

July 16-17 **CRAFT FAIR & TRADE FAIR AT STOWMARKET CARNIVAL 2005**
Recreation Ground, Stowmarket, Suffolk
Stowmarket Carnival

July 16-17 **GAME & COUNTRY FAIR**
Michelham Priory, Upper Dicker, Hailsham, East Sussex
Sussex Past

July 16-17 **ARTS & CRAFT FAIR/St William College, York, North Yorks**
Yorkshire Craft Fairs

July 17 **CRAFT MARQUEE AT ASHBY AGRICULTURAL SHOW**
Measham Lodge Farm, Measham, Swadlincote, Derbys
Ashby-de-la-Zouch Agricultural Society

July 17 **COXWOLD CRAFT FAIR/Village Hall, Coxwold, North Yorks**
Coxwold Craft Fairs

July 17 **CRAFT & GIFT MARQUEE AT ASHBOURNE HIGHLAND GATHERING**
Ashbourne, Derbys
Craft People 2000

July 17 **MILLENNIUM CRAFTS & GIFTS/Community Centre, Lyndhurst, Hants**
Millennium Crafts & Gifts

July 17 **QUALITY CRAFT & GIFT FAIR**
Sun Pavilion, Valley Gardens, Harrogate, North Yorks
Quality Fairs

July 17-18 **CRAFT MARQUEE AT ACKWORTH VINTAGE GATHERING**
Showfield, Ackfield Top, nr Pontefract, West Yorks
Kingfisher Craft Marquee Management

July 18-21 **BEAUTY, HEALTH & LIFESTYLE MARQUEE AT ROYAL WELSH SHOW**
Royal Welsh Showground, Llanelwedd, Builth Wells, Powys
BHLR Ltd

July 18-21	**HEART OF ENGLAND CRAFTWORKERS MARQUEE AT ROYAL WELSH SHOW/Royal Welsh Showground, Llanelwedd, Builth Wells, Powys** Heart of England Craftworkers Ltd
July 18-21	**CRAFTS AT ROYAL WELSH SHOW** **Royal Welsh Showground, Llanelwedd, Builth Wells, Powys** Royal Welsh Agricultural Society Ltd (main event organiser)
July 18-21	**RURAL CRAFTS ASSOCIATION AT ROYAL WELSH SHOW** **Royal Welsh Showground, Llanelwedd, Builth Wells, Powys** Rural Crafts Association
July 18-21	**WELSH CRAFTS AT ROYAL WELSH SHOW** **Royal Welsh Showground, Llanelwedd, Builth Wells, Powys** Wales Craft Council
July 21	**CRAFTS MARQUEE AT LAUNCESTON AGRICULTURAL SHOW** **Kennards House, Launceston, Cornwall** Enterprise Tamar Ltd
July 21-24	**ARTISTS & ILLUSTRATORS EXHIBITION 2005** **Business Design Centre, Upper Street, Islington, London N1** Artists & Illustrators Exhibition
July 21-24	**CRAFT FAIR/Market House, Hawes, Wensleydale, North Yorks** Wensleydale Craft Fairs
July 22	**CRAFT & GIFT FAIR/Evron Centre, Filey, North Yorks** Hardy Fairs Ltd
July 22-24	**BEAUTY, HEALTH & LIFESTYLE MARQUEE AT CLA GAME FAIR** **Belvoir Castle, Belvoir, Leics** BHLR Ltd
July 22-24	**HEART OF ENGLAND CRAFTWORKERS MARQUEE AT CLA GAME FAIR** **Belvoir Castle, Belvoir, Leics** Heart of England Craftworkers Ltd
July 22-24	**LIVE CRAFT SHOW/Ragley Hall, Alcester, Warks** HD Events Ltd
July 22-24	**NETLEY MARSH STEAM & CRAFT SHOW** **Netley Marsh, A326 (from M27 J2), nr Southampton** Netley Marsh Steam & Craft Show Ltd
July 22-24	**RURAL CRAFTS ASSOCIATION AT CLA GAME FAIR** **Belvoir Castle, Belvoir, Leics** Rural Crafts Association
July 22-24	**CRAFT & TRADE STALLS AT WARWICK FOLK FESTIVAL** **Warwick Boys School, Myton Road, Warwick** Warwick Folk Festival Ltd

July 23	**CRAFT MARQUEE AT ANTRIM SHOW** **Greenmount College Grounds, Dublin Road, Antrim, Co Antrim** Antrim Agricultural Society
July 23	**CRAFT STANDS AT BALQUHIDDER, LOCHEARNHEAD & STRATHYRE HIGHLAND GAMES/Games Park, Lochearnhead, Perthshire** Balquhidder, Lochearnhead & Strathyre Highland Games
July 23	**FOCUS CRAFT GROUP/Town Hall, Stonehaven, Aberdeenshire** Festival of Crafts Unique to Scotland (FOCUS)
July 23	**CRAFT MARQUEE AT MID DEVON SHOW** **Hartnoll Farm, Post Hill, Tiverton, Devon** Mid Devon Show
July 23	**ARTS & CRAFT FAIR/Town Hall, Stokesley, nr Middlesbrough** Yorkshire Craft Fairs
July 23-24	**BLAKEMERE CRAFT FAIR** **Blakemere Craft Centre, Chester Road, Sandiway, Northwich, Cheshire** Blakemere Craft Centre
July 23-24	**MARQUEE OF CRAFTS AT SUNDERLAND AIR SHOW** **Seaburn Park, nr Sunderland** Cottage Industries
July 23-24	**CRAFT FAIR/Wheatcroft Garden Centre, Edwalton, Notts** Creative Crafts Association
July 23-24	**JOUST – FESTIVAL OF MEDIEVAL MAYHEM** **Berkeley Castle, Berkeley, Glos** Joust
July 24	**ARTS & CRAFT FAYRE/Hartington Village Hall, Hartington, Derbys** Biddulph Arts & Craft Fayres
July 24	**COXWOLD CRAFT FAIR/Village Hall, Coxwold, North Yorks** Coxwold Craft Fairs
July 24	**CRAFT FAIR AT GLENDALE FESTIVAL/Wooler, Northumberland** Glendale Festival
July 24	**REDESMERE CRAFTS** **Siddington Village Hall, A34, nr Macclesfield, Cheshire** Redesmere Crafts Association
July 26	**CHESTERFIELD MEDIEVAL MARKET** **Market Place, Chesterfield, Derbys** Special Event Organisers (UK) Ltd
July 26-28	**BEAUTY, HEALTH & LIFESTYLE MARQUEE AT NEW FOREST & HAMPSHIRE COUNTY SHOW/The Showground, New Park, Brockenhurst, Hants** BHLR Ltd

July 26-28 **CRAFT FAIR/Town Hall, Lloyd Street, Llandudno, Conwy**
Event~Reality

July 26-28 **BRITISH MADE CRAFTS AT NEW FOREST & HAMPSHIRE COUNTY SHOW/The Showground, New Park, Brockenhurst, Hants**
New Forest Agricultural Show Society (main show organiser)

July 26-Aug 6 **POOLE SUMMER FAIR/Poole Town Centre, Dorset**
Eden Crafts

July 27 **DUNSTER COUNTRY FAIR/The Lawns, Dunster, Minehead, Somerset**
Dunster Country Fair

July 27 **CRAFT MARQUEE AT CARDIGAN AGRICULTURAL SHOW**
Cardigan Show Field, Cardigan, Ceredigion
Ffeiriau Arbennig

July 27 **CRAFT MARQUEE AT STRANRAER SHOW**
London Road Playing Fields, Stranraer, Dumfries & Galloway
Jane McDowall

July 27 **NORTH LONSDALE AGRICULTURAL SHOW**
Bardsea Park, nr Ulverston, Cumbria
North Lonsdale Agricultural Society

July 28 **CRAFT MARQUEE AT TOTNES & DISTRICT SHOW LTD**
Berry Farm, Berry Pomeroy, Totnes, Devon
Totnes & District Show Ltd

July 28-29 **CRAFT FAIR/Market House, Hawes, Wensleydale, North Yorks**
Wensleydale Craft Fairs

July 29 **CRAFT & GIFT FAIR/Evron Centre, Filey, North Yorks**
Hardy Fairs Ltd

July 29-31 **BRANCEPETH CASTLE SUMMER FAIR**
Brancepeth Castle, 5 miles west of Durham City on A690
Brancepeth Castle Fairs

July 29-31 **CRAFT & GIFT FAIR/St Helens Show, Sherdley Park, St Helens, Lancs**
Cheshire Fayre

July 29-31 **CRAFT FAIR/Rivendell Garden Centre, Mill Lane, Widnes, Cheshire**
Creative Crafts Association

July 29-31 **BRITISH MADE CRAFTS AT GATESHEAD FLOWER SHOW**
Central Nursery Complex, Lobbley Hill, Gateshead, Tyne & Wear
Gateshead Metropolitan Council

July 29-31 **THE GREAT NORTH WEST BALLOON & ARTS FESTIVAL**
(formerly Burnley Balloon Festival)/Burnley, Lancs
Initiative Burnley

July 30 **CRAFTS AT BISHOP'S CASTLE AGRICULTURAL SHOW**
Love Lane, Bishop's Castle, Shropshire
Bishop's Castle Agricultural Show

July 30 **FOCUS CRAFT GROUP AT BANCHORY SHOW/Banchory, Aberdeenshire**
Festival of Crafts Unique to Scotland (FOCUS)

July 30-31 **BLAKEMERE CRAFT FAIR/Blakemere Craft Centre, Chester Road, Sandiway, Northwich, Cheshire**
Blakemere Craft Centre

July 30-31 **CRAFT & GARDEN FAIR AT MONTACUTE**
Montacute House, Montacute, nr Yeovil, Somerset
Craft Carnival

July 30-31 **CRAFT & GIFT MARQUEE AT INTERNATIONAL KOI SHOW**
Billing Aquadrome, Northampton
Craft People 2000

July 30-31 **CRAFTS AT HECKINGTON SHOW**
The Showground, off Eastgate, Heckington, Sleaford, Lincs
Heckington Show

July 30-31 **JOUST - FESTIVAL OF MEDIEVAL MAYHEM**
Berkeley Castle, Berkeley, Glos
Joust

July 30-31 **CRAFT MARQUEE AT NOTTINGHAM STEAM & COUNTRY SHOW**
West Park, Long Eaton, Nottingham
Kingfisher Craft Marquee Management

July 30-31 **MARQUEE PRESENTATION OF CRAFTS**
Ullesthorpe Garden Centre, Lutterworth, Leics
Shirecrafts

July 30-31 **SOMERSET GUILD OF SPINNERS & WEAVERS DEMONSTRATION**
Somerset Rural Life Museum, Chilkwell Street, Glastonbury, Somerset
Somerset Rural Life Museum

July 30-31 **SUN & MOON FESTIVAL/Bridgwater, Somerset**
Wessex Fayres

July 30-Aug 6 **WELSH CRAFTS AT NATIONAL EISTEDDFOD**
Faenol Estate, nr Bangor, Gwynedd
Wales Craft Council

July 31-Aug 1 **FOCUS CRAFT GROUP AT TURRIFF AGRICULTURAL SHOW**
The Showfield, Queens Road, Turriff, Aberdeenshire
Festival of Crafts Unique to Scotland (FOCUS)

July 31-Aug 1 **CRAFT FAIR AT TURRIFF AGRICULTURAL SHOW**
The Showfield, Queens Road, Turriff, Aberdeenshire
Turriff District Agricultural Association (main event organiser)

July 31-Aug 6 **OPEN AIR STALLS AT ALNWICK INTERNATIONAL MUSIC FESTIVAL**
Market Place, Alnwick, Northumberland
Alnwick International Music Festival

Aug date tba **TEESDALE FOOD & CRAFT FESTIVAL**
The Bowes Museum, Bowes, Barnard Castle, Co Durham
Bowes Museum

Aug 1-Sept 4 **SPIRIT OF SUMMER/The Harbour Gallery, Le Boulevard, St Aubin, Jersey**
Art in the Frame Foundation

Aug 2-3 **CRAFTS AT FERMANAGH COUNTY SHOW/Enniskillen, Co Fermanagh**
County Fermanagh Farming Society Ltd

Aug 3-4 **HEART OF ENGLAND CRAFTWORKERS MARQUEE AT BAKEWELL SHOW/Bakewell Showground, Derbys**
Heart of England Craftworkers Ltd

Aug 3-7 **CRAFTS AT STOCKTON INTERNATIONAL RIVERSIDE FESTIVAL**
Stockton-on-Tees High Street and Riverside
Stockton-on-Tees Council

Aug 3-7 **RURAL CRAFTS ASSOCIATION AT DUBLIN HORSE SHOW**
Dublin, Republic of Ireland
Rural Crafts Association

Aug 4 **CARMARTHENSHIRE CRAFTS/St Peters Hall, Nott Square, Carmarthen**
Carmarthenshire Crafts

Aug 4-7 **EASTLEIGH FESTIVAL/Fleming Park, Passfield Avenue, Eastleigh, Hants**
Hampshire Music & Arts Festivals

Aug 5 **CRAFT & GIFT FAIR/Evron Centre, Filey, North Yorks**
Hardy Fairs Ltd

Aug 5-6 **CRAFTS AT PERTH SHOW/South Inch, Perthshire**
Perthshire Agricultural Society

Aug 5-7 **CRAFTS AT AYR FLOWER SHOW/Rozelle Estate, Monument Road, Ayr**
Ayr Flower Show

Aug 5-7 **CRAFT FAIR/Grosvenor Garden Centre, Belgrave, nr Chester, Cheshire**
Creative Crafts Association

Aug 5-7 **ART IN CLAY/Hatfield House, Hatfield, Herts**
HD Events Ltd

Aug 5-7 **RURAL CRAFTS ASSOCIATION AT FESTIVAL OF BRITISH EVENTING**
Gatcombe Park, Tetbury, Glos
Rural Crafts Association

Aug 5-7 **RURAL CRAFTS ASSOCIATION AT LOWTHER DRIVING TRIALS**
Penrith, Cumbria
Rural Crafts Association

Aug 5-7 **CRAFT MARQUEE AT INTERNATIONAL KITE FESTIVAL**
Southsea Common, Southsea, Hants
Woodland Crafts

Aug 6 **CRAFT TABLES AT BERWICKSHIRE COUNTY SHOW**
Duns Castle, Duns, Berwickshire
Berwickshire Agricultural Association

Aug 6 **CIRENCESTER CRAFTSMAN'S MARKET**
Corn Hall, Market Place, Cirencester, Glos
Cirencester Craftsman's Market

Aug 6 **CRAFTS AT DUMFRIES & LOCKERBIE AGRICULTURAL SHOW**
The Showfield, Park Farm, New Abbey Road, Dumfries
Dumfries & Lockerbie Agricultural Society

Aug 6 **FOCUS CRAFT GROUP AT ABOYNE HIGHLAND GAMES/Aboyne, Aberdeenshire**
Festival of Crafts Unique to Scotland (FOCUS)

Aug 6 **CRAFTS AT THE FORUM/The Forum, Norwich, Norfolk**
Norfolk Events

Aug 6-7 **BLAKEMERE CRAFT FAIR**
Blakemere Craft Centre, Chester Road, Sandiway, Northwich, Cheshire
Blakemere Craft Centre

Aug 6-7 **CRAFT & GIFT MARQUEE AT NOTTINGHAM RIVERSIDE FESTIVAL**
Nottingham
Craft People 2000

Aug 6-7 **CRAFT SHOW/Woburn Abbey, Woburn, Beds**
Living Heritage Craft Shows

Aug 6-7 **CRAFT MARQUEE AT EVESHAM COUNTRY PARK**
Evesham By-Pass A46, Worcs
Shirecrafts

Aug 6-7 **THURLOW & HAVERHILL STEAM & COUNTRY SHOW**
Horseheath Racecourse, A1307 between Cambridge + Haverhill
Thurlow & Haverhill Steam & Country Show

Aug 6-13 **CRAFT FAIR AT BILLINGHAM INTERNATIONAL FOLKLORE FESTIVAL**
Billingham Town Centre + Forum Theatre
Stockton-on-Tees Council

Aug 7 **CRAFT MARQUEE AT CRANLEIGH SHOW**
The Showground, Bookhurst Road, Cranleigh, Surrey
Cranleigh & South Eastern Agricultural Society

Aug 7 **ARTS & CRAFTS MARQUEE AT 121st SYKEHOUSE SHOW**
Poplars Farm, Sykehouse, Goole, East Yorks
Sykehouse Show Society

Aug 9-10 **CRAFT MARQUEE AT ANGLESEY AGRICULTURAL SHOW**
Mona, Gwalchmai, Ynys Môn
Gwynedd & Clwyd Association of Craftworkers

Aug 9-11 **MILLENNIUM CRAFTS & GIFTS/Community Centre, Lyndhurst, Hants**
Millennium Crafts & Gifts

Aug 11 **CRAFT MARQUEE AT OKEHAMPTON SHOW**
Stoneypark Showground, Okehampton, Devon
Okehampton Agricultural Show

Aug 11-14 **CRAFT & TRADE STALLS AT BRISTOL BALLOON FIESTA**
Ashton Court Estate, Long Ashton, Bristol
Bristol Balloon Fiestas Ltd

Aug 11-14 **COTTAGE INDUSTRIES CRAFT MARQUEE AT BRISTOL BALLOON FIESTA**
Ashton Court Estate, Long Ashton, Bristol
Cottage Industries

Aug 11-14 **CRAFT STANDS AT AIRBOURNE/Western Lawns, Seafront, Eastbourne, East Sussex**
Eastbourne Borough Council

Aug 13 **CRAFT TENT AT PEEBLES SHOW/Hay Lodge Park, Peebles**
Peeblesshire Agricultural Society

Aug 13 **ARTS & CRAFT FAIR/The Milton Rooms, Malton, North Yorks**
Yorkshire Craft Fairs

Aug 13-14 **ARTS & CRAFT FAYRE/Hartington Village Hall, Hartington, Derbys**
Biddulph Arts & Craft Fayres

Aug 13-14 **BLAKEMERE CRAFT FAIR**
Blakemere Craft Centre, Chester Road, Sandiway, Northwich, Cheshire
Blakemere Craft Centre

Aug 13-14 **CRAFT MARQUEE AT CHERTSEY SHOW/The Meads, Chertsey, Surrey**
Chertsey Agricultural Association

Aug 13-14 **DANSON CRAFT & COUNTRY SHOW**
Danson Park, Danson Road, Bexleyheath, Kent
Oakleigh Craft Fairs

Aug 13-14 **SUMMER CRAFT FAIR/Saltram House, Plymouth, Devon**
Saltram House

Aug 13-14 **CRAFT FAIR/Market House, Hawes, Wensleydale, North Yorks**
Wensleydale Craft Fairs

Aug 13-14 **6th ANNUAL SOUTH DORSET GIANT ANTIQUES, CRAFTS & COLLETORS FAIR/Weymouth Pavilion, Esplanade, Weymouth, Dorset**
West Country Craft Fairs

Aug 14 **CRAFT MARQUEE AT BINGLEY SHOW/Myrtle Park, Bingley, West Yorks**
Airedale Agricultural Society

Aug 14 **COXWOLD CRAFT FAIR/Village Hall, Coxwold, North Yorks**
Coxwold Craft Fairs

Aug 14 **FOCUS CRAFT GROUP/Victoria Hall, Ballater, Aberdeenshire**
Festival of Crafts Unique to Scotland (FOCUS)

Aug 14 **FILLONGLEY SHOW/Stonehouse Farm, Stonehouse Lane, Corley, Warks**
Fillongley Show

Aug 14 **MARQUEE + STANDS AT STEAM & VINTAGE RALLY**
Boatside Farm, Hay-on-Wye
Three Cocks Vintage Society Ltd

Aug 14 **ARTS & CRAFT FAIR/Crown Hotel, Harrogate, North Yorks**
Yorkshire Craft Fairs

Aug 16 **MILLENNIUM CRAFTS & GIFTS/Community Centre, Lyndhurst, Hants**
Millennium Crafts & Gifts

Aug 16-18 **CRAFT FAIR/Town Hall, Lloyd Street, Llandudno, Conwy**
Event~Reality

Aug 16-18 **HEART OF ENGLAND CRAFTWORKERS MARQUEE AT PEMBROKESHIRE SHOW/County Showground, Withybush, Haverfordwest, Pembrokeshire**
Heart of England Craftworkers Ltd

Aug 17 **RURAL CRAFTS ASSOCIATION AT GILLINGHAM & SHAFTESBURY AGRICULTURAL SHOW/Gillingham & Shaftesbury Showground, Dorset**
Rural Crafts Association

Aug 17 **CRAFT FAIR AT VALE OF GLAMORGAN AGRICULTURAL SHOW**
Fonmon Castle Grounds, nr Cardiff International Airport
Vale of Glamorgan Agricultural Show

Aug 18-21 **BEAUTY, HEALTH & LIFESTYLE MARQUEE AT SOUTHPORT FLOWER SHOW/Victoria Park, Southport**
BHLR Ltd

Aug 18-21 **FESTIVAL OF QUILTS/NEC, Birmingham**
Creative Exhibitions Ltd

Aug 18-21 **RURAL CRAFTS ASSOCIATION AT SOUTHPORT FLOWER SHOW**
Victoria Park, Southport
Rural Crafts Association

Aug 19 **DUNSTER SHOW/Dunster Castle Lawns, nr Minehead, Somerset**
Dunster Show Society

Aug 19 **CRAFT & GIFT FAIR/Evron Centre, Filey, North Yorks**
Hardy Fairs Ltd

Aug 19-21 **CANFORD SCHOOL HOME DESIGN & INTERIORS EXHIBITION**
Wimborne, Dorset
Buckingham Events

Aug 19-21 **LIVE CRAFT SHOW/Parham Park, Pulborough, West Sussex**
HD Events Ltd

Aug 19-21 **CRAFTS AT PONTARDAWE INTERNATIONAL MUSIC FESTIVAL**
Parc Ynysderw, behind Leisure Centre, Pontardawe, nr Swansea
Pontardawe International Music Festival

Aug 20 **CIRENCESTER CRAFTSMAN'S MARKET/Corn Hall, Market Place, Cirencester, Glos**
Cirencester Craftsman's Market

Aug 20 **CRAFT & GIFT FAIR**
Leconfield Hall, Market Square, Petworth, West Sussex
Craft Developments

Aug 20 **FOCUS CRAFT GROUP/Town Hall, Banchory, Aberdeenshire**
Festival of Crafts Unique to Scotland (FOCUS)

Aug 20 **OUTDOOR STALLS AT ST CATHERINE MEDIEVAL STREET FAIR**
Catherine Street, Catherine Hill + surrounding areas, Frome, Somerset
Frome Town Centre Promotions Group

Aug 20 **CRAFTS AT THE FORUM/The Forum, Norwich, Norfolk**
Norfolk Events

Aug 20 **WHITTINGHAM SHOW/Whittingham, Alnwick, Northumberland**
Whittingham Show

Aug 20 **ARTS & CRAFT FAIR/Crescent Hotel, Ilkley, West Yorks**
Yorkshire Craft Fairs

Aug 20-21 **BLAKEMERE CRAFT FAIR**
Blakemere Craft Centre, Chester Road, Sandiway, Northwich, Cheshire
Blakemere Craft Centre

Aug 20-21 **HOBBIES, MODELS & CRAFT FESTIVAL**
The Spa Royal Hall, Bridlington, East Yorks
Bridlington Model Boat Society

Aug 20-21 **CRAFT MARQUEE AT AMERICAN EXTRAVAGANZA**
Shakespeare County Raceway,
Long Marston, Stratford-upon-Avon, Warks
Cottage Industries

Aug 20-21 **SELBY SUMMER SHOW/Carlton Towers, Carlton, nr Selby**
Exhibition Management

Aug 20-21 **MACCLESFIELD FAMILY FUN DAY**
West Park, Prestbury Road, Macclesfield, Cheshire
Macclesfield Borough Council

Aug 20-21 **BORDE HILL COUNTRY FAIR**
Borde Hill Garden, Balcombe Road, nr Haywards Heath, West Sussex
Nelton Exhibitions Ltd

Aug 20-21 **HAMPSHIRE SUMMER GARDEN & CRAFT SHOW**
Broadlands, Romsey, Hants
RVT Events

Aug 20-21 **SHIRECRAFT MARQUEE AT WOODLANDS/Woodlands Nurseries, Ashby Road, Stapleton, Leics**
Shirecrafts

Aug 21 **COXWOLD CRAFT FAIR/Village Hall, Coxwold, North Yorks**
Coxwold Craft Fairs

Aug 21 **LAKELAND COUNTRY FAIR/Torver, nr Coniston, Cumbria**
Lakeland Country Fair

Aug 21 **LAUDERDALE HOUSE ARTS & CRAFTS**
Lauderdale House, Waterlow Park, Highgate Hill, London N6
Lauderdale Arts & Crafts

Aug 21 **QUALITY CRAFT & GIFT FAIR**
Swallow St George Hotel, Ripon Road, Harrogate, North Yorks
Quality Fairs

Aug 23-29 **CRAFT FAIR/Town Hall, Lloyd Street, Llandudno, Conwy**
Event~Reality

Aug 25-26 **CRAFT FAIR/Market House, Hawes, Wensleydale, North Yorks**
Wensleydale Craft Fairs

Aug 25-27 **COWAL HIGHLAND GATHERING/Sports Stadium, Dunoon, Argyll**
Cowal Highland Gathering

Aug 25-27 **PORT OF DARTMOUTH ROYAL REGATTA – TRADE FAIR**
Coronation Park, Dartmouth, Devon
Port of Dartmouth Royal Regatta

Aug 25-29 **MARQUEE AT TOWERSEY VILLAGE FESTIVAL**
Towersey Playing Fields, Towersey, nr Thame, Oxon
Towersey Village Festival

Aug 26 **CRAFT & GIFT FAIR/Evron Centre, Filey, North Yorks**
Hardy Fairs Ltd

Aug 26-29 **COTTAGE CRAFT FESTIVAL**
Norfolk Showground, Dereham Road, New Costessey, Norwich, Norfolk
Country Cottage Crafts

Aug 26-29 **CHILTERNS CRAFT SHOW/Stonor Park, Henley-on-Thames, Oxon**
ICHF

Aug 26-29 **CRAFT MARQUEE AT STOCKTON SUMMER SHOW**
Preston Hall Museum & Park, Yarm Road, Stockton-on-Tees
Stockton-on-Tees Council

Aug 27 **BRITISH MADE CRAFTS AT BELLINGHAM SHOW**
Bellingham Showfield, Bellingham, Northumberland
Bellingham Show

Aug 27 **CRAFT & COLLECTABLES/Poynton Show, Poynton, Cheshire**
Craft & Collectables

Aug 27 **WENSLEYDALE SHOW/Showfield, Bellerby Road, Leyburn, North Yorks**
Wensleydale Agricultural Society

Aug 27-28 **CRAFT MARQUEE AT CASTLE KENNEDY COUNTRY FAIR & SCOTTISH CARRIAGE DRIVING CHAMPIONSHIPS/Showground, New Luce Road, Castle Kennedy, Stranraer**
Jane McDowall

Aug 27-29 **CRAFT SPACES AT SOUTHEND SUMMER GARDEN SHOW**
Garon Park, Southend-on-Sea, Essex
Aztec Events

Aug 27-29 **ARTS & CRAFT FAYRE/Hartington Village Hall, Hartington, Derbys**
Biddulph Arts & Craft Fayres

Aug 27-29 **BLAKEMERE CRAFT FAIR**
Blakemere Craft Centre, Chester Road, Sandiway, Northwich, Cheshire
Blakemere Craft Centre

Aug 27-29 **BRECON BEACONS SUMMER FAYRE**
National Park Visitor Centre, Libanus, Brecon, Powys
Brecon Beacons National Park Authority

Aug 27-29 **CRAFTS & GIFTS AT SUMMER GARDEN FESTIVAL**
Bodelwyddan Castle, St Asaph, Denbighshire
Cheshire Fayre

Aug 27-29 **BANK HOLIDAY CRAFT MARQUEE AT EVESHAM FISHING CHAMPIONSHIPS/Crown Meadow, Evesham, Worcs**
Cottage Industries

Aug 27-29 **SUMMER CRAFT & GARDEN SHOW AT KINGSTON LACY PARK**
Kingston Lacy, nr Wimborne, Dorset
Craft Carnival

Aug 27-29 **CRAFT FAIR/Gawsworth Hall, Gawsworth, Macclesfield, Cheshire**
Creative Crafts Association

Aug 27-29 **EDEN CRAFTS MARQUEE AT TOWN & COUNTRY FESTIVAL**
NAC, Stoneleigh Park, Warks
Eden Crafts

Aug 27-29 **COUNTRY CRAFT FAYRE/Wakehurst Place, Ardingly, Haywards Heath, West Sussex**
Four Seasons Craft Fayres Ltd

Aug 27-29 **LIVE CRAFT SHOW/Highclere Castle, nr Newbury, Berks**
HD Events Ltd

Aug 27-29 **COUNTRY CRAFTS WEEKEND/Shugborough, Milford, Staffs**
Hobby Horse Events Ltd

Aug 27-29 **CRAFTS AT GARDENERS' WEEKEND**
Audley End House, Saffron Walden, Essex
Hobby Horse Events Ltd

Aug 27-29 **FESTIVAL OF CRAFT, GIFTS & GARDENS**
Golden Acres Garden Centre, Landford, Wilts
IGF Marketing

Aug 27-29 **IWA NATIONAL FESTIVAL & BOAT SHOW**
Preston Brook, Bridgewater Canal, nr Daresbury, Cheshire
IWA Festivals

Aug 27-29 **CRAFT MARQUEE AT TRENT 2005/Stoke Bardolph, Nottingham**
Kingfisher Craft Marquee Management

Aug 27-29 **CRAFT FAIR/Woodgreen, Godmanchester, Cambs**
Kingfisher Promotions

Aug 27-29 **ESSEX CRAFT SHOW/Blake Hall, Ongar, Essex**
Living Heritage Craft Shows

Aug 27-29 **OXFORDSHIRE CRAFT SHOW/Blenheim Palace, Woodstock, Oxon**
Living Heritage Craft Shows

Aug 27-29 **ENGLAND'S MEDIEVAL FESTIVAL & CRAFT FAIR**
Herstmonceux Castle, Herstmonceux, East Sussex
Malcolm Group Events Ltd

Aug 27-29 **AUGUST BANK HOLIDAY CRAFT & COUNTRY SHOW**
Hainault Forest Country Park, Romford Road, Chigwell Row, Essex
Oakleigh Craft Fairs

Aug 27-29 **QUALITY CRAFT & GIFT FAIR/Carlton Towers, Carlton, nr Goole**
Quality Fairs

Aug 27-29 **WREST PARK CRAFTS FESTIVAL/Wrest Park, Silsoe, Beds**
Romor Exhibitions Ltd

Aug 27-29 **MARQUEE AT RUDGWICK STEAM & COUNTRY SHOW**
The Showground, off A281, Rudgwick, nr Horsham, West Sussex
Rudgwick Steam & Country Show

Aug 27-29 **CRAFT MARQUEE AT SOUTH EAST GARDEN SHOW**
The Hop Farm Country Park, Paddock Wood, Kent
WMH Leisure

Aug 27-29 **CRAFT MARQUEE AT RUDGWICK STEAM & COUNTRY SHOW**
The Showground, off A281, Rudgwick, nr Horsham, West Sussex
Woodland Crafts

Aug 27-29 **YORKRAFT CRAFT EVENT/Town Hall, Helmsley, North Yorks**
Yorkraft

Aug 28 **VALE EARTH FAIR – ENVIRONMENTALLY FRIENDLY CRAFTS**
Vale Castle, Vale, Guernsey
Vale Earth Fair

Aug 28-29 **MARQUEE AT SHEFFIELD FAYRE & HORTICULTURAL SHOW**
Norfolk Heritage Park, Guildford Avenue, Sheffield
Allott Agency

Aug 28-29 **CRAFT MARQUEE AT EDENBRIDGE & OXTED SHOW**
Ardenrun, Lingfield, Surrey
BHLR Ltd

Aug 28-29 **MODEL BOAT CONVENTION**
Boat Museum, South Pier Road, Ellesmere Port, Cheshire
Boat Museum

Aug 28-29 **COXWOLD CRAFT FAIR/Village Hall, Coxwold, North Yorks**
Coxwold Craft Fairs

Aug 28-29 **CRAFT & GIFTS MARQUEE AT MOORGREEN AGRICULTURAL SHOW**
Moorgreen Showground, Watnall, Notts
Craft Lincs

Aug 28-29 **EYE SHOW/Showground, Eye, Suffolk**
Eye Show Ltd

Aug 28-29 **CRAFT STALLS AT THE COUNTESS OF WARWICK'S COUNTRY SHOW**
Little Easton Church, Rectory Manor, nr Dunmow, Essex
Five Parishes PCC

Aug 28-29 **CRAFTS AT HARROW SHOW/Headstone Manor Recreation Ground, Pinner View, North Harrow, Middx**
Harrow Show

Aug 28-29 **BRITISH MADE CRAFTS AT HAMPSHIRE PAGEANT OF MOTORING**
Broadlands, Romsey, Hants
H.P.O.M.

Aug 28-29 **CRAFT SHOW/Layer Marney Tower, nr Colchester, Essex**
K.C. Craft Shows

Aug 28-29 **WEYMOUTH SUMMER CRAFT FAIR**
Pavilion Complex, The Esplanade, Weymouth, Dorset
Kevin Murphy Craft Fairs

Aug 28-29 **CRAFT & GIFT MARQUEE AT MOORGREEN COUNTRY SHOW**
Moorgreen Showground, Watnall, Notts
Moorgreen Country Show (main event organiser)

Aug 28-29 **REDESMERE CRAFTS**
Siddington Village Hall, A34, nr Macclesfield, Cheshire
Redesmere Crafts Association

Aug 28-29 **CRAFT MARQUEE AT SANDWELL SHOW/Sandwell Showground, Sandwell Valley Country Park, Salters Lane, West Bromwich, West Midlands**
Sandwell Valley Craft Fairs

Aug 28-29 **WELLS & MID-SOMERSET 7th ANNUAL AUGUST CRAFT FESTIVAL**
Town Hall, Market Square, Wells, Somerset
West Country Craft Fairs

Aug 28-29 **BANK HOLIDAY CRAFTS/Duncombe Park, Helmsley, North Yorks**
Yorkshire Craft Fairs

Aug 29 **3 SHIRES CRAFT GUILD/Courtyard Hall, Pershore, Worcs**
3 Shires Craft Guild

Aug 29 **OUTDOOR CRAFTS AT AYLSHAM AGRICULTURAL SHOW**
Blickling Park, nr Aylsham, Norwich, Norfolk
Aylsham Agricultural Show Association

Aug 29 **CRAFT MARQUEE AT BERKELEY AGRICULTURAL SHOW**
Berkeley Castle, Berkeley, Glos
Berkeley Agricultural Show

Aug 29 **CRAFT STALLS AT CORSLEY SHOW/Corsley Showground, off A362 between Warminster & Frome**
Corsley Show

Aug 29 **CRAFT MARQUEE AT GLENDALE SHOW**
The Showfield, Wooler, Northumberland
Glendale Agricultural Society

Aug 29 **CRAFT & GIFT FAIR/Evron Centre, Filey, North Yorks**
Hardy Fairs Ltd

Aug 29 **CRAFTS AT KESWICK SHOW**
Crossings Field, High Hill, Keswick, Cumbria
Keswick Show

Aug 29 **MUNCASTER COUNTRY FAIR**
Adjacent to Muncaster Castle, Ravenglass, Cumbria
Muncaster Country Fair

Aug 29 **FAMILY DAY & CRAFT FAIR/The Argory, Derrycaw Road, Moy, Co Tyrone**
National Trust – The Argory

Aug 30 **CRAFT & GIFT MARQUEE AT KILNSEY SHOW**
Kilnsey, nr Skipton, North Yorks
Craft People 2000

Aug 31 **CRAFTS MARQUEE AT REETH SHOW**
Showground, Reeth, Swaledale, North Yorks
Wensleydale Craft Fairs

Aug 31-Sept 4 **CRAFT MARQUEES AT GREAT DORSET STEAM FAIR**
South Down, Tarrant Hinton, Blandford, Dorset
Great Dorset Steam Fair Ltd

Sept date tba **CRAFT AT CLASSIC & VINTAGE CAR SHOW**
Capel Manor College, Bullsmoor Lane, Enfield, Middx
Fig Fairs

Sept date tba **CERAMICS IN THE CITY**
Geffrye Museum, Kingsland Road, Shoreditch, London E2
Geffrye Museum

Sept date tba **ENFIELD AUTUMN SHOW/Town Park, Enfield, Middx**
Ubique Leisure Ltd

Sept date tba **ARTS & CRAFT FAIR/Town Hall, Northallerton, North Yorks**
Yorkshire Craft Fairs

Sept 1 **CARMARTHENSHIRE CRAFTS/St Peters Hall, Nott Square, Carmarthen**
Carmarthenshire Crafts

Sept 1-4 **RURAL CRAFTS ASSOCIATION AT BURGHLEY HORSE TRIALS**
Burghley House, Stamford, Lincs
Rural Crafts Association

Sept 2 **CRAFT & GIFT FAIR/Evron Centre, Filey, North Yorks**
Hardy Fairs Ltd

Sept 2-4 **AMBLESIDE FLOWER SHOW & CRAFT FAIR**
The Sports Field, Stock Lane, Grasmere, Cumbria
Ambleside Horticultural & Craft Society

Sept 2-4 **CRAFT SPACES AT SUFFOLK AUTUMN GARDEN SHOW**
Suffolk Showground, Bucklesham Road, Ipswich, Suffolk
Aztec Events

Sept 2-4 **CRAFT MARQUEE AT DUNDEE FLOWER & FOOD FESTIVAL**
Camperdowns Country Park, Dundee
Dundee City Council

Sept 2-4 **LIVE CRAFT SHOW/Missenden Abbey, Great Missenden, Bucks**
HD Events Ltd

Sept 2-4 **STITCH & CREATIVE CRAFTS SHOW/G-MEX, Manchester**
Nationwide Exhibitions (UK) Ltd

Sept 3 **CIRENCESTER CRAFTSMAN'S MARKET/Corn Hall, Market Place, Cirencester, Glos**
Cirencester Craftsman's Market

Sept 3 **FOCUS CRAFT GROUP/Town Hall, Stonehaven, Aberdeenshire**
Festival of Crafts Unique to Scotland (FOCUS)

Sept 3 **HARBOTTLE SHOW/Oak Tree Field, Harbottle, Northumberland**
Harbottle Show

Sept 3 **KEIGHLEY & DISTRICT AGRICULTURAL SHOW**
Marley Fields, Keighley, West Yorks
Keighley & District Agricultural Show

Sept 3 **SALISBURY CRAFT FAIR/Guildhall, Market Place, Salisbury, Wilts**
Kevin Murphy Craft Fairs

Sept 3 **KINGSBRIDGE SHOW**
Borough Farm, East Allington, nr Kingsbridge, Devon
Kingsbridge Agricultural & Horticultural Show

Sept 3 **CRAFTS AT THE FORUM/The Forum, Norwich, Norfolk**
Norfolk Events

Sept 3 **ARTS & CRAFT FAIR/Town Hall, Stokesley, nr Middlesbrough**
Yorkshire Craft Fairs

Sept 3-4 **ART IN THE GARDENS**
Sheffield Botanical Gardens, Clarkehouse Road, Sheffield
Allott Agency

Sept 3-4 **BEAUTY, HEALTH & LIFESTYLE MARQUEE AT CHATSWORTH COUNTRY FAIR/Chatsworth House, Baslow, Derbys**
BHLR Ltd

Sept 3-4 **BLAKEMERE CRAFT FAIR**
Blakemere Craft Centre, Chester Road, Sandiway, Northwich, Cheshire
Blakemere Craft Centre

Sept 3-4 **GARDENERS WEEKEND CRAFT MARQUEE**
Kings Heath Park, Birmingham
Cottage Industries

Sept 3-4 **CRAFTS AT DORSET'S COUNTY SHOW – DORCHESTER SHOW**
Cokers Frome Showground, Dorchester, Dorset
Dorchester Agricultural Society (main event organiser)

Sept 3-4 **EDEN CRAFTS MARQUEE AT BIGGIN HILL AIR SHOW**
Biggin Hill, Kent
Eden Crafts

Sept 3-4 **PARKGATE COUNTRY SHOW/Backwood Hall, Parkgate, Neston, Wirral**
Exhibition Management

Sept 3-4 **HEART OF ENGLAND CRAFTWORKERS MARQUEE AT CHATSWORTH COUNTRY FAIR/Chatsworth House, Baslow, Derbys**
Heart of England Craftworkers Ltd

Sept 3-4 **CRAFT VILLAGE AT BECKENHAM FAMILY SHOW**
Croydon Road Recreation Ground, Beckenham, Kent
Oakleigh Craft Fairs

Sept 3-4 **RURAL CRAFTS ASSOCIATION AT CHATSWORTH COUNTRY FAIR**
Chatsworth House, Baslow, Derbys
Rural Crafts Association

Sept 3-4 **RURAL CRAFTS ASSOCIATION AT DORSET'S COUNTY SHOW – DORCHESTER SHOW/Cokers Frome Showground, Dorchester, Dorset**
Rural Crafts Association

Sept 3-4 **CRAFT MARQUEE AT SHOREHAM AIRSHOW**
Shoreham-by-Sea, West Sussex
Woodland Crafts

Sept 4 **ARTS & CRAFT FAYRE/Hartington Village Hall, Hartington, Derbys**
Biddulph Arts & Craft Fayres

Sept 4 **KENSWORTH VINTAGE & CLASSIC CAR RALLY**
Dovehouse Lane, Kensworth, Dunstable, Beds
Colin Toten

Sept 4 **COXWOLD CRAFT FAIR/Village Hall, Coxwold, North Yorks**
Coxwold Craft Fairs

Sept 4 **CRAFT FAIR/Floral Hall, The Promenade, Southport**
Creative Crafts Association

Sept 4 **KILDALE SHOW/Village Hall Field, Kildale, Whitby, North Yorks**
Kildale Agricultural & Horticultural Show Society

Sept 4 **CRAFT STALLS AT LUTON MELA**
Wardown Park, New Bedford Road, Luton, Beds
Luton Borough Council – Arts Unit

Sept 4 **MILLENNIUM CRAFTS & GIFTS/Community Centre, Lyndhurst, Hants**
Millennium Crafts & Gifts

Sept 4 **READING & WOKINGHAM COUNTRY SHOW**
White House Farm, Spencers Wood, Reading, Berks
Reading & Wokingham Country Show

Sept 4 **ARTS & CRAFT FAIR/Bankfield Hotel, Bingley, West Yorks**
Yorkshire Craft Fairs

Sept 6 **MILLENNIUM CRAFTS & GIFTS/Community Centre, Lyndhurst, Hants**
Millennium Crafts & Gifts

Sept 6-8 **CRAFT FAIR/Town Hall, Lloyd Street, Llandudno, Conwy**
Event~Reality

Sept 7 **CRAFTS MARQUEE AT MUKER SHOW**
Showground, Muker, Swaledale, North Yorks
Wensleydale Craft Fairs

Sept 8 **CRAFT FAIR/Market House, Hawes, Wensleydale, North Yorks**
Wensleydale Craft Fairs

Sept 8-11 **RURAL CRAFTS ASSOCIATION AT BLENHEIM HORSE TRIALS**
Blenheim Palace, Woodstock, Oxon
Rural Crafts Association

Sept 9-11 **CRAFT SPACES AT NORFOLK AUTUMN GARDEN SHOW**
Norfolk Showground, Dereham Road, New Costessey, Norwich, Norfolk
Aztec Events

Sept 9-11 **COTTAGE INDUSTRIES CRAFT EVENT/venue tba**
Cottage Industries

Sept 9-11 **CRAFT MARQUEE AT DERBYSHIRE GARDEN & WOOD FESTIVAL**
The Showground, Bakewell, Derbys
Doug Moore

Sept 9-11 **WEALD OF KENT CRAFT SHOW**
Penshurst Place, nr Tonbridge, Kent
ICHF

Sept 10 **CRAFT MARQUEE AT BOWES SHOW**
Home Farm, Gilmonby, Barnard Castle, Co Durham
Bowes Agricultural Society

Sept 10 **DOLLS HOUSE & MINIATURES + CRAFTS/Somerset Hall, High Street, Portishead, North Somerset**
Dolls House, Miniatures & Crafts

Sept 10 **MARQUEE AT FROME AGRICULTURAL & CHEESE SHOW**
Bunns Lane Showfield, West Woodlands, Frome, Somerset
Frome & District Agricultural Society

Sept 10 **AUTUMN CRAFT MARKET/Commemoration Hall, Huntingdon, Cambs**
Huntingdon Craft Market

Sept 10 **PENISTONE SHOW/Penistone Showground, Penistone, Sheffield**
Penistone Agricultural Society

Sept 10 **RAF LEUCHARS AIRSHOW 2005/RAF Leuchars, St Andrews Fife**
RAF Leuchars Airshow

Sept 10 **ROMSEY SHOW/Broadlands, Romsey, Hants**
Romsey Show

Sept 10 **CRAFT MARQUEE AT USK SHOW/Usk Showground, Usk, Monmouthshire**
Usk Farmers' Club Ltd

Sept 10 **ARTS & CRAFT FAIR/The Milton Rooms, Malton, North Yorks**
Yorkshire Craft Fairs

Sept 10-11 **ESSEX COUNTRY SHOW**
Barleylands Farm, Barleylands Road (off A129), Billericay, Essex
Barleylands Crafts Village

Sept 10-11 **BLAKEMERE CRAFT FAIR**
Blakemere Craft Centre, Chester Road, Sandiway, Northwich, Cheshire
Blakemere Craft Centre

Sept 10-11 **CRAFT FAYRE/Rufford Old Hall, nr Ormskirk, Lancs**
Cheshire Fayre

Sept 10-11 **CRAFT & GIFTS MARQUEE AT LANDROVER OWNERS SHOW**
East of England Showground, Peterborough, Cambs
Craft Lincs

Sept 10-11 **ANNUAL GUILD CRAFT FAYRE**
Cressing Temple Barns, Cressing (B1018), nr Braintree, Essex
Guild of Essex Craftsmen

Sept 10-11 **BRITISH MADE CRAFTS AT HADDENHAM STEAM RALLY**
A1421, nr Ely, Cambs
Haddenham Steam Rally

Sept 10-11 **HUNTON VILLAGE GATHERING & CRAFTS/Hunton, Bedale, North Yorks**
Kingfisher Craft Marquee Management

Sept 10-11 **CRAFTS FESTIVAL/Lamport Hall, Lamport, Northants**
Kingfisher Promotions

Sept 10-11 **CRAFT MARQUEE AT STANHOPE AGRICULTURAL SHOW**
Unthank Park, Stanhope, Bishop Auckland, Co Durham
Stanhope Agricultural Society

Sept 10-11 **CRAFTS AT BILLINGHAM SHOW & CARNIVAL**
Billingham Green, Billingham
Stockton-on-Tees Council

Sept 10-11 **MEDIEVAL WEEKEND/Michelham Priory, Upper Dicker, Hailsham, East Sussex** (only crafts relevant to Medieval period)
Sussex Past

Sept 10-11 **THE WOOD SHOW**
Weald & Downland Open Air Museum, Singleton, Chichester, West Sussex
Weald & Downland Open Air Museum

Sept 11 **COXWOLD CRAFT FAIR/Village Hall, Coxwold, North Yorks**
Coxwold Craft Fairs

Sept 11 **FRAMPTON COUNTRY FAIR**
The Park, Frampton Court, Frampton-on-Severn, Glos
Frampton Country Fair

Sept 11 **REDESMERE CRAFTS**
Siddington Village Hall, A34, nr Macclesfield, Cheshire
Redesmere Crafts Association

Sept 11 **NEWBURY DOLLS HOUSE & MINIATURES FAIR**
Newbury Racecourse, Berks (provisional date)
Warners Dolls House & Miniatures Fairs

Sept 13-15 **CRAFT FAIR/Town Hall, Lloyd Street, Llandudno, Conwy**
Event~Reality

Sept 15 **CRAFT FAIR/Market House, Hawes, Wensleydale, North Yorks**
Wensleydale Craft Fairs

Sept 15-18 **YOURS MAGAZINE LIVE AT NATIONAL STITCH & CREATIVE CRAFTS SHOW/National Exhibition Centre, Birmingham**
Nationwide Exhibitions (UK) Ltd

Sept 16-18 **CRAFT FAIR**
Burnside Garden Centre, New Lane, Thornton Cleveleys, Lancs
Creative Crafts Association

Sept 16-18 **SANDRINGHAM CRAFT SHOW/Sandringham, Norfolk**
Living Heritage Craft Shows

Sept 16-18 **BRITISH MADE CRAFTS AT HARROGATE AUTUMN FLOWER SHOW**
Great Yorkshire Showground, Wetherby Road, Harrogate, North Yorks
North of England Enterprises Ltd

Sept 16-18 **EXHIBITION AT NORTHERN MOTORCARAVAN SHOW**
York Racecourse, York (provisional dates)
Warners Exhibitions

Sept 17 **RNAS YEOVILTON INTERNATIONAL AIR DAY**
RNAS Yeovilton, Yeovil, Somerset
AHA Events Ltd

Sept 17 **CIRENCESTER CRAFTSMAN'S MARKET**
Corn Hall, Market Place, Cirencester, Glos
Cirencester Craftsman's Market

Sept 17 **CRAFTS AT THE FORUM/The Forum, Norwich, Norfolk**
Norfolk Events

Sept 17-18 **BLAKEMERE CRAFT FAIR**
Blakemere Craft Centre, Chester Road, Sandiway, Northwich, Cheshire
Blakemere Craft Centre

Sept 17-18 **STAFFORD CRAFT SHOW**
County Showground, A518 Uttoxeter Road, Stafford
Central Promotions

Sept 17-18 **CRAFT & GIFT MARQUEE AT BEDFORD STEAM & COUNTRY FAYRE**
Old Warden, nr Biggleswade, Beds
Craft People 2000

Sept 17-18 **HEART OF ENGLAND CRAFTWORKERS MARQUEE AT MIDLAND GAME & COUNTRY FAIR/Weston Park, Shifnal, Shropshire**
Heart of England Craftworkers Ltd

Sept 17-18 **CRAFTS AT GARDENERS' WEEKEND/Coughton Court, Studley, Warks**
Hobby Horse Events Ltd

Sept 17-18 **CRAFT SHOW/St Peters Hall, Coggeshall, Essex** (provisional dates)
K.C. Craft Shows

Sept 17-18 **MINIATURA/National Exhibition Centre, Birmingham**
Miniatura

Sept 17-18 **SHIRECRAFTS MARQUEE/Dobbies Garden Centre, Clifton, Lancs**
Shirecrafts

Sept 17-18 **ARTS & CRAFT FAIR/St William College, York, North Yorks**
Yorkshire Craft Fairs

Sept 18 **COXWOLD CRAFT FAIR/Village Hall, Coxwold, North Yorks**
Coxwold Craft Fairs

Sept 18 **ART, CRAFT & GIFT FAIR/Village Hall, Woburn, Beds**
Falcon Fairs

Sept 18 **BRITISH MADE CRAFTS AT VINTAGE & SPECIALIST CAR RALLY**
Tredegar House & Park, Newport
Leukaemia Research Fund - Gwent Branch

Sept 18 **MILLENNIUM CRAFTS & GIFTS/Community Centre, Lyndhurst, Hants**
Millennium Crafts & Gifts

Sept 18 **REDESMERE CRAFTS**
Siddington Village Hall, A34, nr Macclesfield, Cheshire
Redesmere Crafts Association

Sept 18 **WHIRLOW HALL FARM FAYRE**
Whirlow Hall Farm, Whirlow Lane, Whirlow, Sheffield
Whirlow Hall Farm Trust

Sept 18-19 **BEAUTY, HEALTH & LIFESTYLE MARQUEE AT ROYAL COUNTY OF BERKSHIRE SHOW/Newbury Showground, Priors Court, Hermitage, Thatcham, Berks**
BHLR Ltd

Sept 22 **MILLENNIUM CRAFTS & GIFTS/Community Centre, Lyndhurst, Hants**
Millennium Crafts & Gifts

Sept 22 **CRAFT FAIR/Market House, Hawes, Wensleydale, North Yorks**
Wensleydale Craft Fairs

Sept 22-24 **BRIDGEND FESTIVAL/Bridgend Town Centre, South Wales**
Bridgend Festivals

Sept 22-25 **CREATIVE STITCHES & HOBBYCRAFTS**
Westpoint Exhibition Centre, Exeter
ICHF

Sept 23-25 **AVINGTON PARK HOME DESIGN & INTERIORS EXHIBITION**
Itchen Abbas, Winchester, Hants
Buckingham Events

Sept 23-25 **COTTAGE CRAFT FESTIVAL**
Suffolk Showground, Bucklesham Road, Ipswich, Suffolk
Country Cottage Crafts

Sept 23-25 **CRAFT & DESIGN SHOW/Rivermead Leisure Centre, Caversham, nr Reading, Berks** (provisional dates)
Craft in Focus

Sept 24 **3 SHIRES CRAFT GUILD/Memorial Hall, Upton-on-Severn, Worcs**
3 Shires Craft Guild

Sept 24 **ESKDALE SHOW/Eskdale Green, Eskdale, Holmrook, Cumbria**
Fell Dales Association

Sept 24 **FOCUS CRAFT GROUP/Town Hall, Banchory, Aberdeenshire**
Festival of Crafts Unique to Scotland (FOCUS)

Sept 24 **BRITISH MADE CRAFTS AT GRANSDEN & DISTRICT SHOW**
Caxton Road, Great Gransden, nr Sandy, Beds
Gransden & District Agricultural Society

Sept 24 **AUTUMN CRAFT FAIR/Town Hall, Market Square, Wells, Somerset**
West Country Craft Fairs

Sept 24 **ARTS & CRAFT FAIR/Crescent Hotel, Ilkley, West Yorks**
Yorkshire Craft Fairs

Sept 24-25 **BLAKEMERE CRAFT FAIR**
Blakemere Craft Centre, Chester Road, Sandiway, Northwich, Cheshire
Blakemere Craft Centre

Sept 24-25 **CRAFT FAIR/Hawes Market Hall, Hawes, North Yorks**
Cosy Crafts

Sept 24-25 **CRAFT FAIR/Lowther Pavilion, Lytham, Lancs**
Creative Crafts Association

Sept 24-25 **CRAFT MARQUEE AT TEESSIDE HOMES, GARDEN & GIFT SHOW**
Preston Park, Yarm, Tees Valley
Doug Moore

Sept 24-25 **EDEN CRAFTS MARQUEE AT MALVERN AUTUMN SHOW**
Three Counties Showground, Malvern, Worcs
Eden Crafts

Sept 24-25 **LARTINGTON GAMEFAIR/Lartington, Barnard Castle, Co Durham**
Exhibition Management

Sept 24-25 **WOODWORKS – FESTIVAL OF WOOD, WOODLANDS & WOOD PRODUCTS/Millennium Country Park, Station Road, Marston Moretaine, Beds** (provisional dates)
Forest of Marston Vale

Sept 24-25 **CRAFT & GARDEN SHOW/Cressing Temple Barns, Cressing (B1018), nr Braintree, Essex**
Hallmark Craft Fairs

Sept 24-25 **CRAFT MARQUEE AT WORCESTER/Worcester Garden Centre, A38 Droitwich Road, Worcester**
Shirecrafts

Sept 25 **TYNESIDE DOLLS & TEDDY FAIR/Lancastrian Suite, Federation Brewery, Dunston, Gateshead, Tyne & Wear**
Dolly Domain Fairs

Sept 25 **FOCUS CRAFT GROUP/Victoria Hall, Ballater, Aberdeenshire**
Festival of Crafts Unique to Scotland (FOCUS)

Sept 25 **LAUDERDALE HOUSE ARTS & CRAFTS**
Lauderdale House, Waterlow Park, Highgate Hill, London N6
Lauderdale Arts & Crafts

Sept 25 **KENT DOLLS HOUSE & MINIATURES FAIR/Ramada Hotel & Resort, Hollingbourne, nr Maidstone, Kent** (provisional date)
Warners Dolls House & Miniatures Fairs

Sept 25 **ARTS & CRAFT FAIR/Bankfield Hotel, Bingley, West Yorks**
Yorkshire Craft Fairs

Sept 27-29 **RURAL CRAFTS ASSOCIATION AT NATIONAL PLOUGHING CHAMPIONSHIPS/Mogeely, Midleton, Co Cork, Republic of Ireland**
Rural Crafts Association

Sept 30-Oct 2 **STANFORD HALL HOME DESIGN & INTERIORS EXHIBITION**
Lutterworth, Leics
Buckingham Events

Sept 30-Oct 2 **STITCH & CREATIVE CRAFTS SHOW**
Sandown Park Exhibition Centre, Esher, Surrey
Nationwide Exhibitions (UK) Ltd

Oct date tba **CRAFT FAIR/Banbridge Leisure Centre, Banbridge, Co Down**
Banbridge District Arts Committee

Oct date tba **ARTS & CRAFT FAIR/Town Hall, Northallerton, North Yorks**
Yorkshire Craft Fairs

Oct 1 **CIRENCESTER CRAFTSMAN'S MARKET**
Corn Hall, Market Place, Cirencester, Glos
Cirencester Craftsman's Market

Oct 1 **ART, CRAFT & GIFT FAIR/Town Hall, Towcester, Northants**
Falcon Fairs

Oct 1 **FOCUS CRAFT GROUP/Music Hall, Aberdeen**
Festival of Crafts Unique to Scotland (FOCUS)

Oct 1 **CRAFTS AT THE FORUM/The Forum, Norwich, Norfolk**
Norfolk Events

Oct 1 **CHIPPENHAM AUTUMN CRAFT FAIR/The Neeld**
Town Hall, High Street, Chippenham, Wilts
West Country Craft Fairs

Oct 1 **ARTS & CRAFT FAIR/Town Hall, Stokesley, nr Middlesbrough**
Yorkshire Craft Fairs

Oct 1-2 **CRAFT FAIR/Victoria Halls, Hartley Wintney, Hants**
Arts & Craft Fairs

Oct 1-2 **BLAKEMERE CRAFT FAIR**
Blakemere Craft Centre, Chester Road, Sandiway, Northwich, Cheshire
Blakemere Craft Centre

Oct 1-2 **CRAFT MARQUEE AT HATTON COUNTRY WORLD**
A4177 Hatton, between Warwick and Solihull, Warks
Cottage Industries

Oct 1-2 **CRAFT FAIR/Stanford Hall, Swinford, nr Lutterworth, Leics**
Craftworkers Cooperative

Oct 1-2 **EDEN CRAFTS MARQUEE AT SOUTH OF ENGLAND AUTUMN SHOW**
South of England Showground, Ardingly, West Sussex
Eden Crafts

Oct 1-2 **NEWTON ABBOT AUTUMN CRAFT FAIR**
Racecourse, Kingsteignton, Newton Abbot, Devon
Kevin Murphy Craft Fairs

Oct 1-2 **CRAFT & GIFT FAIR/Hoghton Tower, Preston, Lancs**
North West Craft & Gift Fairs

Oct 1-2 **QUALITY CRAFT & GIFT FAIR**
Sun Pavilion, Valley Gardens, Harrogate, North Yorks
Quality Fairs

Oct 1-2	**AUTUMN COUNTRYSIDE CELEBRATION** **Weald & Downland Open Air Museum, Singleton, Chichester, West Sussex** Weald & Downland Open Air Museum
Oct 1-2	**CRAFTS AT FORT PURBROOK** **Fort Purbrook, Portsdown Hill, Cosham, Hants** Woodland Crafts
Oct 2	**BEWDLEY CRAFT SHOW** **Ramada (Heath) Hotel, Habberley Road, Bewdley, Worcs** Central Promotions
Oct 2	**CRAFT FAIR/Rushden & Diamonds FC Sports Centre, Nene Park, Irthlingborough, Northants** DK Fairs
Oct 2	**ART, CRAFT & GIFT FAIR/Village Hall, Denham, Bucks** Falcon Fairs
Oct 2	**REDESMERE CRAFTS** **Siddington Village Hall, A34, nr Macclesfield, Cheshire** Redesmere Crafts Association
Oct 2	**SOMERSET DOLLS HOUSE & MINIATURES FAIR** **Webbington Hotel, Loxton, nr Axbridge, Somerset** Warners Dolls House & Miniatures Fairs
Oct 2	**AUTUMN CRAFT FAIR** **Pavilion Theatre, Marine Parade, Worthing, West Sussex** Worthing Theatres
Oct 2	**ARTS & CRAFT FAIR/Crown Hotel, Harrogate, North Yorks** Yorkshire Craft Fairs
Oct 2-4	**SCOTLAND'S AUTUMN FAIR/SECC, Glasgow** (trade event) Trade Fairs (Scotland) Ltd
Oct 5	**BLAKEMERE CRAFT FAIR/Blakemere Craft Centre, Chester Road, Sandiway, Northwich, Cheshire** Blakemere Craft Centre
Oct 5-8	**CRAFT & GIFT MARQUEE AT NOTTINGHAM GOOSE FAIR/Nottingham** Craft People 2000
Oct 6	**CARMARTHENSHIRE CRAFTS/St Peters Hall, Nott Square, Carmarthen** Carmarthenshire Crafts
Oct 6-9	**CRAFT & DESIGN SHOW** **Rugby Stadium, Twickenham, Middx** (provisional dates) Craft in Focus
Oct 7	**CRAFT FAIR/Market House, Hawes, Wensleydale, North Yorks** Wensleydale Craft Fairs

Oct 7-9 **KNEBWORTH HOUSE HOME DESIGN & INTERIORS EXHIBITION**
Knebworth, Herts
Buckingham Events

Oct 7-9 **LIVE CRAFT SHOW/Stansted Park, Rowlands Castle, Hants**
HD Events Ltd

Oct 7-9 **FASHION & EMBROIDERY/Yorkshire Showground, Harrogate**
ICHF

Oct 8 **3 SHIRES CRAFT GUILD**
St Michaels Church Hall, Bishops Cleeve, Glos
3 Shires Craft Guild

Oct 8 **CRAFT TABLES AT ALWINTON BORDER SHEPHERDS' SHOW**
The Haugh, Alwinton, Rothbury, Northumberland
Alwinton Border Shepherds' Show

Oct 8 **ART, CRAFT & GIFT FAIR/Town Hall, Brackley, Northants**
Falcon Fairs

Oct 8 **FOCUS CRAFT GROUP/Town Hall, Stonehaven, Aberdeenshire**
Festival of Crafts Unique to Scotland (FOCUS)

Oct 8 **AUTUMN CRAFT MARKET/Commemoration Hall, Huntingdon, Cambs**
Huntingdon Craft Market

Oct 8 **CRAFT SHOW/Assembly Hall, Station Road, Chingford, London E4**
Oakleigh Craft Fairs

Oct 8 **ARTS & CRAFT FAIR/The Milton Rooms, Malton, North Yorks**
Yorkshire Craft Fairs

Oct 8-9 **BLAKEMERE CRAFT FAIR**
Blakemere Craft Centre, Chester Road, Sandiway, Northwich, Cheshire
Blakemere Craft Centre

Oct 8-9 **CRAFTS & COUNTRY SHOPPING FAIR**
Tenants Hall, Tatton Park, nr Knutsford, Cheshire
Countrywide Events

Oct 8-9 **CRAFT FAIR/Haydock Park Racecourse, St Helens, Merseyside**
Creative Crafts Association

Oct 8-9 **FINCHCOCKS AUTUMN FAIR/Finchcocks, Goudhurst, Kent**
Finchcocks

Oct 8-9 **CHRISTMAS CRAFTS/Shugborough, Milford, Staffs**
Hobby Horse Events Ltd

Oct 8-9 **WESTON-SUPER-MARE AUTUMN CRAFT FAIR/Winter Gardens Pavilion,**
Royal Parade, Weston-super-Mare, North Somerset
Kevin Murphy Craft Fairs

Oct 8-9 **CRAFTS AT DOBBIES GARDEN CENTRE/Dobbies Garden World, Nuneaton Road, B4111 Mancetter, nr Atherstone, Warks**
Shirecrafts

Oct 8-9 **COUNTRY CRAFTS AT BRITISH NATIONAL PLOUGHING CHAMPIONSHIPS & COUNTRY FESTIVAL/Soham, Cambs**
Society of Ploughmen

Oct 9 **ARTS & CRAFT FAYRE/Hartington Village Hall, Hartington, Derbys**
Biddulph Arts & Craft Fayres

Oct 9 **TEDDY BEAR & DOLL FAIR/Cresta Court Hotel, Altrincham, Cheshire**
Cherish Events

Oct 9 **CRAFTS AT AUTUMN SHOW**
East of England Showground, Peterborough, Cambs
East of England Showground

Oct 9 **CRAFT FAIR/Thurrock Civic Hall, Blackshots Lane, Grays, Essex**
Hallmark Craft Fairs

Oct 9 **MILLENNIUM CRAFTS & GIFTS/Community Centre, Lyndhurst, Hants**
Millennium Crafts & Gifts

Oct 9 **MELTON MOWBRAY FOOD FAYRE/Melton Mowbray Town Centre, Leics**
Special Event Organisers (UK) Ltd

Oct 9 **MANCHESTER DOLLS HOUSE & MINIATURES FAIR**
Civic Centre, Middleton, Manchester
Warners Dolls House & Miniatures Fairs

Oct 9 **SOUTH DORSET AUTUMN CRAFT FAIR**
Weymouth Pavilion, Esplanade, Weymouth, Dorset
West Country Craft Fairs

Oct 9 **ARTS & CRAFT FAIR/Bankfield Hotel, Bingley, West Yorks**
Yorkshire Craft Fairs

Oct 11-16 **CHELSEA CRAFTS FAIR – WEEK ONE**
Chelsea Old Town Hall, King's Road, Chelsea, London SW3
Crafts Council

Oct 12 **BLAKEMERE CRAFT FAIR**
Blakemere Craft Centre, Chester Road, Sandiway, Northwich, Cheshire
Blakemere Craft Centre

Oct 13-16 **KNITTING & STITCHING SHOW**
Alexandra Palace, Wood Green, London N22
Creative Exhibitions Ltd

Oct 14-16 **LOSELEY HOUSE HOME DESIGN & INTERIORS EXHIBITION**
Guildford, Surrey
Buckingham Events

Oct 15 **CIRENCESTER CRAFTSMAN'S MARKET**
Corn Hall, Market Place, Cirencester, Glos
Cirencester Craftsman's Market

Oct 15 **LEEDS DOLL & TEDDY FAIR**
Pudsey Civic Hall, Dawson's Corner, Pudsey, Leeds
Dolly Domain Fairs

Oct 15 **FOCUS CRAFT GROUP/Town Hall, Inverurie, Aberdeenshire**
Festival of Crafts Unique to Scotland (FOCUS)

Oct 15 **WARMINSTER CRAFT FAIR**
Assembly Hall, Sambourne Road, Warminster, Wilts
Kevin Murphy Craft Fairs

Oct 15 **CRAFTS AT THE FORUM/The Forum, Norwich, Norfolk**
Norfolk Events

Oct 15 **CRAFT SHOW/Assembly Hall, Crescent Road, Tunbridge Wells, Kent**
Oakleigh Craft Fairs

Oct 15 **GLASTONBURY AUTUMN CRAFT FAIR**
Town Hall, High Street, Glastonbury, Somerset
West Country Craft Fairs

Oct 15-16 **BLAKEMERE CRAFT FAIR**
Blakemere Craft Centre, Chester Road, Sandiway, Northwich, Cheshire
Blakemere Craft Centre

Oct 15-16 **FESTIVAL OF CRAFTS/Farnham Maltings, Bridge Square, Farnham, Surrey**
Farnham Maltings

Oct 15-16 **CRAFT & GIFT FAIR/Lamport Hall, Lamport, Northants**
Lamport Enterprises Ltd

Oct 15-16 **CRAFT MARQUEE AT ST PETERS**
St Peters Garden Centre, Norton, Worcs
Shirecrafts

Oct 15-16 **ARTS & CRAFT FAIR/St William College, York, North Yorks**
Yorkshire Craft Fairs

Oct 15-20 **MIDLANDS MODEL ENGINEERING EXHIBITION**
International Exhibition Centre, Donington Park, Castle Donington, nr Derby
Meridienne Exhibitions Ltd

Oct 16 **CRAFT & GIFT FAIR/Village Hall, Lewes Road, Ditchling, West Sussex**
Craft Developments

Oct 16 **ART, CRAFT & GIFT FAIR/Village Hall, Woburn, Beds**
Falcon Fairs

Oct 16 **FOCUS CRAFT GROUP/Victoria Hall, Ballater, Aberdeenshire**
Festival of Crafts Unique to Scotland (FOCUS)

Oct 16 **ROSS-ON-WYE AUTUMN CRAFT FAIR**
Chase Hotel, Gloucester Road, Ross-on-Wye, Herefordshire
Kevin Murphy Craft Fairs

Oct 16 **GIFT & FOOD FAIR**
St Bartholomew's School, Andover Road, Newbury, Berks
St Bartholomew's School Parents Association

Oct 18-23 **CHELSEA CRAFTS FAIR – WEEK TWO**
Chelsea Old Town Hall, King's Road, Chelsea, London SW3
Crafts Council

Oct 18-23 **MAURTRAID CRAFTSHOW**
The Centre MK in Middleton Hall, Milton Keynes Shopping Centre, Bucks
Maurtraid Craftshows

Oct 19 **BLAKEMERE CRAFT FAIR**
Blakemere Craft Centre, Chester Road, Sandiway, Northwich, Cheshire
Blakemere Craft Centre

Oct 21-22 **CRAFT MARQUEE AT SCOTTISH PLOUGHING CHAMPIONSHIPS**
Denholm, Hawick, Roxburghshire (possibly Oct 22-23; check with organiser)
Jane McDowall

Oct 21-23 **COBHAM HALL HOME DESIGN & INTERIORS EXHIBITION/Cobham, Kent**
Buckingham Events

Oct 21-23 **CRAFTS FOR SCOTLAND + HOBBYCRAFTS/SECC, Glasgow**
ICHF

Oct 21– Jan 1 2006 **ROYAL KINGSTON FAIR**
Ancient Market Place, Town Square, Kingston upon Thames, Surrey
Eden Crafts

Oct 22 **CRAFT & GIFT FAIR**
Leconfield Hall, Market Square, Petworth, West Sussex
Craft Developments

Oct 22 **SALISBURY CRAFT FAIR/Guildhall, Market Place, Salisbury, Wilts**
Kevin Murphy Craft Fairs

Oct 22 **AUTUMN CRAFT FAIR/Town Hall, Market Square, Wells, Somerset**
West Country Craft Fairs

Oct 22 **ARTS & CRAFT FAIR/Crescent Hotel, Ilkley, West Yorks**
Yorkshire Craft Fairs

Oct 22-23 **BLAKEMERE CRAFT FAIR**
Blakemere Craft Centre, Chester Road, Sandiway, Northwich, Cheshire
Blakemere Craft Centre

Oct 22-23 **CRAFT FAIR/Hawes Market Hall, Hawes, North Yorks**
Cosy Crafts

Oct 22-23 **CHRISTMAS GIFTS FAIR/Tenants Hall, Tatton Park, nr Knutsford, Cheshire**
Countrywide Events

Oct 22-23 **CRAFT FAIR/Woodgreen, Godmanchester, Cambs**
Kingfisher Promotions

Oct 22-23 **AUTUMN ART FAIR**
Landmark Arts Centre, Ferry Road, Teddington, Middx (preview Oct 21)
Landmark Arts Centre

Oct 22-23 **CRAFT WEEKEND AT ULLESTHORPE**
Ullesthorpe Garden Centre, Lutterworth, Leics
Shirecrafts

Oct 22-25 **CRAFT FAIR/Town Hall, Lloyd Street, Llandudno, Conwy**
Event~Reality

Oct 22-30 **GLASTONBURY SPINNERS DEMONSTRATION**
Somerset Rural Life Museum, Chilkwell Street, Glastonbury, Somerset
Somerset Rural Life Museum

Oct 23 **ARTS & CRAFT FAYRE/Hartington Village Hall, Hartington, Derbys**
Biddulph Arts & Craft Fayres

Oct 23 **CRAFT FAIR/Mill Hall, Bellingham Lane, Rayleigh, Essex**
Hallmark Craft Fairs

Oct 23 **CHELTENHAM CRAFT FAIR**
Thistle Hotel, Gloucester Road, Cheltenham, Glos
Kevin Murphy Craft Fairs

Oct 23 **CRAFT & GIFT FAIR/Reebok Stadium, Horwich, nr Bolton, Lancs**
North West Craft & Gift Fairs

Oct 23 **CHRISTMAS CRAFT & GIFT FAIR**
George Hotel, Piercebridge, Darlington, Co Durham
Quality Fairs

Oct 23 **REDESMERE CRAFTS**
Siddington Village Hall, A34, nr Macclesfield, Cheshire
Redesmere Crafts Association

Oct 23 **7th ANNUAL AUTUMN CRAFT FAIR**
Royal Shakespeare Theatre, Stratford-upon-Avon, Warks
West Country Craft Fairs

Oct 23 **ARTS & CRAFT FAIR/Bankfield Hotel, Bingley, West Yorks**
Yorkshire Craft Fairs

Oct 26 **BLAKEMERE CRAFT FAIR**
Blakemere Craft Centre, Chester Road, Sandiway, Northwich, Cheshire
Blakemere Craft Centre

Oct 27-28 **CRAFT FAIR/Market House, Hawes, Wensleydale, North Yorks**
Wensleydale Craft Fairs

Oct 28-29 **SHERBORNE CRAFT MARKET/Digby Hall, Sherborne, Dorset**
Sherborne Craft Market

Oct 28-30 **CRAFT FAIR/Rivendell Garden Centre, Mill Lane, Widnes, Cheshire**
Creative Crafts Association

Oct 28-30 **LIVE CRAFT SHOW/Charterhouse, nr Godalming, Surrey**
HD Events Ltd

Oct 29 **CRAFT & GIFT FAIR**
Steyning Centre, Fletchers Croft, Steyning, West Sussex
Craft Developments

Oct 29 **FOCUS CRAFT GROUP/Music Hall, Aberdeen**
Festival of Crafts Unique to Scotland (FOCUS)

Oct 29 **CRAFT FAIR/Memorial Hall, Chester Road, Wrexham**
Gwynedd & Clwyd Association of Craftworkers

Oct 29-30 **WOODGREEN ANIMAL SHELTER CHRISTMAS GIFT SHOW/Woodgreen Animal Shelter, Godmanchester, Huntingdon, Cambs**
Aztec Events

Oct 29-30 **BLAKEMERE CRAFT FAIR**
Blakemere Craft Centre, Chester Road, Sandiway, Northwich, Cheshire
Blakemere Craft Centre

Oct 29-30 **CRAFT FAYRE/North Stafford Hotel, Station Road, Stoke-on-Trent, Staffs**
Cheshire Fayre

Oct 29-30 **SOUTH EAST OF ENGLAND CHRISTMAS CRAFT SHOW**
Crawley Leisure Centre, Crawley, West Sussex
Craftmaker Events

Oct 29-30 **BEVERLEY CHRISTMAS CRAFT & GIFT FAYRE**
Beverley Racecourse, East Yorks
Doug Moore

Oct 29-30 **FOOD & CRAFT SHOW**
New Hall School, Boreham, nr Chelmsford, Essex (provisional dates)
Penny Farthing Craft Fairs

Oct 29-30 **SHIRECRAFTS MARQUEE WEEKEND**
Worcester Garden Centre, A38 Droitwich Road, Worcester
Shirecrafts

Oct 29-30 **LONDON DOLLS HOUSE & MINIATURES FAIR**
Alexandra Palace, London (inc London Teddy Bear Fair Oct 30)
Warners Dolls House & Miniatures Fairs

Oct 29-30 **CRAFTS AT LANCING COLLEGE/Lancing, West Sussex**
Woodland Crafts

Oct 29-30 **ARTS & CRAFT FAIR/St William College, York, North Yorks**
Yorkshire Craft Fairs

Oct 30 **KINVER CRAFT SHOW**
Community Centre, A449/A458, Kinver, nr Stourbridge
Central Promotions

Oct 30 **EAST MIDLANDS DOLL FAIR/Kelham Hall, Kelham, Newark, Notts**
East Midlands Doll Fairs

Oct 30 **FOCUS CRAFT GROUP/Hilton Tree Tops, Aberdeen**
Festival of Crafts Unique to Scotland (FOCUS)

Oct 30 **CRAFT SHOW/Five Lakes Golf & Country Club, Tolleshunt Knights, nr Tiptree, Essex** (provisional date)
K.C. Craft Shows

Oct 30 **WORCESTER CHRISTMAS CRAFT FAIR**
Bank House Hotel, Bransford, Worcester
Kevin Murphy Craft Fairs

Oct 30 **LAUDERDALE HOUSE ARTS & CRAFTS**
Lauderdale House, Waterlow Park, Highgate Hill, London N6
Lauderdale Arts & Crafts

Oct 30 **MILLENNIUM CRAFTS & GIFTS**
Community Centre, Lyndhurst, Hants
Millennium Crafts & Gifts

Oct 30 **HALLOWEEN CRAFT FAIR/Florence Court, Enniskillen, Co Fermanagh**
National Trust - Florence Court

Oct 31 **CRAFTS AT FRIGHT NIGHT/Fargate, Sheffield City Centre**
Allott Agency

Nov date tba **BOURNEMOUTH ART, CRAFT & GIFT SHOW**
Bournemouth International Centre, Exeter Road, Bournemouth, Dorset
BIC Exhibitions

Nov date tba **CRAFT FAIR/Elton Hall, Elton, nr Peterborough, Cambs**
Craftworkers Cooperative

Nov date tba **CRAFTS FOR CHRISTMAS**
Memorial Hall, The Forebury, Sawbridgeworth, Herts
Fig Fairs

Nov date tba **CHRISTMAS CRAFT FAIR**
Monymusk Arts Centre, Monymusk, by Inverurie, Aberdeenshire
Monymusk Arts Trust

Nov date tba **SWANSEA CHRISTMAS CRAFT MARQUEE**
City Centre, Swansea (may be mid-Dec)
Wales Craft Council

Nov date tba **ARTS & CRAFT FAIR/Town Hall, Northallerton, North Yorks**
Yorkshire Craft Fairs

Nov 2 **BLAKEMERE CRAFT FAIR**
Blakemere Craft Centre, Chester Road, Sandiway, Northwich, Cheshire
Blakemere Craft Centre

Nov 2 **CARMARTHENSHIRE CRAFTS/St Peters Hall, Nott Square, Carmarthen**
Carmarthenshire Crafts

Nov 3-6 **KNITTING & STITCHING SHOW/RDS, Ballsbridge, Dublin, Ireland**
Creative Exhibitions Ltd

Nov 4-6 **THE ART, CRAFT & DESIGN SHOW/Imperial War Museum, Duxford, Cambs**
Art, Craft & Design Show

Nov 4-6 **BRITISH CRAFTS AUTUMN/venue to be confirmed**
British Crafts

Nov 4-6 **WILTSHIRE COUNTY HOME DESIGN & INTERIORS EXHIBITION/Wilts**
Buckingham Events

Nov 4-6 **COTTAGE CRAFT FESTIVAL/Norfolk Showground, Dereham Road, New Costessey, Norwich, Norfolk**
Country Cottage Crafts

Nov 4-6 **CREATIVE STITCHES & HOBBYCRAFTS/International Arena, Cardiff**
ICHF

Nov 4-6 **CRAFTS FOR CHRISTMAS**
Kent County Showground, Detling, nr Maidstone, Kent
Rural Crafts Association

Nov 5 **3 SHIRES CRAFT GUILD/The Community Hall, Churchdown, Glos**
3 Shires Craft Guild

Nov 5 **CRAFTS AT AFTER DARK/Don Valley Bowl, Attercliffe Common, Sheffield**
Allott Agency

Nov 5 **CIRENCESTER CRAFTSMAN'S MARKET**
Corn Hall, Market Place, Cirencester, Glos
Cirencester Craftsman's Market

Nov 5 **CRAFT & GIFT FAIR/Village Hall, High Street, Henfield, West Sussex**
Craft Developments

Nov 5 **ART, CRAFT & GIFT FAIR/Town Hall, Towcester, Northants**
Falcon Fairs

Nov 5 **CRAFTS AT THE FORUM/The Forum, Norwich, Norfolk**
Norfolk Events

Nov 5 **ARTS & CRAFT FAIR/Town Hall, Stokesley, nr Middlesbrough**
Yorkshire Craft Fairs

Nov 5-6 **BRENTWOOD CHRISTMAS CRAFT & GIFT SHOW**
Brentwood Centre, Doddinghurst Road, Brentwood, Essex
Aztec Events

Nov 5-6 **BLAKEMERE CRAFT FAIR**
Blakemere Craft Centre, Chester Road, Sandiway, Northwich, Cheshire
Blakemere Craft Centre

Nov 5-6 **CRAFT FAYRE/Middleton Hall, nr Tamworth, Staffs**
Cheshire Fayre

Nov 5-6 **CHRISTMAS SHOPPING FAIR**
Tenants Hall, Tatton Park, nr Knutsford, Cheshire
Countrywide Events

Nov 5-6 **CRAFT FAIR/The Maltings, Ely, Cambs**
Kingfisher Promotions

Nov 5-6 **CRAFT & GIFT FAIR**
Norcalympia at the Norbreck Castle Hotel, Blackpool, Lancs
North West Craft & Gift Fairs

Nov 5-6 **CRAFT WEEKEND AT DOBBIES OF GAILEY/Dobbies Garden Centre, Gailey Island, Junction A5/A449 Stafford Road, Gailey, Staffs**
Shirecrafts

Nov 6 **ART, CRAFT & GIFT FAIR/Village Hall, Denham, Bucks**
Falcon Fairs

Nov 6 **CHRISTMAS CRAFT & GIFT EVENT**
Brockenhurst College, Brockenhurst, Hants
IGF Marketing

Nov 6 **YEOVIL CHRISTMAS CRAFT FAIR**
Westland Leisure Complex, Westbourne Close, Yeovil, Somerset
Kevin Murphy Craft Fairs

Nov 6 **CHRISTMAS CRAFT & GIFT FAIR**
Cannon Hall, Cawthorne, South Yorks
Quality Fairs

Nov 6 **ARTS & CRAFT FAIR/Bankfield Hotel, Bingley, West Yorks**
Yorkshire Craft Fairs

Nov 9	**BLAKEMERE CRAFT FAIR** **Blakemere Craft Centre, Chester Road, Sandiway, Northwich, Cheshire** Blakemere Craft Centre
Nov 9-13	**COUNTRY LIVING MAGAZINE CHRISTMAS FAIR** **Business Design Centre, Upper Street, Islington, London** Upper Street Events
Nov 10-13	**CRAFTS FOR CHRISTMAS + HOBBYCRAFTS/NEC, Birmingham** ICHF
Nov 10-13	**CRAFTS FOR CHRISTMAS** **Great Yorkshire Showground, Wetherby Road, Harrogate, North Yorks** Rural Crafts Association
Nov 11-13	**COUGHTON COURT HOME DESIGN & INTERIORS EXHIBITION** **Alcester, Warks** Buckingham Events
Nov 11-13	**GIFTS FOR CHRISTMAS/Hatfield House, Hatfield, Herts** HD Events Ltd
Nov 11-13	**INTERNATIONAL MODEL BOAT SHOW/Warwickshire Exhibition Centre,** **Fosse Way, Junction A425/B4455, nr Leamington Spa, Warks** Meridienne Exhibitions Ltd
Nov 11-13	**SPECIAL CHRISTMAS ARTS & CRAFT FAIR** **St William College, York, North Yorks** Yorkshire Craft Fairs
Nov 12	**CRAFT & GIFT FAIR/Adastra Hall, Keymer Road, Hassocks, West Sussex** Craft Developments
Nov 12	**ART, CRAFT & GIFT FAIR/Town Hall, Brackley, Northants** Falcon Fairs
Nov 12	**CHRISTMAS CRAFT MARKET/Commemoration Hall, Huntingdon, Cambs** Huntingdon Craft Market
Nov 12	**SALISBURY CRAFT FAIR/Guildhall, Market Place, Salisbury, Wilts** Kevin Murphy Craft Fairs
Nov 12	**LLANIDLOES CRAFT FAIR/Community Centre, Llanidloes, Powys** Llanidloes Arts & Crafts Fairs
Nov 12	**ART & CRAFT FAIR** **Queens Park Arts Centre, Queens Park, Aylesbury, Bucks** Queens Park Arts Centre
Nov 12	**ARTS & CRAFT FAIR/The Milton Rooms, Malton, North Yorks** Yorkshire Craft Fairs

Nov 12-13 **COLCHESTER CHRISTMAS GIFT SHOW**
Leisure World, Cowdray Road, Colchester, Essex
Aztec Events

Nov 12-13 **BLAKEMERE CRAFT FAIR**
Blakemere Craft Centre, Chester Road, Sandiway, Northwich, Cheshire
Blakemere Craft Centre

Nov 12-13 **CRAFT FAYRE/Buxton Pavilion, Buxton, Derbys**
Cheshire Fayre

Nov 12-13 **CHRISTMAS GIFTS FAIR**
State Rooms, Himley Hall, nr Dudley, West Midlands (provisional dates)
Countrywide Events

Nov 12-13 **CRAFT & GIFTS AT RUFFORD CHRISTMAS FAIR**
Rufford Country Park, Notts
Craft People 2000

Nov 12-13 **CRAFTS AT EAST OF ENGLAND CHRISTMAS FESTIVAL**
East of England Showground, Peterborough, Cambs
East of England Showground

Nov 12-13 **CRAFTS AT CHRISTMAS**
Hylands House, Hylands Park, Chelmsford, Essex
Guild of Essex Craftsmen

Nov 12-13 **CHRISTMAS CRAFTS BROADLANDS/Broadlands, Romsey, Hants**
Living Heritage Craft Shows

Nov 12-13 **CRAFTS AT HARVINGTON HALL/Harvington, nr Kidderminster, Worcs**
Shirecrafts

Nov 12-13 **CHRISTMAS CRAFT FAIR**
South Hill Park Arts Centre, Ringmead, Bracknell, Berks
South Hill Park Arts Centre

Nov 12-13 **12th ANNUAL MID-SOMERSET CHRISTMAS CRAFT FAIR**
Town Hall, Market Square, Wells, Somerset
West Country Craft Fairs

Nov 12-13 **CRAFT MARKET**
Whiteley Village Outlet Shopping, Whiteley, Fareham, Hants
Woodland Crafts

Nov 13 **ARTS & CRAFT FAYRE/Hartington Village Hall, Hartington, Derbys**
Biddulph Arts & Craft Fayres
Nov 13 **CRAFT FAIR/Lancaster University, Lancaster, Lancs**
Creative Crafts Association

Nov 13 **CRAFT FAIR/Rushden & Diamonds FC Sports Centre, Nene Park, Irthlingborough, Northants**
DK Fairs

Nov 13 **FOCUS CRAFT GROUP/Fintry Dyce Village Hall, Aberdeenshire**
Festival of Crafts Unique to Scotland (FOCUS)

Nov 13 **CRAFT FAIR/Castle View School, Meppell Avenue, Canvey Island, Essex**
Hallmark Craft Fairs

Nov 13 **READING AUTUMN CRAFT FAIR**
Calcot Hotel, Bath Road, Calcot, Reading, Berks
Kevin Murphy Craft Fairs

Nov 13 **CRAFT & GIFTS FAIR/Hinchingbrooke House, Huntingdon, Cambs**
Kingfisher Promotions

Nov 13 **REDESMERE CRAFTS**
Siddington Village Hall, A34, nr Macclesfield, Cheshire
Redesmere Crafts Association

Nov 13 **CHRISTMAS CRAFTS & CHARITY FAIR**
Boat Museum, South Pier Road, Ellesmere Port, Cheshire
Boat Museum

Nov 14 **CRAFT FAYRE/Golf Hotel, The Broadway, Woodhall Spa, Lincs**
Woodhall Spa Group of Friends of Cancer Research UK

Nov 15 **INDOOR CHRISTMAS CRAFT MARKET**
Crispin Hall, opp Clark's Village, Street, Somerset
West Country Craft Fairs

Nov 16 **BLAKEMERE CRAFT FAIR**
Blakemere Craft Centre, Chester Road, Sandiway, Northwich, Cheshire
Blakemere Craft Centre

Nov 17 **CHRISTMAS CRAFT & GIFT FAIR/Buttermarket, Retford, Notts**
Quality Fairs

Nov 17-19 **DESIGN & TECHNOLOGY EDUCATION TRADE SHOW/NEC, Birmingham**
ICHF

Nov 17-20 **FESTIVE GIFT FAIR/Hall 12, NEC, Birmingham**
Orchard Events Ltd

Nov 17-20 **CRAFTS FOR CHRISTMAS**
South of England Showground, Ardingly, West Sussex
Rural Crafts Association

Nov 18-20 **LIVE CRAFT SHOW/Sandown Park, Esher, Surrey**
HD Events Ltd

Nov 18-20 **GIFTS FOR CHRISTMAS/Ragley Hall, Alcester, Warks**
HD Events Ltd

Nov 18-20 **HEREFORD CONTEMPORARY CRAFT FAIR**
The Courtyard Centre for the Arts, Edgar Street, Hereford
Herefordshire Council

Nov 18-20 **LIVING CRAFTS FOR CHRISTMAS/Blenheim Palace, Woodstock, Oxon**
Living Crafts Ltd

Nov 18-20 **KENT CHRISTMAS GIFT FAYRE/Farming World, Faversham, Kent**
WMH Leisure

Nov 18–Jan 1 2006 **DEVON GUILD OF CRAFTSMEN CHRISTMAS EXHIBITION**
Devon Guild of Craftsmen, Riverside Mill, Bovey Tracey, Devon
Devon Guild of Craftsmen

Nov 19 **CIRENCESTER CRAFTSMAN'S MARKET**
Corn Hall, Market Place, Cirencester, Glos
Cirencester Craftsman's Market

Nov 19 **CRAFT & GIFT FAIR**
Village Hall, Ferring Street, Ferring, West Sussex
Craft Developments

Nov 19 **CRAFT & GIFT MARQUEE AT DUNSTABLE TUDOR FESTIVAL**
Dunstable, Beds
Craft People 2000

Nov 19 **FOCUS CRAFT GROUP/Town Hall, Banchory, Aberdeenshire**
Festival of Crafts Unique to Scotland (FOCUS)

Nov 19 **CRAFTS AT THE FORUM/The Forum, Norwich, Norfolk**
Norfolk Events

Nov 19-20 **BLAKEMERE CRAFT FAIR**
Blakemere Craft Centre, Chester Road, Sandiway, Northwich, Cheshire
Blakemere Craft Centre

Nov 19-20 **TALL TREES CHRISTMAS CRAFT & GIFT SHOW**
Tall Trees Nightclub, Yarm, Tees Valley
Doug Moore

Nov 19-20 **GORING CHRISTMAS CRAFT FAIR**
Goring Village Hall, High Street, Goring-on-Thames, Oxon
Goring Village Hall Management

Nov 19-20 **ART IN CLAY/Farnham Maltings, Farnham, Surrey**
HD Events Ltd

Nov 19-20 **CHRISTMAS CRAFTS/Lamport Hall, Lamport, Northants**
Hobby Horse Events Ltd

Nov 19-20 **CRAFTS AT CHRISTMAS/Gosfield School, Gosfield, Halstead, Essex**
(provisional dates)
K.C. Craft Shows

Nov 19-20 **NEWTON ABBOT CHRISTMAS CRAFT FAIR/Racecourse, Kingsteignton, Newton Abbot, Devon**
Kevin Murphy Craft Fairs

Nov 19-20	**CRAFT STALLS AT LIGHTING UP LUTON/Luton Town Centre, Luton, Beds** Luton Borough Council
Nov 19-20	**CHRISTMAS CRAFT FAIR/Buckland Abbey, Yelverton, Devon** National Trust - Buckland Abbey
Nov 19-20	**WIMPOLE CHRISTMAS CRAFT FAIR** **Wimpole Hall, Arrington, nr Cambridge** National Trust - Wimpole Hall
Nov 19-20	**CHRISTMAS CRAFT MARQUEE** **Evesham Country Park, Evesham By-Pass A46, Worcs** Shirecrafts
Nov 19-20	**CHRISTMAS GIFT & CRAFT FAIR** **Michelham Priory, Upper Dicker, Hailsham, East Sussex** Sussex Past
Nov 19-20	**CRAFTS AT FORT PURBROOK** **Fort Purbrook, Portsdown Hill, Cosham, Hants** Woodland Crafts
Nov 19-20	**WINTER CRAFT FAIR** **Pavilion Theatre, Marine Parade, Worthing, West Sussex** Worthing Theatres
Nov 19-20	**CHRISTMAS CRAFT FAIR/Duncombe Park, Helmsley, North Yorks** Yorkshire Craft Fairs
Nov 19-21	**WESTONBIRT SCHOOL CHRISTMAS FAYRE/Tetbury, Glos** Buckingham Events
Nov 19-Dec 17	**CHRISTMAS CRAFT FAIR** **Somerset Rural Life Museum, Chilkwell Street, Glastonbury, Somerset** Somerset Rural Life Museum
Nov 20	**CRAFT STANDS AT BECHER MEETING** **Aintree Racecourse, Aintree, Liverpool** Aintree Racecourse Co Ltd
Nov 20	**CRAFT FAIR** **Burgess Civic Hall, St Ivo Leisure Centre, Westwood Road, St Ives, Cambs** Burgess Civic Hall
Nov 20	**CRAFT FAIR/Crown Woods School, Riefield Row, Eltham, London SE9** Cancer Research UK - Greenwich Committee
Nov 20	**TELFORD CRAFT SHOW/Moat House Hotel, M54 J5, Telford Town Centre, Shropshire** - provisional date Central Promotions
Nov 20	**CRAFT FAIR/Floral Hall, The Promenade, Southport** Creative Crafts Association

Nov 20 **ART, CRAFT & GIFT FAIR/Village Hall, Woburn, Beds**
Falcon Fairs

Nov 20 **CRAFT FAIR/Clwyd Theatre Cymru, Mold, Flintshire**
Gwynedd & Clwyd Association of Craftworkers

Nov 20 **LAUDERDALE HOUSE ARTS & CRAFTS/Lauderdale House, Waterlow Park, Highgate Hill, London N6**
Lauderdale Arts & Crafts

Nov 20 **MILLENNIUM CRAFTS & GIFTS/Community Centre, Lyndhurst, Hants**
Millennium Crafts & Gifts

Nov 20 **CRAFT SHOW/Red Lion, Great North Road, Hatfield, Herts**
Oakleigh Craft Fairs

Nov 20 **REDESMERE CRAFTS**
Siddington Village Hall, A34, nr Macclesfield, Cheshire
Redesmere Crafts Association

Nov 20 **HOVE DOLLS HOUSE & MINIATURES FAIR**
Town Hall, Norton Road, Hove, East Sussex
Warners Dolls House & Miniatures Fairs

Nov 22 **MILLENNIUM CRAFTS & GIFTS/Community Centre, Lyndhurst, Hants**
Millennium Crafts & Gifts

Nov 22 **INDOOR CHRISTMAS CRAFT MARKET**
Crispin Hall, opp Clark's Village, Street, Somerset
West Country Craft Fairs

Nov 23 **BLAKEMERE CRAFT FAIR**
Blakemere Craft Centre, Chester Road, Sandiway, Northwich, Cheshire
Blakemere Craft Centre

Nov 23-26 **LLANDUDNO CELTIC WINTER FAYRE/Llandudno, Conwy**
Event~Reality

Nov 24-25 **CRAFTS FOR CHRISTMAS LIGHTS DAY**
Commemoration Hall, Huntingdon, Cambs
Huntingdon Craft Market

Nov 24-27 **KNITTING & STITCHING SHOW**
Harrogate International Centre, King's Road, Harrogate, North Yorks
Creative Exhibitions Ltd

Nov 24-27 **WORCESTER CHRISTMAS FAYRE/City Centre, Worcester**
Worcester City Council

Nov 24-27 **ST NICHOLAS ARTS & CRAFT FAIR/St William College, York, North Yorks**
Yorkshire Craft Fairs

Nov 25 **NEWTON STREET FAYRE**
Community Centre + surrounding streets, Newton, Alfreton, Derbys
Newton Carnival Team

Nov 25-27 **NORFOLK CHRISTMAS CRAFT & GIFT SHOW**
Norfolk Showground, Dereham Road, New Costessey, Norwich, Norfolk
Aztec Events

Nov 25-27 **BRANCEPETH CASTLE CHRISTMAS FAIR**
Brancepeth Castle, 5 miles west of Durham City on A690
Brancepeth Castle Fairs

Nov 25-27 **BRITISH CRAFTS AUTUMN**
Chiswick Town Hall, Heathfield Terrace, London W4
British Crafts

Nov 25-27 **WOBURN ABBEY CHRISTMAS FAYRE/Woburn, Beds**
Buckingham Events

Nov 25-27 **CHRISTMAS SHIBDEN HALL CRAFT FAIR/Shibden Hall, Listers Road, Halifax, West Yorks**
Calderdale MBC

Nov 25-27 **CHRISTMAS SHOPPING FAYRE/Westpoint, Clyst St Mary, Exeter, Devon**
Grandstand Events Ltd

Nov 25-27 **CHRISTMAS GIFT & CRAFT FAIR/Thorpe Park, nr Chertsey, Surrey**
HD Events Ltd

Nov 25-27 **LIVE CRAFT SHOW/Harewood House, Leeds**
HD Events Ltd

Nov 25-27 **CHRISTMAS CRAFTS AT SANDRINGHAM/Sandringham, Norfolk**
Living Heritage Craft Shows

Nov 25-27 **CRAFTS FOR CHRISTMAS/Tatton Country Park, Knutsford, Cheshire**
Rural Crafts Association

Nov 26 **FOCUS CRAFT GROUP/Music Hall, Aberdeen**
Festival of Crafts Unique to Scotland (FOCUS)

Nov 26 **MADE IN THE MARCHES**
St John the Baptist Parish Church, Bishop's Castle, Shropshire
Made in the Marches

Nov 26 **DICKENS NIGHT CELEBRATIONS/Atherston, Nuneaton, Warks**
Shirecrafts

Nov 26-27 **BLAKEMERE CRAFT FAIR**
Blakemere Craft Centre, Chester Road, Sandiway, Northwich, Cheshire
Blakemere Craft Centre

Nov 26-27 **STAFFORD CRAFT SHOW**
County Showground, A518 Uttoxeter Road, Stafford
Central Promotions

Nov 26-27 **CRAFT FAYRE/Quarry Bank Mill, Styal, Cheshire**
Cheshire Fayre

Nov 26-27 **CHRISTMAS SHOPPING FAIR/State Rooms, Himley Hall, nr Dudley, West Midlands** (provisional dates)
Countrywide Events

Nov 26-27 **CRAFT FAIR/Haydock Park Racecourse, St Helens, Merseyside**
Creative Crafts Association

Nov 26-27 **ESSEX CRAFT FAIR**
Cliffs Pavilion Theatre, Station Road, Westcliff-on-Sea, Essex
Hallmark Craft Fairs

Nov 26-27 **INSPIRATION FOR CHRISTMAS ART & CRAFT FAIR**
Bratton Court, Minehead, Somerset
Inspiration for Christmas

Nov 26-27 **IN-HOUSE CRAFT & GOURMET FOOD FAIR**
Landmark Arts Centre, Ferry Road, Teddington, Middx
Landmark Arts Centre

Nov 26-27 **EASTERN ENGLAND CRAFT MARKET**
Rhodes Centre, South Street, Bishop's Stortford, Herts
Oakleigh Craft Fairs

Nov 26-27 **CHRISTMAS FOOD & CRAFT FAIR**
Cressing Temple Barns, Cressing, nr Braintree, Essex
Penny Farthing Craft Fairs

Nov 26-27 **CHRISTMAS CRAFT & GIFT FAIR**
Swallow St George Hotel, Ripon Road, Harrogate, North Yorks
Quality Fairs

Nov 26-27 **CHRISTMAS CRAFT MARQUEE WEEKEND/Dobbies Garden World, Nuneaton Road, B4111 Mancetter, nr Atherstone, Warks**
Shirecrafts

Nov 26-27 **BOLSOVER FESTIVAL OF CHRISTMAS/Bolsover Castle, Bolsover, Derbys**
Special Event Organisers (UK) Ltd

Nov 26-27 **ANNUAL NEW FOREST CHRISTMAS CRAFT FAIR**
Lyndhurst Park Hotel, High Street, Lyndhurst, Hants
West Country Craft Fairs

Nov 26-27 **CRAFTS AT BRIGHTON RACECOURSE**
Freshfield Road, Brighton, East Sussex
Woodland Crafts

Nov 27 **ARTS & CRAFT FAYRE/Hartington Village Hall, Hartington, Derbys**
Biddulph Arts & Craft Fayres

Nov 27 **TEDDY BEAR & DOLL FAIR/Buxton Pavilion, Buxton, Derbys**
Cherish Events

Nov 27 **CRAFT & GIFT FAIR/Village Hall, West Street, Storrington, West Sussex**
Craft Developments

Nov 27 **FAIRFIELD CHRISTMAS CRAFT & GIFT FAIR**
Fairfield Halls, Park Lane, Croydon, Surrey
Fairfield (Croydon) Ltd

Nov 27 **FOCUS CRAFT GROUP/Hilton Tree Tops, Aberdeen**
Festival of Crafts Unique to Scotland (FOCUS)

Nov 27 **CHRISTMAS FAYRE/RHS Hyde Hall, Rettendon, nr Chelmsford, Essex**
Guild of Essex Craftsmen

Nov 27 **ROSS-ON-WYE CHRISTMAS CRAFT FAIR**
Chase Hotel, Gloucester Road, Ross-on-Wye, Herefordshire
Kevin Murphy Craft Fairs

Nov 27 **REDESMERE CRAFTS**
Siddington Village Hall, A34, nr Macclesfield, Cheshire
Redesmere Crafts Association

Nov 27 **ARTS, CRAFTS & HOBBIES FAIR**
University of Southampton Staff Club, Highfield, Southampton, Hants
University of Southampton Staff Club

Nov 27 **YORK DOLLS HOUSE & MINIATURES FAIR/York Racecourse, York**
Warners Dolls House & Miniatures Fairs

Nov 28-29 **CRAFTS AT ROYAL WELSH AGRICULTURAL WINTER FAIR**
Royal Welsh Showground, Llanelwedd, Builth Wells, Powys
Royal Welsh Agricultural Society Ltd

Nov 28-Dec 4 **WOKING CHRISTMAS FAIR/Town Square, Woking, Surrey**
Eden Crafts

Nov 29 **INDOOR CHRISTMAS CRAFT MARKET**
Crispin Hall, opp Clark's Village, Street, Somerset
West Country Craft Fairs

Nov 30 **BLAKEMERE CRAFT FAIR**
Blakemere Craft Centre, Chester Road, Sandiway, Northwich, Cheshire
Blakemere Craft Centre

Nov 30 **CRAFTS AT CHRISTMAS EXTRAVAGANZA/Frome Town Centre (outdoor) & Frome Cheese and Grain (indoor), Somerset**
Frome Town Centre Promotions Group

Dec date tba **CHRISTMAS FESTIVAL**
The Bowes Museum, Bowes, Barnard Castle, Co Durham
Bowes Museum

Dec date tba **CRAFT AT CHRISTMAS CAROUSEL**
Capel Manor College, Bullsmoor Lane, Enfield, Middx
Fig Fairs

Dec 1 **CRAFT & GIFT FAIR (LATE NIGHT SHOP)**
Town Hall, Fisher Street, Lewes, East Sussex
Craft Developments

Dec 2 **CRAFTS FOR CHRISTMAS/Commemoration Hall, Huntingdon, Cambs**
Huntingdon Craft Market

Dec 2-4 **CHRISTMAS GIFT & CRAFT FAIR/Hop Farm, Paddock Wood, Kent**
HD Events Ltd

Dec 2-4 **GIFTS FOR CHRISTMAS/Audley End House, Saffron Walden, Essex**
HD Events Ltd

Dec 2-4 **LIVE CRAFT SHOW/Ascot Racecourse, Berks**
HD Events Ltd

Dec 2-4 **CRAFTS FOR CHRISTMAS**
Suffolk Showground, Bucklesham Road, Ipswich, Suffolk
Rural Crafts Association

Dec 2-4 **CHRISTMAS CRAFT FAIR**
Vaynol Estate, Bangor, Gwynedd (provisional dates)
Vaynol Enterprises Ltd

Dec 2-5 **EAST LONDON DESIGN SHOW**
Shoreditch Town Hall, 380 Old Street, London EC1
East London Design Show

Dec 3 **BOWES SHOW CHRISTMAS CRAFT FAYRE**
Bowes Village Hall, Bowes, Barnard Castle, Co Durham
Bowes Agricultural Society

Dec 3 **CIRENCESTER CRAFTSMAN'S MARKET**
Corn Hall, Market Place, Cirencester, Glos
Cirencester Craftsman's Market

Dec 3 **CRAFT & GIFT FAIR/Civic Centre, Bell Farm Lane, Uckfield, East Sussex**
Craft Developments

Dec 3 **ART, CRAFT & GIFT FAIR/Town Hall, Towcester, Northants**
Falcon Fairs

Dec 3 **HADDENHAM FESTIVAL & CRAFT FAYRE**
Village Hall, Haddenham, nr Aylesbury, Bucks
Haddenham Festival & Craft Fayre

Dec 3 **NATIONAL CHRISTMAS LACEMAKER'S FAIR**
Pavilion, National Exhibition Centre, Birmingham
John & Jennifer Ford

Dec 3 **CRAFT SHOW**
Crook Log Sports Centre, Brampton Road, Bexleyheath, Kent
Oakleigh Craft Fairs

Dec 3 **SHERBORNE CHRISTMAS CRAFT FAIR**
Digby Church Halls, opp Abbey, Sherborne, Dorset
West Country Craft Fairs

Dec 3-4 **CRAFT FAIR/Victoria Halls, Hartley Wintney, Hants**
Arts & Craft Fairs

Dec 3-4 **BLAKEMERE CRAFT FAIR**
Blakemere Craft Centre, Chester Road, Sandiway, Northwich, Cheshire
Blakemere Craft Centre

Dec 3-4 **FESTIVE CHRISTMAS FAIR**
Borde Hill Garden, Balcombe Road, Haywards Heath, West Sussex
Borde Hill Garden

Dec 3-4 **CRAFTS & GIFTS AT ARLEY CHRISTMAS FESTIVAL**
Arley Hall, nr Knutsford, Cheshire
Cheshire Fayre

Dec 3-4 **CRAFT FAIR/Sandon Hall, Sandon, Staffs**
Creative Crafts Association

Dec 3-4 **YORK CHRISTMAS CRAFT & GIFT SHOW**
Knavesmire Suite, York Racecourse
Doug Moore

Dec 3-4 **VICTORIAN CHRISTMAS AT AVONCROFT MUSEUM/Bromsgrove, Worcs**
Hobby Horse Events Ltd

Dec 3-4 **WESTON-SUPER-MARE CHRISTMAS CRAFT FAIR/Winter Gardens**
Pavilion, Royal Parade, Weston-super-Mare, North Somerset
Kevin Murphy Craft Fairs

Dec 3-4 **CRAFT FAIR/The Maltings, Ely, Cambs**
Kingfisher Promotions

Dec 3-4 **MILLENNIUM CRAFTS & GIFTS/Community Centre, Lyndhurst, Hants**
Millennium Crafts & Gifts

Dec 3-4 **CHRISTMAS AT CLUMBER/Clumber Park, Worksop, Notts**
National Trust - Clumber Park

Dec 3-4 **CHRISTMAS CRAFT FAIR**
Sutton House, Homerton High Street, London E9
National Trust - Sutton House

Dec 3-4 **VICTORIAN CHRISTMAS CRAFT FAIR**
The Argory, Derrycaw Road, Moy, Co Tyrone
National Trust - The Argory

Dec 3-4 **YULETIDE CRAFT & FOOD FAIR/Saltram House, Plymouth, Devon**
Saltram House

Dec 3-4 **MATLOCK VICTORIAN WEEKEND/Hall Leys Park, Matlock, Derbys**
Special Event Organisers (UK) Ltd

Dec 3-4 **ARTS & CRAFT FAIR/St William College, York, North Yorks**
Yorkshire Craft Fairs

Dec 3-6 **CHRISTMAS SHOWCASE**
The Harbour Gallery, Le Boulevard, St Aubin, Jersey
Art in the Frame Foundation

Dec 4 **BRENTWOOD CHRISTMAS CRAFT & GIFT SHOW**
Brentwood Centre, Doddinghurst Road, Brentwood, Essex
Aztec Events

Dec 4 **ARTS & CRAFT FAYRE/Hartington Village Hall, Hartington, Derbys**
Biddulph Arts & Craft Fayres

Dec 4 **ART, CRAFT & GIFT FAIR/Village Hall, Denham, Bucks**
Falcon Fairs

Dec 4 **LAUDERDALE HOUSE ARTS & CRAFTS**
Lauderdale House, Waterlow Park, Highgate Hill, London N6
Lauderdale Arts & Crafts

Dec 4 **CRAFT SHOW/Royal Chace Hotel, The Ridgeway, Enfield, Middx**
Oakleigh Craft Fairs

Dec 4 **CHRISTMAS CRAFT FAIR/The Reading Room, Ovingham, Northumberland**
Ovingham Goose Fair

Dec 4 **CHRISTMAS CRAFT & GIFT FAIR/venue to be advised**
Quality Fairs

Dec 4 **10th ANNUAL CHRISTMAS CRAFT FAIR**
Royal Shakespeare Theatre, Stratford-upon-Avon, Warks
West Country Craft Fairs

Dec 5 **TIVERTON CRAFT FAIR/The Pannier Market, Tiverton, Devon**
Tiverton Craft Fair

Dec 6 **INDOOR CHRISTMAS CRAFT MARKET**
Crispin Hall, opp Clark's Village, Street, Somerset
West Country Craft Fairs

Dec 7	**BLAKEMERE CRAFT FAIR** **Blakemere Craft Centre, Chester Road, Sandiway, Northwich, Cheshire** Blakemere Craft Centre
Dec 7	**CARMARTHENSHIRE CRAFTS** **St Peters Hall, Nott Square, Carmarthen** Carmarthenshire Crafts
Dec 7-23	**WINTERLAND** **Bridgend Town Centre, South Wales** Bridgend Festivals
Dec 9-11	**CRAFT & GIFTS AT BEDFORD VICTORIAN MARKET/Bedford, Beds** Craft People 2000
Dec 9-11	**LIVE CRAFT SHOW/Chiltern Open Air Museum, Chalfont St Giles, Bucks** HD Events Ltd
Dec 9-11	**CRAFTS FOR CHRISTMAS/Burghley House, Stamford. Lincs** Rural Crafts Association
Dec 10	**3 SHIRES CRAFT GUILD/Bredon Village Hall, Bredon, Glos** 3 Shires Craft Guild
Dec 10	**BARLEYLANDS CRAFT & FARMERS' MARKET/Barleylands Farm, Barleylands Road (off A129), Billericay, Essex** Barleylands Crafts Village
Dec 10	**BRECON BEACONS CHRISTMAS FAYRE/Market Hall, Brecon, Powys** Brecon Beacons National Park Authority
Dec 10	**CRAFT & GIFT FAIR** **Woodlands Centre, Woodlands Avenue, Rustington, West Sussex** Craft Developments
Dec 10	**ART, CRAFT & GIFT FAIR/Town Hall, Brackley, Northants** Falcon Fairs
Dec 10	**FOCUS CRAFT GROUP/Town Hall, Banchory, Aberdeenshire** Festival of Crafts Unique to Scotland (FOCUS)
Dec 10	**12th ANNUAL DORCHESTER CHRISTMAS CRAFT FAIR** **Corn Exchange, Town Centre, Dorchester, Dorset** West Country Craft Fairs
Dec 10	**ARTS & CRAFT FAIR/The Milton Rooms, Malton, North Yorks** Yorkshire Craft Fairs
Dec 10-11	**BLAKEMERE CRAFT FAIR** **Blakemere Craft Centre, Chester Road, Sandiway, Northwich, Cheshire** Blakemere Craft Centre

Dec 10-11 **CRAFTS & GIFTS AT ARLEY CHRISTMAS FESTIVAL**
Arley Hall, nr Knutsford, Cheshire
Cheshire Fayre

Dec 10-11 **CHRISTMAS GIFT & CRAFT FAIR**
Kempton Park, Sunbury-on-Thames, Middx
HD Events Ltd

Dec 10-11 **SALISBURY CHRISTMAS CRAFT FAIR**
Guildhall, Market Place, Salisbury, Wilts
Kevin Murphy Craft Fairs

Dec 10-11 **CHRISTMAS CRAFT FAIR/Woodgreen, Godmanchester, Cambs**
Kingfisher Promotions

Dec 10-11 **CHRISTMAS AT CLUMBER/Clumber Park, Worksop, Notts**
National Trust - Clumber Park

Dec 11 **ARTS & CRAFT FAYRE/Hartington Village Hall, Hartington, Derbys**
Biddulph Arts & Craft Fayres

Dec 11 **CRAFT FAIR/Blackwater Leisure Centre, Park Drive, Maldon, Essex**
Hallmark Craft Fairs

Dec 11 **CRAFT & GIFT FAIR/Reebok Stadium, Horwich, nr Bolton, Lancs**
North West Craft & Gift Fairs

Dec 11 **CRAFT SHOW/Leisure Centre, Bagshot Road (A322), Bracknell, Berks**
Oakleigh Craft Fairs

Dec 11 **CHRISTMAS CRAFT & GIFT FAIR**
Hilton Leeds Garforth Hotel, Wakefield Road, Garforth, Leeds
Quality Fairs

Dec 11 **REDESMERE CRAFTS**
Siddington Village Hall, A34, nr Macclesfield, Cheshire
Redesmere Crafts Association

Dec 11 **CHRISTMAS PAST CRAFT FAIR/Sandwell Park Farm, Sandwell Valley Country Park, Salters Lane, West Bromwich** (provisional - might be Dec 18)
Sandwell Valley Craft Fairs

Dec 11 **6th ANNUAL SOUTH DORSET CHRISTMAS CRAFT MARKET/Weymouth Pavilion, Esplanade, Weymouth, Dorset**
West Country Craft Fairs

Dec 11 **TANKERTON CHRISTMAS MARKET/Tankerton Road, Whitstable, Kent**
Whitstable Festivals & Events Ltd

Dec 11 **ARTS & CRAFT FAIR/Bankfield Hotel, Bingley, West Yorks**
Yorkshire Craft Fairs

Dec 13 **MILLENNIUM CRAFTS & GIFTS/Community Centre, Lyndhurst, Hants**
Millennium Crafts & Gifts

Dec 13 **INDOOR CHRISTMAS CRAFT MARKET**
Crispin Hall, opp Clark's Village, Street, Somerset
West Country Craft Fairs

Dec 14 **BLAKEMERE CRAFT FAIR**
Blakemere Craft Centre, Chester Road, Sandiway, Northwich, Cheshire
Blakemere Craft Centre

Dec 17 **BARLEYLANDS CRAFT & FARMERS' MARKET**
Barleylands Farm, Barleylands Road (off A129), Billericay, Essex
Barleylands Crafts Village

Dec 17 **CIRENCESTER CRAFTSMAN'S MARKET**
Corn Hall, Market Place, Cirencester, Glos
Cirencester Craftsman's Market

Dec 17 **SNOW FAYRE/Bridgwater, Somerset**
Wessex Fayres

Dec 17 **CITY OF WELLS 7th ANNUAL GIANT CHRISTMAS CRAFT FAIR**
Town Hall, Market Square, Wells, Somerset
West Country Craft Fairs

Dec 17 **ARTS & CRAFT FAIR/Town Hall, Stokesley, nr Middlesbrough**
Yorkshire Craft Fairs

Dec 17-18 **BLAKEMERE CRAFT FAIR**
Blakemere Craft Centre, Chester Road, Sandiway, Northwich, Cheshire
Blakemere Craft Centre

Dec 18 **ART, CRAFT & GIFT FAIR/Village Hall, Woburn, Beds**
Falcon Fairs

Dec 18 **LAUDERDALE HOUSE ARTS & CRAFTS**
Lauderdale House, Waterlow Park, Highgate Hill, London N6
Lauderdale Arts & Crafts

Dec 18 **CRAFT SHOW**
Hilton International Hotel, Round Coppice Road, Stansted Airport, Essex
Oakleigh Craft Fairs

Dec 18 **REDESMERE CRAFTS**
Siddington Village Hall, A34, nr Macclesfield, Cheshire
Redesmere Crafts Association

Dec 21 **BLAKEMERE CRAFT FAIR**
Blakemere Craft Centre, Chester Road, Sandiway, Northwich, Cheshire
Blakemere Craft Centre

CALENDAR 2005

JANUARY

M	T	W	T	F	S	S
					1	2
3	4	5	6	7	8	9
10	11	12	13	14	15	16
17	18	19	20	21	22	23
24	25	26	27	28	29	30
31						

FEBRUARY

M	T	W	T	F	S	S
	1	2	3	4	5	6
7	8	9	10	11	12	13
14	15	16	17	18	19	20
21	22	23	24	25	26	27
28						

MARCH

M	T	W	T	F	S	S
	1	2	3	4	5	6
7	8	9	10	11	12	13
14	15	16	17	18	19	20
21	22	23	24	25	26	27
28	29	30	31			

APRIL

M	T	W	T	F	S	S
				1	2	3
4	5	6	7	8	9	10
11	12	13	14	15	16	17
18	19	20	21	22	23	24
25	26	27	28	29	30	

MAY

M	T	W	T	F	S	S
						1
2	3	4	5	6	7	8
9	10	11	12	13	14	15
16	17	18	19	20	21	22
23	24	25	26	27	28	29
30	31					

JUNE

M	T	W	T	F	S	S
		1	2	3	4	5
6	7	8	9	10	11	12
13	14	15	16	17	18	19
20	21	22	23	24	25	26
27	28	29	30			

JULY

M	T	W	T	F	S	S
				1	2	3
4	5	6	7	8	9	10
11	12	13	14	15	16	17
18	19	20	21	22	23	24
25	26	27	28	29	30	31

AUGUST

M	T	W	T	F	S	S
1	2	3	4	5	6	7
8	9	10	11	12	13	14
15	16	17	18	19	20	21
22	23	24	25	26	27	28
29	30	31				

SEPTEMBER

M	T	W	T	F	S	S
			1	2	3	4
5	6	7	8	9	10	11
12	13	14	15	16	17	18
19	20	21	22	23	24	25
26	27	28	29	30		

OCTOBER

M	T	W	T	F	S	S
					1	2
3	4	5	6	7	8	9
10	11	12	13	14	15	16
17	18	19	20	21	22	23
24	25	26	27	28	29	30
31						

NOVEMBER

M	T	W	T	F	S	S
	1	2	3	4	5	6
7	8	9	10	11	12	13
14	15	16	17	18	19	20
21	22	23	24	25	26	27
28	29	30				

DECEMBER

M	T	W	T	F	S	S
			1	2	3	4
5	6	7	8	9	10	11
12	13	14	15	16	17	18
19	20	21	22	23	24	25
26	27	28	29	30	31	

DIRECTORY OF EVENT ORGANISERS

In preparing this section, we have questionnaired British organisers of craft events and other organisations providing craft fair, show and festival opportunities. The initial contact details which begin each entry (starting opposite) are self-explanatory.

The remaining part of each entry comprises answers to the nine key questions we have posed. We asked for details on the following:

Number of craft events organised each year.

Which months they take place in.

Number of craft stands available at these events.

Admission charges to the general public.

Average stand/space cost for exhibitors.

Details of extra charges (e.g. electricity).

Late booking opportunities.

Whether photographs of crafts need to be submitted by new exhibitors.

Selection policy.

Only the last item really requires any further explanation. Organisers have been asked to designate their selection policy A, B, C or D – signifying the following:

A =
- rigorous quality control of all parameters
- all original craft work; absolutely no bought-in goods
- superior levels of design and execution
- strictly no duplication of crafts on display

B =
- strong quality control
- predominantly original work; some limited exceptions
- high levels of design and execution
- duplication of crafts allowed occasionally; special cases

C =
- good craftwork, but no photos required
- mostly original work, but no bar to third party/imported crafts
- good quality preferred, but stock goods OK
- duplication of crafts can be expected at certain events

D =
- no quality statements required
- non-craft goods permitted and bought-in goods OK
- commercial basis; design quality not an issue
- no policy on duplication (in fact sometimes inevitable)

When dealing with selection policy, we also asked if the organiser expressly insisted on British made crafts only and if there were any other important restrictions; where these apply, they are noted.

Unless otherwise stated, the stand/space costs are the average daily exhibiting costs, net of VAT. Sometimes you will find a range of costs, particularly where organisers operate in a variety of venues.

This has necessarily been a process of self-certification by those listed and so there is still no substitute for our perennial advice to you to visit the events of organisers you have not used previously or in the recent past.

You will in a limited number of cases find information omitted from some entries. This is either because it was not provided by the organiser or it is not relevant in a particular case.

We must emphasise that while every effort has been made to ensure the provision of accurate information, both here and in all other sections of the book, details have been provided by others and we have accepted and printed them in good faith. You should refer to the disclaimer on page two.

The entries that follow constitute a guide to each organiser's policy but all the elements of this need to be double-checked by you before undertaking any financial commitment. We have neither sought nor accepted payment for any standard entry. However, some organisations have chosen to take paid advertising and they are represented in bold type. In some cases these adverts contain additional useful information and an index to them is on page 318 of the book.

3 SHIRES CRAFT GUILD
c/o The Old Bakehouse
Harpley Road
Defford
Worcs WR8 9BL
Tel: 01386 750475
Mobile: 07780 876802
Email: joanstrong@defford52.freeserve.co.uk
Website: www.3-shires-craft-guild.ik.com
Contact: Joan Strong
Number of Events: 12-14
When: All months exc Jan/Feb
Number of Stands: 12-25
Public Admission Price: Nil
Stand/Space Costs: £6 per 6ft table for guild members; £15 for guests (costs under review). No extras.
Late Booking Opportunities: Sometimes
Photographs Needed: Yes
Selection Policy: A/B - British made crafts only. Guests are restricted to one table only. Preference given to members near Christmas.

AHA EVENTS LTD
Mayfair
1 The Square
Barnstaple
Devon EX32 8LS
Tel: 0870 800 4030
Fax: 0870 800 4031
Email: airday@ahagb.co.uk
Website: www.yeoviltonairday.co.uk
Contact: Darren Trick
Number of Events: 1
When: Sept
Number of Stands: 30
Public Admission Price: Adults £20, under-15s £5 (discounts for advanced bookings).
Stand/Space Costs: From £125 to £175 for the event. No power or water supplies available.
Late Booking Opportunities: Sometimes
Photographs Needed: Yes
Selection Policy: B

AINTREE RACECOURSE CO LTD
Aintree
Liverpool L9 5AS
Tel: 0151 523 2600
Fax: 0151 522 2920
Email: aintree@rht.net
Website: www.aintree.co.uk
Contact: Joanne Teare
Number of Events: 2
When: Apr, Nov
Number of Stands: 16
Stand/Space Costs: £750 for Grand National and £230 for Becher Meeting. In both cases price includes shedding-style retail units, positioned outside.
Late Booking Opportunities: Rare
Photographs Needed: Yes
Selection Policy: B

AIREDALE AGRICULTURAL SOCIETY
Russell Court
4 Woolgate
Cottingley Business Park
Bingley
West Yorks BD16 1PE
Tel/Fax: 01274 564400
Email: secretary@bingleyshow.co.uk
Website: www.bingleyshow.co.uk
Contact: Mrs Maggie Marshall
Number of Events: 1
When: Aug
Number of Stands: Approx 20
Public Admission Price: Adults £6, Seniors £4, Children £3, Family £16.
Stand/Space Costs: £30 in the Craft Marquee for 6ft by 2ft with table and two chairs. Trade stands cost a minimum of £60 (10ft frontage by 20ft depth, space only).
Late Booking Opportunities: Trade stands sometimes; usually not in Craft Marquee.
Photographs Needed: No

ALLOTT AGENCY
8 Melbourne Avenue
Dronfield Woodhouse
Dronfield
Derbys S18 8YW
Tel: 01246 412365
Fax: 01246 290338
Mobile: 07733 481005
Email: allottagency@btinternet.com
Contact: Christine Allott
Number of Events: 10
When: May, June, Aug, Sept, Oct, Nov

ALNWICK INTERNATIONAL MUSIC FESTIVAL
c/o Linden House
Lesbury
Alnwick
Northumberland NE66 3QW
Fax: 01670 787986
Website: www.alnwickfestival.com *(cont)*

Contact: Anne Walton
Number of Events: 1
When: July/Aug
Number of Stands: 25
Public Admission Price: Nil
Stand/Space Costs: £20 per day or £120 for whole festival; no extras.
Late Booking Opportunities: Rare
Photographs Needed: Yes
Selection Policy: B/C. As this is an open air market place venue, stallholders need to set up and dismantle stall each day.

ALWINTON BORDER SHEPHERDS' SHOW
Linbrig Farm
Harbottle
Morpeth
Northumberland NE65 7BJ
Tel: 01669 650436
Fax: 01670 515492
Mobile: 07766 747382
Email: katstanners@aol.com
Contact: Katherine Stanners
Number of Events: 1
When: Oct
Number of Stands: 50 Tables
Public Admission Price: Adults £4, Concessions £1.50, under-16s £1.
Stand/Space Costs: £30 for first table and £15 for a second; no extras.
Late Booking Opportunities: Sometimes
Photographs Needed: No
Selection Policy: C – genuine craft items only.

AMBLESIDE HORTICULTURAL & CRAFT SOCIETY
'Latrigg'
Lake Road
Ambleside
Cumbria LA22 0DF
Tel/Fax: 01539 432252
Mobile: 07730 946510
Email: anything@ambleside-show.org.uk
Website: www.ambleside-show.org.uk
Contact: David Capstick
Number of Events: 1
When: Sept
Number of Stands: 40
Public Admission Price: Adults £5, Seniors/under-16s/Concessions £4.
Stand/Space Costs: £95 for the 3 days; electricity extra £20 on request.
Late Booking Opportunities: Nearly always
Photographs Needed: Yes
Selection Policy: B

ANTRIM AGRICULTURAL SOCIETY
660 Antrim Road
Newtownabbey
Co Antrim BT36 4RG
Tel/Fax: 028 9084 9466
Email: antrimshowsec@hotmail.com
Contact: Linda Davis
Number of Events: 1
When: July
Number of Stands: 20–30
Public Admission Price: Adults £5, Seniors £3, under-18s £2 (unaccompanied).
Stand/Space Costs: £20 for 7ft by 7ft; no extras.
Late Booking Opportunities: Nearly always
Photographs Needed: No
Selection Policy: C

APPLIED ARTS SCOTLAND
The Lighthouse
11 Mitchell Lane
Glasgow G1 3NU
Tel: 0141 572 1835
Email: office@appliedartsscotland.org.uk
Number of Events: 2
When: Apr
Stand/Space Costs: On application. See also entry in Representative Bodies section.

THE ART, CRAFT AND DESIGN SHOW
36 High Street
Balsham
Cambs CB1 6DJ
Tel: 01223 895895
Fax: 01223 895891
Email: jannahodgson@hotmail.com
Website: www.artcraftdesignshow.co.uk
Contact: Janna Hodgson
Number of Events: 1
When: Nov
Number of Stands: 170
Public Admission Price: Adults £6, Seniors/Concessions £5, under-14s free.
Stand/Space Costs: Approx £80 per square metre; extra for electricity and tables.
Late Booking Opportunities: Rare
Photographs Needed: Yes
Selection Policy: A – crafts must be of the best quality as must be the display.

ART IN THE FRAME FOUNDATION
Les Anquettes
Clos au Port
La Rocque
Grouville
Jersey JE3 9BZ
Tel: 01534 853395
Fax: 01534 854690
Website: www.mnlg.com
Number of Events: 6 plus 8 smaller markets
When: Apr, May, June, Aug, Sept, Dec
Number of Stands: 55 and 25 at markets
Public Admission Price: Adults £4, Seniors £2, Children £1; free at The Harbour Gallery.
Stand/Space Costs: From £15 to £20 per day, depending on venue. £100 for 4-day event.
Late Booking Opportunities: Sometimes
Photographs Needed: Yes
Selection Policy: B – this is a charity set up to promote local art and craft so most exhibitors are from Jersey. However, there are always some invited exhibitors from England and mainland Europe. The foundation is always happy to hear from craftworkers world-wide.

ARTISTS & ILLUSTRATORS EXHIBITION
Quarto Magazines
Third Floor, 226 City Road
London EC1V 2TT
Tel: 020 7812 8652
Fax: 020 7253 4370
Email: aim@quarto.com
Website: www.aimag.co.uk
Contact: Paul Harris
Number of Events: 1
When: July
Number of Stands: 120
Public Admission Price: Standard £7, concessions £5.50 in advance.
Stand/Space Costs: £176 per square metre for the event; extra for lighting, electrics and furniture.
Late Booking Opportunities: Nearly always
Photographs Needed: No
Selection Policy: C – plus product exclusivity clause.

ARTS & CRAFT FAIRS
Estate House
61 Cranford Avenue
Church Crookham
Fleet
Hants GU52 6QT
Tel: 0870 722 2287
Fax: 0870 722 2288
Email: sarah@artsandcraftfairs.co.uk
Website: www.artsandcraftfairs.co.uk
Contact: Sarah Warrington
Number of Events: 6
When: Feb, Apr, June, Oct, Dec
Number of Stands: 45
Public Admission Price: Adults £2, Seniors £1, Children free.
Stand/Space Costs: £40 per day; no extras.
Late Booking Opportunities: Sometimes
Photographs Needed: Yes
Selection Policy: B – British made crafts only.

ASHBY CANAL TRUST
c/o 9 Dayton Close
Coalville
Leics LE67 3RG
Tel/Fax: 01283 224667
Mobile: 07976 637858
Email: wendyjr@tiscali.co.uk
Contact: Wendy Robinson
Number of Events: 1
When: May
Number of Stands: 10-40
Public Admission Price: Adults £3, under-16s free.
Stand/Space Costs: From £25 to £50 per 3m run outside. A Craft Tent may be available; contact for further details.
Late Booking Opportunities: Sometimes
Photographs Needed: No, but advance notice of display to avoid duplication.
Selection Policy: C/D

ASHBY-DE-LA-ZOUCH AGRICULTURAL SOCIETY
Tithe Farm Livery Stables
Boundary, Swadlincote
Derbys DE11 7BA
Tel: 01283 229225
Fax: 01283 229226
Email: info@ashbyshow.com
Website: www.ashbyshow.com
Contact: Mrs L Ensor
Number of Events: 1
When: July
Number of Stands: 30
Public Admission Price: Adults £6, under-16s/Seniors £3.
Stand/Space Costs: Approx £13 per sq.m.; extra £3 for tables and £1.50 for chairs.
Late Booking Opportunities: Sometimes
Photographs Needed: No
Selection Policy: B/C

AYLSHAM AGRICULTURAL SHOW ASSOCIATION
Lothian Room
Town Hall
Aylsham
Norwich
Norfolk NR11 6EL
Tel: 01263 732432
Fax: 01263 735020
Email: aylshamshow@ewing-self.co.uk
Website: www.aylshamshow.co.uk
Contact: Christopher Self
Number of Events: 1
When: Aug
Number of Stands: 50
Public Admission Price: Adults £9, under-16s free.
Stand/Space Costs: On application; this is on a greenfield site with neither cover nor electricity.
Late Booking Opportunities: Sometimes
Photographs Needed: No
Selection Policy: C

AYR FLOWER SHOW
60 Dalblair Road
Ayr KA7 1UQ
Tel: 01292 618395
Email: info@ayrflowershow.org
Website: www.ayrflowershow.org
Contact: Ian Sloan or Sandra Nixon
Number of Events: 1
When: Aug
Number of Stands: 200+
Public Admission Price: Adults £11, Seniors £9, Children £6, under-5s free, Family £25.
Stand/Space Costs: On application
Late Booking Opportunities: Nearly always
Photographs Needed: No
Selection Policy: C/D – safety regulations to be adhered to.

AZTEC EVENTS
South House
48 South Street
Rochford
Essex SS4 1BQ
Tel: 01702 549623
Fax: 01702 542163
Email: info@aztecevents.co.uk
Website: www.aztecevents.co.uk
Contact: Laura (Craft Shows); Martin or Emma (Garden Shows)
Number of Events: 40
When: Feb, Apr, May, June, Aug, Sept, Oct, Nov, Dec
Number of Stands: Approx 250
Public Admission Price: Varies
Stand/Space Costs: On application
Late Booking Opportunities: Rare
Photographs Needed: No, not normally, but they are welcome
Selection Policy: C

BALQUHIDDER, LOCHEARNHEAD & STRATHYRE HIGHLAND GAMES
Dundhu
Lochearnhead
Perthshire FK19 8PT
Tel/Fax: 01567 830268
Mobile: 07711 368649
Website:
www.lochearnheadhighlandgames.co.uk
Contact: Angus Cameron
Number of Events: 1
When: July
Number of Stands: 30
Public Admission Price: Adults £5, under-16s/Seniors £2.
Stand/Space Costs: £30 for the event; no extras.
Late Booking Opportunities: Nearly always
Photographs Needed: No
Selection Policy: C

BANBRIDGE DISTRICT ARTS COMMITTEE
c/o Banbridge District Council
Civic Building
Downshire Road
Banbridge
Co Down BT32 3JY
Tel: 028 4066 0605
Fax: 028 4066 0601
Email: leah.duncan@banbridge.gov.uk
Website: www.banbridge.com
Contact: Leah Duncan
Number of Events: 1 Craft Fair
When: Oct
Number of Stands: 60+
Public Admission Price: Adults £1, Seniors/under-16s/Concessions 50p.
Stand/Space Costs: £45 for the 2 days (or £35 for one); no extras.
Late Booking Opportunities: Some (late booking fee though)
Photographs Needed: No
Selection Policy: B

BARLEYLANDS CRAFT VILLAGE
Barleylands Farm
Barleylands Road
Billericay
Essex CM11 2UD
Tel: 01268 290229
Fax: 01268 290222
Mobile: 07843 357380
Email: info@barleylands.co.uk
Website: www.barleylands.co.uk
Contact: Beck Wigmore
Number of Events: 2
When: Dec
Number of Stands: Approx 20
Public Admission Price: Nil
Stand/Space Costs: £20 per 6ft width; extra £7 for table and £5 for electric socket.
Late Booking Opportunities: Sometimes
Photographs Needed: No
Selection Policy: B – British made crafts only.

BATH & NORTH EAST SOMERSET COUNCIL
Parks Section
Lower Sports Centre
North Parade Road
Bath BA2 4ET
Tel: 01225 477010
Fax: 01225 480072
Mobile: 07977 228207
Email: sarah_giovannini@bathnes.gov.uk
Contact: Sarah Giovannini
Number of Events: 1
When: Apr/May
Number of Stands: 50
Public Admission Price: Adults £6.50, Seniors/Concessions £5, accompanied under-16s free.
Stand/Space Costs: £175 for the event with minimum 10ft by 10ft stand; extra £10 for table, £3 for chair, £76 for single socket.
Late Booking Opportunities: Sometimes
Photographs Needed: Yes
Selection Policy: B – public liability insurance minimum is £5 million.

BELLINGHAM SHOW
Glendale
Bellingham
Northumberland NE48 2JR
Tel: 01434 220396
Fax: 01434 220815
Mobile: 07989 432921
Email: slocombe@madasafish.com
Contact: Anne Slocombe
Number of Events: 1
When: Aug
Number of Stands: 25
Public Admission Price: Adults £5, Seniors/under-16s/Concessions £2.
Stand/Space Costs: £30 for the event; no extras.
Late Booking Opportunities: Sometimes
Photographs Needed: No
Selection Policy: B – British made crafts only.

BELPER STEAM & VINTAGE EVENT
Tel: 01773 550700
Website: www.belpersteam.co.uk
Contact: Rachel Jeffery
Number of Events: 1
When: June
Number of Stands: Approx 50
Public Admission Price: Adults £4, Seniors/Concessions/under-7s £2, Family £8 (2004).
Stand/Space Costs: On application

BERKELEY AGRICULTURAL SHOW
c/o 13 Turnpike Close
Yate
Bristol BS37 4JF
Tel/Fax: 01454 320067
Contact: Paula Clarke
Number of Events: 1
When: Aug
Number of Stands: Approx 25
Stand/Space Costs: 2004 charges were £27.50 for 8ft frontage, with extra frontage at £4 per foot up to a max of 12ft. Extra £5 for tables £5 and £10 for electric point (2004).
Late Booking Opportunities: Rare
Photographs Needed: No
Selection Policy: C

BERWICKSHIRE AGRICULTURAL ASSOCIATION
The Cottage
Nabdean Farm
Paxton
Berwick-upon-Tweed
TD15 1SZ
Tel: 01289 386412
Fax: 01289 386852
Mobile: 07712 623669
Email: ncormack@farming.co.uk
Contact: Natalie Cormack
Number of Events: 1
When: Aug

(cont)

Number of Stands: 25
Public Admission Price: Adults £5, under-16s/Seniors £1.
Stand/Space Costs: £12.50 per table; power charged extra and also tables at £1 each.
Late Booking Opportunities: Nearly always
Photographs Needed: No
Selection Policy: C

BEVERLEY & EAST RIDING FOLK FESTIVAL
Festival Office
PO Box 296
Matlock
Derbys
DE4 3XU
Tel: 01629 827018
Fax: 01629 821874
Email: info@beverleyfestival.co.uk
Website: www.beverleyfestival.co.uk
Contact: Joe Heap
Number of Events: 1
When: June
Number of Stands: 20-30
Stand/Space Costs: On application
Late Booking Opportunities: Sometimes
Photographs Needed: Yes
Selection Policy: B/C

BHLR LTD
Ash House
26 Tongdean Lane
Brighton
East Sussex
BN1 5JE
Tel: 01273 563382
Fax: 01273 563383
Mobile: 07966 418378
Email: sbproms@aol.com
Website:
www.beautyhealthandlifestyle.co.uk
Contact: David Rothstein
Number of Events: 18
When: May-Sept
Number of Stands: 25
Stand/Space Costs: From £130 to £170 per sq. m. per event, inc lighting. Extra £5 for tables and £45 for power. High quality marquees, carpeted with shell scheme and electrics on all stands. The theme is beauty, health and lifestyle.
Late Booking Opportunities: Rare
Photographs Needed: No
Selection Policy: D

BIC EXHIBITIONS
Bournemouth International Centre
Exeter Road
Bournemouth
Dorset BH2 5BH
Tel: 01202 456501
Fax: 01202 456500
Email:
louise.burridge.bic@bournemouth.gov.uk
Website: www.bic.co.uk
Contact: Louise Burridge
Number of Events: 2
When: Mar, Nov
Number of Stands: 120
Public Admission Price: From Adults £1.50, Seniors £1, under-16s 50p.
Stand/Space Costs: From £105 per event. 2ft extra space offered to demonstrators. Power is charged extra at £25 (inc VAT), but included if crafts are made by the exhibitor.
Late Booking Opportunities: Sometimes
Photographs Needed: Yes
Selection Policy: C

BIDDULPH ARTS & CRAFT FAYRES
35 Scragg Street
Packmoor
Stoke-on-Trent
Staffs ST7 4QJ
Tel: 01782 822713 or 01782 410502
Contact: Jim, Jackie or John
Number of Events: 26
When: Feb-Dec
Number of Stands: 21
Public Admission Price: Adults 50p.
Stand/Space Costs: £17 (inc VAT) per day; no extras.
Late Booking Opportunities: Sometimes
Photographs Needed: No
Selection Policy: B/C

BISHOP'S CASTLE AGRICULTURAL SHOW
c/o 29 Church Street
Bishop's Castle
Shropshire SY9 5AD
Tel: 01588 630070
Fax: 01588 630452
Email: bishopscastle@mccartneys.co.uk
Number of Events: 1
When: July
Public Admission Price: Adults £4, Children £1.50, Family £10.
Stand/Space Costs: £7.80 per sq.m.; no

extras.
Late Booking Opportunities: Sometimes
Photographs Needed: No
Selection Policy: C

BLAIRCRAFT
32 Talisman Crescent
Helensburgh G84 7TE
(this address is due to change, so 'phone first)
Tel: 01436 675750
Contact: Sheila Cairns
Number of Events: 1
When: June
Number of Stands: 20-30
Stand/Space Costs: £17.50 per table; no extras.
Late Booking Opportunities: Rare
Photographs Needed: No
Selection Policy: A – British made crafts only.

BLAKEMERE CRAFT CENTRE
Chester Road
Sandiway
Northwich
Cheshire CW8 2EB
Tel: 01606 883261
Fax: 01606 301495
Email:
info@blakemere-shoppingexperience.com
Website:
www.blakemere-shoppingexperience.com
Contact: Janet Barnes
Number of Events: 64
When: Every month
Number of Stands: 12
Public Admission Price: Nil
Stand/Space Costs: £15 on Wednesdays, £25 for Sat or Sun, £35 for the weekend. Additional charge for electricity used between 250W and 1000W of 50p on Wednesday/one-day booking and £1 at the weekend.
Late Booking Opportunities: Sometimes
Photographs Needed: Yes
Selection Policy: B – Blakemere has 30 permanent shops on site and does not duplicate with their core business and stall bookings.

THE BOAT MUSEUM
South Pier Road
Ellesmere Port
Cheshire CH65 4FW
Tel: 0151 355 5017
Fax: 0151 355 4079
Mobile: 07801 231722
Email:
david.hardman@thewaterwaystrust.org
Website: www.boatmuseum.org.uk
Number of Events: 4
When: Aug, Nov
Number of Stands: 30-90
Public Admission Price: On application
Stand/Space Costs: On application
Late Booking Opportunities: Sometimes
Photographs Needed: Yes
Selection Policy: C

BORDE HILL GARDEN
Balcombe Road
Haywards Heath
West Sussex RH16 1XP
Tel: 01444 450326
Fax: 01444 440427
Email: info@bordehill.co.uk
Website: www.bordehill.co.uk
Contact: Sarah Brook
Number of Events: 1
When: Dec
Number of Stands: 40-150
Public Admission Price: Adults £4, Children free.
Stand/Space Costs: From £60; tables, chairs and electricity charged extra. 20% discount for demonstrators.
Late Booking Opportunities: Sometimes
Photographs Needed: No
Selection Policy: C

BORDER COUNTIES VINTAGE CLUB LTD
c/o 10 Three Crosses Close
Ross-on-Wye
Herefordshire HR9 7EZ
Tel: 01989 562602
Fax: 01432 378359
Mobile: 07919 503126
Email: matiz2000@aol.com
Contact: Andy Vaughton
Number of Events: 1
When: May
Number of Stands: 10+
Public Admission Price: Adults £3, Seniors/under-16s £2.
Stand/Space Costs: £15 for 10ft frontage. No tables provided.
Late Booking Opportunities: Nearly always
Photographs Needed: No
Selection Policy: C

BOWES AGRICULTURAL SOCIETY
c/o West View Farm
Boldron
Barnard Castle
Co Durham DL12 9RQ
Tel: 01833 631125
Website: www.bowesshow.org.uk
Number of Events: 2
When: Sept, Dec.
Number of Stands: 20-30
Public Admission Price: Adults £3, Children £1.50.
Stand/Space Costs: £10 for the one day; no extras.
Late Booking Opportunities: Some
Photographs Needed: No
Selection Policy: C

BOWES MUSEUM
Barnard Castle
Co Durham DL12 8NP
Tel: 01833 690606
Fax: 01833 637163
Email: info@bowesmuseum.org.uk
Website: www.bowesmuseum.org.uk
Number of Events: 2
When: Aug, Dec
Number of Stands: 15-25
Public Admission Price: Adults £6, Seniors/Concessions £5, under-16s free.
Stand/Space Costs: £30 per event; no extras.
Late Booking Opportunities: Sometimes
Photographs Needed: No
Selection Policy: C - sometimes predominantly aimed at locally made crafts.

BRANCEPETH CASTLE FAIRS
Brancepeth Castle
Co Durham DH7 8DF
Tel: 0191 378 0628 or 0191 378 9670
Contact: Mrs F Dobson or Mrs A Hobbs
Number of Events: 2
When: July, Nov
Number of Stands: 90-110
Public Admission Price: Adults £1.50, Seniors £1, under-14s free.
Stand/Space Costs: £16.20 per foot frontage (6ft minimum) for 3-day event. Optional table hire at £2 per ft.
Late Booking Opportunities: Sometimes
Photographs Needed: Yes
Selection Policy: B - British made crafts only.

BRECON BEACONS NATIONAL PARK AUTHORITY
National Park Visitor Centre
Libanus
Brecon
Powys LD3 8ER
Tel: 01874 624979
Fax: 01874 624515
Email: andrew.powell@breconbeacons.org
Website: www.breconbeacons.org
Contact: Andrew Powell
Number of Events: 4-6
When: Apr, Dec
Number of Stands: 50
Public Admission Price: Nil
Stand/Space Costs: £25 per event (equivalent £6 per foot); no extras.
Late Booking Opportunities: Rare
Photographs Needed: Yes
Selection Policy: A/B - British made crafts only.

BRIDGEND FESTIVALS
Festivals Office
The Rhiw Hill
Bridgend CF31 3BL
Tel: 01656 661338
Mobile: 07976 430086
Email: kingbarry@btconnect.com
Website: www.bridgend-events.co.uk
Contact: Barry King or Jo Spensley
Number of Events: 4
When: June, July, Sept, Dec.
Number of Stands: 60
Stand/Space Costs: Ranges from £15 to £30 per day. 25% discount for demonstrators. Tables charged extra at £5 at some events.
Late Booking Opportunities: Sometimes
Photographs Needed: Yes
Selection Policy: B

BRIDLINGTON MODEL BOAT SOCIETY
46 Manorfield Avenue
Driffield
East Yorks
YO25 5HP
Tel: 01377 252550
Mobile: 07960 773940
Email: fozzie46@aol.com
Website: www.bridmodelboats.co.uk
Contact: John Foster
Number of Events: 1
When: Aug
Number of Stands: 70-80

Public Admission Price: Adults £2, under-12s free.
Stand/Space Costs: £25 for the event; no extras.
Late Booking Opportunities: Sometimes
Photographs Needed: No
Selection Policy: C – but British made crafts only.

BRISTOL BALLOON FIESTAS LTD
St Johns Street
Bedminster
Bristol BS3 4NH
Tel: 0117 953 5884
Fax: 0117 953 5606
Email: admin@bristolfiesta.co.uk
Website: www.bristolfiesta.co.uk
Contact: Susan Tanner or Sara Pacey
Number of Events: 1
When: Aug
Number of Stands: 130+
Public Admission Price: Nil
Stand/Space Costs: £380 for 3m by 3m (covered). Open space only starts at £430 for 5m by 5m, rising to £500 for 6m by 5m, £690 for 6m by 6m. The larger open sites include electricity and run from £1,000 for 9m by 6m right up to £3,700 for a 12m by 12m Premier site. Many craft stallholders not eligible for the separately run Cottage Industries marquee book one of these many options.
Late Booking Opportunities: Sometimes
Photographs Needed: Yes
Selection Policy: C/D

BRITISH CRAFTS
4 Riverview Grove
London W4 3QJ
Tel: 020 8742 1697
Mobile: 07941 938427
Email: info@britishcrafts.co.uk
Website: www.britishcrafts.co.uk
Contact: Meg Fisher
Number of Events: 2
When: Apr, Nov
Number of Stands: 50
Public Admission Price: Adults £3, Seniors/Concessions £1, under-16s free.
Stand/Space Costs: From £295 up to £500, depending on stand size. Price includes two spotlights but other electrics are charged extra.
Late Booking Opportunities: Sometimes
Photographs Needed: Yes
Selection Policy: A – British made crafts only.

BROCKLEY SOCIETY
c/o 3 Crescent Way
London SE4 1QL
Tel: 020 8691 7234
Contact: T Kirwan
Number of Events: 1
When: June
Number of Stands: Approx 300 total
Public Admission Price: Nil
Stand/Space Costs: £40 in marquee and £20 outside (2004).
Late Booking Opportunities: Nearly always
Photographs Needed: No
Selection Policy: D

BUCKINGHAM EVENTS
Buckingham House
11 High Street
Old Portsmouth
Hants PO1 2LP
Tel: 023 9229 5555
Fax: 023 9229 5544
Email: su9322@eclipse.co.uk
Website: www.statelyhomeevents.co.uk
Contact: Sales Office
Number of Events: 20
When: Jan, Mar-June, Aug-Nov
Number of Stands: Approx 200
Public Admission Price: Varies
Stand/Space Costs: On application
Late Booking Opportunities: Some
Photographs Needed: Yes
Selection Policy: D

BUGLAWTON HALL SCHOOL VINTAGE FAIR
Buglawton Hall School
Buxton Road
Buglawton
Congleton
Cheshire CW12 3PQ
Tel: 01260 274492
Contact: Alison Williams
Number of Events: 1
When: June
Number of Stands: 45
Public Admission Price: Adults £5, Seniors/Children £2.50.
Stand/Space Costs: £45 for 10ft and £1 per ft thereafter; no extras.
Late Booking Opportunities: Nearly always
Photographs Needed: No
Selection Policy: B

BURGESS CIVIC HALL
St Ivo Leisure Centre
Westwood Road
St Ives
Cambs PE27 6WU
Tel: 01480 388514
Fax: 01480 388513
Email: kelly.norman@huntsdc.gov.uk
Website: www.huntsdc.gov.uk
Contact: Kelly Norman
Number of Events: 1
When: Nov
Number of Stands: 50
Public Admission Price: Adults £1.50, 5-16s/Seniors £1, under-5s free.
Stand/Space Costs: From £25 up to £40 per stand for the event; extra for tables and power.
Late Booking Opportunities: Sometimes
Photographs Needed: No
Selection Policy: D

BURLYN EVENTS LTD
25 Prospect Street
Caversham
Berks RG4 8JB
Tel: 0118 947 8996
Mobile: 07970 759950
Email: burlyn@dircon.co.uk
Website: www.salisburyshow.co.uk
Contact: Evelyn Burt
Number of Events: 1
When: July
Number of Stands: 50
Public Admission Price: Adults £5, Seniors £4.50, under-12s free.
Stand/Space Costs: £150 for the event; extra £25 for power.
Late Booking Opportunities: Sometimes
Photographs Needed: Yes
Selection Policy: C – but still no duplication of crafts.

BURNLEY MAY DAY FESTIVAL
3 Snowden Street, Burnley
Lancs BB12 6JH
Tel: 01282 457456
Email: jack.preston2@ntlworld.com
Contact: Jack Preston
Number of Events: 1
When: May
Number of Stands: Large number available
Public Admission Price: Nil
Stand/Space Costs: On application
Late Booking Opportunities: Nearly always
Photographs Needed: No
Selection Policy: C/D – they have a market charter; only craft/charity.

CALDERDALE MBC
Shibden Hall
Lister's Road, Halifax
West Yorks HX3 6XG
Tel: 01422 352246
Fax: 01422 348440
Email: shibden.hall@calderdale.gov.uk
Website: www.calderdale.gov.uk
Contact: Valerie Stansfield
Number of Events: 2
When: May, Nov
Number of Stands: 30-40
Public Admission Price: Adults £1, Seniors/Concessions/under-16s 50p. These are special concessionary rates at Shibden Hall for the craft fair weekends only.
Stand/Space Costs: £30 for the two-day event and £40 for Christmas three-day event; no extras.
Late Booking Opportunities: Sometimes
Photographs Needed: Yes
Selection Policy: B – British made crafts only.

CAMBRIDGE ARTS & CRAFTS
PO Box 82
Cambridge
Cambs CB2 2XQ
Tel: 01223 247370
Email: ros.myers@clara.co.uk
Contact: Roz Myers
Number of Events: 50
When: Every month
Number of Stands: 30
Public Admission Price: Nil
Stand/Space Costs: £25.50 per day (inc electrics). Table hire £1.50 each extra.
Late Booking Opportunities: Sometimes
Photographs Needed: Yes
Selection Policy: B/C; if goods are imported (limited amount allowed in any fair) they must be good quality work. See programme details in section on Markets etc.

CANCER RESEARCH UK – GREENWICH COMMITTEE
11 Colepits Wood Road
Eltham
London SE9 2QJ

Tel: 020 8850 5901
Email: lesley@advertisebydesign.co.uk
Website:
www.cancerresearchuk-greenwich.co.uk
Contact: Mrs Lesley Corti
Number of Events: 1
When: Nov
Number of Stands: 55
Public Admission Price: 50p all round, under-12s free.
Stand/Space Costs: £17.50 for the one day. Table hire £4.50. Additional free space offered to demonstrators.
Late Booking Opportunities: Sometimes
Photographs Needed: Yes
Selection Policy: B – British made crafts only.

CARMARTHENSHIRE CRAFTS
Tremile, Penybont
Carmarthenshire SA33 6PU
Tel: 01994 484520
Email: sue.holland@tesco.net
Contact: Sue Holland
Number of Events: 9
When: Apr-Dec
Number of Stands: 15
Public Admission Price: Nil
Stand/Space Costs: £12 per day; no extras.
Late Booking Opportunities: Sometimes
Photographs Needed: No
Selection Policy: B/C – but British made crafts only.

CARRICK LOWLAND GATHERING
c/o 15 Smith Crescent
Girvan
Ayrshire KA26 0DU
Tel: 01465 712667
Mobile: 07702 605133
Email: ian@fitzsimmons200.freeserve.co.uk
Contact: Ian Fitzsimmons
Number of Events: 2
Number of Stands: Approx 60
Public Admission Price: Nil
Stand/Space Costs: £25 per event (no covering, but tables supplied).
Late Booking Opportunities: Nearly always
Photographs Needed: No
Selection Policy: D

CARRINGTON RALLY
c/o The Chestnuts
1 Main Road
Little Hale
Sleaford
Lincs NG34
Tel: 01529 462037
Fax: 01754 890172
Contact: Mrs Ann Beever
Number of Events: 1
When: May
Public Admission Price: Adults £6, Seniors £5, under-14s £3.
Stand/Space Costs: £45 for the two-day event; no extras.
Late Booking Opportunities: Rare
Photographs Needed: Yes
Selection Policy: C

CASTLE POINT BOROUGH COUNCIL
Leisure Services
Kiln Road, Benfleet
Essex SS7 1TF
Tel: 01268 882473
Fax: 01268 882464
Mobile: 07748 114906
Email: shickey@castlepoint.gov.uk
Website: www.castlepoint.gov.uk
Contact: Sharon Hickey
Number of Events: 1
When: June
Number of Stands: 75
Public Admission Price: Adults £2, under-10s free.
Stand/Space Costs: £35 per day in Marquee, £28 per day outside. Extra £3 for tables and £5 for power.
Late Booking Opportunities: Nearly always
Photographs Needed: No
Selection Policy: C

CASTLEWELLAN & DISTRICT AGRICULTURAL SHOW
10 Sleepy Valley
Rathfriland
Co Down BT34 5HL
Tel/Fax: 028 4063 0536
Email: castlewellan.show@rdplus.net
Contact: Violet Bell
Number of Events: 1
When: July
Public Admission Price: Adults £5, under-15s free.
Stand/Space Costs: £30 for the event; no extras.
Photographs Needed: No
Selection Policy: D

CDE LTD
PO Box 942
Maidstone
Kent ME15 0YB
Tel: 01622 747325
Fax: 01622 747246
Email: info@craftexperience.co.uk
Website: www.craftexperience.co.uk
Contact: Robert Chapman
Number of Events: 1
When: May
Number of Stands: 200-250
Public Admission Price: Adults £5-£7, Seniors/Concessions £4-£5, Children £1.
Stand/Space Costs: From £345 up to £960, depending on size; power, tables and chairs charged extra. Discount for demonstrations; amount depends on demo.
Late Booking Opportunities: Sometimes
Selection Policy: B - British made crafts only.

CENTRAL PROMOTIONS
24 Stokesay Way
Telford
Shropshire TF7 4QF
Tel/Fax: 01952 588414
Contact: David Bushill
Number of Events: 10
When: Jan, Feb, Mar, Apr, May, Sept, Oct, Nov
Number of Stands: 30-80
Public Admission Price: Adults £1, under-12s free.
Stand/Space Costs: £25 to £35 per day; no extras.
Late Booking Opportunities: Sometimes
Photographs Needed: Yes
Selection Policy: B/C

CERAMIC ART LONDON 2005
3rd Floor
25 Foubert's Place
London W1F 7QF
Email: organiser@ceramics.org.uk
Website: www.ceramics.org.uk
A new UK showcase for contemporary ceramics. Any practising potter, in the UK or from overseas, is eligible to apply for one of the stands and selection is by an independent committee. A fully illustrated catalogue in full colour will serve as a guide to the fair. Advance purchase visitor tickets go on sale from 1 December 2004.

CHERISH EVENTS
PO Box 51
Macclesfield
Cheshire SK10 2WU
Tel/Fax: 01625 431132
Mobile: 07711 585072
Email: cherishevents@ft6.com
Website: www.cherishevents.co.uk
Contact: Sue or John Wainwright
Number of Events: 6
When: Jan, Mar, Apr, May, Oct, Nov
Number of Stands: 20-40
Public Admission Price: Adults £2.50, 5-16s £1.
Stand/Space Costs: £55 per event; no extras.
Late Booking Opportunities: Sometimes
Photographs Needed: Yes
Selection Policy: B

CHERTSEY AGRICULTURAL ASSOCIATION
c/o 157A Kingston Road
New Malden
Surrey KT3 3NT
Tel: 020 8942 3652
Email: frank@stretchers4framing.co.uk
Contact: Frank Hartfree
Number of Events: 1
When: Aug
Number of Stands: 30-40
Public Admission Price: Adults £6, Seniors/Children £3.
Stand/Space Costs: £80 (minimum) for the event; extra for tables, chairs and electricity.
Late Booking Opportunities: Rare
Photographs Needed: Yes
Selection Policy: B - British made crafts only. No bought-in goods.

CHESHIRE AGRICULTURAL SOCIETY
Clay Lane Farm
Marton
Winsford
Cheshire CW7 2QH
Tel: 01829 760020
Fax: 01829 760021
Email: cheshire.show@btinternet.com
Website: www.cheshirecountyshow.org.uk
Contact: David Broster
Number of Events: 1
When: June
Number of Stands: 40-50
Public Admission Price: 2004 was Adults

£12, Seniors £9, under-16s £5, Family £24, under-5s free; discounts for advance purchase.
Stand/Space Costs: Approx £120 for 10ft frontage for the event. Power charged extra.
Late Booking Opportunities: Sometimes
Photographs Needed: Yes
Selection Policy: B/C

CHESHIRE FAYRE
PO Box 51
Macclesfield
Cheshire SK10 2WU
Tel: 01625 430519
Fax: 01625 431132
Mobile: 07711 585072
Email: cheshirefayre@talk21.com
Website: www.cheshirefayre.co.uk
Contact: Sue or John Wainwright
Number of Events: 18
When: Feb-Dec
Number of Stands: 40-80
Public Admission Price: Adults £2, Concessions £1.50.
Stand/Space Costs: £99 per event; no extras.
Late Booking Opportunities: Sometimes
Photographs Needed: Yes
Selection Policy: B - British made crafts only.

CIRENCESTER CRAFTSMAN'S MARKET
The Old Forge
Hampton Street
Tetbury
Glos GL8 8JN
Tel: 01666 504838
Fax: 01666 503079
Website: www.craftsmansmarket.co.uk
Contact: Colin Clark
Number of Events: 23
When: Jan-Dec
Number of Stands: 45
Public Admission Price: Nil
Stand/Space Costs: £23 for one day; no extras.
Late Booking Opportunities: Sometimes
Photographs Needed: Yes
Selection Policy: A - British made crafts only.

CLUN GREENMAN FESTIVAL
c/o The White Horse Inn
The Square
Clun
Shropshire SY7 8JA
Tel: 01588 640305
Fax: 01588 640460 (ring other number first)
Mobile: 07867 788261
Email: jack@whi-clun.co.uk
Website: www.clun.org.uk/greenman.htm
Contact: Jack Limond
Number of Events: 1
When: May
Number of Stands: 60
Public Admission Price: Adults £2, under-14s 50p.
Stand/Space Costs: £20 for the day. Tables charged extra. Discount for demonstrators to be agreed.
Late Booking Opportunities: Nearly always
Photographs Needed: Yes
Selection Policy: B - British made crafts only.

COLIN TOTEN
172 Common Road
Kensworth, Dunstable
Beds LU6 2PH
Tel: 01582 873460
Contact: Colin Toten
Number of Events: 1
When: Sept
Number of Stands: 30
Public Admission Price: Adults £2, Children £1, Parties over 25 get 25% discount.
Stand/Space Costs: £14 for the one day with extra space at £5 per metre; space only supplied.
Late Booking Opportunities: Nearly always
Photographs Needed: No, but details of type of items for sale to be supplied.
Selection Policy: D - but usually no more than two vendors selling the same items.

CORSLEY SHOW
c/o 5 Red Cottages
Corsley
nr Warminster
Wilts BA12 7PS
Tel: 01373 832371
Contact: Kim Brixey
Number of Events: 1
When: Aug
Number of Stands: 60-80
Public Admission Price: Adults £6, Seniors £3, under-17s £2.
Stand/Space Costs: £40 for a 5m by 5m stall, open air, no power provided. Tables and

chairs can be provided on request.
Late Booking Opportunities: Sometimes
Photographs Needed: No
Selection Policy: C

COSY CRAFT
3 Rissington Walk
Thornaby
Stockton-on-Tees TS17 9QJ
Tel: 01642 880727
Email: k.k.holliday@btopenworld.com
Number of Events: 7-10
When: Mar, Apr, May, June, July, Sept, Oct
Number of Stands: 8-12
Stand/Space Costs: £20 per day; no extras.
Late Booking Opportunities: Sometimes
Photographs Needed: No
Selection Policy: C

COTTAGE INDUSTRIES
25 Hughes Avenue
Bradmore
Wolverhampton
West Midlands WV3 7AU
Tel/Fax: 01902 332901
Mobile: 07957 319462 (Jean) or 07960 958161 (John)
Contact: Jean or John Jeater
Number of Events: 12
When: Apr-Oct
Number of Stands: 30-35
Public Admission Price: Nil (main gate charge only)
Stand/Space Costs: Approx £175 to £250 per event (inc 2 tables); power extra at approx £15-£25. Demonstrators should contact organiser about discount possibilities.
Late Booking Opportunities: Sometimes
Photographs Needed: No
Selection Policy: C – no cheap advertising materials permitted (e.g. dayglo posters and tickets) or pitching to public.

COUNTRY COTTAGE CRAFTS
8 Willow Close
Tasburgh
Norwich
Norfolk NR15 1NE
Tel: 01508 471549
Fax: 01508 470957
Email: info@cottagecrafts.fsnet.co.uk
Website: www.cottagecrafts.fsnet.co.uk
Contact: David
Number of Events: 5
When: Mar, Apr, Aug, Sept, Nov
Number of Stands: 100-125
Public Admission Price: Adults £3.50, Seniors £2.50, Children £2.50, under-12s free.
Stand/Space Costs: £160 per event. Extra £5 for tables and £2.50 for chairs; electricity free. Extra space free of charge for demonstrators.
Late Booking Opportunities: Sometimes
Photographs Needed: Yes
Selection Policy: B – British made crafts only.

COUNTRYCRAFT
5 Boucher Place
St Werburghs
Bristol BS2 9YY
Tel: 0117 955 7936
Contact: Sandra Atkins
Number of Events: 40
When: Apr-Dec
Number of Stands: 20
Public Admission Price: Nil
Stand/Space Costs: £20 for one day; no extras.
See Markets section for more details about this programme.

COUNTRY LIFESTYLE EXHIBITIONS LTD
PO Box 477
Belfast BT16 2YA
Tel: 028 9048 3873
Fax: 028 9048 0195
Email: irishcountrylifestyle@btinternet.com
Website: www.irishcountrylifestyle.com
Contact: John McClelland
Number of Events: 1
When: June
Number of Stands: 30 Craft
Public Admission Price: Adults £8, under-16s £4, Family £20.
Stand/Space Costs: £130 for the event; extra £5 for tables and £25 for power points.
Late Booking Opportunities: Rare
Photographs Needed: No
Selection Policy: B

COUNTRYWIDE EVENTS
10 Naseby Drive
Loughborough

Leics LE11 4NU
Tel: 01509 217444
Number of Events: 7
When: Mar, Apr, Oct, Nov
Number of Stands: 50
Public Admission Price: Adults £1.50, Seniors £1, under-16s free.
Stand/Space Costs: Approx £180 per event; no extras.
Late Booking Opportunities: Sometimes
Photographs Needed: Yes
Selection Policy: B/C – high standard of display required.

COUNTY ANTRIM AGRICULTURAL ASSOCIATION
Ballymena Showgrounds
Warden Street
Ballymena
Co Antrim BT43 7DR
Tel/Fax: 028 2565 2666
Email: ballymena.showoffice@virgin.net
Contact: Mrs June Lamont
Number of Events: 1
When: May
Number of Stands: 200
Public Admission Price: Adults £7, Seniors £5.
Stand/Space Costs: £80 for 10ft by 10ft in the floored marquee; extra £10 for electricity.
Late Booking Opportunities: Sometimes
Photographs Needed: No
Selection Policy: D – rules on health and safety, risk assessments and public liability insurance need to be adhered to.

COUNTY FAIRS
PO Box 2
Ratby
Leics LE6 0XT
Tel: 0116 239 4366
Mobile: 07850 394366
Email: countyfairs@btopenworld.com
Contact: Marcus Pateman
Number of Events: 40
When: Jan-Dec, but no dates available at time of printing – contact organiser.
Number of Stands: 40
Public Admission Price: Adults £1.
Stand/Space Costs: £25+ per day; no extras.
Late Booking Opportunities: Nearly always
Photographs Needed: No
Selection Policy: B

COWAL HIGHLAND GATHERING
54 Hillfoot Street
Dunoon
Argyll PA23 7DT
Tel: 01369 702086
Fax: 01369 707172
Email: info@cowalgathering.com
Website: www.cowalgathering.com
Contact: Carol Morrison
Number of Events: 1
When: Aug
Number of Stands: Approx 40
Public Admission Price: Adults £9, Seniors £7, Concessions £6, under-5s £2, Family £20.
Stand/Space Costs: £282 (inc VAT) for the event; no extras.
Late Booking Opportunities: Sometimes
Photographs Needed: Yes
Selection Policy: B

COXWOLD CRAFT FAIRS
28 Windy Hill Lane
Marske-by-the-Sea
Cleveland TS11 7BN
Tel: 01642 472675
Fax: 01642 498908
Email: windyplanter@ntlworld.com
Contact: Stephen or Gloria Lilley
Number of Events: 27
When: Mar–Sept
Number of Stands: 12-16
Public Admission Price: Nil
Stand/Space Costs: £6 to £8 per day; no extras.
Late Booking Opportunities: Sometimes
Photographs Needed: Yes
Selection Policy: A – British made crafts only. All items for sale must be made by the exhibitor. No third party involvement.

CRAFT CARNIVAL
Hill Butts House
Kingston Lacy, Wimborne
Dorset BH21 4DS
Tel/Fax: 01202 842407
Mobile: 07981 883232
Email: info@craftcarnival.co.uk
Contact: Kati Zombory-Moldovan
Number of Events: 7
When: Mar, Apr/May, June, July, Aug
Number of Stands: 100-160
Public Admission Price: Adults £3, Seniors

(cont)

£2.50, under-14s free.
Stand/Space Costs: £90 to £150 per event; extra £20 for electrical points. Free 3ft space for demonstrators.
Late Booking Opportunities: Sometimes
Photographs Needed: Yes
Selection Policy: C

CRAFT DEVELOPMENTS
17 Whittingehame Gardens
Brighton
East Sussex BN1 6PU
Tel: 01273 887596
Contact: Deirdre Cannon
Number of Events: 10-15
When: May, Aug, Oct, Nov, Dec
Number of Stands: 8-45
Public Admission Price: Nil
Stand/Space Costs: £25 per event; no extras.
Late Booking Opportunities: Sometimes
Photographs Needed: Yes
Selection Policy: C

CRAFT IN FOCUS
PO Box 942
Maidstone
Kent ME15 0YB
Tel: 01622 747325
Fax: 01622 747246
Email: info@craftinfocus.com
Website: www.craftinfocus.com
Contact: Robert Chapman
Number of Events: 4
When: Mar, Apr, Sept, Oct
Number of Stands: 100-120
Public Admission Price: Adults £4, Seniors/Concessions £3, under-14s free.
Stand/Space Costs: From £270 to £600 per event, depending on size; extra for power and tables.
Late Booking Opportunities: Sometimes
Photographs Needed: Yes
Selection Policy: B - British made crafts only.

CRAFT LINCS
2 The Croft
Park Street
Alfreton
Derbys DE55 7JR
Tel: 01773 830200
Fax: 01773 831031
Contact: Ian Willis
Number of Events: 10
When: May-Sept
Number of Stands: 35-65
Stand/Space Costs: From £90 to £210 per event for a basic size stall; extra for tables and power. 2ft additional space free for demonstrators.
Late Booking Opportunities: Sometimes
Photographs Needed: No
Selection Policy: C

CRAFTMAKER EVENTS
74 Hazel Way
Crawley Down
West Sussex RH10 4EU
Tel/Fax: 01342 713375
Email: info@jetsevents.co.uk
Website: www.jetsevents.co.uk
Contact: Joyce Edmonds
Number of Events: 2
When: June, Oct
Number of Stands: 50
Late Booking Opportunities: Sometimes
Photographs Needed: Yes
Selection Policy: B

CRAFT PEOPLE 2000
38 Eden Grove
Swallownest
Sheffield
South Yorks S26 4TP
Tel: 0114 287 9671
Fax: 0114 287 3037
Mobile: 07976 964226
Email: info@craftpeople2000.co.uk
Website: www.craftpeople2000.co.uk
Contact: Peter Fox
Number of Events: 25-30
When: All except Jan, Feb, Apr
Number of Stands: 10-70
Stand/Space Costs: On application.
Late Booking Opportunities: Sometimes
Photographs Needed: Yes
Selection Policy: C - with only limited duplication.

CRAFTS & COLLECTABLES
c/o 4 Grosvenor Drive
Poynton
Cheshire SK12 1JF
Tel: 01625 877865 (8am-7pm)
Email: anne@tortuga.fsnet.co.uk
Website: www.poyntonshow.co.uk

Contact: Anne or Louise Campbell
Number of Events: 3-4
When: June, Aug
Number of Stands: 60
Public Admission Price: Advanced tickets (2004) at: Adults £5, Seniors/Children £2.50, Family £14.
Stand/Space Costs: £35 per day; no extras.
Late Booking Opportunities: Sometimes
Photographs Needed: No
Selection Policy: C

CRAFTS AT BOVEY TRACEY
c/o The Devon Guild of Craftsmen
Riverside Mill
Bovey Tracey
Devon TQ13 9AF
Tel: 01626 830612
Email: mail@craftsatboveytracey.co.uk
Website: www.craftsatboveytracey.co.uk
Contact: Sarah James
Number of Events: 1
When: June
Number of Stands: 160
Public Admission Price: Adults £5, Seniors/Concessions £3, under-14s free.
Stand/Space Costs: From £140 for the event. Small booking fee for power; one table free with extras at cost. 10% discount for demonstrators.
Late Booking Opportunities: Sometimes
Photographs Needed: Yes
Selection Policy: A – British made crafts only.

CRAFTS COUNCIL
44a Pentonville Road
London N1 9BY
Tel: 020 7278 7700
Fax: 020 7837 6891
Email: busdev@craftscouncil.org.uk
Website: www.craftscouncil.org.uk
Contact: Stephanie Taylor
Number of Events: 1
When: Oct
Number of Stands: 220 over 2 separate weeks
Public Admission Price: Adults £7 single visit, £10 one visit each week, Concessions £5 and £7 respectively.
Stand/Space Costs: Single stand 1st time exhibitor £545, 2nd/3rd time exhibitors £610, all others £720. Shared stand 1st time £370, 2nd/3rd time £455. Double stand 1st time £1080, 2nd/3rd time £1200, all others £1410.
These prices are all subject to confirmation for 2005.
Late Booking Opportunities: Rare
Photographs Needed: Yes
Selection Policy: A/B

CRAFTWORKERS COOPERATIVE
17 Hopefield
Newport
NP20 5FN
Tel: 07813 581527
Email: potman@tesco.net
Number of Events: 2
When: Oct, Nov
Number of Stands: Approx 100
Public Admission Price: TBC
Stand/Space Costs: From £50 per day inside and from £30 per day outside (power inc); extra for tables/chairs.
Late Booking Opportunities: Sometimes
Photographs Needed: No
Selection Policy: C

CRANLEIGH & SOUTH EASTERN AGRICULTURAL SOCIETY
Oakapple Cottage, Stane Street
Ockley, Dorking
Surrey RH5 5ST
Tel/Fax: 01306 712050
Email: cranleighshow@hotmail.com
Contact: Mrs Troughton
Number of Events: 1
When: Aug
Number of Stands: 230+
Public Admission Price: Adults £9, Seniors/under-16s £5, Family £25.
Stand/Space Costs: Provisionally between £66 and £92.50 for the one day; extra for tables and power.
Late Booking Opportunities: Sometimes
Photographs Needed: No
Selection Policy: B

CREATIVE CRAFTS ASSOCIATION
Primrose Cottage
Howards Lane
Eccleston
St Helens WA10 5QD
Tel/Fax: 01744 750606
Mobile: 07966 499748
Email: sandracca@aol.com
Website: www.creativecrafts-online.co.uk
Contact: Sandra Mather

Number of Events: 40
When: Feb-Dec
Number of Stands: 50-100
Public Admission Price: Adults £2, under-16s free.
Stand/Space Costs: £35 per day. Small charge for electricity at some events.
Late Booking Opportunities: Sometimes
Photographs Needed: Yes
Selection Policy: B/C – British made crafts only.

CREATIVE EXHIBITIONS LTD
8 Greenwich Quay
Clarence Road
London SE8 3EY
Tel: 020 8692 2299
Fax: 020 8692 6699
Email: mail@twistedthread.com
Website: www.twistedthread.com
Number of Events: 5
When: Mar/Apr, Aug, Oct, Nov
Number of Stands: 300+
Public Admission Price: From: Adults £7, Seniors/Concessions £6, under-16s £3.
Stand/Space Costs: From £130 per sq.m; extra for furniture and electricity.
Late Booking Opportunities: Sometimes
Photographs Needed: No
Selection Policy: B

CUMBERLAND AGRICULTURAL SOCIETY
Warcarr
Greenhead, Brampton
Cumbria CA8 7HY
Tel/Fax: 01697 747397
Email: cumberland.show@virgin.net
Website: www.cumberlandshow.co.uk
Contact: Mrs D Rozario
Number of Events: 1
When: July
Number of Stands: 20-30
Public Admission Price: Adults £8, under-16s £3, Family £20.
Stand/Space Costs: £22 for the event.
Late Booking Opportunities: Nearly always
Photographs Needed: Yes
Selection Policy: A/B

DALRY FARMERS' SOCIETY
16 Heronswood
Kilwinning
Ayrshire
KA13 7DP
Tel: 01294 552494
Mobile: 07966 438961
Contact: Anna Reid
Number of Events: 1
When: May
Number of Stands: 30
Stand/Space Costs: £10; no extras.
Late Booking Opportunities: Sometimes
Photographs Needed: No
Selection Policy: C

DEEPING AGRICULTURAL SHOW & COUNTRY FAYRE
Consort House
30 Monks House Lane
Spalding
Lincs
PE11 3LH
Tel: 01775 710606
Fax: 01775 711172
Mobile: 07775 754580
Number of Events: 1
When: June
Stand/Space Costs: From £60 to £216 for the event; some extras charged.
Late Booking Opportunities: Sometimes
Photographs Needed: No
Selection Policy: C

DERBYSHIRE AGRICULTURAL & HORTICULTURAL SOCIETY LTD
5 Willow Park Way
Weston Road
Aston-on-Trent
Derbys
DE72 2DF
Tel/Fax: 01332 793068
Mobile: 07764 849511
Email: anne.james@talk21.com
Website: www.derbyshirecountyshow.org.uk
Contact: Anne James
Number of Events: 1
When: June
Number of Stands: 20
Public Admission Price: Adults £7, Seniors/under-16s £4, Family pre-booked £14.
Stand/Space Costs: £45 for the day; extra £20 for electricity.
Late Booking Opportunities: Sometimes
Photographs Needed: Yes
Selection Policy: B – British made crafts only.

DEVON GUILD OF CRAFTSMEN
Riverside Mill
Bovey Tracey
Devon TQ13 9AF
Tel: 01626 832223
Fax: 01626 834220
Email: jenny@crafts.org.uk
Website: www.crafts.org.uk
Contact: Jenny Plackett

DK FAIRS
4 Boughton Drive
Rushden
Northants NN10 9HX
Tel: 01933 311313
Website: www.dkfairs.co.uk
Contact: David King
Number of Events: 4
When: Mar, Oct, Nov
Number of Stands: 60–88
Public Admission Price: Adults £1.50, Seniors £1.20, under-16s free.
Stand/Space Costs: £25 per day for a single stand and £40 for a double; no extras.
Late Booking Opportunities: Sometimes
Photographs Needed: No
Selection Policy: B – British made crafts only. No pets, no kettles.

DOLLS HOUSE, MINIATURES & CRAFTS
c/o 10 Woodhill Avenue
Portishead
North Somerset BS20 7EX
Tel: 01275 847033
Contact: Mrs Rita Daniels
Number of Events: 2
When: Feb, Sept
Number of Stands: Approx 30
Public Admission Price: Nil
Stand/Space Costs: £35 per event; no extras.
Late Booking Opportunities: Sometimes
Photographs Needed: No
Selection Policy: C

DOLLY DOMAIN FAIRS
45 Henderson Road
South Shields
Tyne & Wear NE34 9QW
Tel/Fax: 0191 424 0400
Email: fairs@dollydomain.com
Website: www.dollydomain.com
Contact: Liz or David Bonner
Number of Events: 6
When: Feb, Mar, May, July, Sept, Oct
Number of Stands: 57 (4) and 92 (2)
Public Admission Price: Adults £3, under-16s 50p.
Stand/Space Costs: £65 per event; no extras.
Late Booking Opportunities: Sometimes
Photographs Needed: Yes
Selection Policy: C

DORCHESTER AGRICULTURAL SOCIETY
Agriculture House
Acland Road
Dorchester
Dorset DT1 1EF
Tel: 01305 264249
Fax: 01305 251643
Email: secretary@dorchestershow.co.uk
Website: www.dorchestershow.co.uk
Contact: Mrs Sam Mackenzie-Green
Number of Events: 1
When: Sept
Number of Stands: 50
Public Admission Price: Adults £10, Seniors £7, under-16s £4, Family £18 (in advance).
Stand/Space Costs: £129 for the event; extra for power.
Late Booking Opportunities: Rare
Photographs Needed: Yes
Selection Policy: B

DOUG MOORE
North View
Haycroft Lane
Fleet, Spalding
Lincs PE12 8LB
Tel/Fax: 01406 490420
Mobile: 07977 134364
Email: doug@gardenfestivals.com
Website: www.gardenfestivals.com
Contact: Doug Moore
Number of Events: 8
When: Apr, May, June, Sept, Oct, Nov, Dec
Number of Stands: 70–120
Stand/Space Costs: On application
Late Booking Opportunities: Sometimes
Photographs Needed: No
Selection Policy: C

DOUNE & DUNBLANE AGRICULTURAL SOCIETY
Parks of Aldie
Fossoway
Kinross

(cont)

Fife KY13 0QH
Tel/Fax: 01577 840045
Contact: Mrs Wilma Sim
Number of Events: 1
When: July
Number of Stands: 24+
Public Admission Price: Adults £6, Seniors/under-15s £3, Family £16.
Stand/Space Costs: £25 for table in Craft Tent and £45 for double table; no extras.
Late Booking Opportunities: Rare
Selection Policy: B – British made crafts only.

DOWNTON CUCKOO FAIR LTD
Leicester House
The Borough
Downton
Salisbury
Wilts SP5 3LY
Tel: 01725 513521
Email: bookings@cuckoofair.co.uk
Website: www.cuckoofair.co.uk
Number of Events: 1
When: April
Number of Stands: 250
Public Admission Price: Nil
Stand/Space Costs: £65 for 8ft x 8ft in Marquee and £35 for same space outside; no extras.
Late Booking Opportunities: Rare
Selection Policy: B/C

DUMFRIES & LOCKERBIE AGRICULTURAL SOCIETY
15 Fruids Park Avenue
Annan
Dumfriesshire DG12 6AY
Tel: 01461 201199
Fax: 01461 206261
Contact: Mrs E Bicket
Number of Events: 1
When: Aug
Number of Stands: 50-60
Stand/Space Costs: £20 for the one day; no extras.
Late Booking Opportunities: Sometimes
Photographs Needed: No
Selection Policy: C

DUNDEE CITY COUNCIL
Leisure & Arts Department
Tayside House
Crichton Street
Dundee DD1 3RA
Tel: 01382 433042
Fax: 01382 433312
Email: peter.sandwell@dundeecity.gov.uk
Website:
www.dundeeflowerandfoodfestival.com
Contact: Peter Sandwell
Number of Events: 2
When: Apr, Sept
Number of Stands: 50
Public Admission Price: Adults £7, Seniors/Concessions £6, under-16s free.
Stand/Space Costs: £100 for 2m by 2m; no extras.
Late Booking Opportunities: Rare
Photographs Needed: Yes
Selection Policy: B – exhibitors must be bona fide craftworkers.

DUNSTER COUNTRY FAIR
c/o Longcombe Lodge
Alcombe
Minehead
Somerset TA24
Tel: 01643 705430
Contact: Mrs Marie McLean-Foreman or Peter Yeandle
Number of Events: 1
When: July
Number of Stands: 40
Public Admission Price: Adults £6, Seniors £5, under-14s free.
Stand/Space Costs: £65 for the event; no extras.
Late Booking Opportunities: Sometimes
Photographs Needed: No
Selection Policy: C

DUNSTER SHOW SOCIETY
c/o Apple Tree House
Higher Vexford
Lydeard St Lawrence
Somerset TA4 3QF
Tel: 01984 556990
Email: rebecca@aliquo.demon.co.uk
Contact: Mrs R Langdon
Number of Events: 1
When: Aug
Public Admission Price: Adults £6, Children £3.
Stand/Space Costs: On application.
Late Booking Opportunities: Rare
Photographs Needed: Yes
Selection Policy: B

EASTBOURNE BOROUGH COUNCIL
Events Development
College Road
Eastbourne
East Sussex BN21 4JJ
Tel: 01323 415442
Fax: 01323 736373
Email: events@eastbourne.gov.uk
Website: www.eastbourne.org/events
Contact: Jo Osborne
Number of Events: 6
When: May, June, July, Aug, Oct
Number of Stands: 20 at Magnificent Motors, Skate & Beer Festival; 40 at Tennis; 200 at Airbourne.
Public Admission Price: All free except Tennis (tba).
Stand/Space Costs: On application
Late Booking Opportunities: Sometimes
Photographs Needed: Yes

EAST LONDON DESIGN SHOW
15 Ellingfort Road
London E8 3PA
Tel: 020 8510 9069
Fax: 020 8986 1116
Mobile: 07971 570577
Email: info@eastlondondesignshow.co.uk
Website: www.eastlondondesignshow.co.uk
Contact: Della Tinsley or Gideon Cleary
Number of Events: 2-4
When: Dec
Number of Stands: 100
Public Admission Price: Adults £2, Concessions £1, under-16s free.
Stand/Space Costs: £420 for small stand and £625 for large stand. 15% discount sometimes offered to demonstrators.
Late Booking Opportunities: Sometimes
Photographs Needed: Yes
Selection Policy: A – all work has to be either designed or made by the exhibitors.

EAST MIDLANDS DOLL FAIRS
5 Arran Close
Holmes Chapel
Cheshire CW4 7QP
Tel/Fax: 01477 534626
Contact: Bruce King
Number of Events: 3
When: Feb, July, Oct
Number of Stands: 110
Public Admission Price: Adults £3.50, Seniors/Concessions £2.50.
Stand/Space Costs: £60 per event; no extras.
Late Booking Opportunities: Rare
Photographs Needed: No
Selection Policy: D – products on sale must be doll/dollshouse related (teddy bears also inc).

EASTNOR CASTLE
Portcullis Office, Eastnor Castle
Ledbury
Herefordshire HR8 1RL
Tel: 01531 633160
Fax: 01531 631776
Email: enquiries@eastnorcastle.com
Website: www.eastnorcastle.com
Contact: Sally Watson
Number of Events: 1
When: May
Number of Stands: 50
Public Admission Price: Adults £7, Seniors £6, 5-15s £4, Family £18.
Stand/Space Costs: On application
Late Booking Opportunities: Sometimes
Photographs Needed: Yes
Selection Policy: B – British made crafts only.

EAST OF ENGLAND SHOWGROUND
Alwalton
Peterborough
Cambs PE2 6XE
Tel: 01733 234451
Fax: 01733 370038
Email: marketing@eastofengland.org.uk
Website: www.eastofengland.org.uk
Contact: Keeley or Jane
Number of Events: 4
When: Mar, June, Oct, Nov
Number of Stands: 50
Public Admission Price: Varies with each event.
Stand/Space Costs: From £45 per event; extra for power.
Late Booking Opportunities: Sometimes
Photographs Needed: No
Selection Policy: C

EASTON FESTIVAL
Ivy Cottage
The Street. Easton
Woodbridge
Suffolk IP13 0ED
Tel: 01728 746162

(cont)

Email: eastonfestival@suffolkonline.net
Website: www.eastonfestival.org.uk
Contact: Carol Davis
Number of Events: 1
When: June
Number of Stands: 50
Public Admission Price: Adults £5.75, Seniors £5.25, under-16s £4.25, Family £18.
Stand/Space Costs: £30 for the event (tables not provided); £10 extra for electricity.
Late Booking Opportunities: Nearly always
Photographs Needed: No
Selection Policy: D – all health and safety and risk assessment requirements must be strictly adhered to.

EDEN CRAFTS LTD
39 Ross Court
Putney Hill
Putney
London SW15 3NZ
Tel: 020 8788 4434
Fax: 020 8780 0993
Mobile: 07729 337485
Email: dina@edencrafts.co.uk
Website: www.edencrafts.co.uk
Contact: Dina Samara
Number of Events: 30
When: Mar–Dec
Number of Stands: Usually around 45
Public Admission Price: Nil
Stand/Space Costs: Ranges from £100 per day to £300 per event; tables, chairs and electrics extra. 25% discount for demonstrators.
Late Booking Opportunities: Sometimes (not christmas)
Photographs Needed: Yes
Selection Policy: B/C – high standard of display required.

ENTERPRISE TAMAR LTD
St Thomas Road
Launceston
Cornwall PL15 8BU
Tel/Fax: 01566 775632
Email: info@e-tamar.org.uk
Website: www.e-tamar.org.uk
Contact: David Stanbury
Number of Events: 4
When: May, June, July
Number of Stands: 35–70
Public Admission Price: Nil
Stand/Space Costs: Ranges between £20 and £70 per day; extra £2 to £7 for tables (electric inc).
Late Booking Opportunities: Rare
Photographs Needed: Yes
Selection Policy: A/B – British made crafts only. Only Cornish residents in Royal Cornwall marquee and West Country residents in Devon County marquee.

ETES LTD
9-11 High Street
Staines
Middx TW18 4QY
Tel: 01784 880891
Fax: 01784 880892
Email: katev@youcanmake-it.co.uk
Website: www.youcanmake-it.co.uk
Contact: Kate Valentine
Number of Events: 1
When: Feb
Number of Stands: Approx 150
Public Admission Price: Adults £6.95, Seniors/Concessions £4.95, under-16s free. Group discount: buy 12 tickets and pay for only 10.

EVENT~REALITY
The Old Garage
Conwy Road
Tal y Bont
Conwy LL32 8SE
Tel/Fax: 01492 660209
Mobile: 07974 121063
Email: esorlegin@aol.com
Contact: Nigel Rose
Number of Events: 25
When: Mar–Dec
Number of Stands: 25
Public Admission Price: Nil; donations collected for local charities.
Stand/Space Costs: £15 to £20 per day; no extras. Tariff varies with each venue and length of fair.
Late Booking Opportunities: Yes, usually
Photographs Needed: Sometimes
Selection Policy: B/C

EXHIBITION MANAGEMENT
The Windmill
Mill Lane, off Sea Lane
Wrangle
Boston
Lincs PE22 9HE

Tel: 01205 871354
Fax: 01205 871747
Mobile: 07905 708493
Email: geoffrey.clutton@btopenworld.com
Website: www.selbygamefair.co.uk
Contact: Geoff
Number of Events: 10
When: Mar, Apr, May, July, Aug, Sept
Number of Stands: 100
Public Admission Price: Adults £7, Seniors/Concessions £3, under-14s free, Family £25.
Stand/Space Costs: £50 per day; no extras.
Late Booking Opportunities: Sometimes
Photographs Needed: Yes
Selection Policy: C

EYE SHOW LTD
17 Victoria Hill
Eye
Suffolk IP23 7HH
Tel: 01379 898816
Fax: 01379 898709
Mobile: 07860 811334
Website: www.eye-show.org.uk
Contact: Tim Seeley
Number of Events: 1
When: Aug
Number of Stands: 40
Public Admission Price: Adults £8, under-14s £4.
Stand/Space Costs: £90 for the event for a 10ft by 10ft site; extra £60 for power.
Late Booking Opportunities: Sometimes
Photographs Needed: No
Selection Policy: C

FABLES EVENTS LTD
Holly Cottage
17 Rose Grove
Keyworth
Notts NG12 5HE
Tel: 0115 937 4147
Fax: 0115 937 6766
Mobile: 07889 808599
Email: simon@fablesevents.freeserve.co.uk
Website: www.fablesevents.co.uk
Contact: Mr S Raine
Number of Events: 1-2
When: Mar
Number of Stands: 50
Public Admission Price: Adults £6, Seniors £4.50, Children £1.50, Family £10 (pre-booked).
Stand/Space Costs: £75 per event. Extra space given to demonstrators. Additional tables cost £3.
Late Booking Opportunities: Rare
Photographs Needed: No
Selection Policy: C

FAIRFIELD (CROYDON) LTD
Fairfield Halls
Park Lane
Croydon
Surrey CR9 1DG
Tel: 020 8603 3930/3812
Fax: 020 8603 3850
Email: marylka@fairfield.co.uk
Website: www.fairfield.co.uk
Contact: Marylka Gowlland
Number of Events: 2
When: Mar, Nov
Number of Stands: Approx 100-120
Public Admission Price: Adults £1.50, Concessions £1.
Stand/Space Costs: £60 for single stall and £102 for double stall, per event; no extras.
Late Booking Opportunities: Nearly always
Photographs Needed: No
Selection Policy: C

FALCON FAIRS
41 Nicholas Way
Northwood
Middx HA6 2TR
Tel/Fax: 01923 823455
Contact: M Morgan
Number of Events: 30
When: Apr-June, Sept-Dec
Number of Stands: 15-30
Public Admission Price: Nil to 50p, depending on venue.
Stand/Space Costs: £25 to £30 per day; no extras.
Late Booking Opportunities: Sometimes
Photographs Needed: No
Selection Policy: C – no smoking in display areas.

FARNHAM MALTINGS
Bridge Square
Farnham
Surrey GU9 7QR
Tel: 01252 726234
Fax: 01252 718177
Email: info@farnhammaltings.com
Website: www.farnhammaltings.com
Contact: Kate Martin

(cont)

Number of Events: 1
When: Oct
Stand/Space Costs: On application
Selection Policy: A

FELL DALES ASSOCIATION
Gill Bank Farm
Boot
Holmrook
Cumbria CA19 1TG
Tel/Fax: 01946 723292
Email: gillbank.temple@virgin.net
Contact: Gillian Temple
Number of Events: 1
When: Sept
Number of Stands: 10-20
Public Admission Price: Adults £2.50.
Stand/Space Costs: £18 for the event; no extras.
Late Booking Opportunities: Nearly always
Photographs Needed: No
Selection Policy: D

FESTIVAL OF CRAFTS UNIQUE TO SCOTLAND (FOCUS)
The Steading
Newpark
Newmachar
Aberdeenshire AB21 7XB
Tel: 01224 770943
Fax: 01224 774047
Email: embeetartans@hotmail.com
Contact: Marjorie Medford
Number of Events: 30-40
When: Apr-Dec
Number of Stands: 20-50
Public Admission Price: Free entry to some; others are outdoor events with showground entrance fees.
Stand/Space Costs: On application
Late Booking Opportunities: Sometimes
Photographs Needed: Yes
Selection Policy: A - British made crafts only.

FFEIRIAU ARBENNIG
Llwyn Helyg
Cnwch Coch
Aberystwyth
Ceredigion SY23 4LQ
Tel: 01974 261131
Mobile: 07811 040457
Email: ffeiriau.arbennig@ukonline.co.uk
Website: www.welshcrafts.co.uk
Contact: Robert Parkinson
Number of Events: 8
When: May, July
Number of Stands: 25
Public Admission Price: Nil
Stand/Space Costs: On application.
Late Booking Opportunities: Rare
Photographs Needed: Yes
Selection Policy: B - British made crafts only, with priority given to Welsh made crafts.

FIG FAIRS
119 West Road
Sawbridgeworth
Herts CM21 0BW
Tel: 01279 835711
Email: fig.fairs@ntlworld.com
Number of Events: 5
When: Apr, July, Sept, Nov, Dec
Number of Stands: 35
Public Admission Price: Adults £1, under-16s free (Nov price only).
Stand/Space Costs: £40 per day; extra £5 for tables and £10 for electric at Capel Manor. Free space offered to demonstrators.
Late Booking Opportunities: Sometimes
Photographs Needed: Yes
Selection Policy: B - British made crafts only. No mixed crafts or joint stalls permitted.

FILLONGLEY SHOW
c/o 162 Stonebury Avenue
Eastern Green
Coventry
Warks CV5 7NX
Tel: 024 7646 0150
Fax: 024 7646 0287
Email: fillongleyshow@fsmail.net
Contact: Cheryl Brookes
Number of Events: 1
When: Aug
Number of Stands: 80
Stand/Space Costs: On application
Late Booking Opportunities: Rare
Photographs Needed: No
Selection Policy: C/D

FINCHCOCKS
Goudhurst
Kent TN17 1HH
Tel: 01580 211702
Fax: 01580 211007
Email: katrina@finchcocks.co.uk

Website: www.finchcocks.co.uk
Contact: Katrina Burnett or Brenda Holbrow
Number of Events: 2
When: May, Oct
Number of Stands: May 70, Oct 100
Public Admission Price: Adults £5, Children £1.
Stand/Space Costs: £40 per day; extra for tables and power.
Late Booking Opportunities: Sometimes
Photographs Needed: Yes
Selection Policy: B/C – photos required and all stands vetted; standholder's insurance mandatory.

FIVE COUNTIES VINTAGE MACHINERY ORGANISATION LTD
c/o 17 Chelford Road
Macclesfield
Cheshire
SK10 3LG
Tel/Fax: 01625 612784
Number of Events: 1
When: June
Number of Stands: 20-30
Public Admission Price: Adults £5, Seniors/12s+ £4, under-12s free.
Stand/Space Costs: £30 for the event; extra £1 for electric lighting.
Late Booking Opportunities: Nearly always
Photographs Needed: No
Selection Policy: B/C

FIVE PARISHES P.C.C.
c/o Old House
The Broadway
Dunmow
Essex
CM6 3BH
Tel: 01371 872894
Fax: 01371 872370
Email: angela.harbottle@virgin.net
Website: www.fiveparishes.co.uk
Contact: Mrs A Harbottle
Number of Events: 1
When: Aug
Number of Stands: 50
Stand/Space Costs: £60 per 6ft trestle table for the two-day event or £100 for open field site; some minimal extras.
Late Booking Opportunities: Nearly always
Photographs Needed: No
Selection Policy: B/C – some safety restrictions to be adhered to.

FOREST OF MARSTON VALE
Forest Centre
Station Road
Marston Moretaine
Beds MK43 0PR
Tel: 01234 767037
Fax: 01234 762606
Email: guy.lambourne@marstonvale.org
Website: www.marstonvale.org
Contact: Guy Lambourne
Number of Events: 1
When: Sept
Number of Stands: 30
Public Admission Price: Nil
Stand/Space Costs: £25 for the event; no extras. Free for demonstrators.
Late Booking Opportunities: Sometimes
Photographs Needed: No
Selection Policy: B – British made, wood related crafts; British wood only.

FORRES HIGHLAND GAMES
c/o 7 Fleurs Road
Forres
Moray IV36 1LY
Tel/Fax: 01309 673289
Mobile: 07901 696855
Email: michaelwscott@lineone.net
Website:
www.forreshighlandgames.fsnet.co.uk
Contact: Mike Scott
Number of Events: 1
When: July
Number of Stands: 30
Public Admission Price: Adults £3.50, under-15s/Seniors £1.50.
Stand/Space Costs: From £25 to £35; traders supply their own tables.
Late Booking Opportunities: Nearly always
Photographs Needed: No
Selection Policy: D

FOUR SEASONS CRAFT FAYRES LTD
1 Kineton Road
Southam
Warks CV47 1HZ
Tel/Fax: 01926 812529
Mobile: 07831 414520
Email: ann@fourseasonscraftfayres.co.uk
Website: www.fourseasonscraftfayres.co.uk
Contact: Ann Turner
Number of Events: 6
When: Apr, May, Aug
Number of Stands: From 30 to 200
Public Admission Price: Adults £4.50, *(cont)*

Seniors £4, 5-15s £2.
Stand/Space Costs: On application
Late Booking Opportunities: Sometimes
Photographs Needed: Yes
Selection Policy: B – British made crafts only.

FRAMLINGHAM SPORTS CLUB
c/o Grove Farm Barns
Easton Road, Framlingham
Suffolk IP13 9LW
Tel: 01728 723320
Fax: 01728 723398
Email: richardbull@suffolkonline.net
Contact: R Bull
Number of Events: 1
When: May
Number of Stands: 30-40
Public Admission Price: Nil
Stand/Space Costs: £30 for two days or £17.50 for one day; no extras.
Late Booking Opportunities: Nearly always
Photographs Needed: No
Selection Policy: C

FRAMPTON COUNTRY FAIR
Estate Office
Manor Farm, Frampton-on-Severn
Glos GL2 7EP
Tel/Fax: 01452 740698
Email: clifford.fce@farming.co.uk
Website: www.framptoncountryfair.org.uk
Contact: Rose Spence
Number of Events: 1
When: Sept
Number of Stands: 40-50
Public Admission Price: Adults £7, under-15s £2.
Stand/Space Costs: £37 per 8ft for the event; extra £7 for tables and £7 for electricity.
Late Booking Opportunities: Sometimes
Photographs Needed: No
Selection Policy: B

FROME & DISTRICT AGRICULTURAL SOCIETY
The Show Office
Rodden Road, Frome
Somerset BA11 2AH
Tel: 01373 463600
Fax: 01373 464861
Email: admin@fromecheeseshow.co.uk
Website: www.fromecheeseshow.co.uk
Number of Events: 1
When: Sept
Number of Stands: Approx 50
Public Admission Price: Adults £8, Seniors £6, under-17s £3, Family £21.
Stand/Space Costs: £54 for the event; extra £6 for tables and £10 for electricity (all provisional costs).
Late Booking Opportunities: Nearly always
Photographs Needed: No
Selection Policy: D

FROME TOWN CENTRE PROMOTIONS GROUP
c/o 21 Paul Street
Catherine Hill
Frome
Somerset BA11 1DT
Tel/Fax: 01373 461352
Email: ftcpg@btinternet.com
Contact: Lyn Waller
Number of Events: 3
When: Feb, Aug, Nov
Number of Stands: Up to 100
Public Admission Price: Nil
Stand/Space Costs: Approx £15 per sq.m. per day; extra £8 for tables, £5 for chairs and £5 for electricity.
Late Booking Opportunities: Sometimes
Photographs Needed: Yes
Selection Policy: Events are themed and appropriate costume and stall decoration is expected.

GATESHEAD METROPOLITAN COUNCIL
Civic Centre
Regent Street
Gateshead
Newcastle upon Tyne
Tyne & Wear NE8 1HH
Tel: 0191 433 3000
Number of Events: 2
When: Apr, July
Number of Stands: 90
Stand/Space Costs: From £75 for 6ft in April and from £95 for July (2004 prices).
Late Booking Opportunities: Rare
Photographs Needed: Yes
Selection Policy: B – British made crafts only.

GEFFRYE MUSEUM
136 Kingsland Road
Shoreditch
London E2 8EA

Tel: 020 7739 9893
Fax: 020 7729 5647
Website: www.geffrye-museum.org.uk
Contact: Karen Bunting, Broadway Ceramics
Number of Events: 1/2
When: Sept
Number of Stands: 50
Public Admission Price: Nil
Stand/Space Costs: From £120 to £150 for the event; no extras. Some discount offered to demonstrators.
Late Booking Opportunities: Rare
Photographs Needed: Yes
Selection Policy: A - British made crafts only.

GLENDALE AGRICULTURAL SOCIETY
Low Bleakhope
Powburn
Alnwick
Northumberland NE66 4NZ
Tel/Fax: 01665 578845
Email: sarah.nelson@ukonline.co.uk
Contact: Sarah Nelson
Number of Events: 1
When: Aug
Number of Stands: Approx 40
Public Admission Price: Adults £6, Seniors £4, 5-14s £2, under-5s free, Family £15.
Stand/Space Costs: £30 per 6ft frontage.
Late Booking Opportunities: Sometimes
Photographs Needed: Yes, sometimes
Selection Policy: C/D

GLENDALE FESTIVAL
Tel: 01668 281462
Email: glendalefestival@hotmail.com
Contact: John Davidson
Number of Events: 1
When: July
The Craft Fair runs from 10am to 4pm and is part of a mix of music and other entertainments as well as a Flower Festival.

GLOBAL FUSION
Pestalozzi International Village
Sedlescombe
East Sussex TN33 0RR
Tel: 01424 870444
Fax: 01424 870655
Email: festival@pestalozzi.org.uk
Website: www.pestalozzi.org.uk
Contact: Mandy Curtis
Number of Events: 1
When: June
Number of Stands: 25
Public Admission Price: For 3 days, Adults £35, Children half price, under-10s free (approx).
Stand/Space Costs: £120 for the event; no extras.
Late Booking Opportunities: Sometimes
Photographs Needed: Yes
Selection Policy: C. The organiser wishes to encourage fairly traded global crafts.

GORING VILLAGE HALL MANAGEMENT
Water Meadow
Long Meadow
Manor Road
Goring-on-Thames
Reading RG8 9EG
Tel: 01491 872884
Contact: Gill Cranshaw
Number of Events: 1
When: Nov
Number of Stands: 30
Public Admission Price: Adults £1, under-16s free.
Stand/Space Costs: £60 for the event; no extras.
Late Booking Opportunities: Sometimes
Photographs Needed: Yes
Selection Policy: B - British made crafts only.

GRAND PROMOTION EVENTS LTD
Unit 1, Michaelmas Barn
Norwich Road
Long Stratton, Norwich
Norfolk NR15 2PY
Tel: 01508 531143
Fax: 01508 536024
Mobile: 07876 567277
Contact: Andy or Tracey Grand
Number of Events: 1
When: Apr
Number of Stands: 50
Public Admission Price: Adults £8, Concessions £4, Children £3, under-5s free.
Stand/Space Costs: From £60 for the event; extra £5 for tables.
Late Booking Opportunities: Sometimes
Photographs Needed: No
Selection Policy: B

GRANDSTAND EVENTS LTD
The Old Coach House
Boutport Street
Barnstaple

(cont)

Devon EX31 1RW
Tel: 01271 378000
Fax: 01271 329133
Email: grahame@grandstandevents.com
Website: www.grandstandevents.com
Contact: Grahame Davidson
Number of Events: 1
When: Nov
Number of Stands: 280
Public Admission Price: Adults £2.50, Seniors £1.50, under-16s free.
Stand/Space Costs: From £160 for the event; extra £5 for tables, £22.50 for lighting and £28 for sockets.
Late Booking Opportunities: Rare
Photographs Needed: No
Selection Policy: C – duplication of products is avoided where possible.

GRANSDEN & DISTRICT AGRICULTURAL SOCIETY
Home Farm
Arrington
Royston
Herts SG8 0AX
Tel: 01223 207313
Fax: 01223 208335
Contact: Mrs A Pearce
Number of Events: 1
When: Sept
Number of Stands: 90
Public Admission Price: Adults £7, under-11s free.
Stand/Space Costs: First table £20 and additional tables £15; no extras.
Late Booking Opportunities: Rare
Photographs Needed: No
Selection Policy: B/C - British made crafts only.

GREAT DORSET STEAM FAIR LTD
Dairy House Farm
Child Okeford
Blandford
Dorset
DT11 8HT
Tel: 01258 860361 or 01258 860186
Fax: 01258 860361
Email: enquiries@steam-fair.co.uk
Website: www.steam-fair.co.uk
Contact: Rowena Ellis
Number of Events: 1
When: Aug/Sept
Number of Stands: 100
Public Admission Price: Adults £14, Seniors £12, 6-15s £6, Family £30. Discount at roughly 20% for advance bookings under 'Saver' ticket scheme.
Stand/Space Costs: £312 per 12ft pitch and £26.00 per extra ft (inc VAT). Extra £7.50 for tables and £60 for electricity. Negotiable space discount for demonstrators.
Late Booking Opportunities: Rare
Photographs Needed: Yes
Selection Policy: B

GREAT ECCLESTON & DISTRICT AGRICULTURAL SOCIETY
Unsworth House
St Michaels-on-Wyre
Preston
Lancs
PR3 0TD
Tel: 01995 679204
Contact: Mrs S Robinson
Number of Events: 1
When: July
Number of Stands: Approx 20
Public Admission Price: Adults £6, Seniors £4, under-14s £1.
Stand/Space Costs: £60 for the event; extra £15 for power.
Late Booking Opportunities: Rare
Photographs Needed: No
Selection Policy: A/B – crafts must be made in Lancashire.

GREEN DAYS CRAFT FAIR
c/o Parish Office
St Michael & All Angels Church
Priory Avenue
London
W4 1TX
Tel: 020 8994 1380
Email: stmichaelandallangels@ukgateway.net
Website: www.bedfordparkfestival.org
Contact: Sara Gronmark
Number of Events: 1
When: June
Number of Stands: 20-30
Public Admission Price: Nil
Stand/Space Costs: £90 for the event; no extras.
Late Booking Opportunities: Sometimes
Photographs Needed: Yes
Selection Policy: B/C – British made crafts only.

GUILD OF ESSEX CRAFTSMEN
c/o 10 The Furlongs
Ingatestone
Essex CM4 0AH
Tel: 01277 356008
Email: reelspin@route56.co.uk
Website: www.essexcraftguild.co.uk
Number of Events: 5
When: Mar, Sept, Nov
Number of Stands: 30-60
Stand/Space Costs: Nominal costs; only available to guild members. Extra cost for table hire.
Selection Policy: B - British made crafts only.

GWYNEDD & CLWYD ASSOCIATION OF CRAFTWORKERS
c/o 7 Grosvenor Crescent
Rossett
Wrexham LL12 0HX
Tel: 01244 570354
Contact: Wendy Edwards
Number of Events: 7
When: Mar, May, Aug, Oct, Nov
Number of Stands: 12-32
Public Admission Price: Nil
Stand/Space Costs: £30 to £40 per event for a 6ft by 8ft stand. Extra for tables at some events.
Late Booking Opportunities: Sometimes (Members)
Photographs Needed: Yes
Selection Policy: A/B - British made crafts only (Guild Members).

HADDENHAM FESTIVAL & CRAFT FAYRE
3 Church Street
Aylesbury
Bucks HP20 2QP
Tel: 01296 415333
Fax: 01296 397092
Contact: John or Jackie Weller
Number of Events: 1
When: Dec
Number of Stands: 25
Public Admission Price: Adults £1, Seniors/Children 50p.
Stand/Space Costs: £26 per day for those exhibiting their own, hand-made goods; otherwise £36 is the general fee. Public liability insurance, if not already held, available for additional £2.
Late Booking Opportunities: Sometimes
Photographs Needed: No
Selection Policy: C

HADDENHAM STEAM RALLY
Darkin
Meadow Lane, Earith
Cambs PE28 3QE
Tel/Fax: 01487 841893
Email: denise.young@tesco.net
Contact: Denise Young
Number of Events: 1
When: Sept
Number of Stands: 24
Stand/Space Costs: On application
Late Booking Opportunities: Rare
Photographs Needed: Yes
Selection Policy: C - British made crafts only.

HALE EVENTS LTD
Premier House
Old Church Road
Axbridge
Somerset BS26 2BQ
Tel: 01934 733433
Fax: 01934 733233
Email: mail@selectwest.co.uk
Website: www.selectwest.co.uk
Number of Events: 1
When: Apr
Number of Stands: Approx 250
Public Admission Price: N/A - Select 2005 is a trade only fair.
Stand/Space Costs: £125 per sq.m. (min 3 sq.m.), inc shell scheme of walls, fascia, nameboard and carpet.
Selection Policy: To qualify to exhibit at Select, your product must be produced /manufactured in Britain.

HALLMARK CRAFT FAIRS
PO Box 5434
Westcliff-on-Sea
Essex SS0 8RA
Tel: 01702 477300
Fax: 01702 710383
Email: hallmarkcraftfairs@talk21.com
Website: www.ridgewebb.co.uk
Contact: Charles Jackson
Number of Events: 12-14
When: Feb-June and Oct-Dec
Number of Stands: 30-120
Public Admission Price: Adults from £1.50 to £3, Seniors from £1 to £2, under-14s free.
Stand/Space Costs: From £30 to £50 per day; no extras.
Late Booking Opportunities: Sometimes
Photographs Needed: No
Selection Policy: C

HAMPSHIRE MUSIC & ARTS FESTIVALS
51 Russell Street
Gosport
Hants PO12 3JD
Tel/Fax: 023 9252 8017
Email: chegwyn@talk21.com
Website: www.gosportfestival.co.uk and www.eastleighfestival.co.uk
Contact: Peter Chegwyn
Number of Events: 2
When: Mar, Aug
Number of Stands: 20
Public Admission Price: Ranges from £7 to £20.
Stand/Space Costs: From £150 to £200 per event; no extras.
Late Booking Opportunities: Sometimes
Photographs Needed: No
Selection Policy: D

HARBOTTLE SHOW
c/o Lanternside House
Morpeth
Northumberland NE65 7AX
Tel: 01669 650318
Email: secretary@harbottleshow.com
Website: www.harbottleshow.com
Contact: Joanna Wood
Number of Events: 1
When: Sept
Number of Stands: Up to 20
Public Admission Price: Adults £2, Children 50p.
Stand/Space Costs: £10 for the one day.
Late Booking Opportunities: Nearly always
Photographs Needed: No
Selection Policy: C

HARDY FAIRS LTD
4 Granville Road
Scarborough
North Yorks YO11 2RA
Tel: 01723 350419
Mobile: 07734 407030
Email: hardyfairs@beeb.net
Contact: Stuart or Jane
Number of Events: 20-30
When: Mar, May, July, Aug, Sept
Number of Stands: 8-20
Public Admission Price: Nil
Stand/Space Costs: Varies, but around £25 for 6ft per day.
Late Booking Opportunities: Sometimes
Selection Policy: B/C

HARROW SHOW
88 Weald Lane
Harrow Weald
Middx HA3 5EY
Tel: 020 8863 0340
Website: www.harrowshow.org.uk
Contact: Mrs Sandra Gilmore
Number of Events: 1
When: Aug
Number of Stands: 45
Public Admission Price: Adults £4, Seniors/Children £2, Family £10.
Stand/Space Costs: From £70 to £90 for the event; extra £5 for chairs and £20 for electricity.
Late Booking Opportunities: Sometimes
Photographs Needed: No
Selection Policy: C

HD EVENTS LTD
Events House
Wycombe Air Park, Marlow
Bucks SL7 3DP
Tel: 01494 450504
Fax: 01494 450245
Email: hdfairs@aol.com
Website: www.reflexexhibitionsteam.co.uk
Contact: Sarah Miller
Number of Events: Approx 25
When: Mar-Dec
Number of Stands: 100-200
Public Admission Price: £5.
Stand/Space Costs: Approx £350 per event.
Late Booking Opportunities: Yes
Photographs Needed: Yes
Selection Policy: B - British made crafts only for the Live Crafts events.

HEART OF ENGLAND CRAFTWORKERS LTD
105 St George's Lane
Worcester
Worcs WR1 1QS
Tel: 01905 21702
Fax: 01905 29285
Mobile: 07974 000175
Email: info@heartofenglandcraftworkers.com
Website: www.heartofenglandcraftworkers.com
Contact: Eddie or Betty Carless
Number of Events: Approx 14
When: May-Sept
Number of Stands: 40+

Stand/Space Costs: On application
Late Booking Opportunities: Sometimes
Photographs Needed: Yes
Selection Policy: B

HECKINGTON & DISTRICT AGRICULTURAL SOCIETY
Home Farm
East Heckington
Boston
Lincs PE20 3QF
Tel/Fax: 01529 461823
Email: secretary@heckingtonshow.org.uk
Website: www.heckingtonshow.org.uk
Contact: Ann Beever
Number of Events: 1
When: July
Public Admission Price: Adults £6, under-16s £2.
Stand/Space Costs: On application
Late Booking Opportunities: Rare
Photographs Needed: No
Selection Policy: B/C

HEREFORDSHIRE COUNCIL
PO Box 4
Plough Lane
Hereford
Herefordshire HR4 0XH
Tel: 01432 260129
Fax: 01432 383031
Email: pnorton@herefordshire.gov.uk
Website: www.craftfair.uk.com
Contact: Peter Norton
Number of Events: 1
When: Nov
Number of Stands: 50
Public Admission Price: Adults £1, under-14s free.
Stand/Space Costs: £180 for the event (provisional costing); includes stand, lighting, power etc.
Late Booking Opportunities: Rare
Photographs Needed: Yes
Selection Policy: A/B - British made crafts only.

HISTORIC VEHICLE GATHERING
c/o 5 Holcombe Road
Teignmouth
Devon TQ14 8UP
Tel: 01626 778960
Email: peterj_smallwood@hotmail.com
Website: www.crashboxclub.co.uk
Contact: Sue Smallwood
Number of Events: 1
When: July
Number of Stands: 100+
Stand/Space Costs: On application
Late Booking Opportunities: Nearly always
Photographs Needed: No
Selection Policy: D

HMS SULTAN SUMMER SHOW
Lt Collins, Rutherford Block
HMS Sultan
Military Road
Gosport
Hants PO12 3BY
Tel: 023 9254 2425
Fax: 023 9254 6018
Email: sultan-tdn@nrta.mod.uk
Website: www.sultan.org.uk
Contact: Lt D Collins RN
Number of Events: 1
When: June
Number of Stands: 80
Public Admission Price: Adults £5 (£3.50), under-18s/Seniors £2.50 (£2), Family £12 (£9); advance purchase price in brackets.
Stand/Space Costs: £75 for the two days in the marquee. Outside are full plots at £115 and half-plots at £75. No extras.
Late Booking Opportunities: Sometimes
Photographs Needed: No
Selection Policy: B/C

HOBBY HORSE EVENTS LTD
PO Box 3751
Solihull
West Midlands B91 3QF
Tel: 0121 711 4728
Fax: 0121 709 1012
Website: www.hobbyhorseevents.com
Contact: Jane Kimberley
Number of Events: 20
When: Mar, Apr, May, July, Aug, Sept, Oct, Nov, Dec
Number of Stands: 20-130
Stand/Space Costs: On application
Late Booking Opportunities: Sometimes
Photographs Needed: Yes
Selection Policy: B - British made crafts only.

HOLLOWELL STEAM & HEAVY HORSE SHOW
Brickle House
Hollowell Road

(cont)

Creaton
Northants NN6 8NU
Tel/Fax: 01604 505422
Mobile: 07802 570590
Contact: Allen Eaton
Number of Events: 1
When: July
Number of Stands: 30-35
Public Admission Price: Adults £6, Seniors/Children £3.
Stand/Space Costs: Around £45; no extras. £5 discount for demonstrators.
Late Booking Opportunities: Sometimes
Photographs Needed: No
Selection Policy: D

HONLEY AGRICULTURAL SHOW LTD
c/o Winwood, Dove House
Pell Lane
Wooldale
Holmfirth
West Yorks HD9 1QL
Tel: 01484 689755
Fax: 01484 689744
Email: nigel@winwood.co.uk
Website: www.honleyshow.co.uk
Contact: Nigel Stansfield
Number of Events: 1
When: June
Number of Stands: 30
Public Admission Price: Adults £6, Seniors/Concessions £4, Children £2, Family £12.
Stand/Space Costs: £50 for the one day; extra £5 for power.
Late Booking Opportunities: Sometimes
Photographs Needed: No
Selection Policy: B

H.P.O.M.
PO Box 7815
Chelmsford
Essex CM1 2WL
Tel: 01245 344813
Fax: 01245 281240
Contact: C Ankers
Number of Events: 1
When: Aug
Number of Stands: 40-50
Public Admission Price: Adults £7, Seniors £6, under-16s £1.
Stand/Space Costs: From £45 to £65 for the event; no extras.
Late Booking Opportunities: Rare
Selection Policy: A – British made crafts only.

HUNTINGDON CRAFT MARKET
5 Huckleberry Close
Luton
Beds LU3 4AN
Tel: 01582 598442
Mobile: 07798 538568
Email: michael.kelly17@ntlworld.com
Contact: Mike Kelly
Number of Events: 7
When: Mar, May, Sept, Oct, Nov, Dec
Number of Stands: 20
Public Admission Price: Nil
Stand/Space Costs: From £25 to £35 per day; no extras.
Late Booking Opportunities: Sometimes
Photographs Needed: Yes
Selection Policy: B – British made crafts only.

ICHF
Dominic House
Seaton Road
Highcliffe
Dorset BH23 5HW
Tel: 01425 272711
Fax: 01425 279369
Email: marketing@ichf.co.uk
Website: www.ichf.co.uk
Contact: Simon Burns
Number of Events: 19
When: All except Jan, July, Dec
Number of Stands: 200-250
Public Admission Price: Varies
Stand/Space Costs: On application
Late Booking Opportunities: Rare
Photographs Needed: Yes
Selection Policy: B

IGF MARKETING
45 Hawkers Close
Testwood Farm
Totton
Southampton
Hants SO40 3GG
Tel: 023 8066 1466
Email: nustart@tiscali.co.uk
Contact: Gail Ingram
Number of Events: 5
When: Mar + Aug confirmed
Number of Stands: 30-60
Public Admission Price: Adults £1.50, Seniors £1.
Stand/Space Costs: From £45 per day. Some outside sites; prices on application. Electricity available; price on application.

Late Booking Opportunities: Sometimes
Photographs Needed: Yes
Selection Policy: B – stands to be manned at all times when event is open.

INITIATIVE BURNLEY
Lodge House, Cow Lane
Burnley
Lancs BB11 1NN
Tel: 01282 414800
Fax: 01282 428718
Email: info@initiativeburnley.co.uk
Website: www.burnleyballoonfestival.co.uk or www.initiativeburnley.co.uk
Contact: Karin Wilson or Paul Howard
Number of Events: 1
When: July
Number of Stands: 40
Public Admission Price: Adults £2.50, Children free.
Stand/Space Costs: £30 for the event; extra for power and lighting.
Late Booking Opportunities: Sometimes
Photographs Needed: Yes
Selection Policy: B – some restrictions on food crafts.

INSPIRATION FOR CHRISTMAS
Bratton Court
Minehead
Somerset TA24 8SL
Tel/Fax: 01643 705797
Website: www.inspirationforchristmas.co.uk
Contact: Caroline Lytton
Number of Events: 1
When: Nov
Number of Stands: 25
Public Admission Price: Nil
Stand/Space Costs: £50 for the event; no extras.
Late Booking Opportunities: Sometimes
Photographs Needed: Yes
Selection Policy: A/B – British made crafts only and if possible, local.

IWA FESTIVALS
Inland Waterways Association
PO Box 114
Rickmansworth
Herts WD3 1ZY
Tel: 0870 241 0237
Fax: 01283 716158
Email: exhibition@waterways.org.uk
Website: www.waterways.org.uk
Contact: Jerry Sanders
Number of Events: 2
When: Apr/May, Aug
Number of Stands: 60
Public Admission Price: Cavalcade nil. Festival: Adults £7.50, Seniors £6, Children free.
Stand/Space Costs: £17.50 per sq.m. for Cavalcade and £24 per sq.m. for Festival. Extra for tables, power and lighting.
Late Booking Opportunities: Nearly always
Photographs Needed: No
Selection Policy: C – no generators.

JANE MCDOWALL
Culroy Cottage
Glenluce, Newton Stewart
Dumfries & Galloway DG8 0LE
Tel: 01776 702254
Fax: 01581 500327
Mobile: 07702 488179
Email: culroy@btinternet.com
Website: www.stranraershow.com + www.castlekennedydriving.com + www.scotplough.co.uk
Contact: Jane McDowall
Number of Events: 3
When: July, Aug, Oct
Number of Stands: 20-60
Public Admission Price: Adults £5, Seniors £4, 5-14s £2, under-5s free, Family £15.
Stand/Space Costs: £15 per day; £5 extra for electricity.
Late Booking Opportunities: Sometimes
Photographs Needed: No
Selection Policy: C

JOHN & JENNIFER FORD
October Hill
Upper Longdon
Rugeley
Staffs WS15 1QB
Tel: 01543 491000
Email: j.ford@lace-making.com
Website: www.lace-making.com
Contact: Jennifer Ford
Number of Events: 2
When: Mar, Dec
Number of Stands: NEC 90, Harrogate 36
Stand/Space Costs: On application.
Late Booking Opportunities: Sometimes
Photographs Needed: Yes
Selection Policy: B – exhibitors must have own third party liability insurance.

JOUST
271 Royal College Street
London NW1 9LU
Tel: 020 7482 0115
Fax: 020 7267 1169
Email: info@joust.info
Website: www.joust.info
Contact: David Crompton
Number of Events: 2
When: July
Number of Stands: 100
Public Admission Price: Adults £12, Seniors £11, Children £5, under-4s free, Family £30.
Stand/Space Costs: £120 per event; discount for booking both weekends (consecutive). Extra £30 for power, £6.50 for table and £2.50 for chair.
Late Booking Opportunities: Rare
Photographs Needed: No
Selection Policy: B

K.C. CRAFT SHOWS
Acer House
109B Tilkey Road
Coggeshall
Essex
CO6 1QN
Tel/Fax: 01376 561459
Contact: Carole Mills
Number of Events: 7
When: Apr, May, June, Aug, Oct, Nov, Dec
Number of Stands: 35-45
Public Admission Price: Adults £1.50, under-15s free.
Stand/Space Costs: From £38 up to £68 per event; no extras.
Late Booking Opportunities: Sometimes
Photographs Needed: Yes
Selection Policy: C – but British made crafts only, good quality and attractively displayed.

KEIGHLEY & DISTRICT AGRICULTURAL SHOW
c/o Lynden Barn
Sawood Lane
Oxenhope
nr Keighley
West Yorks BD22 9SP
Tel: 01535 643206
Contact: Mrs I Spencer
Number of Events: 1
When: Sept
Number of Stands: 10-15
Public Admission Price: Adults £6, Seniors/under-15s/Concessions £3, Family £12.
Stand/Space Costs: £40 for the event. Extra £5 for 6ft table and £1 for chair.
Late Booking Opportunities: Nearly always
Photographs Needed: No
Selection Policy: B/C

KENILWORTH & DISTRICT AGRICULTURAL SOCIETY
12 High Street
Warwick
Warks
CV34 4AP
Tel: 01926 402222
Fax: 01926 401464
Mobile: 07703 352089
Email: dbussey@margetts.co.uk
Website: www.kenilworthshow.org.uk
Contact: David Bussey
Number of Events: 1
When: June
Number of Stands: Up to 50
Public Admission Price: Adults £6, under-16s £3.50.
Stand/Space Costs: Outside open ground cost is £80 for 6m by 6m rising to £333 for 12m by 24m. Inside covered shopping cost is £50 for 2m by 2m space rising to £130 for 2m by 6m. Extra £20 for generators.
Late Booking Opportunities: Sometimes
Photographs Needed: No
Selection Policy: C

KENT & SUSSEX BORDER LIONS
Easter Cottage
Three Leg Cross
Ticehurst
East Sussex
TN5 7HL
Tel: 01580 200672
Fax: 01580 200690
Contact: David Francis
Number of Events: 1
When: June
Number of Stands: 14 inside; many outside
Public Admission Price: £5 per car.
Stand/Space Costs: Approx £3.75 per ft of frontage by 24ft depth outside; more charged inside (all inclusive).
Late Booking Opportunities: Sometimes
Photographs Needed: No
Selection Policy: C/D – garden and hand-made products preferred.

KESWICK SHOW
Gateway
The Craggs
Bothel
Wigton
Cumbria CA7 2JN
Tel/Fax: 01697 323418
Contact: Mrs J Hildreth
Number of Events: 1
When: Aug
Number of Stands: 28
Public Admission Price: Adults £4.50, Seniors £3, 11-16s £1.
Stand/Space Costs: £8 per yard; no extras.
Late Booking Opportunities: Rare
Photographs Needed: No
Selection Policy: A

KEVIN MURPHY CRAFT FAIRS
Chapel Farm
St John's Chapel
Eastacombe
Barnstaple
Devon EX31 3PB
Tel/Fax: 01271 343160
Mobile: 07774 904027
Email: info@kevinmurphycraftfairs.co.uk
Website: www.kevinmurphycraftfairs.co.uk
Contact: Kevin Murphy
Number of Events: 30
When: Mar, May, Aug, Sept, Oct, Nov, Dec
Number of Stands: 30-90
Public Admission Price: Adults £1, Concessions 80p, under-14s free.
Stand/Space Costs: £36 per day; no extras.
Late Booking Opportunities: Sometimes
Photographs Needed: Yes
Selection Policy: B – British made crafts only.

KILDALE AGRICULTURAL & HORTICULTURAL SHOW SOCIETY
c/o The Cottage
Dundale Beck Farm
Kildale
Whitby
North Yorks YO21 2RL
Tel: 01642 724214
Contact: Alison Dent
Number of Events: 1
When: Sept
Number of Stands: 20
Public Admission Price: Adults £2.50, Seniors/Concessions/Children £1.
Stand/Space Costs: £18; no extras.
Late Booking Opportunities: Sometimes
Photographs Needed: No
Selection Policy: C

KINGFISHER CRAFT MARQUEE MANAGEMENT
6 Hill Croft
Thornton
Bradford
West Yorks BD13 3QR
Tel/Fax: 01274 833180
Mobile: 07778 473404
Email: davetheleather@aol.com
Contact: Dave Harrison
Number of Events: 10
When: May, July, Aug, Sept
Number of Stands: 40
Public Admission Price: Main show entry fees may apply, but none to marquees.
Stand/Space Costs: Ranges from £45 to £70 per event; no extras. Extra space offered free to demonstrators.
Late Booking Opportunities: Sometimes
Photographs Needed: No
Selection Policy: C

KINGFISHER PROMOTIONS
6 School Lane
Wilburton
Cambs CB6 3RW
Tel/Fax: 01353 740725
Email: anita.foster@talk21.com
Contact: Anita or Bob Foster
Number of Events: 14
When: All months except Jan and June
Number of Stands: 40+
Late Booking Opportunities: Sometimes
Photographs Needed: Yes
Selection Policy: B

KINGSBRIDGE AGRICULTURAL & HORTICULTURAL SHOW
The Crescent
East Allington
Totnes
Devon TQ9 7RA
Tel/Fax: 01548 521406
Website: www.kingsbridgeshow.co.uk
Contact: Jacqueline Broad
Number of Events: 1
When: Sept
Public Admission Price: Adults £5, under-16s £2.
Stand/Space Costs: £30 per 10ft including one 6ft table for the event. Extra tables

(cont)

charged at £5.
Late Booking Opportunities: Sometimes
Photographs Needed: No
Selection Policy: C

KINGSTON UPON HULL CITY COUNCIL
Hull Events, 2nd Floor
79 Ferensway
Hull
East Yorks
Tel: 01482 615624
Fax: 01482 615673
Email: michelle.kidd@hullcc.gov.uk
Website: www.hullcc.gov.uk
Contact: Michelle Kidd
Number of Events: 1
When: June
Number of Stands: 20
Stand/Space Costs: On application
Late Booking Opportunities: Sometimes
Photographs Needed: No
Selection Policy: C

LAKELAND COUNTRY FAIR
c/o Downfield House
Leece
Ulverston
Cumbria LA12 0RD
Tel: 01229 837680
Email: aboltpv@aol.com
Website: www.lakelandcountryfair.co.uk
Number of Events: 1
When: Aug
Number of Stands: 30-40
Public Admission Price: Adults £4, Children £2.
Stand/Space Costs: £25 for 10ft frontage, £35 for 20ft, £45 for 30ft and £55 for 40ft (max). Tables charged extra at £5; there is no electricity/lighting on site.
Late Booking Opportunities: Sometimes
Photographs Needed: No
Selection Policy: C

LAMPORT ENTERPRISES LTD
Lamport Hall
Lamport
Northants NN6 9HD
Tel: 01604 686272
Fax: 01604 686224
Email: admin@lamporthall.co.uk
Website: www.lamporthall.co.uk
Contact: Kate Worrall
Number of Events: 2
When: May, Oct
Number of Stands: Approx 80
Public Admission Price: Adults £3-£6, Seniors £2.50-£3 (£4-£5 in May), 11-16s £2-£3, under-11s free.
Stand/Space Costs: From £80 to £140 per day (all inc except lighting and electrical leads). £10 off for demonstrators.
Late Booking Opportunities: Sometimes
Photographs Needed: Yes
Selection Policy: C/D – all electrics brought in must be PAT tested.

LANCHESTER AGRICULTURAL SOCIETY
Acorn Cottage
Cornsay Colliery
Co Durham DH7 9BN
Tel: 0191 373 4565
Fax: 0191 373 7321
Email: ccarolcliffe@aol.com
Contact: Carol Cliffe
Number of Events: 1
When: July
Number of Stands: 60
Public Admission Price: Adults £3, Children/Seniors/Concessions £2.
Stand/Space Costs: £30 for the two days; no extras.
Late Booking Opportunities: Sometimes
Photographs Needed: No
Selection Policy: C/D

LANDMARK ARTS CENTRE
Ferry Road
Teddington
Middx TW11 9NN
Tel: 020 8977 7558
Fax: 020 8977 4830
Email: landmarkartfairs@aol.com
Website: www.landmarkartscentre.org
Contact: Barbara Robertson or Lorna Henderson
Number of Events: 4
When: Mar, June, Oct, Nov
Number of Stands: 70+
Public Admission Price: Adults £4, Seniors/Concessions £2, under-14s free.
Stand/Space Costs: From £100 to £300 per event; extra for additional power points. Discount offered for demonstrators.
Late Booking Opportunities: Rare
Photographs Needed: Yes
Selection Policy: A – open to individual

designers/artists in the UK and beyond; no groups or galleries.

LAUDERDALE ARTS & CRAFTS
22A Calabria Road
London N5 1JA
Tel: 020 7354 0140
Mobile: 07711 419788
Website:
www.london-northwest.com/lauderdalearts/
Contact: Elizabeth Nelson
Number of Events: 12
When: Feb-Dec
Number of Stands: 30-70 (max at Xmas)
Public Admission Price: Voluntary donation (guide, Adults £1).
Stand/Space Costs: Ranges from £30 to £48 for the day (depending on time of year and part of building); no extras. 40% discount for demonstrators.
Late Booking Opportunities: Nearly always
Photographs Needed: Yes
Selection Policy: B/C – high quality is the overriding factor.

LEICESTERSHIRE AGRICULTURAL SOCIETY
Dishley Grange Farm
Derby Road
Loughborough
Leics LE11 5SF
Tel: 01509 646786
Fax: 01509 646787
Email: info@leicestershireshow.co.uk
Website: www.leicestershireshow.co.uk
Contact: Andy Hardy-Smith or Michelle Davies
Number of Events: 1
When: May
Number of Stands: Averages 300
Public Admission Price: Adults £7, Seniors/Concessions/Children £5,Family £20.
Stand/Space Costs: £105 for 10ft by 10ft in the marquee for the event; otherwise £12 per sq.ft.
Late Booking Opportunities: Sometimes
Photographs Needed: No
Selection Policy: C – clashes with existing products avoided.

LEUKAEMIA RESEARCH FUND - GWENT BRANCH
8 Cwm Cwddy Drive
Bassaleg
Newport NP10 8JA
Tel: 01633 895145
Contact: Bruce or Mandy Womack
Number of Events: 1
When: Sept
Number of Stands: 20-30
Public Admission Price: Adults £5, Seniors £3, Children £2, Family £12.
Stand/Space Costs: £4 per ft frontage (min 5ft) for the event; extra £2.50 for electricity, £4 for 6ft table and £6 for 10ft table.
Late Booking Opportunities: Sometimes
Photographs Needed: No
Selection Policy: C – British made crafts only.

LICHFIELD MEDIEVAL MARKET
7 The Close
Lichfield
Staffs WS13 7LD
Tel: 01543 306275
Fax: 01543 306274
Email: megan.barr@lichfield-arts.org.uk
Website: www.lichfieldfestival.org
Contact: Megan Barr
Number of Events: 1
When: July
Number of Stands: 140
Public Admission Price: Nil
Stand/Space Costs: £50 for 8ft for the event. Extra £10 for every additional 1ft frontage. Discount available for demonstrators, by negotiation.
Late Booking Opportunities: Sometimes
Photographs Needed: No
Selection Policy: C/D – arrival times given must be adhered to. Payment must be received before day of event.

LISKEARD STEAM & VINTAGE CLUB
'Wychecroft'
Gypsy Lane, Liskeard
Cornwall PL14 4HQ
Tel: 01579 342148 (day) or 01579 344126 (evenings).
Fax: 01579 342148
Contact: Mrs S M Matthews
Number of Events: 1
When: July
Public Admission Price: Show admission charge; no charge to marquee.
Stand/Space Costs: £5 per ft frontage in the large marquee for the 3-day fair; no extras
Late Booking Opportunities: Sometimes
Photographs Needed: No
Selection Policy: B

LIVING CRAFTS LTD
66 Penny Street
Portsmouth
Hants PO1 2NL
Tel/Fax: 023 9286 3871
Email: admin@livingcrafts.co.uk
Website: www.livingcrafts.co.uk
Number of Events: 2
When: May, Nov
Number of Stands: 400 (May), 60 (Nov)
Stand/Space Costs: On application
Late Booking Opportunities: Rare
Photographs Needed: Yes
Selection Policy: A - British made crafts only.

LIVING HERITAGE CRAFT SHOWS
PO Box 36
Uttoxeter
Staffs ST14 8PY
Tel: 01283 820548
Fax: 01283 821200
Email: marge@livingheritage.fsnet.co.uk
Website: www.craft-show.co.uk
Contact: Marge Needham
Number of Events: Approx 40
When: Apr-Dec

LLANDUDNO TRANSPORT FESTIVAL
48 Church Road
Rhos-on-Sea
Colwyn Bay
Conwy LL28 4YS
Tel/Fax: 01492 545053
Contact: Sandra Ricketts
Number of Events: 1
When: Apr/May
Number of Stands: 100
Public Admission Price: Adults £4, Seniors £3, Children £1.
Stand/Space Costs: £2 per ft per day; no extras. Book two days, third day free.
Late Booking Opportunities: Sometimes
Photographs Needed: No
Selection Policy: D

LLANIDLOES ARTS & CRAFTS FAIRS
Bryn Afon
Aberhafesp
Newtown
Powys SY16 3HU
Tel/Fax: 01686 688653
Contact: Julie Akehurst
Number of Events: 2
When: Mar, Nov
Number of Stands: 32
Public Admission Price: Nil
Stand/Space Costs: 8ft table in March is £22 and in Nov £25. Half tables available at £11 and £12 respectively. Extra £2 for electricity.
Late Booking Opportunities: Sometimes
Photographs Needed: Yes, if possible.
Selection Policy: A/B - British made crafts only. No packing away before advertised closing time.

LUTON BOROUGH COUNCIL - ARTS UNIT
65-67 Bute Street
Luton
Beds LU1 2EY
Tel: 01582 878100
Fax: 01582 878109
Email: artsunit@luton.gov.uk
Website: www.luton.gov.uk
Contact: Janet Parker
Number of Events: 2-3
When: May, Sept
Number of Stands: Approx 25
Public Admission Price: Usually nil
Stand/Space Costs: Approx £25 per event, usually for open air space with market type stall; no extras.
Late Booking Opportunities: Sometimes
Photographs Needed: No
Selection Policy: C

LUTON BOROUGH COUNCIL
Town Hall
George Street, Luton
Beds LU1 2BQ
Tel: 01582 546416
Fax: 01582 547058
Email: irelandt@luton.gov.uk
Website: www.luton.gov.uk
Contact: Tony Ireland
Number of Events: 5
When: Mar, Apr, May, Nov
Number of Stands: Unlimited
Public Admission Price: Nil
Stand/Space Costs: £25 per day; no extras.
Late Booking Opportunities: Sometimes
Selection Policy: D

MABE SHINDIG
c/o Eathorne Manor
Constantine

Falmouth
Cornwall TR11 5PJ
Tel: 01326 340754
Email: david_charles@compuserve.com
Contact: Mrs P Charles
Number of Events: 1
Number of Stands: 8-12
Public Admission Price: Adults £4, Seniors £3, under-16s £2, Family £10 (tbc).
Stand/Space Costs: £25 per 6ft table plus 2ft; no extras.
Late Booking Opportunities: Sometimes
Photographs Needed: No
Selection Policy: B – British made crafts only.

MACCLESFIELD BOROUGH COUNCIL
Community Directorate
Town Hall
Macclesfield
Cheshire SK10 1EA
Tel: 01625 504508
Fax: 01625 504515
Mobile: 07764 778951
Email: b.north@macclesfield.gov.uk
Website: www.macclesfield.gov.uk
Contact: Bill North or Roy Lowndes
Number of Events: 1
When: Aug
Number of Stands: 100
Public Admission Price: Nil
Stand/Space Costs: £33.50 per day; tables £25 returnable deposit. Market stall at cost.
Late Booking Opportunities: Rare
Photographs Needed: Yes
Selection Policy: B/C

MACHEN AGRICULTURAL SHOW
Cefn Llwyd Farm
Abertridwr
Caerphilly CF83 4FH
Tel: 029 2083 0278
Mobile: 07811 445284
Contact: Emma Tamplin
Number of Events: 1
When: July
Number of Stands: 25
Public Admission Price: Adults £4, under-14s/Seniors £2, Family £10.
Stand/Space Costs: £20 per 6ft trestle table for the event.
Late Booking Opportunities: Nearly always
Photographs Needed: No
Selection Policy: C

MADE IN THE MARCHES
Englefield
The Cabin
Bishop's Castle
Shropshire SY9 5JG
Tel: 01588 638269
Contact: Patricia Jones
Number of Events: 1
When: Nov
Number of Stands: 30
Stand/Space Costs: £15; no extras.
Late Booking Opportunities: Sometimes
Photographs Needed: No
Selection Policy: C

MALCOLM GROUP EVENTS LTD
36 Acacia Close
Stanmore
Middx HA7 3JR
Tel/Fax: 020 8416 0398
Email: info@mgel.com
Website: www.englandsmedievalfestival.com
Contact: Clive Geisler
Number of Events: 2
When: Aug
Number of Stands: 100+
Public Admission Price: Adults £14, Seniors/Concessions £13, Children £9.
Stand/Space Costs: £175 per event; some extras.
Late Booking Opportunities: Nearly always
Photographs Needed: No
Selection Policy: D – medieval costume required.

MALTON AGRICULTURAL SOCIETY
1 The Shambles Offices
The Cattle Market
Malton
North Yorks YO17 7LZ
Tel: 01653 693382
Fax: 01653 699910
Contact: Mrs J Bird
Number of Events: 1
When: June
Number of Stands: 25
Public Admission Price: Adults £6, under-16s/Seniors £4.
Stand/Space Costs: £30 for the event; no extras.
Late Booking Opportunities: Sometimes
Photographs Needed: No
Selection Policy: B

MARY HOLLAND CRAFT FAIRS LTD
PO Box 43
Abingdon
Oxon
OX14 2EX
Tel/Fax: 01235 521873
Email: paulineburren@maryholland.co.uk
Website: www.maryholland.co.uk
Contact: Pauline Burren
Number of Events: 1
When: Oct
Number of Stands: Up to 150
Public Admission Price: To be confirmed
Stand/Space Costs: From £250; negotiable discount for demonstrators sometimes possible.
Late Booking Opportunities: Some
Photographs Needed: Yes
Selection Policy: A/B – no imports.

MAURTRAID CRAFTSHOWS
202 Buckingham Road
Bletchley
Milton Keynes
Bucks
MK3 5JB
Tel/Fax: 01908 271833
Contact: Susan Preedy
Number of Events: 4
When: Feb, Apr, July, Oct
Number of Stands: 60–100
Public Admission Price: Nil
Stand/Space Costs: On application. Discount for demonstrators to be confirmed.
Late Booking Opportunities: Sometimes
Photographs Needed: Yes
Selection Policy: B – British made crafts only; tidy and smart exhibits. See also section on 'Crafts Selling in Shopping Centres'.

MERIDIENNE EXHIBITIONS LTD
The Fosse
Fosse Way
Radford Semele
Leamington Spa
Warks
CV31 1XN
Tel: 01926 614101
Fax: 01926 614293
Email: info@meridienne.co.uk
Website: www.meridienneexhibitions.co.uk
Number of Events: 6
When: Jan, Apr, Oct, Nov

MID DEVON SHOW
Dudley's Corner
Whitnage
Tiverton
Devon EX16 7DS
Tel: 01392 499036
Fax: 01884 821815
Email: carolyn@middevonshow.fsnet.co.uk
Website: www.middevonshow.co.uk
Contact: Jim Dowling ('phone) or Carolyn Branton (fax/email)
Number of Events: 1
When: July
Number of Stands: 40
Public Admission Price: Adults £8, Seniors £6, under-16s £2.
Stand/Space Costs: On application
Late Booking Opportunities: Rare
Photographs Needed: Yes
Selection Policy: A – British made crafts only.

MIDDLEWICH FOLK & BOAT FESTIVAL
PO Box 141
Winsford
Cheshire CW10 9WB
Tel: 0709 239 0501
Email: stalls@middlewichfestival.org
Website: www.middlewichfestival.org
Contact: Dorothy Basford
Number of Events: 1
When: June
Number of Stands: 40
Public Admission Price: Nil
Stand/Space Costs: On application
Late Booking Opportunities: Sometimes; check for cancellations
Photographs Needed: No
Selection Policy: B/C

MID SHROPSHIRE VINTAGE CLUB LTD
c/o Woodville
Pontesford
Shrewsbury
Shropshire SY5 0UF
Tel/Fax: 01743 790446
Email: badgerss@msn.com
Website: www.msvintageclub.org.uk
Number of Events: 1
When: June
Number of Stands: 70
Public Admission Price: Adults £6, Seniors £5, Children £2.
Stand/Space Costs: One table inside Pavilion for the two days costs £20 with two tables

costing £40; no extras. Outside in own tent at £30 for first 10ft and then £2 per ft.
Late Booking Opportunities: Sometimes
Photographs Needed: No
Selection Policy: B/C – all exhibitors must hold public liability insurance.

MILLENNIUM CRAFTS & GIFTS
23 Wood Road
Ashurst
Southampton
Hants SO40 7BD
Tel: 023 8029 2907
Mobile: 07887 731155
Email: daverobertyoung@aol.com
Contact: Mrs June Young
Number of Events: 36
When: Feb-Dec
Number of Stands: Approx 38
Public Admission Price: 40p generally.
Stand/Space Costs: £13 per day for 6ft and £24 for 12ft; no extras.
Late Booking Opportunities: Sometimes
Photographs Needed: No
Selection Policy: B/C

MINIATURA
41 Eastbourne Avenue
Birmingham B34 6AR
Tel/Fax: 0121 783 9922
Email: office@miniatura.co.uk
Website: www.miniatura.co.uk
Contact: Andy Hopwood
Number of Events: 5
When: Mar, Apr, June, Sept
Number of Stands: 150-300
Public Admission Price: Varies
Stand/Space Costs: On application
Late Booking Opportunities: Rare
Photographs Needed: Yes
Selection Policy: B – these are for one-twelfth and related scale crafts for dolls houses, except bears and dolls events where products are all sizes.

MITCHAM CARNIVAL
Mitcham Carnival Office
Civic Centre
London Road
Morden
Surrey SM4 5DX
Tel: 020 8545 4888
Fax: 020 8545 3242
Email: mitcham.carnival@merton.gov.uk
Website:
www.merton.gov.uk/mitchamcarnival/
Contact: Marie McCann
Number of Events: 1
When: June
Number of Stands: 300
Public Admission Price: Nil
Stand/Space Costs: £40 for the event for 12ft by 12ft pitch; £30 extra per 12ft additional frontage. No extras.
Late Booking Opportunities: Nearly always
Photographs Needed: No
Selection Policy: D

MONYMUSK ARTS TRUST
Monymusk, by Inverurie
Aberdeenshire AB51 7HJ
Tel: 01467 651220
Fax: 01467 651250
Website: www.artstrust.org
Contact: Mrs Fairly Taylor
Number of Events: 2
When: May to Sept; Nov
Number of Stands: Approx 40
Public Admission Price: Nil
Stand/Space Costs: For Craft Sale, either 5 days help to man the centre or £50 for the 5 months.
Late Booking Opportunities: Sometimes
Photographs Needed: Sometimes
Selection Policy: A/B – all crafts must be hand-made.

MOORGREEN COUNTRY SHOW
Chapter Six
Hall Lane
Old Brinsley
Notts NG16 5AN
Tel: 01773 711767
Email: moorgreenshow@btopenworld.com
Website: www.moorgreenshow.co.uk
Number of Events: 1
When: Aug
Number of Stands: 120
Public Admission Price: Adults £7, Seniors £5, under-15s free.
Late Booking Opportunities: Nearly always
Photographs Needed: No

MOTOR CARAVAN JAMBOREE
51 Abbey Road
Belvedere
Kent
DA17 5DG

(cont)

Tel: 020 8311 3500
Fax: 020 8311 2607
Email: clairedoman@orange.net
Website: www.motorcaravanjamboree.com
Contact: Laura Doman
Number of Events: 1
When: May
Number of Stands: 50+
Public Admission Price: Day visitors free.
Stand/Space Costs: £195 for 3m by 3m inside space; lighting/power extra.
Late Booking Opportunities: Sometimes
Photographs Needed: No
Selection Policy: C/D

MOULTON VILLAGE FESTIVAL
8 Chater Street
Moulton
Northants NN3 7UD
Tel: 01604 646818
Fax: 01604 643984
Email: barrycare@tiscali.co.uk
Contact: Barry Care
Number of Events: 1
When: May
Number of Stands: 50-60
Public Admission Price: Nil
Stand/Space Costs: £30 for the one day for 6ft of space; no extras.
Late Booking Opportunities: Some
Photographs Needed: No
Selection Policy: D

MUNCASTER COUNTRY FAIR
Riverholme
Holmrook
Cumbria CA19 1UH
Tel: 01946 724606
Contact: Jan Mark
Number of Events: 1
When: Aug
Number of Stands: Approx 40-50
Public Admission Price: Flat rate of £3.
Stand/Space Costs: £10 per sq.m.; no extras.
Late Booking Opportunities: Nearly always
Photographs Needed: No
Selection Policy: D

NATIONAL TRUST – BUCKLAND ABBEY
Buckland Abbey
Yelverton
Devon PL20 6EY
Tel: 01822 853607
Fax: 01822 855448
Email: bucklandabbey@nationaltrust.org.uk
Website: www.nationaltrust.org.uk/regions/devoncornwall
Number of Events: 1
When: Nov
Number of Stands: 20-25
Public Admission Price: Nil
Stand/Space Costs: £50 for the event; no extras.
Late Booking Opportunities: Sometimes
Photographs Needed: Yes
Selection Policy: B – British made crafts only.

NATIONAL TRUST – CLUMBER PARK
The Estate Office
Clumber Park
Worksop
Notts S80 3AZ
Tel: 01909 476592
Fax: 01909 500721
Email: carol.white@nationaltrust.org.uk
Website: www.nationaltrust.org.uk
Contact: Carol White
Number of Events: 2
When: June, Dec
Number of Stands: 26
Public Admission Price: Adults £5, Children £3, under-5s free, Family £12.
Stand/Space Costs: £38 per event; no extras. 10% discount for demonstrators.
Late Booking Opportunities: Rare
Photographs Needed: Yes
Selection Policy: A/B – British made crafts only. No vehicle movement during event hours.

NATIONAL TRUST – FLORENCE COURT
Florence Court
Enniskillen
Co Fermanagh BT92 1DB
Tel: 028 6634 8249
Fax: 028 6634 8873
Email: florencecourt@nationaltrust.org.uk
Website: www.ntni.org.uk
Contact: Jim Chestnutt
Number of Events: 2
When: May, Oct
Number of Stands: 25
Stand/Space Costs: On application
Late Booking Opportunities: Sometimes
Photographs Needed: No
Selection Policy: C

NATIONAL TRUST – SUTTON HOUSE
2 & 4 Homerton High Street
London
E9 6JQ
Tel: 020 8525 9055
Fax: 020 8525 9051
Email: suttonhouse@nationaltrust.org.uk
Website: www.nationaltrust.org.uk
Contact: Lucy Sage
Number of Events: 2
When: May, Dec
Number of Stands: 20-30
Public Admission Price: Adults £2, under-16s free.
Stand/Space Costs: £60 for one day or £90 for two days; no extras.
Late Booking Opportunities: Rare
Photographs Needed: Yes
Selection Policy: B

NATIONAL TRUST – THE ARGORY
Derrycaw Road
Moy
Co Tyrone
BT71 6NA
Tel: 028 8778 4753
Fax: 028 8778 9598
Email: argory@nationaltrust.org.uk
Website: www.ntni.org.uk/argory
Contact: Derek Forshaw
Number of Events: 3
When: Mar, Aug, Dec
Number of Stands: 35 for 2 events, 56 the third.
Public Admission Price: Adults £3.50, Children £1.50.
Stand/Space Costs: £35 per day; no extras.
Late Booking Opportunities: Rare
Selection Policy: C

NATIONAL TRUST – WIMPOLE HALL
Arrington
nr Royston
Cambs
SG8 0BW
Tel: 01223 206000
Fax: 01223 207838
Email: wimpolehall@nationaltrust.org.uk
Website: www.wimpole.org.uk
Number of Events: 1
When: Nov
Public Admission Price: Adults £2.50.
Late Booking Opportunities: Rare
Selection Policy: B – British made crafts only.

NATIONWIDE EXHIBITIONS (UK) LTD
PO Box 20, Fishponds
Bristol BS16 5QU
Tel: 0117 907 1000
Fax: 0117 907 1001
Email: user@nwe.co.uk
Website: www.nwe.co.uk
Contact: Mrs Nadine Lingard
Number of Events: 8
When: Jan, Feb, Apr, Sept/Oct
Number of Stands: 100-200
Public Admission Price: Adults £6, Seniors/Concessions £5, under-16s free.
Stand/Space Costs: From £90 to £115 per sq.m. Extra for furniture and electrics. 10% discount for demonstrators.
Late Booking Opportunities: Sometimes
Photographs Needed: No
Selection Policy: C/D

NELTON EXHIBITIONS LTD
The Old Sun
Crete Hall Road
Northfleet
Kent DA11 9AA
Tel: 01474 536535
Fax: 01474 536552
Mobile: 07946 855445
Email: tc@nelton.co.uk
Website: www.nelton.com
Contact: Tony Cox
Number of Events: 1
When: Aug
Number of Stands: 50
Public Admission Price: Adults £6, Seniors/Concessions £5, 3-15s £3.50, Family £15.
Stand/Space Costs: From £130 to £150 for the event; extra for power, lighting and furniture. 10% discount for demonstrators.
Late Booking Opportunities: Sometimes
Photographs Needed: No
Selection Policy: C

NETLEY MARSH STEAM & CRAFT SHOW LTD
38 Water Lane
Totton
Southampton
Hants SO40 3DN
Tel: 023 8086 7882
Fax: 023 8086 4000
Email: tonygreenham@supanet.com
Website:
www.netleymarshsteamandcraftshow.org

Contact: Tony or Pat Greenham
Number of Events: 1
When: July
Number of Stands: 75
Public Admission Price: Adults £9, Seniors/under-16s £5, Family £22.
Stand/Space Costs: £70 for the event; electricity charged extra.
Late Booking Opportunities: Nearly always
Photographs Needed: No
Selection Policy: B

NEW FOREST AGRICULTURAL SHOW SOCIETY
The Showground
New Park
Brockenhurst
Hants SO42 7QH
Tel: 01590 622400
Fax: 01590 622637
Email: info@newforestshow.co.uk
Website: www.newforestshow.co.uk
Number of Events: 1
When: July
Number of Stands: 90
Stand/Space Costs: £170 for the event; extra £6 for table and £65 for electricity. Free of charge areas outside available for demonstrators.
Late Booking Opportunities: Rare
Photographs Needed: Yes
Selection Policy: A/B – British made crafts only, made by exhibitors themselves.

NEWTON CARNIVAL TEAM
Briar House
55 Main Street
Newton
Alfreton
Derbys DE55 5TE
Tel: 01773 779237
Fax: 01623 824255
Email: lisa.dexter@virgin.net
Contact: Mrs Lisa Bullock
Number of Events: 4
When: July, Nov
Number of Stands: 20-60
Public Admission Price: Nil
Stand/Space Costs: £15 per event; no extras.
Late Booking Opportunities: Sometimes
Photographs Needed: No
Selection Policy: C – no pressure selling via demonstrators.

NORFOLK EVENTS
26 Elm Grove
Garboldisham
Diss
Norfolk
IP22 2RY
Tel: 01953 681715
Email: rholland@norfolkevents.co.uk
Website: www.norfolkevents.co.uk
Contact: Rita Holland
Number of Events: 40
When: All months except Dec
Number of Stands: 20
Public Admission Price: Nil
Stand/Space Costs: £35 per day; no extras. Special rates for block booking.
Late Booking Opportunities: Sometimes
Photographs Needed: Yes
Selection Policy: B – British made crafts only.

NORTH ANTRIM AGRICULTURAL ASSOCIATION LTD
58 Carrowreagh Road
Armoy
Ballymoney
Co Antrim
BT53 8RS
Tel: 028 2075 1327
Fax: 028 2075 1162
Contact: Mrs Anne Morrison
Number of Events: 1
When: June
Number of Stands: Unlimited
Public Admission Price: Adults £4, Children £2.
Stand/Space Costs: £35 for the event; no extras.
Late Booking Opportunities: Nearly always
Photographs Needed: No
Selection Policy: C

NORTH EAST HANTS AGRICULTURAL ASSOCIATION
c/o 33 Highland Road
Emsworth
Hants
PO10 7JL
Tel: 01243 430926
Fax: 01243 430806
Email: jan@janbutler.plus.com
Website: www.altonshow.info
Contact: Mrs J M Butler
Number of Events: 1
When: July

Number of Stands: 40
Public Admission Price: Adults £6, under-15s/Seniors/Concessions £4, Family £15.
Stand/Space Costs: £30 for 6ft frontage in Craft Marquee; £54 for 12ft. Additional frontage at £4 per ft. Larger sites outside (trade) priced at £90 for 20ft frontage by 30ft depth. Some 10ft plots at £45.50. Extra £10 for electricity.
Late Booking Opportunities: Nearly always
Photographs Needed: No
Selection Policy: A/B – strictly maker only crafts in the Craft Marquee, with the aim of highlighting traditional British crafts. There is also a Countryside Area where demonstrations of traditional rural crafts such as thatching, besom broom making and trug making are featured. Importers of crafts can request outside trade stand positioned near to Craft Marquee.

NORTHERN EXHIBITIONS
Clent House
Back Lane
Hunsingore
Wetherby
West Yorks
LS22 5JB
Tel/Fax: 01423 359259
Number of Events: 2
When: Jan
Public Admission Price: N/A – Trade Only Events.
Stand/Space Costs: On application (trade)

NORTH LONSDALE AGRICULTURAL SOCIETY
c/o 16 Oakwood Drive
Ulverston
Cumbria
LA12 9HH
Tel: 01229 585832
Email: nla.show@virgin.net
Contact: Mrs Sandra Wells
Number of Events: 1
When: July
Number of Stands: Approx 100
Stand/Space Costs: £10 per sq.m. inside or £6.50 per sq.m. outside; 8ft tables charged £3 extra.
Late Booking Opportunities: Nearly always
Photographs Needed: No, but specific details requested with booking form.
Selection Policy: C

NORTH OF ENGLAND ENTERPRISES LTD
4A South Park Road
Harrogate
North Yorks HG1 5QU
Tel: 01423 561049
Fax: 01423 536880
Email: info@flowershow.org.uk
Website: www.flowershow.org.uk
Contact: Roger Brownbridge
Number of Events: 2
When: Apr/May, Sept
Number of Stands: 50-60
Public Admission Price: Adults £9-£13, under-16s free.
Stand/Space Costs: £250 for 2.4m by 1.8m; inc electricity supply and two trestle tables. Additional space available at £25 per 0.3m. Additional space available for demonstrating free of charge up to 0.9m.
Late Booking Opportunities: Sometimes
Photographs Needed: Yes
Selection Policy: A/B – British made crafts only.

NORTH SOMERSET SHOW
c/o Hippisley's Farm
Wick St Lawrence
Weston-super-Mare
North Somerset BS22 7YG
Tel: 0845 634 2464
Fax: 01934 514764
Email: office@nsas.org.uk
Website: www.nsas.org.uk
Contact: Katie Hutchins
Number of Events: 1
When: May
Number of Stands: 30
Late Booking Opportunities: Rare
Photographs Needed: No
Selection Policy: B/C – local craft exhibitors preferred.

NORTHUMBERLAND COUNTY SHOW
PO Box 17
Brampton
Cumbria CA8 7GA
Tel: 01697 747848
Fax: 01697 747847
Email: admin@northcountyshow.co.uk
Website: www.northcountyshow.co.uk
Contact: Kathleen Walton
Number of Events: 1
When: May
Number of Stands: 30

(cont)

Public Admission Price: Adults £8, Seniors £5, 4-16s £2.
Stand/Space Costs: £42 for 6ft or £73.50 for 12ft for the event; extra £5.25 for table and £90 for electricity.
Late Booking Opportunities: Rare
Photographs Needed: Yes
Selection Policy: B/C

NORTH WEST CRAFT & GIFT FAIRS
Primrose Cottage
Howards Lane, Eccleston
St Helens WA10 5QD
Tel/Fax: 01744 750606
Mobile: 07966 499748
Email: sandracca@aol.com
Website: www.creativecrafts-online.co.uk
Contact: Sandra Mather
Number of Events: 8
When: Mar, Apr/May, June, Oct, Nov, Dec
Number of Stands: 100-200
Public Admission Price: Adults £2, under-16s free.
Stand/Space Costs: £40 per day. Small extra charge for power.
Late Booking Opportunities: Sometimes
Photographs Needed: No
Selection Policy: D – although open events, the organiser is still looking for quality products.

OAKLEIGH CRAFT FAIRS
Old Tithe Hall
Start Hill
Bishop's Stortford
Herts CM22 7TF
Tel: 01279 871110
Fax: 01279 870844
Email: olltd@aol.com
Number of Events: 25
When: Mar-Sept
Number of Stands: 30-150
Public Admission Price: From 50p to £4.
Stand/Space Costs: Ranges from £32 up to £145 per event. Additional space given free to demonstrators.
Late Booking Opportunities: Nearly always
Photographs Needed: No
Selection Policy: C

OKEHAMPTON AGRICULTURAL SHOW
Forge House
Pool Hill
Bridestowe
Devon EX20 4EW
Tel: 01837 861536
Number of Events: 1
When: Aug
Number of Stands: 35-40
Public Admission Price: Adults £6, Children £4, Family £15.
Stand/Space Costs: £28 for the event; extra for tables/chairs.
Late Booking Opportunities: Some
Photographs Needed: No
Selection Policy: B/C – British made crafts only.

ORCHARD EVENTS LTD
Pond House
1 Priory Road
Kew Green
Richmond
Surrey TW9 3DQ
Tel: 020 8332 9595
Fax: 020 8332 1444
Mobile: 07810 222444
Email: orchardevents01@aol.com
Website: www.festivegiftfair.co.uk
Contact: Nicky Stephenson
Number of Events: 1
When: Nov
Number of Stands: 350
Public Admission Price: Details available from Ticket Hotline on 0121 767 4151.
Stand/Space Costs: £222 per sq.m.; extra for power.
Late Booking Opportunities: Sometimes
Photographs Needed: Yes
Selection Policy: C

OVINGHAM GOOSE FAIR
c/o 12 Horsley Road
Ovingham
Northumberland NE42 6AL
Tel: 01661 832460
Email: goosefair@hotmail.com
Number of Events: 2
When: June, Dec
Number of Stands: 10-20
Public Admission Price: Adults £1, under-16s/Concessions 50p.
Stand/Space Costs: From £6 to £15 per day; no extras.
Late Booking Opportunities: Sometimes
Photographs Needed: No
Selection Policy: C

PEEBLESSHIRE AGRICULTURAL SOCIETY
c/o Easter Happrew
Stobo
Peebles
EH45 8NT
Tel: 01721 760266
Email: campbelljacqui@hotmail.com
Contact: Jacqui Campbell
Number of Events: 1
When: Aug
Number of Stands: 30-40
Stand/Space Costs: On application
Late Booking Opportunities: Sometimes
Photographs Needed: No
Selection Policy: B

PEMBROKESHIRE CRAFT MAKERS
c/o Waterfront Gallery
The Old Sail Loft
The Docks
Milford Haven
Pembrokeshire
SA73 3AF
Tel: 01646 699556
Email: julie.randell@btopenworld.com
Website:
www.pembrokeshirecraftmakers.co.uk
Number of Events: 15
When: Apr to Oct + Dec
These are events which only showcase the group's own members, i.e. crafts made in Pembrokeshire. Contact David Randell (above contact details) for details of membership. Shows take place in Laugharne, Manorbier, Newport, St David's, Dale, Narberth and other venues. See also in the guilds division of the Representative Bodies section of this book.

PENISTONE AGRICULTURAL SOCIETY
Huthwaite Bank
Old Mill Lane
Thurgoland
Sheffield S35 7EG
Tel: 0114 288 7816
Contact: Mrs D Clegg
Number of Events: 1
When: Sept
Number of Stands: 60
Stand/Space Costs: On application.
Late Booking Opportunities: Rare
Photographs Needed: No
Selection Policy: B/C

PENNY FARTHING CRAFT FAIRS
'Ridgeway'
Maldon Road
Steeple
Essex CM0 7RT
Tel/Fax: 01621 773403
Mobile: 07808 422406
Contact: Richard Berry
Number of Events: 10
When: Apr, June, Oct, Nov
Number of Stands: 45-130
Public Admission Price: Adults from £1.50 to £2.50, under-14s free.
Stand/Space Costs: From £38 to £45 or £65 to £80 per event; no extras. Free space available for demonstrators.
Late Booking Opportunities: Sometimes
Photographs Needed: Yes
Selection Policy: B – with some limited exceptions, British made crafts only.

PENSTHORPE
Fakenham Road
Fakenham
Norfolk NR21 0LN
Tel: 01328 851465
Fax: 01328 855905
Email: info@pensthorpe.com
Website: www.pensthorpe.com
Contact: Brigid Harrison
Number of Events: 2
When: Mar, June
Public Admission Price: Adults £2.75, Children £1.50.
Stand/Space Costs: The stands are free of charge and Pensthorpe levy a commission on pieces sold.
Late Booking Opportunities: Sometimes
Photographs Needed: Yes
Selection Policy: A – for the March event, must be wildlife carvings or sculptures.

PERTHSHIRE AGRICULTURAL SOCIETY
26 York Place
Perth PH2 8EH
Tel: 01738 623780
Fax: 01738 621206
Mobile: 07834 980073
Email: secretary@perthshow.co.uk
Website: www.perthshow.co.uk
Contact: Neil Forbes
Number of Events: 1
When: Aug
Number of Stands: 40

(cont)

Public Admission Price: TBC
Stand/Space Costs: £100 for the event.
Late Booking Opportunities: Sometimes
Photographs Needed: No
Selection Policy: C

PONTARDAWE INTERNATIONAL MUSIC FESTIVAL
c/o 44 Swansea Road
Pontardawe
Swansea SA8 4AL
Tel: 01792 830200
Email: info@pontardawefestival.org.uk
Website: www.pontardawefestival.org.uk
Contact: David Hammond-Williams
Number of Events: 1
When: Aug
Number of Stands: 80-100
Stand/Space Costs: From £80 to £150 for the 3-day event.
Late Booking Opportunities: Nearly always
Photographs Needed: No
Selection Policy: C

PORTCHESTER GALA
c/o 23-25 West Street
Portchester
Fareham
Hants PO16 9XB
Tel: 023 9220 1629
Fax: 023 9261 0051
Mobile: 07712 575733
Contact: Alan Simpson
Number of Events: 1
When: June
Number of Stands: Approx 100
Public Admission Price: Nil
Stand/Space Costs: £12 for 4m width (inc vehicle); no extras.
Late Booking Opportunities: Nearly always
Photographs Needed: No
Selection Policy: D

PORT OF DARTMOUTH ROYAL REGATTA
c/o 17 Mount Boone Way
Dartmouth
Devon TQ6 9PL
Tel: 01803 834861
Mobile: 07792 753343
Contact: John Light
Number of Events: 1
When: Aug
Number of Stands: 80-100
Public Admission Price: Nil
Stand/Space Costs: £145 per 2.5 sq.m. for the three-day event; extra £5 for 13A electrical socket.
Late Booking Opportunities: Rare
Photographs Needed: Yes, if possible
Selection Policy: B/C – copies of insurance required beforehand.

PSM LTD
Hammonds Barn
London Road
Burgess Hill
West Sussex
RH15 9QJ
Tel: 01273 833884
Email: info@primarysport.co.uk
Website: www.bctf.co.uk
Contact: Alex Coombes or Philip Bunn
Number of Events: 1
When: Apr
Public Admission Price: N/A; this is trade only
Stand/Space Costs: £125 per sq.m. Furniture etc is extra and available from the show contractor at a cost of approx £60.
Late Booking Opportunities: Rare
Photographs Needed: Yes
Selection Policy: A – British made crafts only. Work must be displayed in a professional manner.

QUALITY FAIRS
(formerly Quality Craft & Gift Fairs)
The Granary
Wintersett
Wakefield
West Yorks
WF4 2EB
Tel: 01924 865055
Fax: 01924 864039
Email: enquiries@qualityfairs.co.uk
Website: www.qualityfairs.co.uk
Contact: Jane Forsyth
Number of Events: 26
When: Mar-Aug and Oct-Dec
Public Admission Price: The majority are free entry events.
Stand/Space Costs: £40 per day; no extras. Larger stands where available cost £50 for 8ft, £60 for 10ft, £70 for 12ft and £100 for 18ft. Free additional space is offered to demonstrators.

Late Booking Opportunities: Nearly always
Photographs Needed: Yes
Selection Policy: B/C – the right is reserved to turn stallholders away who display different stock to which they have previously stated (if this breaches Quality Fairs' duplication policies).

QUEENS PARK ARTS CENTRE
Queens Park
Aylesbury
Bucks
HP21 7RT
Tel: 01296 424332/431272
Fax: 01296 337363
Email: qpc@ukonline.co.uk
Website: www.qpc.org
Contact: Sarah Hinckley or Louise Griffiths-Kimber
Number of Events: 1
When: Nov
Number of Stands: 30-40
Public Admission Price: Adults £1, Children 50p.
Stand/Space Costs: £25 for the one-day event; no extras..
Late Booking Opportunities: Some
Photographs Needed: Yes
Selection Policy: B/C; for artists and crafters working locally.

RAF LEUCHARS AIRSHOW
1 Tutor Road
Leuchars
St Andrews
Fife KY16 0JW
Tel: 01334 839000
Fax: 01334 838986
Email: info@airshow.co.uk
Website: www.airshow.co.uk
Contact: Jane McCulloch
Number of Events: 1
When: Sept
Number of Stands: 60
Public Admission Price: Adults £12-£15, Seniors/under-15s £7-£8, Family £30-£40 (2004, advance and on the day).
Stand/Space Costs: Approx £60 for the event (2004 cost); extra £5 for table – electricity free, by arrangement.
Late Booking Opportunities: Nearly always
Photographs Needed: No
Selection Policy: C – public liability insurance cover is mandatory.

READING & WOKINGHAM COUNTRY SHOW
10 Beech Hill Road
Spencers Wood
Reading
Berks
RG7 1HL
Tel/Fax: 0118 988 8721
Mobile: 07879 472078
Email: lizstorey2000@hotmail.com
Website: www.countryshow.net
Contact: Liz Storey
Number of Events: 1
When: Sept
Number of Stands: 60
Public Admission Price: Adults £6, Seniors £4, under-14s £3, Family £15.
Stand/Space Costs: £30 for minimum frontage of 8ft and £6.50 per 2ft thereafter; extra £3 for chairs, £6 for tables and £10 for electricity.
Late Booking Opportunities: Nearly always
Photographs Needed: No
Selection Policy: A, but with some duplication of crafts possible.

REDESMERE CRAFTS ASSOCIATION
c/o 17 Beechwood Drive
Eaton Village
nr Congleton
Cheshire CW12 2NQ
Tel: 01260 297087
Contact: Wenda Dobson
Number of Events: Approx 17
When: Each month exc Jan, May, June
Number of Stands: 12-13
Public Admission Price: Nil
Stand/Space Costs: £19 per fair; no extras.
Late Booking Opportunities: Rare
Photographs Needed: Yes
Selection Policy: B – British made crafts only and no mixed displays (unless there's an obvious theme or link). Redesmere Crafts Association organises events at Siddington Village Hall. Guest craftworkers are invited to complement these events with their own crafts, thereby adding variety.

ROMOR EXHIBITIONS LTD
PO Box 448
Bedford
Beds MK40 2ZP
Tel: 01234 345725
Fax: 01234 328604
Website: www.romorexhibitions.co.uk

(cont)

Contact: Anthony or Miriam Rose
Number of Events: 1
When: Aug
Number of Stands: 150
Public Admission Price: TBC
Stand/Space Costs: £253+ for the event; extra for electricity and tables.
Late Booking Opportunities: Rare
Photographs Needed: Yes
Selection Policy: A

ROMSEY SHOW
2A Market Place
Romsey
Hants SO51 8NB
Tel: 01794 517521
Fax: 01794 517615
Contact: Annie Carder
Number of Events: 1
When: Sept
Number of Stands: 50
Public Admission Price: TBC
Stand/Space Costs: On application
Late Booking Opportunities: Rare
Photographs Needed: Yes
Selection Policy: B - British made crafts only, with majority to have been made by the exhibitor.

ROTARY CLUB OF HORBURY & OSSETT PHOENIX
c/o Chestnut House
Daw Lane
Horbury
Wakefield
West Yorks WF4 5DR
Tel: 01274 472676
Fax: 01274 472251
Mobile: 07785 385594
Email: cjohn.faulkner@btopenworld.com
Website: www.horburyshow.plus.com
Contact: Ian Rayner
Number of Events: 1
When: June
Number of Stands: 50-60
Public Admission Price: Nil
Stand/Space Costs: Approx £8 per metre frontage for space only; exhibitors provide their own stalls and tables etc. Make direct contact to discuss discount for demonstrators.
Late Booking Opportunities: Sometimes
Photographs Needed: No
Selection Policy: C/D

ROTHBURY STREET FAIR
Coquetdale Round Table
East Oaktree House
High Street
Rothbury
Northumberland NE65 7TL
Tel/Fax: 01669 620593
Mobile: 07801 320721
Email: crt443@btopenworld.com
Website: www.rothbury.com
Contact: Simon Caple on 01669 621173
Number of Events: 1
When: May
Number of Stands: 40+
Public Admission Price: Nil
Stand/Space Costs: Approx £50 for a 12ft pitch. Price negotiation for first timers. Discount for demonstrators considered. Some stalls available within the price, on a first come, first served basis.
Late Booking Opportunities: Nearly always
Photographs Needed: No
Selection Policy: C - crafts are an important part of the fair, comprising about 50% of the stands.

ROYAL HIGHLAND SHOW
Royal Highland Centre
Ingliston
Edinburgh EH28 8NF
Tel: 0131 335 6200
Fax: 0131 333 5236
Email: info@rhass.org.uk
Website: www.royalhighlandshow.org
Number of Events: 1
When: June

ROYAL INTERNATIONAL AIR TATTOO
Douglas Bader House
Horcott Hill
Cirencester
Glos GL7 5RE
Tel: 01285 713300
Fax: 01285 713268
Email: exhibition@rafbfe.co.uk
Website: www.airtattoo.com
Contact: Avril Swainsbury
Number of Events: 1
When: July
Number of Stands: 30-50
Public Admission Price: Adults £24-£35, under-16s free.
Stand/Space Costs: On application
Late Booking Opportunities: Sometimes

Photographs Needed: Yes
Selection Policy: B/C – no replica weapons.

ROYAL WELSH AGRICULTURAL SOCIETY LTD
Llanelwedd
Builth Wells
Powys LD2 3SY
Tel: 01982 553683/554402
Fax: 01982 553563
Email: info@rwas.co.uk
Website: www.rwas.co.uk
Contact: John Richards or Simon Gittoes
Number of Events: 3
When: May, July, Nov
Number of Stands: Varies
Stand/Space Costs: On application
Late Booking Opportunities: None
Photographs Needed: No
Selection Policy: B

RUDGWICK STEAM & COUNTRY SHOW
Windacres Barn
Rudgwick
Horsham
West Sussex RH12 3EG
Tel: 01403 822378 or 01403 823262
Mobile: 07803 581415
Email: chanaburi@hotmail.com
Website: www.rudgwicksteamshow.co.uk
Contact: Terry Hand
Number of Events: 1
When: Aug
Number of Stands: 100-200
Public Admission Price: Adults £6.50, Seniors £5.50, Children £3.
Stand/Space Costs: £100 for all three days; extra for tables/chairs. Large Craft Tent or outside space available. 25% discount for demonstrators.
Late Booking Opportunities: Rare
Photographs Needed: No
Selection Policy: C

RURAL CRAFTS ASSOCIATION
Brook Road
Wormley
Godalming
Surrey GU8 5UA
Tel: 01428 682292
Fax: 01428 685969
Email: ruralcraftsassociation@btinternet.com
Website: www.ruralcraftsassociation.co.uk
Contact: Karen Hall-Sears or Trevor Sears
Number of Events: 40+
When: Mar-Sept, Nov, Dec
Number of Stands: From 40 to 200+
Stand/Space Costs: On application
Late Booking Opportunities: Sometimes
Photographs Needed: Yes
Selection Policy: B – European craftworkers and their work are permitted.

RVT EVENTS
PO Box 6369
Chelmsford
Essex CM1 2FW
Tel: 01245 350830
Fax: 01245 281240
Contact: R Trickett
Number of Events: 2
When: Mar, Aug
Number of Stands: 40-50
Public Admission Price: Adults £6, Seniors £5, under-16s free.
Stand/Space Costs: From £110 to £145 per event; no extras.
Late Booking Opportunities: Rare
Photographs Needed: Yes
Selection Policy: A – British made crafts only.

SALTRAM HOUSE
Plympton
Plymouth
Devon PL7 1UH
Tel/Fax: 01752 347852
Email: kirsty.eales@nationaltrust.org.uk
Contact: Kirsty Eales
Number of Events: 3
When: May, Aug, Dec
Number of Stands: 40
Public Admission Price: Adults £2.50, under-16s free.
Stand/Space Costs: From £70 to £110 per event; no extras.
Late Booking Opportunities: Sometimes
Photographs Needed: Yes
Selection Policy: B – British made crafts only.

SANDWELL VALLEY CRAFT FAIRS
Sandwell Park Farm
Salters Lane
West Bromwich
West Midlands B71 4BG
Tel: 0121 553 0220
Fax: 0121 525 9435
Email: pippa.hallett@sandwell.gov.uk *(cont)*

Website: www.sandwell.gov.uk
Contact: Pippa Hallett
Number of Events: 4
When: Mar, May, Aug, Dec
Number of Stands: 20-30
Public Admission Price: Varies; some are free.
Stand/Space Costs: On application
Late Booking Opportunities: Sometimes
Photographs Needed: Yes
Selection Policy: B/C

SELWOOD STEAM & VINTAGE VEHICLE PRESERVATION SOCIETY
45 Stonebridge Drive
Frome
Somerset BA11 2TW
Tel: 01373 466846 (evenings only)
Contact: Mrs P Francis
Number of Events: 1
When: May
Public Admission Price: Adults £4, Seniors £3, 5-16s £1.50.
Stand/Space Costs: £25 for one day, £40 for two days or £50 for three days; no extras.
Late Booking Opportunities: Nearly always
Photographs Needed: No
Selection Policy: D

SHERBORNE CASTLE COUNTRY FAIR
c/o Willowtree Barn
Sandford Orcas
Dorset DT9 4SE
Tel: 01963 220490
Fax: 01963 220069
Email: jan@jelowe.com
Website: www.sherbornecountryfair.com
Contact: Jan Lowe
Number of Events: 1
When: May
Number of Stands: 40 in Craft Courtyard
Public Admission Price: Adults £7, Seniors £5, Children £3, under-5s free, Family £15.
Stand/Space Costs: £50 for 10ft by 10ft; some extras.
Late Booking Opportunities: Rare
Photographs Needed: Yes
Selection Policy: A/B – no parking on site without permission. All profits from this fair go to children's charities.

SHERBORNE CRAFT MARKET
The Old Forge
Holton
Wincanton
Somerset BA9 8AY
Tel/Fax: 01963 33384
Email: memoryimb@aol.com
Contact: Susan Higginson
Number of Events: 1
When: Oct
Number of Stands: 42
Public Admission Price: Adults £1.50, under-16s free.
Stand/Space Costs: £11 per ft of frontage for two days; no extras.
Late Booking Opportunities: Rare
Photographs Needed: Yes
Selection Policy: B – British made crafts only; all original hand-made work.

SHIBDEN HALL
see 'Calderdale MBC'

SHIRECRAFTS
25 Hughes Avenue
Wolverhampton
West Midlands WV3 7AU
Tel/Fax: 01902 332901
Mobiles: 07957 319462 (Jean) or 07960 958161 (John)
Contact: Jean or John Jeater
Number of Events: 30-35
When: Feb-Nov
Number of Stands: 30-35
Public Admission Price: Adults 50p, Children free.
Stand/Space Costs: £70-£75 per event; extra £7 for power. Extra tables £5, space 8ft by 6ft or to be agreed. Contact organiser for details of discounts for demonstrators.
Late Booking Opportunities: Sometimes
Photographs Needed: No
Selection Policy: C – no cheap advertising, dayglo posters or tickets.

SHROPSHIRE & WEST MIDLANDS AGRICULTURAL SOCIETY
The Agricultural Showground
Berwick Road
Shrewsbury
Shropshire SY1 2PF
Tel: 01743 289831
Fax: 01743 289920
Email: mail@west-mid-show.org.uk
Website: www.west-mid-show.org.uk
Number of Events: 1
When: June

SOCIETY OF PLOUGHMEN
Quarry Farm
Loversall
Doncaster
South Yorks DN11 9DH
Tel: 01302 852469
Fax: 01302 859880
Email: info@ploughmen.co.uk
Website: www.ploughmen.co.uk
Contact: Susan Frith
Number of Events: 1
When: Oct
Number of Stands: 20+
Public Admission Price: Adults £6, under-16s/Seniors £3.
Stand/Space Costs: Approx £50 for the event; extra for tables/chairs.
Late Booking Opportunities: Sometimes
Photographs Needed: No
Selection Policy: C/D

SOMERSET RURAL LIFE MUSEUM
Abbey Farm
Chilkwell Street
Glastonbury
Somerset BA6 8DB
Tel: 01458 831197
Fax: 01458 834684
Email: county-museums@somerset.gov.uk
Website: www.somerset.gov.uk/museums
Contact: Mary Gryspeerdt
Number of Events: 3
When: July, Oct, Nov/Dec
Number of Stands: 15-20 (Christmas)
Public Admission Price: Nil
Stand/Space Costs: 20% commission on sales (Christmas).
Late Booking Opportunities: Rare
Photographs Needed: Yes
Selection Policy: B – Somerset crafts preferred.

SOUTHAMPTON CITY COUNCIL
Tourism & Event Management Services
Civic Centre
Southampton
Hants
SO14 7LP
Tel: 023 8083 2525
Fax: 023 8083 2929
Email: events@southampton.gov.uk
Website: www.southampton.gov.uk
Contact: Stella May
Number of Events: 1
When: June
Number of Stands: Approx 30 in Arts & Crafts Marquee
Public Admission Price: Nil
Stand/Space Costs: Approx £145 for the event; extra for power.
Late Booking Opportunities: Sometimes
Photographs Needed: Yes
Selection Policy: C

SOUTH HILL PARK ARTS CENTRE
Ringmead
Bracknell
Berks
RG12 7PA
Tel: 01344 484858
Fax: 01344 411427
Email: tom.freshwater@southhillpark.org.uk
Website: www.southhillpark.org.uk
Contact: Tom Freshwater
Number of Events: 1
When: Nov
Number of Stands: Approx 90
Public Admission Price: Adults £3.50, Seniors/Children £2, under-10s free (all subject to change).
Stand/Space Costs: Range of pitch sizes and locations available for the event at costs from £162 to £208; no extras.
Late Booking Opportunities: Sometimes
Photographs Needed: Yes
Selection Policy: B – full rights of exhibit selection reserved by organiser; reselection required each year.

SOUTH SUFFOLK AGRICULTURAL SHOW
c/o 35 Dalham Road
Moulton
Newmarket
Suffolk
CB8 8SB
Tel: 01638 750879
Email: geoff@southsuffolkshow.co.uk
Website: www.southsuffolkshow.co.uk
Contact: Geoff Bailes
Number of Events: 1
When: May
Number of Stands: 40
Public Admission Price: Adults £7, under-14s/Seniors/Concessions £5.
Stand/Space Costs: £32.50 for the one day; extra for table and chair hire.
Late Booking Opportunities: Sometimes
Photographs Needed: No
Selection Policy: C

SOUTH WEST EVENTS LTD
9 Granary Lane
Budleigh Salterton
Devon EX9 6ES
Tel: 01395 446695
Fax: 01395 446605
Email: sales@southwestevents.co.uk
Website: www.southwestevents.co.uk
Number of Events: 10
When: Only Mar confirmed
Number of Stands: 50
Public Admission Price: Adults £4, Seniors £3, under-12s free.
Stand/Space Costs: £50 per sq.m. per event; extra £45 for 13A Socket, £35 for 2 150W Spots, £55 for 13A Socket + Spots and £10 for table.
Late Booking Opportunities: Sometimes
Photographs Needed: Yes
Selection Policy: C

SOVEREIGN FAIRS
12 Samoa Way
Sovereign Harbour North
Eastbourne
East Sussex BN23 5BA
Tel: 01323 471018
Fax: 01323 472688
Email: sovereignfairs@supanet.com
Website: www.sovereignfairs.co.uk
Contact: Kate Pitcher
Number of Events: 8
When: May, July
Number of Stands: 25-50
Stand/Space Costs: £50 per day; book two fairs and get 10% discount. Extra for tables, chairs and power. Extra free space for demonstrators.
Late Booking Opportunities: Sometimes
Photographs Needed: Yes
Selection Policy: C – no dogs allowed, no smoking, strict pitch sizing.

SPECIAL EVENT ORGANISERS (UK) LTD
Event House
31 Ray Street
Heanor
Derbys DE75 7GE
Tel/Fax: 01773 534414
Mobile: 07889 455715
Contact: Alan Scaife
Number of Events: 4
When: July, Oct, Nov, Dec
Number of Stands: 50
Public Admission Price: Nil
Stand/Space Costs: From £55 to £60 per event; extra £5 for tables.
Late Booking Opportunities: Sometimes
Photographs Needed: No
Selection Policy: C

STANHOPE AGRICULTURAL SOCIETY
Moor View
Blackston
Eggleston
Barnard Castle
Co Durham DL12 0AY
Tel: 01833 650309
Contact: Helen Beadle
Number of Events: 1
When: Sept
Number of Stands: Approx 40
Public Admission Price: Adults £5, Seniors/under-16s £2.
Stand/Space Costs: £12 per 6ft table per day (subject to increase).
Late Booking Opportunities: Sometimes
Photographs Needed: No
Selection Policy: C

ST BARTHOLOMEW'S SCHOOL PARENTS' ASSOCIATION
c/o 79 Gloucester Road
Newbury
Berks RG14 5JN
Tel: 01635 49672 or 01635 299147
Email: elisehirst@aol.com
Contact: Mrs B Williams or Mrs E Hirst
Number of Events: 1
When: Oct
Number of Stands: 60-65
Public Admission Price: Adults £2.50, Seniors/Concessions £1.50, under-16s free.
Stand/Space Costs: £30 for 6ft table; no extras.
Late Booking Opportunities: Sometimes
Photographs Needed: No
Selection Policy: D

STITHIANS AGRICULTURAL ASSOCIATION
The Showground
Stithians
Truro
Cornwall TR3 7BB
Tel: 01209 861073
Fax: 01209 861288
Email: information@stithiansshow.org.uk

Website: www.stithiansshow.org.uk
Contact: Mrs Tremayne
Number of Events: 1
When: July
Number of Stands: 19
Public Admission Price: Adults £7, Seniors £4, Children £2 (2004).
Stand/Space Costs: £45 for the one day (2004). Tables need to be provided by exhibitors.
Late Booking Opportunities: Rare
Photographs Needed: Yes, or good explanation of goods.
Selection Policy: B/C – British made crafts only. Stands must be set up before 10pm on the day prior to the show.

STOCKTON-ON-TEES BOROUGH COUNCIL
Events Team
Sun Street Depot
Sun Street, Thornaby
Stockton-on-Tees TS17 6HB
Tel: 01642 527344/5/6
Fax: 01642 393663
Email: events@stockton.gov.uk
Website: www.stockton.gov.uk
Contact: Derek Batchelor or Carol Croft
Number of Events: 5
When: June, Aug, Sept
Public Admission Price: Adults £2.50, Seniors/5-16s £1.50, Family £6.
Stand/Space Costs: £25 for one day, £40 for two days, £55 for three days (makers); £5 per day surcharge for craft traders. Extra flat rate charge of £5 for power for low level lighting (no high wattage appliances).
Late Booking Opportunities: Nearly always
Photographs Needed: No
Selection Policy: C – Council insists on health certification and proper handling of foodstuffs (where applicable); it tries to work through farmers' market organisations to ensure quality.

STOWMARKET CARNIVAL
c/o 67 Kipling Way
Stowmarket
Suffolk IP14 1TS
Tel: 01449 775327
Fax: 01449 615586
Mobile: 07836 289376
Contact: Mark Cook
Number of Events: 1
When: July
Number of Stands: 50
Public Admission Price: Adults £1 (tbc)
Stand/Space Costs: Craft Fair is £20 per 10ft pitch inside for one day or £30 for both days. Craft & Trade is £18 per 10ft pitch outside for one day or £27 for both days.
Late Booking Opportunities: Nearly always
Photographs Needed: No
Selection Policy: C – you must have public liability insurance to £2 million.

STRATHMORE VINTAGE VEHICLE CLUB
81 North Street
Forfar
Angus DD8 3BL
Tel: 01307 462496
Fax: 01307 467279
Email: dvbowler@btopenworld.com
Contact: Derek Bowler
Number of Events: 1
When: July
Public Admission Price: Adults £7, under-16s/Seniors/Concessions £5, Family £17.
Stand/Space Costs: On application
Late Booking Opportunities: Rare
Photographs Needed: Yes
Selection Policy: B

SURREY FEDERATION OF YOUNG FARMERS CLUBS
Unit G11, The Mayford Centre
Smart Heath Road
Woking
Surrey GU22 0PP
Tel/Fax: 01483 768786
Email: amanda@surreyyfc.co.uk
Website: www.cowpie.co.uk
Contact: Amanda Colebrook
Number of Events: 1
When: May
Public Admission Price: Adults £7, Seniors £5, Children £3, Family £18.
Stand/Space Costs: £12 per sq.m. £20 extra for electrical socket.
Late Booking Opportunities: Sometimes
Photographs Needed: Yes
Selection Policy: B

SUSAN ADAMS BUSINESS SERVICES LTD
161 High Street
Tonbridge
Kent TN9 1BX
Tel: 01732 357872

Fax: 01732 360178
Email: tgs@netcomuk.co.uk
Website: www.tonbridgegardenshow.co.uk
Contact: Mrs Susan Adams
Number of Events: 1
When: Apr/May
Number of Stands: 30
Public Admission Price: Adults £4, Seniors £3, under-14s free.
Stand/Space Costs: £105 for single stand and £195 for a double for the event; extra £12 for tables and £70 for electricity.
Late Booking Opportunities: Sometimes
Photographs Needed: No
Selection Policy: B/C

SUSSEX PAST
Michelham Priory
Upper Dicker
Hailsham
East Sussex BN27 3QS
Tel: 01323 844224
Fax: 01323 844030
Email: adminmich@sussexpast.co.uk
Website: www.sussexpast.co.uk
Contact: Frances Preedy
Number of Events: 6
When: Apr, May, July, Aug, Sept, Nov
Number of Stands: 25-50
Public Admission Price: Adults £5.40, Seniors/Concessions £4.50, 5-16s £2.80, Family £13.80.
Stand/Space Costs: Approx £50 (inc VAT) per event; extra for tables and large use of power.
Late Booking Opportunities: Nearly always
Photographs Needed: Yes
Selection Policy: B/C

SYKEHOUSE SHOW SOCIETY
c/o Wayside Cottage
Sykehouse
Goole DN14 9AQ
Tel: 01405 785349
Email: show@jatsykehouse.fsnet.co.uk
Contact: Mrs J Threadgold
Number of Events: 1
When: Aug
Number of Stands: Approx 24
Public Admission Price: Adults £3, Children £2.
Stand/Space Costs: £16 for 6ft table in Arts & Crafts Marquee; no extras.
Late Booking Opportunities: Sometimes
Photographs Needed: No
Selection Policy: C – nevertheless, seldom if ever two stalls with same product.

T.C.T.C.
80 Lime Road
Wednesbury
West Midlands WS10 9NF
Tel/Fax: 0121 556 4281
Email: email@thimblehouse.com
Contact: David or Jacqui Duffill
Number of Events: 1
When: Apr/May
Number of Stands: 20
Stand/Space Costs: From £45 for the event; no extras.
Late Booking Opportunities: Sometimes
Photographs Needed: Yes
Selection Policy: B – British made crafts only. All exhibitors must have public liability insurance.

TENDRING HUNDRED SHOW
The Oaks
Hunters Chase
Ardleigh
nr Colchester
Essex CO7 7LN
Tel: 01206 231821
Fax: 01206 231409
Email: info@tendringshow.co.uk
Website: www.tendringshow.co.uk
Contact: Mrs Romany Foster
Number of Events: 1
When: July
Number of Stands: 30+
Public Admission Price: Adults £10, Seniors £8, Children £6, Family £25,
Stand/Space Costs: £60 for the event, based on a per table rate; extra for electricity
Late Booking Opportunities: Rare
Photographs Needed: Yes
Selection Policy: B – British made crafts only

THREE COCKS VINTAGE SOCIETY LTD
Colebrook Villa
Bronllys
Brecon
Powys LD3 0RU
Tel: 01874 711110 or 01497 847738
Contact: Mrs M James or Mr G Lewis
Number of Events: 1
When: Aug

Public Admission Price: Adults £5, Seniors £3.
Stand/Space Costs: On application. Free for demonstrators in marquee.
Late Booking Opportunities: Rare
Photographs Needed: No
Selection Policy: C – there is also trade stand space available outdoors.

THURLOW & HAVERHILL STEAM & COUNTRY SHOW
114A The Street
Thurlow
Haverhill
Suffolk
CB9 7LA
Tel: 01440 783457
Contact: Don Loveday
Number of Events: 1
When: Aug
Public Admission Price: Adults £4, Seniors/Concessions £3, 5-15s £1.
Stand/Space Costs: £25 for the event. Gazebos available at £33 for the weekend outside.
Late Booking Opportunities: Nearly always
Photographs Needed: No
Selection Policy: C/D

TIVERTON CRAFT FAIR
c/o 29 Old Road
Tiverton
Devon
EX16 4HJ
Tel: 01884 253556
Email: celiarufey@eclipse.co.uk
Contact: Celia Rufey
Number of Events: 1
When: Dec
Number of Stands: Approx 60
Stand/Space Costs: £37.50 inc table, socket for lighting (if required) and all-day parking.
Photographs Needed: Yes
Selection Policy: A - British made crafts only; only quality crafts by professional makers. Everything is vetted before a stand is offered.

TOTNES & DISTRICT SHOW LTD
c/o Little Beeches
Holsome Lane
Diptford
Totnes
Devon TQ9 7NU
Tel/Fax: 01548 821070
Email: tom@jenkins67.freeserve.co.uk
Contact: Tom Jenkins
Number of Events: 1
When: July
Number of Stands: 80
Stand/Space Costs: £50 for 12ft by 6ft and £65 for 18ft by 6ft in Craft Marquee. Tables £3; no electricity on site.
Late Booking Opportunities: Very rare
Photographs Needed: Helpful and may be requested on receipt of application.
Selection Policy: B/C

TOWERSEY VILLAGE FESTIVAL
Festival Office
PO Box 296
Matlock
Derbys DE4 3XU
Tel: 01629 827017
Fax: 01629 821874
Email: info@towerseyfestival.com
Website: www.towerseyfestival.com
Contact: Joe Heap
Number of Events: 1
When: Aug
Number of Stands: Approx 50
Public Admission Price: Adults £4, under-18s £1.
Stand/Space Costs: On application
Late Booking Opportunities: Sometimes
Photographs Needed: Yes
Selection Policy: B/C

TRADE FAIRS (SCOTLAND) LTD
Station Road
Beauly
Inverness-shire IV4 7EH
Tel: 01463 782578
Fax: 01463 782409
Email: mis@enterprise.net
Website: www.madeinscotland.uk.com
Contact: Jane, Margaret, Avril or Paula
Number of Events: 2
When: Jan, Oct
Number of Stands: Jan 800, Oct 350
Public Admission Price: N/A - trade only.
Stand/Space Costs: Jan: £149 per sq.m. for shell scheme or £129 per sq.m. for space. Oct: £115 and £95 per sq.m. respectively. Extra for furniture and power.
Late Booking Opportunities: Sometimes
Photographs Needed: Yes
Selection Policy: D

TURRIFF DISTRICT AGRICULTURAL ASSOCIATION
c/o Ardmiddle Mains
Turriff
Aberdeenshire AB53 8AG
Tel/Fax: 01888 568830
Mobile: 07977 505246
Email: bruce@turriffshow.org
Website: www.turriffshow.org
Contact: Bruce Ferguson
Number of Events: 1
When: July/Aug
Number of Stands: 20
Public Admission Price: Adults £7, Seniors £5, Concessions £3.50, under-14s £2, Family £17.
Stand/Space Costs: From £100 to £150 for the event, inc table and power.
Late Booking Opportunities: Rare
Photographs Needed: Yes
Selection Policy: B

UBIQUE LEISURE LTD
11 Fincudean Road
Rowlands Castle
Hants PO9 6DA
Tel/Fax: 023 9241 3713
Email: sales@ubiqueleisure.co.uk
Website: www.ubiqueleisure.co.uk
Contact: Emma Braden or Nigel Stewart
Number of Events: 2-4
When: July, Sept
Number of Stands: 75
Stand/Space Costs: On application
Late Booking Opportunities: Nearly always
Photographs Needed: Yes
Selection Policy: C

UNIVERSITY OF SOUTHAMPTON STAFF CLUB
Staff Club Office
Building 38, Highfield
Southampton
Hants SO17 1BJ
Tel: 023 8059 3600
Fax: 023 8059 4560
Email: staffclub@soton.ac.uk
Website: www.staffclub.soton.ac.uk
Contact: Eileen Richmond
Number of Events: 1
When: Nov
Number of Stands: 120
Public Admission Price: £1.50.
Stand/Space Costs: £30 plus 10% commission on sales; no extras.
Late Booking Opportunities: Rare
Photographs Needed: Yes
Selection Policy: A – crafts must be made by the exhibitor.

UPPER STREET EVENTS
52 Upper Street
Islington
London
N1 0QH
Tel: 020 7288 6000
Fax: 020 7288 6446
Email: suzyp@upperstreetevents.co.uk
Website: www.countrylivingfair.com
Contact: Suzy Pallett
Number of Events: 3
When: Mar, Apr, Nov
Number of Stands: 400
Public Admission Price: Adults £12.
Stand/Space Costs: £260 per event; lighting and electrics charged extra. 35% discount for demonstrators.
Late Booking Opportunities: Sometimes
Photographs Needed: Yes
Selection Policy: B – British made crafts only.

USK FARMERS' CLUB LTD
Llanerthil Mill
Llandenny
Usk
Monmouthshire NP15 1DJ
Email: usk.show@virgin.net
Contact: Fiona Jenkins
Number of Events: 1
When: Sept (Craft Marquee)

VALE EARTH FAIR
La Cachette
New Place
Vauvert
St Peter Port
Guernsey GY1 1ND
Tel: 01481 747333
Fax: 01481 720968
Mobile: 07781 107698
Email: rob.roussel@gov.gg
Website: www.valeearthfair.org
Contact: Rob Roussel
Number of Events: 1
When: Aug
Number of Stands: 10
Public Admission Price: Adults £10, under-

14s free.
Stand/Space Costs: Levy of 20% of takings.
Late Booking Opportunities: Nearly always
Photographs Needed: No
Selection Policy: C – environmentally friendly crafts; no plastics.

VALE OF GLAMORGAN AGRICULTURAL SHOW
c/o Ty Gwyn
Maendy
Cowbridge
Vale of Glamorgan
Tel: 01446 773258
Email: nicola@valeshow.fsnet.co.uk
Website: www.valeofglamorganshow.co.uk
Contact: Ann Arnott by mail/'phone or Nicola Gibson by e-mail.
Number of Events: 1
When: Aug
Number of Stands: 80
Public Admission Price: Adults £7, Seniors £5, Children £3, Family £18 (tbc).
Stand/Space Costs: £45 for the event inside; extra for power if high wattage is required.
Late Booking Opportunities: Sometimes
Photographs Needed: Yes
Selection Policy: A – British made crafts only and maker only presentations.

VAYNOL ENTERPRISES LTD
Vaynol Hall
Vaynol Estate
Bangor
Gwynedd LL57 4BP
Tel/Fax: 01248 670444
Mobile: 07816 001979
Email: shaunvaynol@yahoo.com
Website: www.vaynol.co.uk
Contact: Shaun Casey
Number of Events: 3-4
When: May and Dec confirmed
Number of Stands: 30-100
Public Admission Price: Varies
Stand/Space Costs: On application
Late Booking Opportunities: Sometimes
Photographs Needed: Yes
Selection Policy: C

WALES CRAFT COUNCIL
Henfaes Lane
Welshpool
Powys SY21 7BE
Tel: 01938 555313
Fax: 01938 556237
Email: info@walescraftcouncil.co.uk
Website: www.walescraftcouncil.co.uk
Contact: Helen Francis
Number of Events: 7-10
When: Jan, Apr, May, June, July, Aug, Nov, Dec
Number of Stands: Varies between Trade and Direct
Public Admission Price: Not generally applicable (trade shows).
Stand/Space Costs: Varies
Late Booking Opportunities: Sometimes
Photographs Needed: Yes
Selection Policy: C – Welsh made crafts only.

WARNERS DOLLS HOUSE & MINIATURE FAIRS
The Maltings
West Street
Bourne
Lincs PE10 9PH
Tel: 01778 391123
Fax: 01778 392079
Email: dollshousefairs@warnersgroup.co.uk
Website: www.dollshousemag.co.uk
Contact: Anne Hind
Number of Events: 10
When: Mar, Apr, June, Sept, Oct, Nov
Number of Stands: 70-150
Public Admission Price: Adults £2.50-£5, Seniors £2-£3.50, 5-16s £1-£1.50.
Stand/Space Costs: Average 6ft stand starts at £68; no extras.
Late Booking Opportunities: Rare
Photographs Needed: Yes
Selection Policy: B – 80% hand-made items required.

WARNERS EXHIBITIONS
address, tel and fax as entry above
Email: sallyb@warnersgroup.co.uk
Website: www.warnersgroup.co.uk
Contact: Sally Beresford
Number of Events: 4
When: Apr, May, July, Sept
Number of Stands: Approx 20 Craft Stands
Public Admission Price: Adults £6, 5-16s £1.50, Family £12.
Stand/Space Costs: On application
Late Booking Opportunities: Sometimes
Photographs Needed: No
Selection Policy: C

WARWICK FOLK FESTIVAL LTD
PO Box 1533
Harbury
Warks CV33 9ZU
Tel: 01844 354269
Email: angi@swfpc.co.uk
Website: www.warwickfolkfest.demon.co.uk
Contact: Angi Cole
Number of Events: 1
When: July
Number of Stands: Approx 40
Public Admission Price: Adults £4.
Stand/Space Costs: From £70 to £100 for the event; no extras.
Late Booking Opportunities: None
Photographs Needed: Yes
Selection Policy: C

WEALD & DOWNLAND OPEN AIR MUSEUM
Singleton
Chichester
West Sussex PO18 0EU
Tel: 01243 811363
Fax: 01243 811475
Email: office@wealddown.co.uk
Website: www.wealddown.co.uk
Contact: Carol Brinson
Number of Events: 2
When: Sept, Oct
Number of Stands: 40
Public Admission Price: Adults £7.70, Seniors £6.70, under-16s £4.10, Family £21.
Stand/Space Costs: From £20 for the event; some extras charged. 50% discount for demonstrators.
Late Booking Opportunities: Sometimes
Photographs Needed: Yes
Selection Policy: B – British made crafts only.

WEETING STEAM RALLY & COUNTRY SHOW
Fengate Farm
Weeting
Brandon
Suffolk IP27 0QF
Tel: 01842 810317
Fax: 01842 815831
Website: www.weetingrally.co.uk
Contact: Mr R N Parrott
Number of Events: 1
When: July
Number of Stands: 20
Public Admission Price: Adults £6, Seniors £5, under-14s free.
Stand/Space Costs: £9 per ft (minimum 10ft) by 25ft depth; no extras.
Late Booking Opportunities: Nearly always
Photographs Needed: Yes
Selection Policy: B

WELSH GAME FAIR
Afondale
Cynwyl Elfed
Carmarthen SA33 6TL
Tel: 01267 281410
Contact: Colin Evans
Number of Events: 1
When: June
Number of Stands: 60
Public Admission Price: Adults £7.
Stand/Space Costs: £45 for the event; extra for tables and chairs.
Late Booking Opportunities: Sometimes
Photographs Needed: No
Selection Policy: C

WENSLEYDALE AGRICULTURAL SOCIETY
c/o Hillside House
Thornton Rust
Leyburn
North Yorks DL8 3AN
Tel: 01969 663797
Email: gill@wensleydaleshow.org.uk
Website: www.wensleydaleshow.org.uk
Contact: Gillian Harrison
Number of Events: 1
When: Aug
Number of Stands: 100
Public Admission Price: Adults £5, Children/Seniors £2.50, under-5s free.
Stand/Space Costs: £3 per ft inside or £5 per ft outside; no extras.
Late Booking Opportunities: Sometimes
Photographs Needed: No
Selection Policy: D

WENSLEYDALE CRAFT FAIRS
57 Kelsey Gardens
Doncaster
South Yorks DN4 7QA
Tel: 01302 370988
Email: berny@inkycalligraphy.co.uk
Contact: Bernard Parkin
Number of Events: 37
When: All months except Jan/Dec

Number of Stands: 12
Public Admission Price: Nil
Stand/Space Costs: £24 for 6ft table and access. Free 2ft extra for demonstrators. Extra £5 for electricity at the Reeth and Muker shows.
Late Booking Opportunities: Nearly always
Photographs Needed: No
Selection Policy: B/C

WESSEX FAYRES
128 Station Road
Ilminster
Somerset TA19 9PW
Tel: 01460 52770
Email: wessexfayres@fsmail.net
Website: www.wessexfayres.com
Contact: Jennifer Wain
Number of Events: 2
When: July, Dec
Number of Stands: 50+
Public Admission Price: Adults £5, under-12s/Seniors £2.50.
Stand/Space Costs: £30 per day; no extras.
Late Booking Opportunities: Sometimes
Photographs Needed: No
Selection Policy: D

WEST COUNTRY CRAFT FAIRS
PO Box 2603
Wells
Somerset BA5 2YL
Tel/Fax: 01749 677049
Website: www.westcountrycraftfairs.co.uk
Contact: Fred Wilcox
Number of Events: 40
When: All months except Jan
Number of Stands: 25-100
Public Admission Price: Adults £1, Seniors/Concessions 80p, under-12s free.
Stand/Space Costs: £18.50 per day; no extras. Complimentary demo space given to demonstrators.
Late Booking Opportunities: Sometimes
Photographs Needed: Yes
Selection Policy: B/C

WEST OF ENGLAND EVENTS
The Old Vicarage, Bourton
Gillingham
Dorset
SP8 5BJ
Tel: 01747 840213
Fax: 01747 840724
Email: wellheadbooks@aol.com
Website: www.westofenglandevents.co.uk
Number of Events: 3
When: May, June
Number of Stands: 30
Public Admission Price: Adults £3.50, under-16s free.
Stand/Space Costs: £60 per table per event; no extras.
Late Booking Opportunities: Rare
Photographs Needed: Yes
Selection Policy: A/B

WHARFEDALE AGRICULTURAL SOCIETY
15 Bridge Street
Otley
West Yorks
LS21 1BQ
Tel: 01943 462541
Mobile: 07961 966952
Email: janet.raw@otleyshow.org.uk
Website: www.otleyshow.org.uk
Contact: Mrs Janet Raw
Number of Events: 1
When: May
Number of Stands: 150
Public Admission Prices: Adults £6, Seniors £3, Children £2.
Stand/Space Costs: From £60 up to £260; no extras.
Late Booking Opportunities: Sometimes
Photographs Needed: No
Selection Policy: C

WHIRLOW HALL FARM TRUST
Whirlow Lane
Whirlow
Sheffield
S11 9QF
Tel: 0114 235 2678
Fax: 0114 262 1015
Email:
admin@whirlowhallfarm.freeserve.co.uk
Website: www.whirlowhallfarm.co.uk
Contact: Rachel Robinson
Number of Events: 2
Number of Stands: 150-200
Public Admission Price: Adults £3.50, Seniors/Concessions £2.50, Children £1.
Stand/Space Costs: On application
Late Booking Opportunities: Sometimes
Photographs Needed: No
Selection Policy: D

WHITSTABLE FESTIVALS & EVENTS LTD
30 Millstrood Road
Whitstable
Kent CT5 1QF
Tel/Fax: 01227 263595
Email: 106270.2734@compuserve.com
Website:
www.tankertonchristmasmarket.co.uk
Contact: Mrs P Thomas
Number of Events: 3
When: June, Dec
Number of Stands: Approx 50
Public Admission Price: Nil
Stand/Space Costs: From £15 upwards, depending on event; small extra cost for tables and chairs.
Late Booking Opportunities: Sometimes
Photographs Needed: No
Selection Policy: C/D

WHITTINGHAM SHOW
c/o Chesterford Cottage
Whittingham
Alnwick
Northumberland
NE66 4UP
Tel: 01665 574274
Website: www.whittinghamshow.co.uk
Contact: Karen Bartlett
Number of Events: 1
When: Aug
Number of Stands: 20+
Public Admission Price: Adults £2, Children 50p.
Stand/Space Costs: £10 per day or 10% of the day's takings, whichever is the greater. Exhibitors' own stands etc outside on show-field.
Late Booking Opportunities: Nearly always
Photographs Needed: No
Selection Policy: C

WILMSLOW SHOW
c/o 16 Lacey Green
Wilmslow
Cheshire
SK9 4BA
Tel: 01625 251126
Email: a.elizm@ntlworld.com
Contact: Miss A E Myers
Number of Events: 1
When: July
Number of Stands: 80+
Public Admission Price: Adults £3.50, 5-16s/Seniors £2, under-5s free, Family £9.
Stand/Space Costs: £20 for 50 sq.ft. in the Craft Marquee. Also outside space at £25 for 20ft by 20ft. Charities welcome at £15 per space (all costs tbc). £3 extra for tables; limited generator power available on request.
Late Booking Opportunities: Nearly always
Photographs Needed: No, but brief description on booking form.
Selection Policy: C/D - exhibitors must have public liability insurance.

WIMBORNE FOLK FESTIVAL
c/o 32 Shillito Road
Parkstone
Poole
Dorset
BH12 2BN
Tel: 01202 743465
Fax: 01202 718488
Mobile: 07729 415719
Email:
maria.bisp@wimbornefolkfestival.co.uk
Website: www.wimbornefolkfestival.co.uk
Contact: Maria Bisp
Number of Events: 1
When: June
Number of Stands: 90
Public Admission Price: Nil
Stand/Space Costs: £125 per 3m by 3m. Stall space is open air and you supply your own stall and tables; no electricity available.
Late Booking Opportunities: Sometimes
Photographs Needed: Yes
Selection Policy: A - organiser tries not to duplicate crafts in the same area. Catering operators are not required.

WIRRAL SHOW CRAFT MARQUEE
142 Sandbrook Lane
Moreton
Wirral
CH46 0QL
Tel: 0151 677 7095
Contact: Ann Cordon
Number of Events: 1
When: July
Number of Stands: 52-63
Public Admission Price: Nil
Stand/Space Costs: £90 for the event; lighting charged extra at £10.
Late Booking Opportunities: Sometimes
Photographs Needed: No
Selection Policy: C

WMH LEISURE
71 West Street
Sittingbourne
Kent ME10 1AN
Tel: 01795 474660
Fax: 01795 474819
Mobile: 07768 555321
Email: wmh@gardenshows.com
Website: www.gardenshows.com
Contact: Will Chesson
Number of Events: 6
When: Apr, May, Aug, Nov
Number of Stands: 20-70
Public Admission Price: Adults £6, Seniors/Concessions £5, under-16s free.
Stand/Space Costs: £120 per event; extra for tables and power. 50% discount for demonstrators.
Late Booking Opportunities: Rare
Photographs Needed: Yes
Selection Policy: B/C

WOODHALL SPA GROUP OF FRIENDS OF CANCER RESEARCH UK
c/o 21 Heather Close
Woodhall Spa
Lincs LN10 6YD
Tel/Fax: 01526 352825
Email: roblind.good@btinternet.com
Number of Events: 1
When: Nov
Number of Stands: 35-40
Public Admission Price: Adults £1, Children free.
Stand/Space Costs: From £18 to £25; no extras.
Late Booking Opportunities: Nearly always
Photographs Needed: No
Selection Policy: B

WOODLAND CRAFTS
'Butskiln'
Street End
Sidlesham Common
Chichester
West Sussex PO20 7QD
Tel/Fax: 01243 641306
Email: info@woodlandcrafts.co.uk
Website: www.woodlandcrafts.co.uk
Number of Events: 25
When: Feb-Nov
Number of Stands: 40-100
Public Admission Price: Adults £2-£2.75, Seniors £1.50-£2.25, under-16s free.
Stand/Space Costs: Basic stand charges range from £70 to £180. Extra for electricity supply, tables and chairs. Free extra space available for demonstrators.
Late Booking Opportunities: Sometimes
Photographs Needed: Yes
Selection Policy: B (maker-only events); C (craft events); D (some marquee events).

WORCESTER CITY COUNCIL
Community Services
Orchard House
Farrier Street
Worcester
Worcs WR1 3BB
Tel: 01905 722320
Fax: 01905 722350
Email: ccollier@cityofworcester.gov.uk
Website: www.visitworcester.com
Contact: Clare Collier
Number of Events: 1
When: Nov
Number of Stands: 100
Public Admission Price: Nil
Stand/Space Costs: On application
Late Booking Opportunities: Rare
Photographs Needed: Yes
Selection Policy: B

WORTHING THEATRES
Union Place
Worthing
West Sussex BN11 1HQ
Tel: 01903 231799
Fax: 01903 215337
Email: theatres@worthing.gov.uk
Website: www.worthingtheatres.co.uk
Contact: Stephanie Anscomb or Rosie Gray
Number of Events: 3
When: Mar, Oct, Nov
Number of Stands: 65
Public Admission Price: Nil
Stand/Space Costs: £28 or £30 per day; no extras.
Late Booking Opportunities: Sometimes
Photographs Needed: No
Selection Policy: C

YARDLEY HASTINGS SOCIETY
62 Castle Ashby Road
Yardley Hastings
Northants NN7 1EL
Tel: 01604 696521
Fax: 01604 696521
Email: debs@yh62.freeserve.co.uk

Contact: Debbie Smith
Number of Events: 1
When: July
Number of Stands: 35
Public Admission Price: Adults £6.
Stand/Space Costs: £37 for the event; no extras.
Late Booking Opportunities: Sometimes
Photographs Needed: No
Selection Policy: B - British made crafts only.

YORKRAFT
35 Thrushwood Crescent
Marske-by-the-Sea
Redcar
Cleveland TS11 7JA
Tel: 01642 275821
Contact: Marion Wallace
Number of Events: 20
When: Mar, May, Aug
Number of Stands: 6
Public Admission Price: Nil
Stand/Space Costs: £15 per day; no extras.
Late Booking Opportunities: Sometimes
Photographs Needed: Yes
Selection Policy: A - British made crafts only.

YORKSHIRE CRAFT FAIRS
Parkside House
17 East Parade
Harrogate
North Yorks HG1 5LF
Tel: 01423 545377
Fax: 01423 545677
Email: info@yorkshirefairs.co.uk
Website: www.yorkshirefairs.co.uk
Contact: Donald Olley
Number of Events: 60
When: Feb-Dec
Number of Stands: 25-65 according to venue
Public Admission Price: Strict policy of free admission, except at stately home/historical building venues.
Stand/Space Costs: From £27 to £45 depending on venue; no extras. Free extra space for demonstrators. Special terms for new exhibitors.
Late Booking Opportunities: Sometimes
Selection Policy: B/C

YORKSHIRE GARDEN SHOW
Bankwood Centre
Church Lane
Welburn
North Yorks YO60 7EG
Tel: 01653 618262
Mobile: 07787 566330
Email: info@ygshow.co.uk
Website: www.ygshow.co.uk
Number of Events: 2
When: May
Number of Stands: 30
Public Admission Price: Adults £5, Seniors £4.50, under-12s free.
Stand/Space Costs: In the Craft Marquee, first 6ft table is £99 for the event with extra 6ft tables at £60. Outside Area offers 3m by 3m at £97 or 6m by 6m at £160. Power Points charged extra; £35 inside, £45 outside. Each exhibitor receives 10 free tickets. Extra space will be provided free for those who demonstrate.
Late Booking Opportunities: Sometimes
Photographs Needed: Yes
Selection Policy: A/B

CALENDAR 2005

JANUARY

M	T	W	T	F	S	S
					1	2
3	4	5	6	7	8	9
10	11	12	13	14	15	16
17	18	19	20	21	22	23
24	25	26	27	28	29	30
31						

FEBRUARY

M	T	W	T	F	S	S
	1	2	3	4	5	6
7	8	9	10	11	12	13
14	15	16	17	18	19	20
21	22	23	24	25	26	27
28						

MARCH

M	T	W	T	F	S	S
	1	2	3	4	5	6
7	8	9	10	11	12	13
14	15	16	17	18	19	20
21	22	23	24	25	26	27
28	29	30	31			

APRIL

M	T	W	T	F	S	S
				1	2	3
4	5	6	7	8	9	10
11	12	13	14	15	16	17
18	19	20	21	22	23	24
25	26	27	28	29	30	

MAY

M	T	W	T	F	S	S
						1
2	3	4	5	6	7	8
9	10	11	12	13	14	15
16	17	18	19	20	21	22
23	24	25	26	27	28	29
30	31					

JUNE

M	T	W	T	F	S	S
		1	2	3	4	5
6	7	8	9	10	11	12
13	14	15	16	17	18	19
20	21	22	23	24	25	26
27	28	29	30			

JULY

M	T	W	T	F	S	S
				1	2	3
4	5	6	7	8	9	10
11	12	13	14	15	16	17
18	19	20	21	22	23	24
25	26	27	28	29	30	31

AUGUST

M	T	W	T	F	S	S
1	2	3	4	5	6	7
8	9	10	11	12	13	14
15	16	17	18	19	20	21
22	23	24	25	26	27	28
29	30	31				

SEPTEMBER

M	T	W	T	F	S	S
			1	2	3	4
5	6	7	8	9	10	11
12	13	14	15	16	17	18
19	20	21	22	23	24	25
26	27	28	29	30		

OCTOBER

M	T	W	T	F	S	S
					1	2
3	4	5	6	7	8	9
10	11	12	13	14	15	16
17	18	19	20	21	22	23
24	25	26	27	28	29	30
31						

NOVEMBER

M	T	W	T	F	S	S
	1	2	3	4	5	6
7	8	9	10	11	12	13
14	15	16	17	18	19	20
21	22	23	24	25	26	27
28	29	30				

DECEMBER

M	T	W	T	F	S	S
			1	2	3	4
5	6	7	8	9	10	11
12	13	14	15	16	17	18
19	20	21	22	23	24	25
26	27	28	29	30	31	

CRAFT SELLING IN SHOPPING CENTRES & MALLS

This section in The Craftworker's Year Book takes a look at some of the British shopping centres and malls that have sites available to craftworkers for the coming year, as well as some of the principal promotional agents in this field. Opportunities in a whole host of different sites are covered. All the costs quoted here are net of VAT unless otherwise stated. It is usually safe to assume that Public Liability Insurance (often with a set minimum of £1 million; sometimes more than this) is a prerequisite for exhibiting in shopping centres and malls.

BROADWAY SHOPPING CENTRE, HAMMERSMITH
c/o Plus Shops Ltd
The Management Suite
The Broadway Shopping Centre
Hammersmith
London W6 9YE
Tel: 020 8563 0137
Fax: 020 8741 3764
Email: jhall@hammersmithbroadway.co.uk
Contact: Joanna Hall - Centre Manager

The Broadway Shopping Centre is right in the heart of Hammersmith and incorporates both the Bus and Tube Stations, making it a bustling and vibrant centre.
There are around 40 stores including a Tesco Metro, Boots, Accessorize and Benetton.
There are 7 Mobile Retail Units which are available to rent for £2,500 plus VAT per calendar month. Those interested in renting a Mobile Retail Unit need to send details of their proposed product lines to Joanna Hall. This is a very popular centre and advanced booking is highly recommended.

CANNON PARK SHOPPING CENTRE
Centre Manager's Office
Lynchgate Road
Coventry
Warks CV4 7EH
Tel: 024 7641 7392
Fax: 024 7669 0833
Email:
cannonpark@centremanagement.fsnet.co.uk
Contact: Keith Allsopp

There is one main promotional space and three smaller concession areas at Cannon Park Shopping Centre. Ranging in size from 16ft by 6ft to 20 square metres and priced from £75 to £350 depending on the size of exhibition or promotion required.
Exhibitors are expected to display their promotions in a professional manner. A more detailed promotional pack is available upon request.
All promoters must supply public liability insurance cover of a minimum of £1 million. Please notify the Centre Manager's Office in advance of all products that you will be displaying or selling on site.

CASTLEGATE SHOPPING CENTRE
Centre Management Offices
High Street
Stockton-on-Tees
Teesside TS18 1BG
Tel: 01642 672783
Fax: 01642 616022
Email: john.clift@dtzms.com
Contact: John Clift - Centre Manager

Castlegate is a six-acre shopping centre spanning a quarter mile of Stockton High Street. It regularly attracts over 12 million visitors a year. The bright and airy indoor centre offers 60 retail units, a market hall and over 800 car parking spaces (including designated disabled bays) with free car parking for the first two hours in the short-term roof top car park and three hours free in the multi-storey car park.
Conveniently situated lifts link all car parks to the shopping malls. A Shopmobility assisted service is also available within the centre. Castlegate's retail mix combines High Street names with small specialist retailers with the emphasis on value for money for today's discerning shoppers.
Free-standing or small exhibition sites are occasionally available and Castlegate is always interested in approaches from businesses producing high quality crafts and merchandising. Managing agents are DTZ Debenham Tie Leung.

THE CENTRE: MK - MIDDLETON HALL
See under 'Maurtraid Craftshows'.

CHERRY TREE SHOPPING CENTRE
Management Suite
Cherry Square

(continued)

The Mall Retail Merchandise Unit (RMU)

Wallasey
Wirral CH44 5XU
Tel: 0151 691 0121
Fax: 0151 637 1822
Email: colin.mccrory@cherrytreecentre.co.uk
Contact: Pauline Smith - Centre Administrator

The centre comprises 140,000 square feet of retail space made up of 41 units, 5 stores, 4 RMUs and a mall café. Pay & Display surface car parking providing 560 spaces, a bus station and two taxi ranks serve the centre. Disabled customers' needs are met by suitable car parking, disabled conveniences, pay phones, ramped access to the shops and a mobility scheme.
The centre has a strong shopper loyalty from the local catchment area of 97,000 residents who live within 10 minutes' travel time. Footfall averages 130,000 per week. Cherry Tree Shopping Centre has mall promotional space available, in addition to the 4 RMUs, throughout the year at competitive rates. A copy of your public liability insurance certificate is required and a licence will be issued.

COCKHEDGE SHOPPING PARK
Centre Manager's Office
17 Cockhedge Way
Warrington
Cheshire WA1 2QQ
Tel: 01925 572219
Fax: 01925 234822
Email: tlc@cockhedge.co.uk
Contact: Tracy or Linda

The Cockhedge Shopping Park comprises a covered mall and an outside retail development. Both promotional spaces are undercover and space is rented on a 7-day weekly basis at prices starting from £500 plus VAT. There are also two barrows on the mall for rental at prices starting at £150 plus VAT payable fortnightly. Anchor tenants at this site include Asda, Argos, Wilkinsons and TK Maxx.
A copy of your public liability insurance will be required and also the signing of the centre's terms and conditions. All exhibitors are expected to display their wares in a professional manner.

CORBY TOWN CENTRE
Corby Town Centre Management
Chisholm House
9 Queen's Square
Corby
Northants NN17 1PD
Tel: 01536 200073
Fax: 01536 401368
Contact: David Ross

This is an open, pedestrianised town centre with several locations in and adjacent to prime shopping, some with covering and including a prominent bandstand. There are areas suitable for mobile display units and large vehicles. There are also standard size market stalls in a busy seven day per week market. Typical rates range from £50 per day to £300 per week (six days).
There are big concessions available for approved registered charities. Payment is due in advance. Exhibitors need to book well in advance as this is a well established, popular pitch.

CORNHILL WALK SHOPPING CENTRE
Management Suite
Brentgovel Street
Bury St Edmunds
Suffolk IP33 1EJ
Tel: 01284 767577
Fax: 01284 769645
Contact: Ms C Harrod - Centre Manager

Cornhill Walk is a small but busy shopping centre in the heart of Bury St Edmunds. Spaces measuring 8ft by 10ft are available at a cost of £200 plus VAT. There are three of these spaces on offer. The centre trades seven days a week (Sundays from 11am to 4pm).

CRAVEN COURT SHOPPING CENTRE
Centre Management Office
High Street
Skipton
North Yorks BD23 1DG
Tel: 01756 700048
Fax: 01756 796522
Email: karen@cravencourt.com
Contact: Karen Hulatt - Centre Manager

Craven Court Shopping Centre is situated on the High Street of Skipton, the 'Gateway to the Dales', with original buildings dating back to the 16th century. The centre is covered with a glass roof with stunning wrought iron work and a York Stone flag floor and was developed in 1988, beautifully incorporating the old and the new and is open seven days

per week throughout the year. Tenants include Laura Ashley, Hawkshead, Wallis, Julian Graves and many more independent shops.
Craven Court is interested in hearing from people producing high quality crafts and merchandise to retail from two well situated retail sites in the centre of the Mall. Charges range from £100 to £225 per week, dependent on the site and the time of year.
These charges include provision of electricity if required. However, all exhibitiors are expected to provide all their own equipment. A copy of your public liability insurance will be required and all exhibitors are required to sign a licence agreement. Payment terms are 14 days prior.

DARWIN SHOPPING CENTRE
Raven Meadows
Shrewsbury
Shropshire SY1 1PL
Tel: 01743 272322
Fax: 01743 272062

The Darwin Shopping Centre, which is attached by Bridge Link to the Raven Meadows multi-storey car park, has a 16ft by 16ft display area for daily/weekly hire for promotions and displays. The centre also has retail merchandising units for short-term or long-term use. Occasionally Darwin is also able to offer retail units for short-term occupancy. Charges are from £70 per day depending upon the time of year and area taken.
Darwin is an indoor centre with 52 units including retailers such as Marks & Spencer, TK Maxx, QVC, River Island, Perfume Shop and Woolworths. The centre is renowned for putting on various art events and exhibitions, together with other community events. Trading is seven days a week.

FREEPORT HORNSEA RETAIL & LEISURE OUTLET VILLAGE
Rolston Road
Hornsea
East Yorks HU18 1UT
Tel: 01964 534211
Fax: 01964 536363
Email: info@freeporthornsea.com
Contact: Meera Patel - Marketing Executive

Freeport Hornsea is a shopping village offering both retail and leisure facilities, with over 40 shops selling famous high street brands at hugely discounted prices. These include Laura Ashley, Moss, Wrangler, Alexon, Waterford Wedgwood, Thornton's and many more.
The centre sometimes holds a Craft Fayre on the site and you will need to contact them to find out when the next one is scheduled and how much participation costs. There is also promotional space available at a cost of £30 a day.
In addition to the retailing side, Freeport Hornsea offers a selection of cafés and restaurants; Neptune's Kingdom, a large soft play area for children; Freeport Hornsea Pottery where adults and children alike can try their hand on the potter's wheel; and arcade machines. Outside there are World of Wings birds of prey flying displays; Butterfly World; Model Village; Adventureland; Children's Rides; Bouncy Castle; Crazy Golf and Games. Free parking, easy access, disabled parking and coach parking all add to the package.

GREEN LANES SHOPPING CENTRE
Management Suite
40 Green Lanes
Barnstaple
Devon EX31 1UL
Tel: 01271 322278
Fax: 01271 324863
Email: p.hill@greenlanes.co.uk
Website: www.greenlanes.co.uk
Contact: Patricia Hill - Centre Administrator

Green Lanes Shopping Centre opened in 1991 and is situated in the heart of Barnstaple. The covered shopping environment has 40 shops which include fashion, sports, individual retailers as well as larger national stores such as Woolworths and BHS. There is a pay-on-foot multi-level shoppers' car park with 411 spaces and parking bays for the disabled.
There are two main display areas for exhibitions. An exhibition space booking is required to be signed to secure an event with payment made in advance. A trading barrow is available for hire for smaller promotions. The centre is open seven days a week; Monday to Saturday 9am to 5.30pm and 10.30am to 4.30pm on Sundays.

THE GRAFTON
46 The Management Suite
The Grafton Centre
Cambridge

(continued)

Cambs CB1 1PS
Tel: 01223 316201
Fax: 01223 460752
Email: liz.mcmanus@prupim.com
Website: www.graftoncentre.co.uk
Contact: Liz McManus - Marketing & Promotions Manager

There is one prime promotional area which goes under the name of Great Court. This area is for promotional purposes only and retail is not allowed to take place in this space. Great Court is 21ft by 21ft and is priced depending on the duration of a promotion, event or exhibition. For more information, or to book Great Court, please contact SpaceandPeople on 0705 900 3144. Retail merchandising units (RMUs) are also available in the centre. All applications to rent a unit must go through Retail Profile Ltd. For more information, call 020 7291 9530.

THE GROVE SHOPPING CENTRE
Centre Management Suite
17A The Grove
Witham
Essex CM8 2YT
Tel: 01376 519440
Fax: 01376 501964
Email: manager@groveshopping.co.uk
Website: www.groveshopping.co.uk
Contact: Wendy Harlow - Centre Manager

The Grove Shopping Centre is a single level, outdoor centre built to the highest standards in an old world style, set within the conservation area of Witham Town Centre, Essex. The centre has a wide range of quality multiple and independent shops and stores.
The Witham Farmers' Market takes place within the centre on the second and fourth Tuesday of each month. Stall space is available from £10 per day. Stall space with electricity costs £15 per day.
Generous promotional and general stall space, which is available all year round, starts from £50 per day. All promotions and goods must be of a professional standard and must not conflict with the goods sold by the centre's tenants. Photographs need to be submitted with applications for sites, for which there is generally good availability. Public liability insurance cover of a minimum of £1 million is required.

GUILDHALL SHOPPING CENTRE
Management Offices
Unit 40, Guildhall Shopping Centre
Exeter
Devon EX4 3HP
Tel: 01392 201910
Contact: Sheryel Ashwell - Centre Administrator

The Guildhall Shopping Centre in Exeter has a unique mix of famous and local names under one roof. The largest shopping centre in Devon & Cornwall, it has a footfall of 250,000 per week.
There are six beautiful, purpose built craft barrows for hire in prime locations and these are available at costs ranging from £10 to £44 on a daily basis.
All goods must be of a professional standard being of a high quality craft or merchandise item and must not conflict with the goods sold by the centre's tenants. Public liability insurance of a minimum of £1 million will be required.

HALTON LEA SHOPPING CENTRE
205 Upper Sales Level
Halton Lea
Runcorn
Cheshire WA7 2EU
Tel: 01928 716363
Fax: 01928 713359
Email: lindsaybeaumont@halton-lea.co.uk
Website: www.halton-lea.co.uk
Contact: Lindsay Beaumont - Promotions

Halton Lea Shopping Centre invites 300,000 customers through its doors each week and is situated in the heart of Runcorn, Cheshire. It is an indoor centre with 85 retail tenants including Argos, Woolworths, JD Sports, New Look and WH Smith. There are four car parks providing 2,200 free parking spaces.
There are three 12ft by 12ft promotional sites costing between £300 and £400 depending on position. Halton Lea is looking forward to hearing from those people offering top quality craftwork exhibitions that can be displayed professionally in Town Square - a focal point of the centre.

HARPUR SHOPPING CENTRE
Management Office
Horne Lane
Bedford
Beds MK40 1TJ
Tel: 01234 357330
Fax: 01234 352117
Email: patc@harpursc23.freeserve.co.uk

Website:
www.harpurshopping-bedford.co.uk
Contact: Pat Combes

The Harpur Centre is an enclosed medium-sized, busy shopping centre with two promotional areas approximately 2.5m wide by 1.5m deep. There must be no product clashes with tenants. All promotions are licensed and public liability insurance of at least £2 million is required. The centre has 24-hour security.

THE MALL

The Mall operates 21 shopping centres throughout the UK (visit the website at: www.themall.co.uk). The Mall is looking for companies with great products, a real flair for retail and excellent customer service. In return, you will have access to 3.7 million shoppers a week and the benefits of the company's innovative management and marketing style.
Opportunities are available in all the malls on a weekly and monthly basis and prices vary per mall. Mall Management requires full details - including photographs of all goods proposed for sale - before approval can be provided. Please call for further information or write requesting preferred dates with a photograph of your merchandise and stand presentation.
Several of the company's malls also have new Retail Merchandising Units which are excellent for displaying products - be sure and ask when you call if these are available.

Malls currently on the list are noted below. Contact The Mall headquarters (details in advert at the beginning of this section and inside front cover) for the up-to-date situation.

The Mall, Aberdeen - Footfall 181,000 per week
Contact: Linda Stewart
Email: linda.stewart@themall.co.uk
Tel: 01224 580076

The Mall, Barnsley, South Yorks - Footfall 158,000 per week
Contact: Ian Fisher
Email: ian.fisher@themall.co.uk
Tel: 01226 295355

The Mall, Bexleyheath, Kent - Footfall 170,000 per week
Contact: Christine Barton
Email: chris.barton@themall.co.uk
Tel: 020 8301 2956

The Mall, Birmingham - Footfall 379,000 per week
Contact: Diane Nicklin
Email: diane.nicklin@themall.co.uk
Tel: 0121 633 3070

The Mall, Blackburn, Lancs - Footfall 315,000 per week
Contact: Janice Chambers
Email: janice.chambers@themall.co.uk
Tel: 01254 54455

The Mall, Bristol - Footfall 250,000 per week
Contact: Lisa Butterworth
Email: lisa.butterworth@themall.co.uk
Tel: 0117 929 0569

The Mall, Chester, Cheshire - Footfall 187,000 per week
Contact: Julie Williams
Email: julie.williams@themall.co.uk
Tel: 01244 342942

The Mall, Edgware, Middx - Footfall 137,000 per week

(continued)

Contact: Alasdair Currie
Email: alasdair.currie@themall.co.uk
Tel: 020 8905 6303

The Mall, Epsom, Surrey - Footfall 131,000 per week
Contact: Paul Clifford
Email: paul.clifford@themall.co.uk
Tel: 01372 742548

The Mall, Falkirk - Footfall 161,000 per week
Contact: Beatrice Pringle
Email: beatrice.pringle@themall.co.uk
Tel: 01324 631985

The Mall, Gloucester - Footfall 172,000 per week
Contact: Jean Wilkins
Email: jean.wilkins@themall.co.uk
Tel: 01452 520023

The Mall, Ilford, Essex - Footfall 275,000 per week
Contact: Jayne Irwin
Email: jayne.irwin@themall.co.uk
Tel: 020 8553 3000

The Mall, Maidstone, Kent - Footfall 220,000 per week
Contact: Paul Alcock
Email: paul.alcock@themall.co.uk
Tel: 01622 691130

The Mall, Middlesbrough - Footfall 281,000 per week
Contact: Patricia Passman
Email: patricia.passman@themall.co.uk
Tel: 01642 244682

The Mall, Norwich, Norfolk - Footfall 203,000 per week
Contact: Sophie Hallett
Email: sophie.hallett@themall.co.uk
Tel: 01603 766430

The Mall, Preston, Lancs - Footfall 186,000 per week
Contact: Ros Harrington
Email: ros.harrington@themall.co.uk
Tel: 01772 204202

The Mall, Romford, Essex - Footfall 112,000 per week
Contact: Pat Shippey
Email: pat.shippey@themall.co.uk
Tel: 01708 733620

The Mall, Southampton, Hants - Footfall 130,000 per week
Contact: Jackie Beazley
Email: jackie.beazley@themall.co.uk
Tel: 023 8033 9164

The Mall, Sutton Coldfield, West Midlands - Footfall 135,000 per week
Contact: Fiona Faizy
Email: fiona.faizy@themall.co.uk
Tel: 0121 355 1112

The Mall, Walthamstow, London - Footfall 150,000 per week
Contact: Shasta Nirwaz
Email: shasta.nirwaz@themall.co.uk
Tel: 020 8509 0016

The Mall, Wood Green, London - Footfall 190,000 per week
Contact: Jackie Webb
Email: jackie.webb@themall.co.uk
Tel: 020 8888 6667

MAURTRAID CRAFTSHOWS
202 Buckingham Road
Bletchley
Milton Keynes
Bucks MK3 5JB
Tel/Fax: 01908 271833
Contact: Susan Preedy

In 2005 Maurtraid has scheduled three events at The Centre: MK (in Middleton Hall) in Central Milton Keynes in Buckinghamshire. The first Maurtraid Craftshow runs from 22-27 February, the second runs from 14-17 April and the third runs from 18-23 October. There are typically between 60 and 100 craft stands available at these long established events and prices are obtainable on application. Top class craftwork and quality demonstrations are sought for the Maurtraid Craftshows. A fourth event is being scheduled for July, with firm dates to be confirmed. See display advertisement.

MAYLORD SHOPPING CENTRE
Management Suite
Hereford
Herefordshire HR1 2DT
Tel: 01432 278083
Fax: 01432 263122

The Maylord Shopping Centre is situated right in the heart of the historic city of Hereford. The shopping centre comprises a mix of pretty, pedestrianised streets and a welcoming, two-level enclosed Atrium boasting a good tenant mix with over 40 shops including names such as TKMaxx, Next, Argos, Laura Ashley, Wallis and a variety of smaller independent retailers.

The centre has both internal and external exhibition space. SpaceandPeople is now responsible for the letting of mall space and can be contacted by telephone on 0705 900 3144 or via the internet at www.spaceandpeople.com

You will need to submit details of your craft product and a copy of your public liability insurance details. All exhibitors are expected to present their displays professionally, providing all their own equipment.

MILL GATE SHOPPING CENTRE

Centre Management Suite
24A The Mall
Bury
Lancs BL9 0QQ
Tel: 0161 763 4593
Fax: 0161 763 4594
Email: vicky.mckay@westfield-uk.com
Website: www.westfield.com/millgate
Contact: Vicky McKay - Sales & Promotions Manager

Mill Gate Shopping Centre is situated in the heart of Bury's thriving market town and attracts 16 million customers per year. The centre's covered malls contain 149 retailers trading from just under 33,000 sq.m. on one level. Situated adjacent to the bus and Metrolink stations, the centre has excellent transport links.

Mill Gate is anchored by some of the UK's largest retailers including Marks & Spencer, Bhs, Littlewoods and Boots, which are supported by leading high street fashion brands New Look, Next, River Island, Burtons, Next, Morgan and Oasis.

Whether you want to sell or promote your product, Mill Gate Shopping Centre can offer you the perfect opportunity to showcase your products. Retail Merchandising Units (RMUs) are state-of-the-art sales units designed to drive sales from passing shoppers in the malls. The RMU offers a flexible short-term agreement with low start-up costs and overheads at competitive rates to suit all budgets. Whatever your promotional requirements, Mill Gate features 12 excellent Exhibition Areas of various sizes, all in high customer flow locations and adjacent to major stores. All sites have central mall locations offering the per-

(continued)

fect opportunity to interact with thousands of customers on a daily basis. Electricity can be supplied to all areas to enhance the display further and the centre's dedicated team are on hand to assist with all service requirements.
You will need to submit details - including photographs - of your merchandise along with a copy of your public and employers liability insurance details. Following approval by the centre management, a licence will be issued.

ONE STOP SHOPPING CENTRE
The Management Suite
2 Walsall Road
Perry Barr
Birmingham
West Midlands B42 1AA
Tel: 0121 344 3697
Fax: 0121 344 3966
Email: natal.chapman@btconnect.com
Contact: Natal Chapman - Promotions Coordinator

The One Stop Shopping Centre was opened to the public in August 1990 and now has a current footfall rate of 200,000 per week. It offers 1,000 free car parking spaces and easy access from the M6, a bus terminus and a railway station round the corner, making public transport simple.
There are currently 68 retailers. The centre offers two main exhibition areas at a cost of £550 and £750 per week. Smaller areas may be available upon request. All enquiries should be made in writing, giving full details of your promotion.

PAISLEY SHOPPING CENTRE
The Management Suite
The Paisley Shopping Centre
23 High Street
Paisley
Renfrewshire PA1 2AQ
Tel: 0141 848 5666
Fax: 0141 848 6667
Email: s.wilson@thepaisleycentre.co.uk and a.mackinnon@thepaisleycentre.co.uk
Contact: Susan Wilson or Andrew MacKinnon

Handcart units and mall promotional space are available within this fully let and successful scheme, anchored by Marks & Spencer, Littlewoods, Co-op Department Store and Boots.
Craft rates for promotions are weekly based. Operators are required to complete a licence, which details the type of goods to be sold. Space is at a premium in this busy centre and traders should book well in advance to secure a promotion.

PARK MALL SHOPPING CENTRE
Management Suite
19A Park Mall
Ashford
Kent TN24 8RY
Tel: 01233 630811
Fax: 01233 646680
Email: paul-stone@park-mall.co.uk
Website: www.parkmallshopping.co.uk
Contact: Paul Stone (quote ref: 'Craftworkers 2005' when writing/e-mailing)

There are two exhibition sites available at Park Mall at a cost approximating to £55 per day or £220 per week. The centre also has a craft barrow, suitably furnished for various uses. Where necessary, plans, drawings and photographs for all promotions/displays must be submitted to the Centre Manager (Paul Stone) for approval. Other regulations apply, which are all confirmed on booking. You will be asked to confirm that the exhibition is to be of a very high standard.

THE PAVILIONS SHOPPING CENTRE - UXBRIDGE, MIDDX
See under 'Uxbridge Craft Market'.

PRINCES MEAD SHOPPING CENTRE
Management Offices
Farnborough
Hants GU14 6YB
Tel: 01252 375520
Fax: 01252 522045
Email: vanessa@princes-mead.co.uk
Contact: Vanessa Johnson - Assistant Centre Manager

Princes Mead Shopping Centre *is* the centre of Farnborough, catering for the local community with an average weekly footfall of 98,000. Opened in 1990, it has 38 shop units including Boots, WH Smith, Blockbuster Video, a fitness club and a food court.
There is space on the mall for approximately 12 stalls of various sizes and prices vary from £200 to £400 per week. Daily rates on application. Public liability insurance is required and all exhibitors are expected to present

their displays professionally.
Princes Mead is always interested in welcoming new licencees to Farnborough.

ROEBUCK CENTRE
54/56 High Street
Newcastle-under-Lyme
Staffs ST5 1SW
Tel/Fax: 01782 627843
Email: roebuck.centre@dial.pipex.com
Contact: Philip Howard - Centre Manager

The Roebuck Centre is centrally located in the historic market town of Newcastle-under-Lyme. Footfall averages 100,000 per week, although the potential catchment is greater. The centre boasts some well known national retailers like Argos, Next and Boots and is completely enclosed and trading on one level.
It has one exhibition area available for rent on a weekly basis and another area available for rent on a longer term. Exhibitors will be required to complete a licence as well as produce a copy of their public liability insurance.

SHAWLANDS SHOPPING CENTRE
Centre Manager's Office
Kilmarnock Road
Glasgow G41 3NN
Tel: 0141 636 8550
Fax: 0141 636 8689
Email: shawlands_shopcentre@talk21.com
Contact: Bill Michie - Centre Manager

Shawlands Shopping Centre sits on the south side of Glasgow among a population of over 130,000. There are two anchor stores, Sainsbury's and Somerfield, and the retail mix includes Farmfoods, Boots the Chemist, Birthdays and Your More Store, among others. The busy mall also extends onto the main thoroughfare of Kilmarnock Road.
The centre has internal exhibition space within both the mall and the atrium areas. All stallholders taking promotional space should be covered by their own public liability and traders insurance. A licence for mall space will be issued under the Fire Regulations and all contact should be made through the centre manager.

SWAN SHOPPING CENTRE
Centre Manager's Office
High Street
Leatherhead
Surrey KT22 8AH
Tel: 01372 376358
Fax: 01372 363880
Email:
patlawless@swan-shoppingcentre.co.uk
Contact: Pat Lawless - Centre Manager

Craft Markets are held on a Saturday once a month throughout October and November and every Saturday in December at a charge of £15 per day. There must be no product conflicts with existing tenants.
Mall concession space is charged at £60 (inclusive) per day. The centre is not locked at night, so exhibitors must dismantle their displays and remove them from the site each day.

UXBRIDGE CRAFT MARKET AT THE PAVILIONS SHOPPING CENTRE
Tel: 01480 456008
Fax: 01480 458977
Email:
enquiries@uxbridge-craft-market.co.uk
Website: www.uxbridge-craft-market.co.uk
Contact: Leon Coleman

The weekly Uxbridge Craft Market is open on Wednesdays till 7 December with extra Mondays and Tuesdays throughout November and at other seasonal periods. Those extra days in 2005 will be: 28 Feb, 1 March, 26-27 Sept, 24-25 Oct, 31 Oct, 1 Nov, 7-8 Nov, 14-15 Nov, 21-22 Nov, 28-29 Nov and 5-6 Dec.
With an ongoing programme of community craft activities and the popular 'Artists in Residence' scheme, the market attracts visitors from all around the Middlesex, Berkshire and Hertfordshire areas.
Trading facilities are excellent with large 8ft by 4ft pitches inclusive of table. There are easy, straightforward unloading arrangements with free parking for traders. The market is in a prime site in the heart of the Pavilions Shopping Centre. Apply for current prices and availability.

VICARAGE FIELD SHOPPING CENTRE
Management Suite, Ripple Road
Barking
IG11 8DQ
Tel: 020 8270 7100
Fax: 020 8270 7101
Email: jkb@vicfield.co.uk
Website: www.vicfield.co.uk
Contact: Mrs J Bones

(continued)

Vicarage Field is a modern, fully enclosed shopping facility at the heart of Barking town centre, in the Greater London catchment area. At 275,000 square feet and a giant Asda superstore, the centre benefits from a constant level of footfall throughout the week. Prime mall promotional sites are available at competitive rates with significant discounts for sole traders retailing quality 'craft' style manufactured product.

WELLINGTON SHOPPING CENTRE
34 The Wellington Centre
Victoria Road
Aldershot
Hants
GU11 1DB
Tel: 01252 315315
Fax: 01252 350363
Email: cgangadeen@lcpproperties.co.uk
Contact: Caroline Gangadeen

The Wellington Shopping Centre is the main retail centre within Aldershot's pedestrianised town centre, providing two large covered malls of retail units with attached 300-space multi-storey car park. Tenants include Boots, WH Smith, Clinton Cards, Roseby's, Wilkinsons, Mothercare, Mark One, New Look and Argos.
There are three promotional sites in varying size located within the centre, costing £60 per day/£215 per week. There is also a glass-fronted kiosk costing £70 per day/£250 per week. Footfall data and further details are available on request.

WESTGATE SHOPPING CENTRE
Management Suite
Stevenage
Herts SG1 1QR
Tel/Fax: 01438 740696
Email: hollyhall@btconnect.com
Contact: Holly Hall - Office Manager

The Westgate Shopping Centre is located in the heart of Stevenage Town Centre and has an average weekly footfall of 140,000. Westgate is a fully enclosed community shopping centre that is covered by 24-hour security and is open seven days a week. The Centre contains 34 retail units and tenants include large national retailers and small specialist shops. Westgate does not cater for commercial displays and only accepts 'art and crafts' style stalls.
Promotional space is available in three different sizes, with the largest being 24ft by 12ft. Rent is charged on a weekly basis and starts at £250 plus VAT. Public liability insurance and electrical test certificates are required and exhibitors must provide all their own equipment.

WEST SWINDON SHOPPING CENTRE
Management Suite
Tewkesbury Way
Swindon
Wilts
SN5 7DL
Tel: 01793 872987
Website: www.swindonweb.com/wssc/
Contact: Julian Leggett

The West Swindon Shopping Centre is convenient for Junction 16 on the M4 as well as for Swindon town centre. The centre's promotion emphasises the lack of problems associated with in-town shopping as there is plenty of free and secure parking, all on the ground level. Being on the one level, the centre is suitable for the disabled. There is a wide range of shops, a McDonald's and three takeaway units, as well as banking, a Post Office, travel agency etc.
For more information on opportunities for craftworkers at West Swindon, please see their display advertisement in this section.

MARKETS, SHOWCASES, SELLING & UNITS

These few pages highlight a range of different craft marketing and exhibiting opportunities not covered in the previous sections of the book. All charges quoted here are net of VAT unless otherwise stated. Given the nature of some of the options described here, such as themed shows, changing exhibitions/sales and the availability of workshops and retail spaces, you will find that it is always worthwhile to telephone the contacts to get a clearer picture of how things are developing through the year.

AMBERLEY WORKING MUSEUM

Amberley
Arundel
West Sussex BN18 9LT
Tel: 01798 831370
Fax: 01798 831831
Email: office@amberleymuseum.co.uk
Website: www.amberleymuseum.co.uk

Amberley Working Museum is a 36-acre open-air site dedicated to the industrial heritage of the south-east. Exhibits include a narrow-gauge railway and vintage bus collection (which provide free travel around the site), the Connected Earth telecommunications hall, the EDF ENERGY Electricity Hall and much more.
The museum is also home to a range of traditional craftspeople, such as the broom-maker, blacksmith, walking stick maker, potter and clay pipe maker. A number of volunteers also undertake craft activities, such as woodturners, wheelwrights and the Print Workshop.
The museum is open from March until late October, Wednesday to Sunday (plus Bank Holiday Mondays and every day during West Sussex School Holidays), from 10am to 5.30pm (last entry 4.30pm). For further details, including the availability of craftspeople, contact the museum.

APPLE CRAFT CENTRE

Macknade
Selling Road
Faversham
Kent ME13 8XF
Tel: 01795 590504
Contact: Ian or Sue Sandford

Only selling the hand-crafted products of selected craftworkers living in Kent, the craft shop occupies the heavily beamed barn between two pairs of former oast houses. The complex offers craftworkers units to rent and presently accommodates a stringed instrument music shop specialising in banjos, a holistic therapist and a woodturner.
The coffee shop and restaurant is situated on the first floor and is accessed by stairs in the craft shop. Specialising in home-made food, the coffee shop and restaurant is open seven days a week, as is the craft shop (9.30am to 5.30pm). Additionally, the Apple Oast Restaurant is open Friday and Saturday evenings from 7pm. On the first floor, above the craft shop, there is an open space suitable for exhibitions, displays, lectures and club meetings.

ARTSWAY

Station Road
Sway
Hants SO41 6BA
Tel: 01590 682260
Fax: 01590 681989
Email: mail@artsway.org.uk
Website: www.artsway.org.uk

ArtSway is a contemporary visual arts venue based in the New Forest. It presents a high quality exhibition programme and also displays a selection of craft for sale in its craft cabinets. The craft work is changed throughout the year and ArtSway invites craftmakers to send in details of their work for selection.
Please include images, a small statement about your work and an SAE.
Opportunities for craft related workshops and exhibitions are also available. Contact the gallery for more details.

BARLEYLANDS CRAFT VILLAGE

Barleylands Road
Billericay
Essex CM11 2UD
Tel: 01268 290219
Fax: 01268 290222
Email: info@barleylands.co.uk
Website: www.barleylands.co.uk
Contact: Kerry Summers

Barleylands Craft Village has over 30 individual specialist workshops providing excellent

rental facilities. Local craftspeople have the opportunity to work and sell their products to the visiting public. Craft workshop studios surround the beautifully landscaped courtyards which invite visitors to relax and enjoy a cream tea in the farmhouse tearoom.
The Craft Village has been awarded the Visitor Attraction Quality Assurance Service by the East of England Tourist Board. Free entry and free parking all year round (closed Mondays).
Christmas Craft Markets are held alongside Farmers' Markets on 10 Dec and 17 Dec. Also on site is a children's animal farm centre open March until October; a small entrance fee applies here.
For further details on how you can base your craft business at Barleylands, contact Kerry Summers.

BILSTON CRAFT GALLERY
Mount Pleasant
Bilston
Wolverhampton
West Midlands WV14 7LU
Tel: 01902 552507
Fax: 01902 552504
Email: bilstoncraftgallery@dial.pipex.com
Website: www.wolverhamptonart.org

Bilston Craft Gallery is the largest craft dedicated venue in the West Midlands region. It has a lively programme of temporary exhibitions which feature the very best in contemporary ceramics, glass, jewellery, textiles and woodwork.
Craftsense, the gallery's new permanent exhibition, provides an introduction to craft for everyone. Tracing craftmaking in the region, Craftsense displays fine, local, historical items including the internationally renowned Bilton Enamels alongside contemporary pieces.
Craftplay is the award winning early years gallery offering workshops for nurseries and pre-school groups. Encouraging exploration and creativity in the very young, Craftplay features specially commissioned craft pieces and an exciting range of sensory materials and environments.
First Floor is a hireable gallery space for the community to show exhibitions of craft and art. Contact the gallery for more information and to book in a slot.
The Craft Shop has specially selected crafts for the visitor to buy. Bilston Craft Gallery is free admission and is open from Tuesday to Friday from 10am to 4pm and on Saturdays from 11am to 4pm.

BLAKEMERE CRAFT CENTRE
Chester Road
Sandiway
Northwich
Cheshire CW8 2EB
Tel: 01606 883261
Email:
info@blakemere-shoppingexperience.com
Website:
www.blakemere-shoppingexperience.com
Contact: Janet Barnes

Blakemere is situated in the beautiful Cheshire countryside yet easily accessible on the junction of the A49/A556 at Sandiway. Based in and around sympathetically restored Edwardian Stables, Blakemere consists of over 30 craft shops and workshops, a large garden centre, children's indoor playbarn, aquatic and falconry centre with bird of prey aviaries and flying arena and a restaurant and coffee shop.
Business opportunities for craftworkers to rent shop or workshop units are offered, subject to craft and availability. Initial three-year leases, with the option to terminate by giving six months' notice.
Further opportunities available for craftworkers at the centre's craft fairs which are held every weekend throughout the year plus every Wednesday from October through to Christmas. Free admission to all fairs, with 12 stalls to rent at reasonable prices. See display advertisement.
Blakemere is open throughout the year, Tuesday to Friday 10am to 5pm, Saturday, Sunday and Bank Holidays 10am to 5.30pm.

BLUECOAT DISPLAY CENTRE
Bluecoat Chambers
School Lane
Liverpool
Merseyside L1 3BX
Tel: 0151 709 4014
Fax: 0151 707 8106
Email: crafts@bluecoatdisplaycentre.com
Website: www.bluecoatdisplaycentre.com
Contact: Maureen Bampton

Situated in the walled garden of the Bluecoat Chambers in the heart of Liverpool, this centre says it has come to represent the best in contemporary crafts from throughout the British Isles. It specialises in exhibiting and selling contemporary hand-made glass, ceramics, studio pottery, jewellery, wood and textiles by over 400 professional craftmakers. Its challenging exhibition programme reflects

both emerging talent and established craftsmanship. The Bluecoat Display Centre offers an interest-free credit scheme to purchasers through its participation in TAPS and it allows original and innovative craftwork to be commissioned simply, with the help of its experienced staff.
Purchasers can also now buy on-line from the centre's craft gift shop and exhibitions on the website.

BROADFIELD HOUSE GLASS MUSEUM
Compton Drive
Kingswinford
West Midlands DY6 9NS
Tel: 01384 812745
Fax: 01384 812746
Email: glass.museum@dudley.gov.uk
Website: www.glassmuseum.org.uk

Craftworkers are welcome to send information on their work to this well known centre. The work will be considered for exhibition in the Glassmakers Gallery; there is, understandably, a bias towards glass, but all media are welcome.

CAMBRIDGE ARTS & CRAFTS
PO Box 82
Cambridge
Cambs CB2 2XQ
Tel: 01223 247370
Email: ros.myers@clara.co.uk
Contact: Roz Myers

Cambridge Arts & Crafts takes place every Saturday throughout the year, except for the first Saturday in June and the last Saturday in December. There are extra weekdays in the run-up to 25 December. The market is held at Fisher Hall, Guildhall Place, Cambridge CB2. The standard cost is £25.50 per day (which includes electricity), plus £1.50 if you need to hire a table. Good quality craftwork is sought for these events and new exhibitors will need to send in photographs. A limited amount of imported goods are permitted, but these must be good quality ethnic work. There is sometimes late availability of space so it is always worth giving Roz Myers a call. There are roughly 30 exhibitors showing each week.

CANDID ARTS TRUST
3 Torrens Street
London EC1V 1NQ
Tel: 020 7837 4237
Email: info@candidarts.com
Website: www.candidarts.com
Contact: Duncan Barlow

Candid Arts Trust is a thriving arts centre based in the heart of Angel (sited just behind the Underground station) in London. The centre consists of three interconnected warehouse style gallery spaces of a combined total of 6,000 square feet, café, banquet room and 25 artists' studios. All spaces are available for hire for exhibitions, events, rehearsals, conferences, meetings, location filming and parties.
The main aim of the Trust is the promotion of Art and Design Graduates through an exhibition programme and internet based services and databases such as Network A.D. and degreeshow.com (services are not exclusive to recent graduates).
Candid runs a programme of events and classes, including life drawing and painting courses, a weekly experimental film screening evening on Tuesdays, singing classes and poetry evenings.

CLERKENWELL GREEN ASSOCIATION
Pennybank Chambers
33-35 St John's Square
London EC1M 4DS
Tel: 020 7251 0276
Email: info@cga.org.uk
Website: www.cga.org.uk
Contact: Claire Gutteridge

Clerkenwell Green Association (CGA) is a unique charity set up to maintain and promote fine craft and design. Through a number of initiatives, including well managed studio spaces, the Clerkenwell Award, Clerkenwell Designers Network and the Pennybank Showcase facilities, CGA continues to protect many traditional and contemporary craft skills.
There are 65 individual studios in two well maintained buildings in the heart of Clerkenwell. There is also a shared space which can be booked for one or more days a week at £9 per day.
The Clerkenwell Designers Network supports designer makers based across London. The Network allows members - many of whom are isolated or have no contact with creative businesses - to meet and share their ideas and experiences. Annual membership is £35 and is currently non-selective. Members also have access to CGA's comprehensive business development programme of seminars,

workshops and one-to-one surgeries, designed to develop and enhance the business skills of those running a small creative business. CGA runs around two to three different training sessions each week, which are either subsidised or free.
The Clerkenwell Award is a scheme that offers a package of financial and business support to help those wanting to set up in a studio in the London Boroughs of Hackney, Camden, Islington or Tower Hamlets. The award lasts for an 18-month period, during which time those supported receive up to 50% of their studio costs, free business support and a business advisor to help guide them through their early stages.
The Pennybank Showcase is an exhibition area with excellent display facilities. Each year, CGA hosts a number of exhibitions which are open to the general public - aiming to demystify and make accessible the work of designer makers to as wide an audience as possible. Regular events include two open studio and design fair weekends and a biannual fashion, accessory and jewellery exhibition aimed at the fashion retail industry.

COCKINGTON COURT CRAFT STUDIOS
Cockington Court
Cockington
Torquay
Devon
TQ2 6XA
Tel: 01803 606035
Email:
info@countryside-trust.org.uk
Website:
www.countryside-trust.org.uk/cockington

Set among 450 acres of beautiful parkland and gardens, the 16th century manor house of Cockington Court is home to a vibrant community of craftspeople, keeping the craft heritage alive and enabling visitors to buy direct from the maker.
All the craftspeople can be seen working in their own individual studios. The crafts currently here include glassblowing, studio pottery, blacksmithing, calligraphy & art, patchwork, aromatherapy, jewellery, woodturning and framing/prints.
Also at the Court is 'Creations' licensed café and restaurant. The surrounding grounds are full of interest with a Norman church close by and behind the house the peaceful walled Rose Garden and Organic Kitchen Garden. There is also a children's play area. Walks and ancient paths lead from the Court all around the estate and these are well signposted. Horse and carriage rides operate to and from the Court and village from Easter to October while the Cockington Bus runs daily from May to September.

COLETTE HAZELWOOD CONTEMPORARY JEWELLERY
Studio 4
Manchester Craft & Design Centre
17 Oak Street
Northern Quarter
Manchester
M4 5JD
Tel: 0161 839 0030
Fax: 0161 832 3416
Email: colettehazelwood@tiscali.co.uk
Website: www.colettehazelwood.com

Colette (winner of a Shell Livewire Young Entrepreneur Award 2002) set up her contemporary jewellery studio/shop in 1999. Since then it has gone from strength to strength and she now shows other designers' work as well. The emphasis is on the modern, incorporating both precious and non-precious materials. It is open from 10am to 5.30pm, Monday to Saturday plus Sundays in December.

COUNTRYCRAFT
5 Boucher Place
St Werburghs
Bristol
BS2 9YY
Tel: 0117 955 7936
Contact: Sandra Atkins

Countrycraft has staged West Country Crafts for 18 years at the Lacock Village Hall, National Trust Village of Lacock, near Chippenham, Wilts. These fairs take place every Sunday and Bank Holiday Monday from the week preceding Easter up to mid-December. At the time of going to press the programme had not been confirmed for 2005, so please contact Sandra Atkins to make sure that all details remain the same.
The cost of participation is around £20 per day but space does tend to get booked up fast. There are about 20 stands at each fair. Photographs/samples are required from exhibitors who have not participated before. Crafts of the very highest standard are required and no mixed crafts on any one stand are permitted. Also, all crafts on display must be both British made and made by the person actually selling them.

THE CRAFT CENTRE & DESIGN GALLERY
City Art Gallery
The Headrow
Leeds
West Yorks LS1 3AB
Tel: 0113 247 8241
Email: information@craftcentreleeds.co.uk
Website: www.craftcentreleeds.co.uk
Contact: Hayley Walker

Established in 1982, The Craft Centre & Design Gallery is ideally situated in Leeds city centre, underneath Leeds City Art Gallery. The gallery promotes contemporary craft by designers based in Britain through a comprehensive exhibition plan. These exhibitions and showcases feature contemporary jewellery, ceramics, glass, applied art, limited edition prints and hand-made cards.

CRAFTMARK
Enterprise House
The Ramparts
Dundalk
Co Louth
Republic of Ireland
Tel: 00 353 42 932 6944
Fax: 00 353 42 932 7101
Email: enquiries@craftmark.ie
Website: www.craftmark.ie
Contact: Sarah Daly

also at:
11 Scotch Street
Downpatrick
Co Down BT30 6AQ
Tel: 028 4461 7214
Fax: 028 4461 7133
Email/Website as above
Contact: Jan Irwin

Craftmark came into being as a result of two networks meeting through The Network of Craft Development Officers Ireland - North & South and realising that there were great advantages and economies of scale in forming a partnership between the two networks.
Craftmark's main objective is to improve cross-border network structures and projects that strengthen the network of Craft Enterprises which produce, promote and present craft and broaden the range of audiences and participation in the Craft, Applied Art and Design sector.
Craftmark offers a three-year events, training and support programme 2003-2006. It has two part-time coordinators (Sarah Daly in Dundalk and Jan Irwin in Downpatrick) and the two offices as noted above. These will double as information libraries and resource centres. The Craftmark Project started in September 2003.

CRAFTS STUDY CENTRE
Surrey Institute of Art & Design, University College
Falkner Road
Farnham
Surrey GU9 7DS
Tel: 01252 891450
Fax: 01252 891451
Email: craftscentre@surrart.ac.uk
Website: www.craftscentre.surrart.ac.uk

The Crafts Study Centre is the new UK museum for modern and contemporary crafts. Housed in a purpose-built museum and study centre at the front of the Farnham campus of The Surrey Institute of Art & Design, it opened in June 2004. There are two galleries: the Tanner Gallery presents work from the Centre's remarkable permanent collections of ceramics, textiles, lettering, archives and furniture. The first exhibition - Crafts in the 20th Century - revisits the first exhibition of the centre at the Holburne Museum, Bath, in 1972.
A temporary exhibition gallery shows work by contemporary craft practitioners, with the focus for the first year on ceramics. Major shows of new work by Magdalene Odundo, Takeshi Yasuda and Emmanuel Cooper lead into a textiles year in the summer of 2005, with the first planned show being 'Sophie Roet: rediscovering textiles'.
A research room enables study visits (on an appointment basis) to the collection and archive. Digital images from the collection can viewed on the Arts & Humanities Data Service website (www.ahds.ac.uk). There is a small shop, with objects sourced by the New Ashgate Gallery and publications relating to the centre and its craft collections.

ELSECAR HERITAGE CENTRE
Wath Road
Elsecar
Barnsley
South Yorks S74 8HJ
Tel: 01226 740203
Fax: 01226 350239
Email:
elsecarheritagecentre@barnsley.gov.uk
Website: www.barnsley.gov.uk
Contact: Asst Manager (units for hire) or Promotions Officer (events)

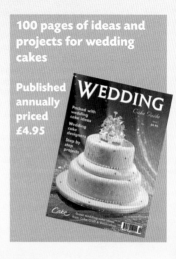

The Elsecar Heritage Centre is an Antique, History and Craft Centre offering something for everyone, with easy access from the M1. Set within the attractive conservation village of Elsecar, the centre is located within the former ironworks and colliery workshops of the Earls of Fitzwilliam.

Restored buildings now house an antique centre, individual craft workshops and exhibitions of Elsecar's past. The site also comprises its own steam railway line, exhibition venue and the world famous Newcomen Beam Engine.

Craft and starter units are available to rent; please contact for latest situation.

The centre also hosts a year-round series of events such as craft shows, children's events and history weekends, with stall booking forms on request.

The site is open from 10am to 5pm daily. For Exhibitions and Craft Shops, please ring to confirm. There is free entry to the site and free car parking (admission charges apply to exhibitions and during special events).

FARNHAM MALTINGS

Bridge Square
Farnham
Surrey GU9 7QR
Tel: 01252 726234
Fax: 01252 718177
Email: info@farnhammaltings.com
Website: www.farnhammaltings.com
Contact: Kate Martin

Situated in the beautiful town of Farnham in Surrey, Farnham Maltings hosts regular art and craft exhibitions in the gallery. Festival of Crafts is the annual craft event held in October (15-16 Oct in 2005) at which established craft practitioners show alongside first-time graduate exhibitors.

Monthly craft based workshops are organised for both adults and children. Also on site is a range of working studios that include jewellery and textile designers, some of which have work on sale. The gallery and other rooms are available for hire.

Other events include cinema, theatre and music evenings. Farnham Maltings has a café and bar open for lunches and early evening drinks.

THE HARBOUR GALLERY

Le Boulevard
St Aubin, Jersey
Tel: 01534 743044
Fax: 01534 854690
Website: www.mnlg.com

The Harbour Gallery was opened in November 2002 by the Art in the Frame Foundation and is run totally by volunteers. It exhibits the work of over 80 local artists and craftworkers, holds monthly exhibitions, runs workshops, demonstrations, lectures and is the home of the Contemporary Textile Group 2003.

Items stocked include paintings, prints, photographs, ceramics, jewellery, enamel, wood, cards, candles etc. The gallery is open seven days a week from 10.30am to 5.30pm.

HOLMFIRTH CRAFT & TREASURE MARKET

Holmfirth Market Hall
38 Huddersfield Road + Hollowgate
Holmfirth
West Yorks
HD9 3JH
Tel: 01484 223730 (Mon-Sat)
or 01484 222437 (Thurs and Sat mornings only)
Fax: 01484 223735
Email: markets@kirklees.gov.uk

Holmfirth is situated in the heart of 'Last of the Summer Wine' country south of Huddersfield in West Yorkshire. It is ideally placed for traders and visitors from West Yorkshire, South Yorkshire, Greater Manchester and Derbyshire.

The Craft & Treasure Market is held in Holmfirth Market Hall every Saturday and Bank Holiday Monday and has up to 40 stalls available. Prices per day range from £10.15 to £13.80 and all traders must have public liability insurance cover. The market is operated by Kirklees Council Markets Department.

HUB

Navigation Wharf
Carre Street
Sleaford
Lincs NG34 7TW
Tel: 01529 308710
Fax: 01529 308711
Email: hub@leisureconnection.co.uk
Website: www.thehubcentre.org

The Hub's home is a newly refurbished four-storey warehouse on the River Slea in Sleaford in the heart of Lincolnshire and now claims to be the largest centre in the UK for

craft design and making. The Hub will hold five exhibitions a year in its main Gallery, with complementary shows in its Roof Gallery.
From the functional to the decorative and from the traditional to the conceptual, exhibitions will explore contemporary craft design and making from all over the UK and from around the world. The work of up and coming designers and makers will be shown alongside that of celebrated artists and makers and the Hub will promote the work of exhibitors at a national and international level.
The centre will have six designer-makers in residence at the on-site workshops throughout the year. These makers will sell their work from the gallery shop, adding to the range of work on sale and on view.

THE MALL GALLERIES
Administration Office
17 Carlton House Terrace
London SW1Y 5BD
Tel: 020 7930 6844
Fax: 020 7839 7830
Email: info@mallgalleries.com
Website: www.mallgalleries.org.uk
Contact: John Deston or Briony Chaplin

The Mall Galleries are home to the Federation of British Artists, an incorporated charity founded in 1961 to promote the visual arts in Britain. It is the umbrella organisation for nine national art societies. Election to membership of these societies is on merit, though non-members are entitled to submit works for selection for the annual exhibitions held in the Mall Galleries. Programmes of exhibition tours, lectures, demonstrations and workshops are arranged throughout the year to complement the exhibitions.
The three interlinked galleries on the Mall, in the heart of London's West End, open onto the ride near Admiralty Arch and provide a total of 500 square metres of exhibition space available for hire by individuals and groups. Other services include a commissions consultancy and an education outreach scheme.

MONYMUSK ARTS CENTRE
Monymusk
by Inverurie
Aberdeenshire
AB51 7HJ
Tel: 01467 651220
Fax: 01467 651250
Website: www.artstrust.org
Contact: Mrs F Taylor

Monymusk Arts Centre stages a five-month Crafts Sale from May to September inclusive. Some of the selected craftspeople are in residence every day, with their ware representing an enormous variety of local crafts.
Those participating in 2004 came from all around the local area, including craftworkers from Kinellar, Lumpanan, Lonmay, Aberdeen, Inverurie, Strathdon, Kintore, Kemnay, Insch and Kinmuck. The Crafts Sale is open daily from 10am to 4pm.
Craftworkers wishing to participate usually commit themselves to a set number of days working at the sale; there is also an exhibiting payment arrangement with details available on application to Mrs Taylor. Admission for the public is free throughout the season. There is also generally a Christmas Craft Fair held at the centre in November.

OTTERTON MILL GALLERY
Otterton
Budleigh Salterton
Devon
EX9 7HG
Tel: 01395 568008
Email: escape@ottertonmill.com
Website: www.ottertonmill.com
Contact: Lisa Scattergood

Set beside the River Otter in one of Devon's loveliest valleys, ottertonmill is a very special place; celebrating the best that the county has to offer. In the unique setting of the historic mill building, visitors will find the work of over 150 leading artists and craftspeople from Devon, Dorset and Somerset.
The gallery has a constantly changing selection of beautiful pottery and glassware, finely crafted jewellery, metalwork, textiles and woodwork. The gallery also displays a wide choice of paintings, drawings, sculpture, prints and photography - with something for all tastes and for all budgets. On the ground floor, the gallery shop holds a good stock of cards and small items which make excellent gifts at any time of the year.
The mill is also home to three artists studios that are open to the public; a centuries old working water mill that supplies flour exclusively to the centre's famous bakery; and a fabulous restaurant serving food to die for. The centre also has a fast growing reputation as a superb live music venue - with blues, folk, jazz or classical events on most Thursday nights. These events normally sell out well in advance so early booking is recommended.

The owners add: "At Otterton we have worked to create an overall atmosphere designed to revive the soul and satisfy the senses. ottertonmill is a place to relax, to unwind, to explore, to escape to and most of all to enjoy".

PICCADILLY MARKET
St James's Church
197 Piccadilly
London W1J 9LL
Tel: 020 7292 4864
Fax: 020 7734 7449
Email: joel@sjcp.fsnet.co.uk
Website: www.st-james-piccadilly.org
Contact: Joel Lewis - Market Manager

Piccadilly Market is held in the courtyard of St James's Church, one of Christopher Wren's finest churches and reputed to be his favourite. The Arts & Crafts Market was first held at St James's as part of the Piccadilly Arts Festival in August 1981 and it opened permanently in 1984.
The Arts & Crafts Market opens from 10am to 6pm from Wednesday to Saturday (Tuesdays are dedicated to antiques and collectables). There are between 45 and 50 stalls each week. Go to the website for a downloadable application form.

THE PLATFORM GALLERY
Station Road
Clitheroe
Lancs BB7 2JT
Tel: 01200 443071
Fax: 01200 414556
Email: platform.gallery@ribblevalley.gov.uk
Website: see art section at
www.ribblevalley.gov.uk
Contact: Grace Whowell

The Platform Gallery is situated in the historic market town of Clitheroe in the heart of the Ribble Valley in Lancashire. It is located in a prime position in the old railway station building, built in 1870. Awarded an Arts Lottery Grant in 2001, the gallery was totally refurbished to provide an airy contemporary craft exhibition space, shop and education facilities operated by Ribble Valley Borough Council.
The Platform Gallery hosts eight exhibitions per year, including solo, group and themed shows. The emphasis is on high quality work by both national and local makers. The shop features an ever-changing selection of ceramics, glass, wood, textiles as well as smaller showcase exhibitions. It offers the Arts Council interest free credit scheme on purchases between £100 and £2,000.
The gallery has a strong education programme and workshops and talks run alongside every exhibition throughout the year. Throughout August there are also children's craft workshops. The education room is available for hire to artists and community groups for creative activities, talks, workshops, exhibitions etc.
The Platform Gallery welcomes approaches from makers or designers of high quality work. You will need to send your name and contact details, a statement about yourself and your work, four to six good quality images with description and size and an SAE for the return of the images.
The gallery is open Monday to Saturday, 10am to 4.30pm (call for Sunday/Bank Holiday times). Admission is free and there is disabled access. The Craft Shop remains open while exhibitions are being changed and operates Monday to Friday from 10am to 4.30pm.

SHEFFIELD CRAFT MARKETS
Sheffield Markets/Sheffield City Council
5th Floor, Castle Market Building
Exchange Street
Sheffield
S1 2AH
Tel: 0114 273 5281
Fax: 0114 275 4299
Email: marketsinfo@sheffield.gov.uk
Website: www.sheffieldmarkets.co.uk
Contact: Anna Sheppard

Sheffield Markets operates approximately 10 Craft Markets per year at various major events and locations throughout the city, including the City Centre (Fargate) and major parks in the city (Norfolk Park and Hillsborough Park). Between 30 and 60 traders attend these markets, exhibiting and selling a variety of excellent quality craft and home-made items, including glass, ceramics, jewellery, wood carvings, cards, toys and textiles.
Sheffield Markets provides stalls and counters for all traders and prices vary, depending on the event.

STAPEHILL ABBEY, CRAFTS & GARDENS
276 Wimborne Road West
Stapehill
Wimborne

Dorset BH21 2EB
Tel: 01202 861686
Fax: 01202 894589
Contact: Lin Tuck

Stapehill Abbey is a beautifully restored Cistercian Abbey set in acres of award winning gardens. The building houses the Nuns chapel and cloisters, Victorian parlour and kitchens, a working craft centre and licensed coffee shop.
The country world museum tells the story of the history of farming through the ages and has a cobbler's and blacksmith's shop, village chemist and hardware shop.
Beyond the walled garden is a lake and waterfalls, a large picnic area, a Japanese garden and a working farmyard and children's play area.
Special events are held all year, including an Autumn Craft Fair and weekend Christmas Craft Markets during December. Craft units are available for rent. Stapehill is open all year round except January. It is closed on Mondays and Tuesdays during the winter months. It is situated between Wimborne and Ferndown on the old A31.

STOCKWOOD PARK MUSEUM
Farley Hill
Luton
Beds LU1 4BH
Tel: 01582 738714
Email: museum.gallery@luton.gov.uk
Website: www.lutonline.gov.uk/museums

Step back in time to pre-industrial Bedfordshire. Stockwood Park Museum has unrivalled displays of rural life which include hand tools and farming equipment, market gardening and fruit growing, countryside crafts such as hedging and hurdle making and important local crafts such as basket making, lace making and rush mat making. The displays are enhanced by traditional craft demonstrations.
The Craft Courtyard offers visitors the opportunity to watch craftspeople at work as well as buying or commissioning crafts. The museum is also home to the Mossman Carriage Collection and the Hamilton Finlay Sculpture Garden.
The Conservatory Tea Rooms are open all year round and are set in beautiful period gardens. Stockwood Park Museum Gift shop is contained within the frame of a 16th century building and offers visitors a variety of affordable gifts and cards.
Opening hours are 10am to 5pm, Tuesday to Sunday between April and October and 10am to 4pm, weekends only, between November and March. Admission is free.

WALFORD MILL CRAFT CENTRE
Stone Lane
Wimborne
Dorset BH21 1NL
Tel: 01202 841400
Fax: 01202 841460
Email: info@walfordmillcrafts.co.uk
Website: www.walfordmillcrafts.co.uk

This is a converted mill about a quarter of a mile north of Wimborne, Dorset, in a quiet riverside setting. There is a craft shop which has a wide range of contemporary craftwork, much of it from local craftspeople, and a gallery which has about eight different exhibitions each year. A number of classes in various crafts are run throughout the year.
Also on the site are three workshops - silk weaving, stained glass and silver jewellery - which all have work for sale as well as working to commission. The Mill has a licensed restaurant, an adjacent car park and there are facilities for disabled visitors.
Open daily from 10am to 5pm (12 noon to 5pm on Sundays) but closed on Mondays during January to March and also on Christmas Day and New Year's Day. Entry is free.

WROXHAM BARNS
Tunstead Road
Hoveton
Norfolk NR12 8QU
Tel: 01603 783762
Email: info@wroxham-barns.co.uk
Website: www.wroxham-barns.co.uk

Housed in beautifully restored 18th century barns and surrounded by the beauty of the Norfolk countryside, Wroxham Barns is one of the finest collections of traditional and contemporary crafts in East Anglia.
Many of the craftsmen at Wroxham Barns take commissions and most offer mail order and home delivery services for bigger items or for personalised gifts. Visitors can wander around the workshops at their own pace and can also visit the Clothes Shop, Country Food Shop, Gift Shop and Fudge Shop.
Friendly, helpful staff are always happy to assist with finding something to suit every taste and budget. A number of the goods on

display are only available at Wroxham Barns, from hand-painted stationery to traditional games and puzzles, ceramic house name plates to scented candles.

Also on offer is a tearoom, Junior Farm and a brand new Fun Fair. Open every day from 10am to 5pm except Christmas Day, Boxing Day and New Year's Day. Admission is free and there is ample free parking for cars and coaches (entry to the Junior Farm is £2.65, free for under-3s).

YORKSHIRE SCULPTURE PARK

West Bretton
Wakefield
West Yorks WF4 4LG
Tel: 01924 832515
Fax: 01924 832600
Website: www.ysp.co.uk

Yorkshire Sculpture Park opened its Christmas Craft Show on 13 November 2004 but despite the name, this runs all the way through until the end of February 2005. It features the work of over 70 makers of contemporary craft and design and can be found in the Bothy Gallery and the YSP Centre. The Bothy Gallery has largely been given over to ceramics, while the YSP Centre stages a major jewellery show.

All the work in the Christmas Craft Show is for sale. The Arts Council National Arts Purchase Interest Free Scheme is available for purchases over £100. The show in the Bothy Gallery opens daily from 11am to 4pm until 27 February 2005 (closed 23-26 Dec). The Jewellery Show is open from 10am to 5pm.

Craft at Yorkshire Sculpture Park is also available online for international as well as national buyers. The dedicated website - www.shop-ysp.co.uk - features a regularly changing collection of individual work by established and emerging artists. This virtual shop enables YSP to expand its support for makers of contemporary craft and design by assisting them in marketing their products to a wider audience. The current selection includes jewellery, ceramics, textiles, paintings, leather, wood, glass and metal work.

Best Wis

SUPPLIERS OF MATERIALS, COMPONENTS & EQUIPMENT

Listed below are over 350 of the UK's principal suppliers to craftworkers and artists in a fully classified directory. In a few cases (e.g. 'buttons') the classification does quite clearly refer to a finished piece. However, in the majority of cases we are referring to supplies *for* a particular craft and not items *of* that craft. So, for instance, under 'jewellery' the companies listed provide the various materials and components for sale to the jewellery maker and not finished pieces *of* jewellery for final retail.

Aside from listing and classifying suppliers, we have also tried to offer guidelines on how they sell and to whom they sell. We've asked them whether they have a shop, use mail order, supply direct to craftworkers or just to retailers/wholesalers etc. We've also asked whether they operate a secure internet sales site. In italic script after each entry you will find what each company has told us.

3D DECOUPAGE

CORNISH HAND CRAFTS
Tamarisk
Perran Downs
Penzance
Cornwall TR20 9HL
Tel: 01736 711262
mail order only

HOUSE OF CARDS
11 Foxlands Avenue
Penn
Wolverhampton
West Midlands WV4 5LX
Tel: 01902 343231
Fax: 01902 330843
Email: janekeith2002@btopenworld.com
mail order only

MASTERART
29 Eastwood Boulevard
Westcliff-on-Sea
Essex SS0 0BY
Tel: 01702 341184
Email: masterart@onetel.net.uk
retail premises and mail order

ORINOCO
Hall Lane
Mawdesley
Ormskirk
Lancs L40 2QZ
Tel: 01704 822604
Fax: 01704 823137
Email: sales@orinoco.free-online.co.uk
mail order only

ACCOUNTANCY & BUSINESS SERVICES

A.B.S.
8 Windsor Avenue
Normacot
Longton
Stoke-on-Trent
Staffs ST3 4RS
Tel: 01782 321860

SIMIA WALL
Sir Robert Peel House
178 Bishopsgate
London EC2M 4NJ
Tel: 020 7283 1604
Fax: 020 7283 0240
Email: mail@simiawall.co.uk
Website: www.simiawall.com

ART SUPPLIES

ART CENTRE
Howard Street
Bedford
Beds MK40 3HS
Tel: 01234 344784
Fax: 01234 360237
Email: info@artcentre.biz
retail premises and mail order

ARTSCENE
35 Chesterfield Road
Sheffield
South Yorks S8 0RL
Tel: 0114 255 5299
retail premises and mail order

Please tell all suppliers you saw their entry in The Craftworker's Year Book

ARTSTAT
PO Box 4
621 Liverpool Road
Irlam
Manchester M44 5BB
Tel: 0161 777 9543
wholesale to trade
WHOLESALE distributor of Artists Materials, Craft and Stationery products. Cash and Carry warehouse and showroom open Monday to Friday, 8am-4pm. Also dispatch by carrier. Family-run business established in 1978.

ART VAN GO
The Studios
1 Stevenage Road
Knebworth
Herts SG3 6AN
Tel: 01438 814946
Fax: 01438 816267
Email: art@artvango.co.uk
Website: www.artvango.co.uk
retail premises and mail order
Art/Textile materials for surface and structural embellishment. Fron Isaf hand-dyed yarns and fibres. Photographic reproduction of 2D and 3D work including textiles. Extensive range of workshops and exhibitions.

CREATIVE CRAFTS
11 The Square
Winchester
Hants SO23 9ES
Tel: 01962 856266
Email: sales@creativecrafts.co.uk
Website: www.creativecrafts.co.uk
retail premises and mail order
Large range of art and craft material supplies. Try us for batik, encaustic, pergamano, cardmaking, instructional books etc. Also find us at www.creativecrafts.co.uk

FOURMARK ART & CRAFT CENTRE
Bayshill Lodge
Montpellier Street Top
Cheltenham
Glos GL50 1SY
Tel/Fax: 01242 231515
retail premises only

Think your company should be listed in this section? Go to last page for details

GLOWSHOP LTD
582-584 Hagley Road West
Birmingham
West Midlands B68 0BS
Tel: 0121 423 2000
Email: sales@glowshop.com
Website: www.glowshop.com
retail premises and mail order; secure internet sales site

GLYNSWOOD OF THAME
11 High Street
Thame
Oxon OX9 2BZ
Tel: 01844 213739
Fax: 01844 213662
Email: sales@glynswood.co.uk
retail premises

GREAT ART
Normandy House
1 Nether Street
Alton
Hants GU34 1EA
Tel: 01420 593332
Fax: 01420 593333
Email: welcome@greatart.co.uk
Website: www.greatart.co.uk
mail order only; secure internet sales site

JACKSON'S ART SUPPLIES
1 Farleigh Place
London N16 7SX
Tel: 020 7254 0077
Fax: 020 7254 0088
Email: sales@jacksonsart.com
Website: www.jacksonsart.com
retail premises and mail order; secure internet sales site

JAKAR INTERNATIONAL LTD
Hillside House
2-6 Friern Park
London N12 9BX
Tel: 020 8445 6376
Fax: 020 8445 2714
Email: info@jakar.co.uk
Website: www.jakar.co.uk
wholesale to trade and retail

LONDON GRAPHIC CENTRE
16-18 Shelton Street
Covent Garden
London WC2H 9JL

Tel: 020 7759 4500
Fax: 020 7759 4585
Email: info@londongraphics.co.uk
Website: www.londongraphics.co.uk
retail premises and mail order; secure internet sales site

MILLER'S CREATIVITY SHOP
28 Stockwell Street
Glasgow
G1 4RT
Tel: 0141 553 1660
Fax: 0141 553 1583
Email: info@millers-art.co.uk
Website: www.millers-art.co.uk
retail premises and mail order
Scotland's largest and most exciting art and craft supply shop. Established 1834. Excellent on-line website. Workshops available. Regular exhibitor at Hobbycraft and Rubber Stamping shows. Visit us soon!

PAINTWORKS
99-101 Kingsland Road
Hoxton
London E2 8AG
Tel: 020 7729 7451
Fax: 020 7739 0439
Email: shop@paintworks.biz
Website: www.paintworks.biz
retail premises and mail order

PHILIP & TACEY LTD
North Way
Andover
Hants SP10 5BA
Tel: 01264 332171
Fax: 01264 384808
Email: sales@philipandtacey.co.uk
Website: www.philipandtacey.co.uk
mail order only

R K BURT & CO LTD
57 Union Street
London SE1 1SG
Tel: 020 7407 6474
Fax: 020 7403 3672
Website: www.rkburt.co.uk
wholesale to trade

SHINGLERS
Compston Road
Ambleside
Cumbria LA22 9DR
Tel: 01539 433433
Fax: 01539 434634
retail premises and mail order

SIOP GELF Y WIBER ART SHOP
7 Sycamore Street
Newcastle Emlyn
Carmarthenshire SA38 9AP
Tel/Fax: 01239 712946
retail premises only

SPECIALIST CRAFTS LTD
PO Box 247
Leicester
Leics LE1 9QS
Tel: 0116 269 7711
Fax: 0116 269 7722
Email: rob@speccrafts.co.uk
Website: www.speccrafts.co.uk
mail order only
For the UK's largest range of arts and crafts, look no further! Over 12,000 products in one catalogue plus franchise opportunities for retailers. Call for your 600-page catalogue today!

STUDIO ARTS
50 North Road
Lancaster
Lancs LA1 1LT
Tel: 01524 68014
Fax: 01524 68013
Website: www.studioarts.co.uk
retail premises and mail order

TRI-CHEM UK
3 Rectory Close
Slapton
Leighton Buzzard
Beds LU7 9BZ
Tel: 01525 220393
Email: email@tri-chem.co.uk
Website: www.tri-chem.co.uk
mail order only

BATIK

TEXTILE TECHNIQUES
37 High Street
Bishop's Castle
Shropshire
SY9 5BE

Tel/Fax: 01588 638712
Email: enquiries@textiletechniques.co.uk
retail premises and mail order; secure internet sales site

BEADS & BEADWORK

21st CENTURY BEADS
Craft Workshops
South Pier Road
Ellesmere Port
Cheshire CH65 4FW
Tel: 0151 356 4444
Fax: 0151 355 3377
Email: sales@beadmaster.com
Website: www.beadmaster.com
retail premises and mail order
Suppliers by retail and wholesale of a vast range of loose beads and jewellery-making supplies. Glossy colour brochure and secure online ordering available. All by mail order or via our shop.

BARBIE CAMPBELL COLE – SILVER FINDINGS
7 Churton Place
London SW1V 2LN
Tel/Fax: 020 7834 7474
Email: barbiecc@mail.com
mail order only

BEAD AS U LIKE
47 Calvados Park
Kingsteignton
Newton Abbot
Devon TQ12 3EE
Tel/Fax: 01626 334046
mail order only

THE BEAD MERCHANT
PO Box 5025
Coggeshall
Essex CO6 1HW
Tel: 01376 563567
Fax: 01376 563568
Email: info@beadmerchant.co.uk
Website: www.beadmerchant.co.uk
mail order only; secure internet sales site

BEADS FOR BEAUTY
32 Babbacombe Road
Torquay
Devon TQ1 3SN
Tel/Fax: 01803 328902
Email: fab_beads@btopenworld.com
mail order only

BEADWORKS + GROSVENOR STONES LTD
16 Redbridge Enterprise Centre
Thompson Close
Ilford
Essex IG1 1TY
Tel: 020 8553 3240
Fax: 020 8478 6248
Website: www.beadworks.co.uk
retail premises and mail order; secure internet sales site

BLACK DRAGON CRAFTS
Bryn Talog
Pencader
Carmarthenshire SA39 9BD
Tel/Fax: 01559 384624
Email: trade@blackdragon.co.uk
Website: www.blackdragon.co.uk
original manufacturer and sells to retail only

CHARISMA BEADS
25 Churchyard Walk
Hitchin
Herts SG5 1HP
Tel: 01462 454054
Email: vivien@charismabeads.co.uk
Website: www.charismabeads.co.uk
retail premises and mail order

CONSTELLATION BEADS
The Coach House
Barningham
nr Richmond
North Yorks DL11 7DW
Tel: 01833 621094
Fax: 01833 621098
Email: info@constellationbeads.co.uk
Website: www.constellationbeads.co.uk
wholesale to trade and retail; secure internet sales site
Fantastic range of beads...glass...ceramic ...metal...silver...in all shapes and sizes. Wholesale and retail prices, secure online ordering. Fast and friendly mail order service.

CRAFTS 'N' SEW ON
1427 Pershore Road

Stirchley
Birmingham B30 2JL
Tel: 0121 433 3855
Email: craftsnsewon@btinternet.com
retail premises and mail order

DAISY CHAINS
The Twll
Kerry
Newtown
Powys SY16 4LU
Tel: 01686 670495
Email: sarah@artsandcrafts.co.uk
mail order only

GJ BEADS
Units 1-3, Court Arcade
The Wharf, St Ives
Cornwall TR26 1LG
Tel: 01736 793886
Fax: 01736 799142
Email: info@gjbeads.co.uk
Website: www.gjbeads.co.uk
retail premises and mail order

GLASS BEADMAKERS UK + JAZZY LILY HOT GLASS
Middle House, 34 Grecian Street
Aylesbury
Bucks HP20 1LT
Tel: 01296 437406
Email: mail@gbuk.fsworld.co.uk or pauline@jazzylily.freeserve.co.uk
Website: www.gbuk.org or www.jazzylily.com
original manufacturer and direct seller

HALFPENNEYS
Email: gandt@halfpenney.co.uk
Website: www.halfpenney.co.uk
mail order only

J.E.M.'S SEWING MACHINE & NEEDLECRAFT CENTRE
19 Sun Street
Canterbury
Kent CT1 2HX
Tel: 01227 457723
Email: canterburysewing@btconnect.com
retail premises and mail order

MARCIA LANYON LTD
PO Box 370
London W6 7NJ
Tel: 020 7602 2446
Fax: 020 7602 0382
Email: sales@marcialanyon.com
Website: www.marcialanyon.co.uk
wholesale to trade

NEW ERA DIRECT
PO Box 6361
Wellingborough
Northants NN29 7ZR
Tel/Fax: 01933 223509
Email: sales@neweradirect.co.uk
Website: www.neweradirect.co.uk
mail order only; secure internet sales site

SPANGLES
1 Casburn Lane
Burwell
Cambs CB5 0ED
Tel/Fax: 01638 742024
Email: spangles4beads@ntlworld.com
Website: www.spangles4beads.co.uk
mail order only

THE SPELLBOUND BEAD CO
45 Tamworth Street
Lichfield
Staffs WS13 6JW
Tel/Fax: 01543 417650
Email: info@spellboundbead.co.uk
Website: www.spellboundbead.co.uk
retail premises and mail order; also wholesale to trade

STITCH 'N' CRAFT LTD
Swan's Yard
High Street
Shaftesbury
Dorset SP7 8JQ
Tel: 01747 852500
Fax: 01747 850751
Email: enquiries@stitchncraft.co.uk
Website: www.stitchncraft.co.uk
retail premises and mail order plus wholesale to trade and retail; secure internet sales site

SWANSTITCH
82-84 High Street
Deal
Kent CT14 6EG
Tel/Fax: 01304 366915
Email: swanstitch@btinternet.com
Website: www.swanstitch.com
retail premises and mail order

TUFFNELL GLASS
38 Wansford Road
Driffield
East Yorks YO25 5NE
Tel: 01377 240745
Fax: 01377 240746
Email: martin@tuffnellglass.freeserve.co.uk
Website: www.tuffnellglass.co.uk
wholesale to trade and retail of glass beads and equipment

WITCH BEADS
11 Randolph Close
Bradville
Milton Keynes
Bucks MK13 7JN
Tel: 01908 311243
Email: witch.beads@btconnect.com
Website: www.witchbeads.com
mail order only

BLANKS (BOXES ETC)

A.B. WOODWORKING
Unit C1, Bank Top Industrial Estate
St Martins
Oswestry
Shropshire SY10 7HB
Tel: 01691 777147
Fax: 01691 777886
Email: sales@abwoodworking.co.uk
Website: www.abwoodworking.co.uk
original manufacturer and direct seller
GOOD QUALITY BIRCH PLY BLANKS; suitable for most finishes. Shaker Boxes (15 sizes), trays, wastepaper bins, hat boxes. Trade enquiries welcome. All our timber is from sustainable sources.

BOXY LADY
Timbers
Aysshton Gardens
Callington
Cornwall PL17 7DW
Tel: 01579 384376
Email: orders@boxylady.co.uk
Website: www.boxylady.co.uk
mail order only

Do you know a good supplier who is not listed here? Get them to e-mail the editor at: charles.wallin@btclick.com to ensure their free entry for the 2006 Edition.

S-PRINT SIMPLE BOXES
Squire White's Cottage
West Bank
Winster
Derbys DE4 2DQ
Tel: 01629 650403
Email: mail@simplepages.org
Website: www.simplepages.org
original manufacturer and direct seller

BOOKBINDING

COCKERELL MARBLED PAPERS
94 Wimpole Road
Barton
Cambridge
Cambs CB3 7AD
Tel/Fax: 01223 262430
Website: www.cockerellpapers.com
original manufacturer and direct seller

HARMATAN LEATHER LTD
Westfields Avenue
Higham Ferrers
Northants NN10 8AX
Tel: 01933 412151
Fax: 01933 412242
Email: info@harmatan.co.uk
Website: www.harmatan.co.uk
retail premises and mail order

RUSSELLS
Unit 1, Bluntswood Hall
Throcking
Buntingford
Herts SG9 9RN
Tel: 01763 281430
Fax: 01763 281431
Email: office@russels.com
Website: www.russels.com
retail premises and mail order

BOOKS (SECOND-HAND)

AVRIL WHITTLE BOOKSELLER
Whittle's Warehouse
7-9 (rear) Bainbridge Road
Sedbergh
Cumbria LA10 5AU
Tel/Fax: 01539 621770
Email: avrilsbooks@aol.com
retail premises and mail order

FELICITY J WARNES
The Old Bookshop
36 Gordon Road
Enfield
Middx EN2 0PZ
Tel: 020 8367 1661
Fax: 020 8372 1035
Email: felicity@fjwarnes.u-net.com
Website: www.fjwarnes.u-net.com
retail premises and mail order

LESLEY JONES
23 Gadesden Road
West Ewell
Epsom
Surrey KT19 9LB
Tel: 020 8394 2431
mail order only

BUTTONS

THE BUTTON LADY
16 Hollyfield Road South
Sutton Coldfield
West Midlands B76 1NX
Tel/Fax: 0121 329 3234
wholesale to trade and retail

DUTTONS FOR BUTTONS
Oxford Street
Harrogate
North Yorks HG1 1QE
Tel: 01423 502092
Fax: 01423 528777
Email: michelle@duttonsforbuttons.co.uk
Website: www.duttonsforbuttons.co.uk
retail premises and mail order

HANDMADE BUTTONS BY PATRICIA
Townsend Cottage
Woonton
Almeley
Herefordshire HR3 6QW
Tel: 01544 340412
Email: golfbag@compuserve.com
mail order only

J.E.M.'S SEWING MACHINE & NEEDLECRAFT CENTRE
19 Sun Street
Canterbury
Kent CT1 2HX
Tel: 01227 457723
Email: canterburysewing@btconnect.com
retail premises and mail order

L NICHOLS VINTAGE GLASS BUTTONS
35 Addington Square
London SE5 7LB
Tel: 020 7701 3433
Email: nicbutns@lineone.net
Website: www.nicholsbuttons.co.uk
original manufacturer and direct seller; secure internet sales site

CALLIGRAPHY MATERIALS

PENMANDIRECT
1 Towneley Road West
Longridge
Lancs PR3 3AB
Tel/Fax: 01772 784444
mail order only

CANDLEMAKING

ARTCRAFTS
107-109 Johnston Street
Blackburn
Lancs BB2 1HY
Tel/Fax: 01254 55871
Email: info@artcraftsuk.com
Website: www.artcraftsuk.com
retail premises and mail order (original manufacturer and direct seller) plus wholesale to trade and retail; secure internet sales site

FULLMOONS CAULDRON
PO Box 2173
Ascot
Berks SL5 0PQ
Tel: 01344 627945
Fax: 0709 210 3111
Email: info@fullmoons-cauldron.co.uk
Website: www.fullmoons-cauldron.co.uk
direct mail and via website
Large range of quality Candlemaking Materials, including gel, paraffin and natural waxes, moulds, etc. Encaustic wax art supplies, Precious Metal Clay plus much more!! Excellent products, service and quick delivery. Secure online shopping.

CANE & BASKETMAKING

THE CANE WORKSHOP
The Gospel Hall
Westport
Langport
Somerset TA10 0BH
Tel/Fax: 01460 281636
retail premises and mail order

JACOBS YOUNG & WESTBURY
Bridge Road
Haywards Heath
West Sussex RH16 1UA
Tel: 01444 412411
Fax: 01444 457662
Email: sales@jyw-uk.com
wholesale to trade and retail
UK's leading importer of cane, bamboo, seagrass, chair rush and willow. The range is complemented with stool frames, picture tray bases, natural and coloured raffia and ready manufactured cane seating.

P H COATE & SON
Meare Green Court
Stoke St Gregory
Taunton
Somerset TA3 6HY
Tel: 01823 490249
Fax: 01823 490814
Email: phcoate@globalnet.co.uk
Website: www.coates-willowbaskets.co.uk
original manufacturer and direct seller

CARDMAKING

ARTS & GRAPHICS + DRAFTLINE
21 Fore Street
Redruth
Cornwall TR15 2BD
Tel: 01209 213534
Fax: 01209 211222
Email: sales@artsand.co.uk
Website: www.artsand.co.uk
retail premises and mail order
Visiting Cornwall? Explore our historic mining town and visit our shop selling a huge range of art and craft materials. Open Monday to Saturday 9am to 5pm. Craft Workshops on Saturdays.

ARTSCENE
35 Chesterfield Road
Sheffield
South Yorks
S8 0RL
Tel: 0114 255 5299
retail premises and mail order

ARTSTAT
PO Box 4
621 Liverpool Road
Irlam
Manchester
M44 5BB
Tel: 0161 777 9543
wholesale to trade
WHOLESALE distributor of Artists Materials, Craft and Stationery products. Cash and Carry warehouse and showroom open Monday to Friday, 8am-4pm. Also dispatch by carrier. Family-run business established in 1978.

CARD INSPIRATIONS
The Old Dairy
Tewin Hill Farm, Tewin
Welwyn
Herts
AL6 0LL
Tel: 01438 717000
Fax: 01438 717477
Website: www.cardinspirations.co.uk
retail premises and mail order

THE CRAFT BARN
9 East Grinstead Road
Lingfield
Surrey
RH7 6EP
Tel: 01342 836097
Fax: 01342 836716
Email: mailorder@craftbarn.co.uk
Website: www.craftbarn.co.uk
retail premises only

CRAFT CRAZY
2 Barley Road
Thelwall
Warrington
Cheshire
WA4 2EZ
Tel: 01925 263263
Email: hilary@craftcrazy.co.uk
Website: www.craftcrazy.co.uk
retail premises and mail order

CRAFT CREATIONS LTD
Ingersoll House
Delamare Road
Cheshunt
Herts
EN8 9HD
Tel: 01992 781900
Fax: 01992 634339
Email: enquiries@craftcreations.com
Website: www.craftcreations.com
retail premises and mail order
Craft Creations manufacture a large range of greeting card blanks. We also sell a superb range of accessories for craftworkers. Other items we stock include Gold Label peel-off stickers, 3D découpage, mini picture sheets, background papers and collage sheets. Please call for a free colour catalogue!

CRAFTWORK CARDS LTD
Unit 2, The Moorings
Waterside Road
Stourton
Leeds
West Yorks
LS10 1RW
Tel: 0113 276 5713
Fax: 0113 270 5986
Email: info@craftworkcards.com
Website: www.craftworkcards.com
retail premises and mail order

CRANBERRY CARD CO
Unit 4, Greenway
Bedwas House Industrial Estate
Bedwas
Caerphilly
CF83 8DW
Tel: 029 2080 7941
Fax: 029 2080 7900
Email: info@cranberrycards.co.uk
Website: www.cranberrycards.co.uk
mail order only; secure internet sales site

DOOLITTLE TASSELS LTD
3 Kitchener Close
Daventry
Northants
NN11 5AJ
Tel: 01327 300227
Fax: 08702 203763
Email: chris@doolittletassels.com
Website: www.doolittletassels.com
tassels, cords and elastics for dressing cards etc

ECLIPSE EXPRESS LTD
The Market Hall
Balcony Shops 3+4
Tennant Street
Derby
Derbys DE1 2DB
Tel: 01332 208308
Fax: 08700 519195
Email: eclipse.cards@virgin.net
Website: www.eclipsecardcraft.co.uk
retail premises and mail order; secure internet sales site

FANCY THAT CRAFTS LTD
Basildon Enterprise Centre
33 Nobel Square
Unit 1 Burnt Mills
Basildon
Essex SS13 1LT
Tel: 01268 457410
Email: sales@fancythatcrafts.com
Website: www.fancythatcrafts.com
retail premises; secure internet sales site

FISKARS BRANDS UK LTD
Newlands Avenue
Bridgend
Mid Glam CF31 2XA
Tel: 01656 655595
Fax: 01656 649425
Website: www.fiskars.com
original manufacturer and direct seller

GREGORY KNOPP
PO Box 158
Gillingham
Kent ME7 3HF
Tel: 01634 375706
Fax: 01634 263155
Email: info@gregory-knopp.co.uk
Website: www.gregory-knopp.co.uk
mail order only

IMPRESS CARDS & CRAFT MATERIALS
Slough Farm
Westhall
Halesworth
Suffolk
IP19 8RN
Tel: 01986 781422
Fax: 01986 781677
Email: sales@impresscards.co.uk
Website: www.impresscards.com
original manufacturer and direct seller; secure internet sales site

J.E.M.'S SEWING MACHINE & NEEDLECRAFT CENTRE
19 Sun Street
Canterbury
Kent CT1 2HX
Tel: 01227 457723
Email: canterburysewing@btconnect.com
retail premises and mail order

JGD CRAFTS
108 Outram Street
Sutton-in-Ashfield
Notts NG17 4FS
Tel/Fax: 01623 466919
Email: j.g.decoupage@btinternet.com
Website: www.jgdcrafts.com
retail premises and mail order; secure internet sales site

KTD COLOURCRAFT
71 Highgate
Kendal
Cumbria LA9 4ED
Tel/Fax: 01539 735311
retail premises only

L.A. DESIGNS
25 High Street
Milford-on-Sea
Lymington
Hants SO41 0QF
Tel/Fax: 01590 644445
retail premises only

M.I.C.
The io Centre
Unit 3, Hearle Way
Hatfield Business Park
Hatfield
Herts AL10 9EW
Tel: 01707 269999
Fax: 01707 269911
Email: sales@micdirect.net
wholesale to trade and retail

MULTICRAFT CABIN
Spring Green Nurseries
Pontefract Road
Crofton
Wakefield
West Yorks WF4 1LW
Tel/Fax: 01924 865301
Email: gillian.whaley@btinternet.com
Website: www.multi-craft.co.uk

NEWNHAM COURT CRAFTS
Newnham Court
Bearsted Road
Maidstone
Kent
ME14 5LH
Tel/Fax: 01622 630886
Email: newnham-court.crafts@virgin.net
Website: www.newnhamcourtcrafts.co.uk
retail premises and mail order

OVER THE MOON CRAFTS
58 Becketts Lane
Boughton Heath
Chester
Cheshire
CH3 5RW
Tel/Fax: 01244 409258
retail premises only

PASTIMES
853 Chesterfield Road
Woodseats
Sheffield S8 0SQ
Tel/Fax: 0114 274 8105
retail premises only

RAINBOW STAMPS
34 Baker Street
Brighton
East Sussex
BN1 4JN
Tel: 01273 621177
Fax: 01273 558442
retail premises and mail order

THE SCRAPBOOKHOUSE LTD
Unit 9, Cromwell Business Park
Chipping Norton
Oxon
OX7 5SR
Tel: 0870 770 7717
Fax: 01608 643430
Email: sales@thescrapbookhouse.com
Website: www.thescrapbookhouse.com
original manufacturer, wholesale (trade and retail), retail premises and mail order; secure internet sales site. Papercrafts: the largest scrapbooking supplier to trade in the UK. We craft, so we know what your customers will buy! Retail workshops, free colour catalogues; order online and fast, friendly service. We also run large craft events.

THE SMITHFIELD COMPANY
Unit 9, Lake Park
Caton Road
Lancaster
Lancs
LA1 3NX
Tel: 01524 762883
Email: info@smithfieldgallery.co.uk
Website: www.smithfieldgallery.co.uk
supplier of raw materials such as papers, metals and fabrics via retail premises and mail order; secure internet sales site

STABLE OF IMAGINATION
Squires Garden Centre
Brentford
Middx
TW17 8RU
Tel: 01932 788052
Fax: 01932 787848
Website: www.stableofimagination.co.uk
retail premises and mail order

STAMPEEZEE
2 Cedars Avenue
Coundon
Coventry
Warks CV6 1DR
Tel/Fax: 024 7644 8085
Email: stampeezee@hotmail.com
retail premises only

SWANSTITCH
82-84 High Street
Deal
Kent CT14 6EG
Tel/Fax: 01304 366915
Email: swanstitch@btinternet.com
Website: www.swanstitch.com
retail premises and mail order

CERAMICS

CROMARTIE KILNS LTD
Park Hall Road
Longton
Stoke-on-Trent
Staffs ST3 5AY
Tel: 01782 313947
Fax: 01782 599723
Email: enquiries@cromartie.co.uk
Website: www.cromartie.co.uk
original manufacturer and direct seller

COUNTRY LOVE CERAMICS
59A Milton Park
Abingdon
Oxon
OX14 4RY
Tel: 01235 861700
Fax: 01235 861900
Email: sales@countryloveceramics.co.uk
Website: www.countryloveceramics.com
wholesale to trade and retail; secure internet sales site

ESSEX KILNS LTD
Woodrolfe Road
Tollesbury
Maldon
Essex
CM9 8SE
Tel: 01621 869342
Fax: 01621 868522
Email: sales@essexkilns.co.uk
Website: www.essexkilns.co.uk
original manufacturer and direct seller

HOBBY CERAMICRAFT
Odiham Road
Heckfield
Hook
Hants
RG27 0LS
Tel/Fax: 0118 932 6153
Email: enquiry@hobbyceramicraft.co.uk
Website: www.hobbyceramicraft.co.uk
wholesale to trade and retail

SCIENTIFIC WIRE COMPANY
18 Raven Road
London
E18 1HW
Tel: 020 8505 0002
Fax: 020 8559 1114
Email: wire@enterprise.net
Website: www.wires.co.uk
wholesale to trade and retail; secure internet sales site

Do you know a good supplier who is not listed here? Get them to e-mail the editor at: charles.wallin@btclick.com to ensure their free entry for the 2006 Edition.

VALENTINE CLAYS LTD
The Sliphouse
18-20 Chell Street
Hanley
Stoke-on-Trent
Staffs ST1 6BA
Tel: 01782 271200
Fax: 01782 280008
Email: sales@valentineclays.co.uk
Website: www.valentineclays.co.uk
original manufacturer and direct seller
Suppliers of an extensive range of prepared clay bodies and powdered clays, including fine bone china, porcelains, stonewares, terracottas, Scarva Earthstones(tm), Flax paper clays and air hardening clay.

CLOCK & WATCH MAKING

MEGA-QUARTZ UK LTD
25 Boshers Gardens
Egham
Surrey TW20 9NZ
Tel: 01784 437072
Fax: 01784 435793
Email: megaquartzuk@aol.com
Website: www.megaquartz.co.uk
mail order only
Supplier of Hermle and Kienzle quartz clock mechanisms, hands, barometer and weather instruments. Also pendulums, dials, sand glasses, alcohol thermometers and ships cases.

DECOUPAGE

MAMELOK PRESS LTD
Northern Way
Bury St Edmunds
Suffolk IP32 6NJ
Tel: 01284 762291
Fax: 01284 703689
Email: info@mamelok.co.uk
Website: www.mamelok.co.uk
original manufacturer and direct seller; secure internet sales site
Manufacturers of an extensive range of embossed and diecut scrapbook pictures (scraps) for 3D/flat découpage, card making, scrapbooking and all your decorative crafting activities.
***Try them, they're special*!**

KNICK KNACK KNOVELTIES
PO Box 55
Barnet
Herts EN4 0HF
Tel: 020 8441 4920
Fax: 020 8449 2626
Email: golf@london.com
wholesale to trade

DOLLS HOUSES & ASSOCIATED MINIATURES

GOODIES
11 East Street
Coggeshall
Essex
CO6 1SH
Tel: 01376 562885
Fax: 01376 563885
Email:
staff@goodies-dollshouse-miniatures.co.uk
Website:
www.goodies-dollshouse-miniatures.co.uk
retail premises and mail order; secure internet sales site

LITTLE TRIMMINGS
PO Box 2267
Reading
Berks
RG4 8NL
Tel/Fax: 0118 947 3155
Email: christine@littletrimmings.com
Website: www.littletrimmings.com
mail order only

MINIATURA
Office C18, HRS House
Garretts Green Lane
Birmingham B33 0UE
Tel/Fax: 0121 783 9922
Email: office@miniatura.co.uk
Website: www.miniatura.co.uk
retail premises only

THE ORIGINAL DOLLS HOUSE COMPANY
The Old Printworks
Streatfield Road
Heathfield
East Sussex TN21 8LA
Tel: 01435 864155
Fax: 01435 865708
Email: info@dijon.co.uk

Website: www.dijon.co.uk
wholesale to trade and retail; secure internet sales site

DYES

KEMTEX EDUCATIONAL SUPPLIES LTD
Chorley Business & Technology Centre
Euxton Lane, Chorley
Lancs PR7 6TE
Tel: 01257 230220
Fax: 01257 230225
Website: www.kemtex.co.uk
mail order only

EGGCRAFT

EGG CRAFTERS GUILD
The Studio, 7 Hylton Terrace
North Shields
Tyne & Wear NE29 0EE
Tel/Fax: 0191 258 3648
Email: joanccutts@aol.com
Website:
http://uk.geocities.com/eggcraftersguild
original manufacturer and seller to retail only

LINDA MARTIN EGG DESIGNS
173 High Cross Road
Poulton-le-Fylde
Lancs FY6 8BX
Tel/Fax: 01253 893540
Email: l.martin@btinternet.com
Website: www.eggdesign.freeserve.co.uk
mail order only

EMBROIDERY/NEEDLEWORK

ARTEFACTS OF WHITBY
159 Church Street
Whitby
North Yorks YO22 4AS
Tel/Fax: 01947 820682
Email: amanda.artefacts@btinternet.com
retail premises and mail order

BRANCH
Drapers House, 71 Connaught Avenue
Frinton-on-Sea
Essex CO13 9PP
Tel: 01255 674456
Email: sewbranch@aol.com
Website: www.sewmuchmore.co.uk
retail premises and mail order; secure internet sales site

BURFORD NEEDLECRAFT
117 High Street
Burford
Oxon OX18 4RG
Tel: 01993 822136
Fax: 01993 824740
Email: rbx20@dial.pipex.com
Website: www.needlework.co.uk
retail premises and mail order; secure internet sales site

CANNYCRAFTS
70 High Street
Banchory
Aberdeenshire
AB31 5SS
Tel: 01330 824979
Email: cannycrafts@hotmail.com
Website: www.cannycrafts.co.uk
retail premises and mail order

CAREY COMPANY
Summercourt
Ridgeway
Ottery St Mary
Devon
EX11 1DT
Tel/Fax: 01404 813486
Email: carey@careycompany.com
Website: www.careycompany.com
original manufacturer and direct seller

CHAMPAGNE COLLECTIONS
The Firs
Smithy Corner
Ashwellthorpe
Norfolk
NR16 1EN
Tel/Fax: 01508 488408
Email: champagne.coll@ndirect.co.uk
Website: www.countedcrossstitch.co.uk
wholesale to trade and retail; secure internet sales site

CHERYL HART TEXTILES
Studio 5, Pyle Enterprise Centre
Village Farm
Pyle
Bridgend CF33 6BL

Tel: 07709 051358
Email: cheryl@cheryl-hart-textiles.com
Website: www.cheryl-hart-textiles.com
original manufacturer and direct seller; secure internet sales site

CLEOPATRA'S NEEDLE
Sharpes Mill
White Cross
Lancaster
Lancs
LA1 4XQ
Tel: 01524 848626
Fax: 01524 848525
Email: sales@cleopatrasneedle.co.uk
Website: www.cleopatrasneedle.co.uk
original manufacturer and direct seller; secure internet sales site

CRAFT FRAMES LTD
21 West Hill
Dartford
Kent DA1 2EL
Tel: 01322 278703
Fax: 01322 278710
retail premises only

THE CRAFT SHOP
2 Main Street
Grassington
Skipton
North Yorks BD23 5AP
Tel: 01756 753576
retail premises and mail order

THE CRAFTY PATCH
3 South Street
Bourne
Lincs PE10 9LY
Tel: 01778 422666
retail premises and mail order

CRAFTY SEW AND SEW
67 City Road
Roath
Cardiff CF24 3BL
Tel: 029 2046 3453
retail premises and mail order

CREATIVE CRAFTS & NEEDLEWORK
18 High Street
Totnes
Devon TQ9 5RY
Tel: 01803 866002
retail premises only

CROSSED THREADS
168 Tankerton Road
Tankerton
Whitstable
Kent CT5 2AP
Tel: 01227 772282
Email: bionicpixie@supanet.com
retail premises and mail order

DESIGNER ARTS TAPESTRIES & NEEDLEWORK KITS
Empire House, 6th Floor,
175 Piccadilly
London W1J 9TB
Tel: 020 7499 9192
Fax: 020 7499 7517
Email: joannenestor@hotmail.com
wholesale to trade and mail order (apply for catalogue)

DESIGNER FORUM LTD
PO Box 565
London SW1V 3PU
Tel: 020 7798 8151
Fax: 020 7233 8118
Email: info@bethrussellneedlepoint.com
Website: www.bethrussellneedlepoint.com
wholesale to trade and retail by mail order; secure internet sales site

DINSDALE EMBROIDERIES
13 Castle Close
Middleton-St-George
Darlington
Co Durham DL2 1DE
Tel: 01325 332592
Fax: 01325 335704
Email: admin@dinsdaleembroideries.co.uk
Website: www.dinsdaleembroideries.co.uk
original manufacturer and direct seller; secure internet sales site

DON'T TELL MOTHER
4 Regent Road
Lowestoft
Suffolk NR32 1PA
Tel: 01502 512555
Email: pemshore@aol.com
retail premises only

THE EMBROIDERY SHOP
7 Market Street
Tenbury Wells
Worcs WR15 8BH
Tel: 01584 810906

Email: embroidery.shop@btinternet.com
retail premises and mail order

THE HOBBY SHOP
1 Denton Hill
Gosforth
Seascale
Cumbria CA20 1AS
Tel: 01946 725702
retail premises only

HOUSE OF SMOCKING
1 Ryeworth Road
Charlton Kings
Cheltenham
Glos
GL52 6LG
Tel: 01242 245204
Email: chris@smocking.co.uk
Website: www.smocking.co.uk
mail order only

IN STITCHES
48 Kings Road
Brentwood
Essex CM14 4DW
Tel: 01277 230448
retail premises only

ISIS DESIGNS
Dept CYB, PO Box 268
Bridgwater
Somerset TA6 6YJ
Tel: 07831 733652
mail order – send 4 1st class stamps for brochure

J.E.M.'S SEWING MACHINE & NEEDLECRAFT CENTRE
19 Sun Street
Canterbury
Kent CT1 2HX
Tel: 01227 457723
Email: canterburysewing@btconnect.com
retail premises and mail order

KNITTERS & SEWERS WORLD
21-22 Park Street
Swansea SA1 3DJ
Tel: 01792 456444
Fax: 01792 644535
Email: sales@knittersandsewersworld.co.uk
Website: www.knittersandsewersworld.co.uk
wholesale to trade and retail

LEICESTER THREAD & TRIMMING MANUFACTURERS LTD
105 Barkby Road
Leicester
Leics LE4 9LG
Tel: 0116 276 5858
Fax: 0116 246 0451
Email: sales@lttm.co.uk
Website: www.lttm.co.uk
wholesale to trade

MACLEOD CRAFT
West Yonderton
Warlock Road
Bridge of Weir
Renfrewshire
PA11 3SR
Tel: 01505 612618
Fax: 01505 690780
Email: mcm@callnetuk.com
wholesale to trade

MADEIRA UK LTD
12 Hallikeld Close
Barker Business Park
Melmerby
Ripon
North Yorks
HG4 5GZ
Tel: 01765 640003
Fax: 01765 641707
Email: info@madeira.co.uk
Website: www.madeira.co.uk
wholesale of threads to trade/retail shops only

MARATHON THREADS UK LTD
Marathon House
Tavistock Avenue
Ripley
Derbys
DE5 3SE
Tel: 01773 741442
Fax: 01773 741443
Email: info@marathonthreads.co.uk
Website: www.marathonthreads.co.uk
wholesale to trade and retail

MEARNSCRAFT
2 Cumberland Close
Kirriemuir
Angus DD8 4EF
Tel: 01575 572640
Email: mdt@mearnscraft.co.uk
Website: www.mearnscraft.co.uk
original manufacturer and direct seller; secure internet sales site

MEINECK DESIGN GROUP
Camelford
Cornwall PL32 9SG
Tel: 01840 261270
Email: sherry@meineck.com
Website: www.meineck.com
wholesale to trade and retail; secure internet sales site

MULBERRY SILKS
Silkwood
4 Park Close
Tetbury
Glos GL8 8HS
Tel: 01666 503438
Fax: 01666 503439
Email: patricia.wood@rdplus.net
Website:
www.mulberrysilks-patriciawood.com
mail order only

NEWNHAM COURT CRAFTS
Newnham Court
Bearsted Road
Maidstone
Kent ME14 5LH
Tel/Fax: 01622 630886
Email: newnham-court.crafts@virgin.net
Website: www.newnhamcourtcrafts.co.uk
retail premises and mail order

NIFTY NEEDLES
56 High Street
Linlithgow
West Lothian EH49 7AQ
Tel: 01506 670435
Email: niftyneedles@tiscali.co.uk
retail premises and mail order

PETIT POINT
12 Montpellier Parade
Harrogate
North Yorks HG1 2TJ
Tel: 01423 565632
Fax: 01423 503464
Email: needlecraft@petitpoint.co.uk
Website: www.petitpoint.co.uk
retail premises and mail order

THE PINCUSHION
1 St Marks Crescent
Maidenhead
Berks SL6 5DA
Tel/Fax: 01628 777266
Email: info@thepincushion.co.uk
Website: www.thepincushion.co.uk
retail premises and mail order

PRINCESS PLEATERS
Checkley Fields
Checkley
Herefordshire HR1 4ND
Tel: 01432 851040
Fax: 01432 851180
Email: sales@princess-pleaters.com
Website: www.princess-pleaters.com
original manufacturer and direct seller

READICUT CRAFTS
Terry Mills
Westfield Road
Horbury
Wakefield
West Yorks
WF4 6HD
Tel: 01924 810812
Fax: 01924 810815
Email: customerservice@readicut.co.uk
mail order only

RESTORE PRODUCTS
2 Talbot Road
Bowdon
Altrincham
Cheshire WA14 3JD
Tel/Fax: 0161 928 0020
Email: products@textilerestoration.co.uk
Website: www.restore-products.co.uk
mail order only

SAMANTHAS WORKBASKET
Enterprise Centre
Station Parade
Eastbourne
East Sussex
BN21 1BE
Tel: 01323 430390
retail premises only

SEW-IN OF MARPLE
46 Market Street
Marple
Cheshire
SK6 7AD
Tel: 0161 427 2529
Email: enquiries@knitting-and-needlework.co.uk
Website: www.knitting-and-needlework.co.uk
retail premises and mail order

THE SMITHFIELD COMPANY
Unit 9, Lake Park
Caton Road
Lancaster
Lancs LA1 3NX
Tel: 01524 762883
Email: info@smithfieldgallery.co.uk
Website: www.smithfieldgallery.co.uk
supplier of raw materials such as fabrics, metals and papers via retail premises and mail order; secure internet sales site

SPINNING JENNY
The Old Smithy
Kildwick
Keighley
West Yorks BD20 9BD
Tel/Fax: 01535 632469
Email: info@spinningjenny.co.uk
Website: www.spinningjenny.co.uk
retail premises and mail order

STITCHES
355 Warwick Road
Solihull
West Midlands B91 1BQ
Tel/Fax: 0121 706 1048
Email: enquiries@needle-craft.com
Website: www.needle-craft.com
retail premises and mail order

STITCHING TIME
14 Haddow Street
Hamilton
Lanarkshire ML3 7HX
Tel: 01698 424025
Fax: 01698 424099
Email: getit@stitchingtime.co.uk
Website: www.stitchingtime.co.uk
retail premises and mail order; secure internet sales site

SWANSTITCH
82-84 High Street
Deal
Kent CT14 6EG
Tel/Fax: 01304 366915
Email: swanstitch@btinternet.com
Website: www.swanstitch.com
retail premises and mail order

T.C. THREADS
Edward House
King Edward Street
Hucknall
Notts NG15 7JR
Tel: 0115 968 0089
Email: sales@tcthreads.ltd.uk
Website: www.tcthreads.ltd.uk
wholesale to trade and retail; secure internet sales site

THREADNEEDLE HOUSE
9 Nuneham Courtenay
Oxford
Oxon OX44 9NX
Tel/Fax: 01865 343407
retail premises and mail order

VARI-GALORE
5 Bennet Close
Alton
Hants GU34 2EL
Tel/Fax: 01420 80595
Email: lorna@varigalore.com
Website: www.varigalore.com
wholesale to trade and retail

ENCAUSTIC ART

ARTS ENCAUSTIC LTD
Trem ar Daf
Glogue
Pembrokeshire SA36 0ED
Tel: 01239 831401
Fax: 01239 831767
Email: info@encaustic.com
Website: www.encaustic.com
original manufacturer and direct seller; secure internet sales site

ARTSTAT
PO Box 4
621 Liverpool Road
Irlam
Manchester M44 5BB
Tel: 0161 777 9543
wholesale to trade
WHOLESALE distributor of Artists Materials, Craft and Stationery products. Cash and Carry warehouse and showroom open Monday to Friday, 8am-4pm. Also dispatch by carrier. Family-run business established in 1978.

WAKES WAXES
Loveneys Farm
Wakes Colne

Colchester
Essex CO6 2BJ
Tel: 01787 227320
Email: barry@waxes.co.uk
Website: www.waxes.co.uk
mail order only

FABRICS/TEXTILES

ABERDARE SPINNERS
The Market Hall
Aberdare
Rhondda Cynon Taff
CF44 7EB
Tel: 01685 876759
Fax: 01685 873083
Email: darespin@fsbdial.co.uk
Website: www.aberdarespinners.co.uk
retail premises only

BLANCHARDS FABRICS
21 Wallingford Street
Wantage
Oxon OX12 8AU
Tel/Fax: 01235 762465
Email: blanchards@tiscali.co.uk
retail premises only

CAMBRIAN WOOLLEN MILL
Top Floor Weaving Unit
Llanwrtyd Wells
Powys LD5 4SD
Tel: 01591 610473
Fax: 01591 610314
Email: cambrianwool@tiscali.co.uk
original manufacturer and direct seller

ESBERGER FABRICS
Unit 33, Market Hall
Low Pavement
Chesterfield
Derbys S40 1AR
Tel: 01246 201330
Fax: 01909 772296
Website: www.chesterfieldshops.uk
retail premises only

FABRIC LAND (BOURNEMOUTH) LTD
Fabric Towers, Kingfisher Park
Headlands, Salisbury Road
Ringwood
Hants BH24 3NX
Tel: 01425 461444
Fax: 01425 463055
Email: marnie.fabricland@lineone.net
Website: www.fabricland.co.uk
retail premises and mail order

FABRIC MAGIC
Station Approach
off Stallard Street
Trowbridge
Wilts BA14 8HW
Tel: 01225 768833
Email: info@fabricmagic.co.uk
Website: www.fabricmagic.co.uk
retail premises and mail order

FANTASY FABRICS
68 Southdown Road
Great Yarmouth
Norfolk
NR31 0DY
Tel/Fax: 01493 309040
Email: susan.ray5@btinternet.com
Website: www.fantasyfabrics.co.uk
mail order only

FIBRECRAFTS
Old Portsmouth Road
Peasmarsh
Guildford
Surrey GU3 1LZ
Tel: 01483 565800
Fax: 01483 565807
Email: sales@fibrecrafts.com
Website: www.fibrecrafts.com
retail premises and mail order

HANGZHOU SILKS
3 Station Approach
Stoneleigh
Surrey
KT19 0QZ
Tel: 020 8393 1888
Fax: 020 8393 4888
wholesale to trade and retail

J.E.M.'S SEWING MACHINE & NEEDLECRAFT CENTRE
19 Sun Street
Canterbury
Kent CT1 2HX
Tel: 01227 457723
Email: canterburysewing@btconnect.com
retail premises and mail order

MINERVA FABRICS LTD
26 Market Hall
Ainsworth Street
Blackburn
Lancs
BB1 6AF
Tel: 01254 664168
Email: ormerodan@aol.com
retail premises only

ODDIES TEXTILES
Unit 3, Bank House
Greenfield Road
Colne
Lancs
BB8 9NL
Tel: 01282 868600
Fax: 01282 871787
Email: oddies.textiles@calderglen.net
Website: www.oddies-textiles.co.uk
wholesale to trade

PONGEES LTD – SPECIALIST IN SILK
28-30 Hoxton Square
London
N1 6NN
Tel: 020 7739 9130
Fax: 020 7739 9132
Email: info@pongees.co.uk
Website: www.pongees.co.uk
wholesale to trade

SHERWOODS FABRICS LTD
39 Church Street
Malvern
Worcs
WR14 2AA
Tel: 01684 572379
Email: sherwoodsfabrics@tiscali.co.uk
Website: www.sherwoodsfabrics.co.uk
retail premises and mail order

THE SMITHFIELD COMPANY
Unit 9, Lake Park
Caton Road
Lancaster
Lancs
LA1 3NX
Tel: 01524 762883
Email: info@smithfieldgallery.co.uk
Website: www.smithfieldgallery.co.uk
supplier of raw materials such as fabrics, metals and papers via retail premises and mail order; secure internet sales site

TEXERE YARNS
College Mill
Barkerend Road
Bradford
West Yorks BD14 4AU
Tel: 01274 722191
Fax: 01274 393500
Email: info@texere.co.uk
Website: www.texere.co.uk
retail premises and mail order; secure internet sales site

TEXTILE HARVEST
21 Ennismore Avenue
Guildford
Surrey GU1 1SR
Tel: 01483 533657
Email: info@textileharvest.co.uk
Website: www.textileharvest.co.uk
mail order only

THREADS OF TIME
Beeston Farm
Marhamchurch
Cornwall EX23 0ET
Tel: 01288 381638
Email: jane@threadsoftime.co.uk
Website: www.threadsoftime.com
original manufacturer and direct seller

WHALEYS (BRADFORD) LTD
Harris Court
Great Horton
Bradford
West Yorks BD7 4EQ
Tel: 01274 576718
Fax: 01274 521309
Email: whaleys@btinternet.com
Website: www.whaleys.co.uk
mail order only; secure internet sales site

FELTMAKING

MORAL FIBRE
The Chapel
Brierley Hill
Presteigne
Powys LD8 2NA
Tel: 01544 267997
Email: info@moralfibre.uk.com
Website: www.moralfibre.uk.com
mail order only

FLOWER PRESERVING

THE GREENHOUSE STUDIO/FLOWER DRY
64 Hackney Road
Matlock
Derbys DE4 2PX
Tel/Fax: 01629 581026
Email: moiraclinch@hotmail.com
wholesale to trade and retail; mail order only

FLOWERS, PRESSED

AVONSIDE FLOWERS
Avonside
54 Ashford Road
Bearsted
Kent ME14 4LP
Email:
lorraine@avonsideflowers.fsnet.co.uk
mail order only
Ready to use pressed flowers and leaves; over 150 varieties available yearly. Make your own gifts, cards and pictures. Send SAE for details.

THE PRESSED FLOWER GARDEN
Poole Farm
Raddington
Taunton
Somerset TA4 2QN
Tel: 01398 361331
Fax: 01398 361551
Email:
thepressedflowergarden@btinternet.com
Website:
www.thepressedflowergarden.co.uk
mail order only
Press an amazing range of flowers and leaves with success. Series of books available with easy instructions for beginners and enthusiasts; make cards, pictures and gifts (including pressing wedding bouquets).

FRAMES

THE FRAME WORKSHOP
151-153 Marsh Street North
Hanley
Stoke-on-Trent
Staffs ST1 5HR
Tel/Fax: 01782 286730
retail premises only

GEMSTONES

MARCIA LANYON LTD
PO Box 370
London W6 7NJ
Tel: 020 7602 2446
Fax: 020 7602 0382
Email: sales@marcialanyon.com
Website: www.marcialanyon.co.uk
wholesale to trade

GENERAL CRAFT SUPPLIES

ARTS & GRAPHICS + DRAFTLINE
21 Fore Street
Redruth
Cornwall TR15 2BD
Tel: 01209 213534
Fax: 01209 211222
Email: sales@artsand.co.uk
Website: www.artsand.co.uk
retail premises and mail order
Visiting Cornwall? Explore our historic mining town and visit our shop selling a huge range of art and craft materials. Open Monday to Saturday 9am to 5pm. Craft Workshops on Saturdays.

ARTSCENE
35 Chesterfield Road
Sheffield
South Yorks S8 0RL
Tel: 0114 255 5299
retail premises and mail order

ARTSTAT
PO Box 4
621 Liverpool Road
Irlam
Manchester M44 5BB
Tel: 0161 777 9543
wholesale to trade
WHOLESALE distributor of Artists Materials, Craft and Stationery products. Cash and Carry warehouse and showroom open Monday to Friday, 8am-4pm. Also dispatch by carrier. Family-run business established in 1978.

C&H FABRICS LTD
21-23 Church Road
Tunbridge Wells
Kent TN1 1HT

Tel: 01892 773600
Fax: 01892 773621
Email: candh@candh.demon.co.uk
seven retail stores

CALICO PIE
15 Queens Drive
Sedbergh
Cumbria LA10 5DP
Tel/Fax: 0845 1662 678
Email: carol@calicopie.co.uk
Website: www.calicopie.co.uk
mail order only

CERES CRAFTS LTD
Lansdown Road
Bude
Cornwall EX23 8BH
Tel: 01288 354070
retail premises only

COLOURS & CRAFTS
61 London Road
Alderley Edge
Cheshire SK9 7DY
Tel/Fax: 01625 586100
Email: seahorse6259@aol.com
retail premises only

THE CRAFT CENTRE
31 Palace Avenue
Paignton
Devon TQ3 3EQ
Tel: 01803 663607
retail premises only

CREATIVE CRAFTS
11 The Square
Winchester
Hants SO23 9ES
Tel: 01962 856266
Email: sales@creativecrafts.co.uk
Website: www.creativecrafts.co.uk
retail premises and mail order
Large range of art and craft material supplies. Try us for batik, encaustic, pergamano, cardmaking, instructional books etc. Also find us at www.creativecrafts.co.uk

DAINTY SUPPLIES LTD
Unit 35, Phoenix Road
Crowther Industrial Estate
Washington
Tyne & Wear NE38 0AD
Tel: 0191 416 7886
Fax: 0191 417 6277
Email: sales@daintysupplies.com
Website: www.daintysupplies.co.uk
retail premises and mail order; secure internet sales site

EVANGELINES
58-61 Covered Market
St Nicholas Markets
Bristol BS1 1LJ
Tel: 0117 925 7170
Fax: 0117 970 2604
Email: info@evangelines.co.uk
retail premises only

EVERGLADES INTERNATIONAL LTD
PO Box 1215
Cheddar
Somerset BS27 3ZX
Tel: 01934 744051
Fax: 01934 743184
Email: sales@everglades-int.com
Website: www.craftmaterialsupplies.co.uk
retail premises and mail order; secure internet sales site
An extensive range of craft products, including exotic woods, epoxy resin, clock motors and accessories, clock inserts, craft kits, Crayola and Winsor & Newton artists' materials, including paints and brushes.

FRED ALDOUS LTD
37 Lever Street
Manchester M1 1LW
Tel: 0161 236 2477
Fax: 0161 236 6075
Email: aldous@btinternet.com
Website: www.fredaldous.co.uk
retail store and mail order; secure internet sales site
Why not visit our shop? It's open from 8.15am until 5.15pm each day (closed Sunday). We are situated in the city centre of Manchester (UK). Art and craft catalogue free on request.

GLYCAR GLASS PAPERWEIGHTS
3 Rushton Road
Cheadle Hulme
Cheshire SK8 6NS
Tel: 0161 355 3052
Email: glycar@aol.com
Website: www.retailfranchise.co.uk/blanks

HOLBURN CRAFTS
10 Broomhill
Aberdeen
AB10 6HS
Tel: 01224 588450
retail premises and mail order

JACOBS YOUNG & WESTBURY
Bridge Road
Haywards Heath
West Sussex RH16 1UA
Tel: 01444 412411
Fax: 01444 457662
Email: sales@jyw-uk.com
wholesale to trade and retail
UK's leading importer of cane, bamboo, seagrass, chair rush and willow. The range is complemented with stool frames, picture tray bases, natural and coloured raffia and ready manufactured cane seating.

KALEIDOSCOPE SUPPLIES
North Street, Langport
Somerset TA10 9RQ
Tel: 01458 253631
Fax: 01458 252655
Email: sales@kal-supplies.co.uk
Website: www.kal-supplies.co.uk
retail premises and mail order

KATHYS CORNER CRAFTS
26 North Street + Mill Lane Mews
Ashby-de-la-Zouch
Leics LE65 1HS
Tel: 01530 416928
retail premises only

KAY KRAFTS
3 Chapel Lane
Bingley
West Yorks BD16 2NG
Tel: 01274 511820
retail premises and mail order

LAINE'S FLORAL ART & HOBBY CRAFTS
60 Commerce Street
Insch
Aberdeenshire AB52 6JB
Tel: 01464 820335
Fax: 0870 133 8209
Email: info@lainesworld.co.uk
Website: www.lainesworld.co.uk

MEYNELL'S LTD
2 Southfield Road
Middlesbrough
TS1 3BZ
Tel/Fax: 01642 247863
Email: sales@meynells.co.uk
Website: www.meynells.co.uk
retail premises and mail order

MILLER'S CREATIVITY SHOP
28 Stockwell Street
Glasgow
G1 4RT
Tel: 0141 553 1660
Fax: 0141 553 1583
Email: info@millers-art.co.uk
Website: www.millers-art.co.uk
retail premises and mail order
Scotland's largest and most exciting art and craft supply shop. Established 1834. Excellent on-line website. Workshops available. Regular exhibitor at Hobbycraft and Rubber Stamping shows. Visit us soon!

NEWNHAM COURT CRAFTS
Newnham Court
Bearsted Road
Maidstone
Kent ME14 5LH
Tel/Fax: 01622 630886
Email: newnham-court.crafts@virgin.net
Website: www.newnhamcourtcrafts.co.uk
retail premises and mail order

NUTSHELL SERVICES
6 Blake House Craft Centre
Blake End, Braintree
Essex CM77 6SH
Tel: 01376 328313
retail premises only
An established business, set in a unique craft centre which is open all the year round. The diversity of units and a licensed tea room gives a good day out.

PAINTERS
6 Windsor Place
Liskeard
Cornwall
PL14 4BH
Tel/Fax: 01579 347237
Email: shop@craft-box.com
Website: www.craft-box.com
retail premises and mail order; secure internet sales site

PANDURO HOBBY
Westway House
Transport Avenue
Brentford
Middx
TW8 9HF
Email: order@panduro.co.uk
Website: www.panduro.co.uk
mail order only; call 08702 422 874 to order 420-page catalogue

PASTIMES
13 Market Place
Brigg
North Lincs
DN20 8ES
Tel/Fax: 01652 653500
Email: pastimesbrigg@btinternet.com
Website: www.craftforall.co.uk

PEAR TREE YARD
Town Street
Sandiacre
Nottingham
Notts NG10 5DN
Tel: 0115 949 7411
Fax: 0115 939 0504
Email: claire@peartreeyard.co.uk
retail premises and mail order

RARE BIRD
61 Shelford Road
Radcliffe-on-Trent
Notts NG12 1AJ
Tel: 0115 933 6268
Fax: 0115 933 6591
Email: rarebird@dial.pipex.com
Website: www.rarebird.co.uk
mail order only

SPECIALIST CRAFTS LTD
PO Box 247
Leicester
Leics
LE1 9QS
Tel: 0116 269 7711
Fax: 0116 269 7722
Email: rob@speccrafts.co.uk
Website: www.speccrafts.co.uk
mail order only
For the UK's largest range of arts and crafts, look no further! Over 12,000 products in one catalogue plus franchise opportunities for retailers. Call for your 600-page catalogue today!

STS NORTH WALES
School Bank Road
Llanrwst
Gwynedd LL26 0HU
Tel: 01492 640664
Fax: 01492 641643
Email: sts.northwales@virgin.net
Website: www.glasseyes.com
mail order only; secure internet sales site

W WILLIAMS & SON LTD
Regent House
1 Thane Villas
London N7 7PH
Tel: 020 7263 7311
Fax: 020 7281 0345
Email: sales@wwilliams.co.uk
Website: www.wwilliams.co.uk
wholesaler
W Williams are the oldest haberdashery and craft distributor in the UK, spanning 185 years. Our ranges include all basic haberdashery items from elastic to dress lining. Our craft section includes traditional needlework through to the popular card making. We have eleven representatives covering the UK.

GIFT BOXES
see 'Packaging/Presentation'

GLASS ENGRAVING, FUSING & MAKING SUPPLIES

DECORATIVE GLASS SUPPLIES LTD
Essex Mill
Essex Street
Bradford
West Yorks BD4 7PG
Tel: 01274 773801
Fax: 01274 773802
Email: dgsuk@aol.com
Website: www.decorativeglass.co.uk
wholesale to trade and retail

DICHROIC-GLASS.CO.UK
Unit 12, Burnett Industrial Park
Wrington
Bristol BS40 5QR
Tel: 01934 863344
Fax: 01934 863333
Email: info@dichroic-glass.co.uk

Website: www.dichroic-glass.co.uk
retail premises and mail order (glass fusing)

GLASSWORKS SERVICES LTD
Unit 7+8, Broomhouse Lane Industrial Estate
Edlington
Doncaster
South Yorks
DN12 1EQ
Tel: 08700 110801
Fax: 08700 110803
Email: enquiries@glassworksservices.co.uk
Website: www.glassworksservices.co.uk
wholesale to trade and retail

TEMPSFORD STAINED GLASS
The Old School
Tempsford
Beds SG19 2AW
Tel: 01767 641014
Fax: 01767 641124
Email: tsg@dial.pipex.com
Website: http://tempsford.ngt
retail premises and mail order; secure internet sales site
Open to shop callers including mail ordering service. Suppliers of coloured glasses, tools, materials and instructional books for all your stained glass requirements. Experienced, trained staff on hand.

GLASS (STAINED)

DECORATIVE GLASS SUPPLIES LTD
Essex Mill
Essex Street
Bradford
West Yorks BD4 7PG
Tel: 01274 773801
Fax: 01274 773802
Email: dgsuk@aol.com
Website: www.decorativeglass.co.uk
wholesale to trade and retail
Huge stock - call, phone or order with our on-line shop. The largest warehouse in the UK for colour glass and tools.

KANSA CRAFT
The Flour Mill
Wath Road
Elsecar
Barnsley
South Yorks
S74 8HW
Tel: 01226 747424
Fax: 01226 743712
Email: stainedglass@kansacraft.co.uk
Website: www.kansacraft.co.uk
wholesale to trade and retail

SUNRISE STAINED GLASS
58-60 Middle Street
Southsea
Hants PO5 4BP
Tel: 023 9275 0512
Email: sunrise@stained-windows.co.uk
Website: www.stained-windows.co.uk
retail premises and mail order

HOT FOIL PRINTERS' SUPPLIES

SPEE-DEE
34C Clwyd Close
Hawarden Industrial Park
Hawarden
Flintshire CH5 3PZ
Tel: 01244 539638
Fax: 01244 539930
Email: speedeeltd@aol.com
original manufacturer and wholesale to trade
Full-service supplier (blanks, blocks and foils) to hot-foilers. Blanks include large range of business (and greetings) cards - including gloss, metallic, pearl, mirri, holocard, irry-dissy, chameleon, 3D and plastics - plus promotional products.

INSURANCE

IAN W WALLACE
PO Box 5063
Verwood
Dorset BH31 6WB
Tel: 0800 919359
Fax: 01202 813001
Email: iwallace@ianwwallace.co.uk
Website: www.craftinsurance.co.uk

Do you know a good supplier who is not listed here? Get them to e-mail the editor at: charles.wallin@btclick.com to ensure their free entry for the 2006 Edition.

JEWELLERY/LAPIDARY

CAVERSWALL MINERALS
PO Box 555
Longton
Stoke-on-Trent
Staffs ST11 9DY
Tel: 01782 393838
Fax: 01782 398239
wholesale to trade of silver jewellery castings

JENCEL
621 Eccleshall Road
Hunters Bar
Sheffield
South Yorks S11 8PT
Tel: 0114 267 9633
Email: jc@jencel.freeserve.co.uk
Website: www.jencel.co.uk
retail premises only

KERNOWCRAFT ROCKS & GEMS LTD
Bolingey
Perranporth
Cornwall TR6 0DH
Tel: 01872 573888
Fax: 01872 573704
Email: info@kernowcraft.com
Website: www.kernowcraft.com
retail premises and mail order; secure internet sales site

MANCHESTER MINERALS
Georges Road
Stockport
Cheshire SK4 1DP
Tel: 0161 477 0435
Fax: 0161 480 5095
Email: gemcraft@btconnect.com
Website: www.gemcraft.co.uk
wholesale to trade and retail; secure internet sales site

PJ MINERALS
583C Liverpool Road
Ainsdale
Southport PR8 3LU
Tel: 01704 575461
Fax: 01704 576181
Email: info@beads.co.uk
Website: www.beads.co.uk
wholesale to trade and retail; secure internet sales site

R HOLT & CO LTD
98 Hatton Garden
London EC1N 8NX
Tel: 020 7405 5286
Fax: 020 7430 1279
Email: info@rholt.co.uk
Website: www.rholt.co.uk
retail premises and mail order
Jewellery and Gem suppliers to the trade since 1948, Holts stock a vast range of gemstones. Lapidary and Stringing services at the company's Central London premises. Educational courses available.

SPECIALITY METALS
Liverpool
L18 3EX
Tel/Fax: 0151 722 9570
Email: enquire@smetals.co.uk
Website: www.smetals.co.uk
original manufacturer and direct seller; mail order only

STONE CORNER
42A High Street
Hastings
East Sussex TN34 3EN
Tel: 01424 431318
Fax: 01424 439915
Email: info@stonecorner.co.uk
Website: www.stonecorner.co.uk (under construction)
retail premises and mail order

KNITTING & CROCHET

COLDSPRING MILL
Haworth Road
Cullingworth
Bradford
West Yorks BD13 5EE
Tel: 01535 275646
Fax: 01535 271541
Email: sales@coldspringmill.co.uk
retail premises and mail order

CROCHET DESIGN
11 North Street
Morecambe
Lancs LA4 5DL
Tel: 01524 831752
Email: paulineturner@crochet.co.uk
Website: www.crochet.co.uk

DOUNESYDE CRAFT SHOP
Drumawill
Sligo Road
Enniskillen
Co Fermanagh BT74 5QN
Tel: 028 6632 3751
retail premises only

SHADES OF CASHMERE
Grove Farm
Wolvey
Hinckley
Leics LE10 3LL
Tel: 01455 220767
Fax: 01455 221246
Email: shadesofcashmere@hotmail.co.uk
mail order only

SIRDAR SPINNING LTD
Flanshaw Lane
Alverthorpe
Wakefield
West Yorks WF2 9ND
Tel: 01924 371501
Fax: 01924 290506
Email: enquiries@sirdar.co.uk
Website: www.sirdar.co.uk
original manufacturer and seller to retail only

SOFT BYTE LTD
Quarry Lane
Nantmawr
Oswestry
Shropshire SY10 9HH
Tel: 01691 828556
Fax: 01691 828195
Email: softbyte@softbyte.co.uk
Website: www.softbyte.co.uk
original manufacturer and direct seller

SPINDLEBERRY ANGORA FIBRE CENTRE
16 Braithwaite Road
Keighley
West Yorks BD22 6PA
Tel: 01535 602033
Email: gillian.sharp@btinternet.com
Website: www.spindleberrycrafts.co.uk
original manufacturer and direct seller; mail order only

TEASELS YARNCRAFTS
842 High Road
Leyton
London E10 6AE
Tel: 020 8539 7947
Email: janet@teasels.co.uk
Website: www.teasels.co.uk
retail premises and mail order

UPPINGHAM YARNS
30 North Street East
Uppingham
Rutland
LE15 9QL
Tel: 01572 823747
Email: uppyarn@wools.co.uk
Website: www.wools.co.uk
retail premises and mail order

WENSLEYDALE LONGWOOL SHEEPSHOP
Cross Lanes Farm
Garriston
Leyburn
North Yorks
DL8 5JU
Tel/Fax: 01969 623840
Email: sheepshop@lineone.net
Website: www.wensleydalelongwool-sheepshop.co.uk
retail premises and mail order

WOOLLY THOUGHTS
166 Keighley Road
Colne
Lancs
BB8 0PJ
Tel: 01282 864273
Email: mail@woollythoughts.com
Website: www.woollythoughts.com
mail order only; secure internet sales site

YEOMAN YARNS LTD
36 Churchill Way
Fleckney
Leics
LE8 8UD
Tel: 0116 240 4464
Fax: 0116 240 2522
Email: sales@yeomanyarns.co.uk
Website: www.yeoman-yarns.co.uk
mail order only; secure internet sales site
Stockist for hand and machine knitting yarns.
Cottons/Acrylics/Fancies/Metallics/Wools.
Shade card sets - h/k £3.50, m/k £4.95.
Both £6.50 (UK), outside UK £7.50. Mail order available - UK postage free.

LACE CRAFT

CHURCH MEADOW CRAFTS
Lady Heyes Craft Centre
Kingsley Road
Frodsham
Cheshire
WA6 6SU
Tel/Fax: 01928 789053
Email: lynn@lacemaking.co.uk
Website: www.lacemaking.co.uk
wholesale to trade and retail

ELIZABETH KNIGHT LACEMAKING SUPPLIES
18 Bridge Street
Olney
Bucks MK46 4AB
Tel: 01234 713719
retail premises and mail order

JOHN & JENNIFER FORD
October Hill
Upper Longdon
Rugeley
Staffs WS15 1QB
Tel: 01543 491000
Email: j.ford@lace-making.com
Website: www.lace-making.com
mail order only

TATTING & DESIGN
47 Breedon Hill Road
Derby
Derbys
DE23 6TH
Tel/Fax: 01332 383841
Email: enquiry@tatting.co.uk
Website: www.tatting.co.uk
wholesale to trade and retail; secure internet sales site

LEATHERCRAFT

BITS & PIECES
4 Thorold Road
Bitterne Park
Southampton
Hants
SO18 1JB
Tel/Fax: 023 8055 3334
mail order only

THE IDENTITY STORE LTD
Billing Park, Northampton
Northants NN3 9BG
Tel: 01604 407177
Fax: 01604 407644
Email: roy@theidentitystore.co.uk
Website: www.theidentitystore.co.uk
retail premises and mail order

JACK CHEYETTE
55 Pine Tree Avenue
Leicester
Leics LE5 1AL
Tel/Fax: 0116 276 8056
Email: ncheyette@aol.com
mail order only
Excellent range of leather blanks for Pyrography and Painting. New lines added monthly. Bookmarks, keyrings, purses and handbags, all in high quality natural leather.

MAUGHAM'S LEATHER CELLAR
5-7 Fazakerley Street
Liverpool
Merseyside L3 9DN
Tel/Fax: 0151 236 1872
retail premises and mail order; also wholesale to trade and retail

LIGHTING

THE DAYLIGHT CO LTD
89-91 Scrubs Lane
London NW10 6QU
Tel: 020 8964 1200
Fax: 020 8964 1300
Email: info@daylightcompany.com
Website: www.daylightcompany.com
original manufacturer and direct seller

MACHINE KNITTING

METROPOLITAN
The Pinfold
Poole, Nantwich
Cheshire
CW5 6AL
Tel: 01270 628414
Fax: 01270 610038
Email: metromachineknit@btconnect.com

Website:
www.metropolitanmachineknitting.co.uk
retail premises and mail order

MARQUETRY

ARTSTAT
PO Box 4, 621 Liverpool Road
Irlam
Manchester M44 5BB
Tel: 0161 777 9543
wholesale to trade
WHOLESALE distributor of Artists Materials, Craft and Stationery products. Cash and Carry warehouse and showroom open Monday to Friday, 8am-4pm. Also dispatch by carrier. Family-run business established in 1978.

MATCHSTICK KITS

W HOBBY LTD
Knights Hill Square
London SE27 0HH
Tel: 020 8761 4244
Fax: 020 8761 8796
Email: mail@hobby.uk.com
Website: www.hobby.uk.com
retail premises plus mail order and wholesale to trade; secure internet sales site

MOULDING/CASTING

ARTSTAT
PO Box 4
621 Liverpool Road
Irlam
Manchester M44 5BB
Tel: 0161 777 9543
wholesale to trade
WHOLESALE distributor of Artists Materials, Craft and Stationery products. Cash and Carry warehouse and showroom open Monday to Friday, 8am-4pm. Also dispatch by carrier. Family-run business established in 1978.

Please tell all suppliers you saw their entry in The Craftworker's Year Book

CFS PARTNERSHIP
Unit A, United Downs Industrial Park
St Day
Redruth
Cornwall
TR16 5HY
Tel: 01209 821028
Fax: 01209 822191
Email: admin@cfsnet.co.uk
Website: www.cfsnet.co.uk
retail premises and mail order; wholesale to trade and retail; secure internet sales site

MUSICAL INSTRUMENT MAKING & REPAIRING

PROOPS BROTHERS LTD
Technology House
24 Saddington Road
Fleckney
Leics
LE8 8AW
Tel: 0116 240 3400
Fax: 0116 240 3300
Email: jessica@proopsbrothers.co.uk
Website: www.proopsbrothers.com
original manufacturer, wholesaler, retail premises and mail order; secure internet sales site
The original Proops Brothers supplies everything for the craft and hobby enthusiast. A vast range of specialist hand tools perfect for woodworking, modelmaking, dollshouse making and lots, lots more!

TOUCHSTONE TONEWOODS
44 Albert Road North
Reigate, Surrey
RH2 9EZ
Tel: 01737 221064
Fax: 01737 242748
Email: sales@touchstonetonewoods.co.uk
Website: www.touchstonetonewoods.co.uk
retail premises and mail order

PACKAGING & PRESENTATION

THE BAG 'N' BOX MAN LTD
Unit 1, West Street
Shutford. Banbury
Oxon
OX15 6PH

Tel: 01295 788522
Fax: 01295 788523
Email: sales@bagnboxman.co.uk
Website: www.bagnboxman.co.uk
original manufacturer and direct seller; secure internet sales site

CROMER BOX COMPANY LTD
15 Church Street
Cromer
Norfolk
NR27 9ES
Tel/Fax: 01263 514905
mail order only
Versatile, quality gift boxes. Plain white - ideal for self decoration. Very strong. Flat packed for easy storage. Small minimum order requirement.

ITALIAN OPTIONS
Unit 8, Stretton Business Park
Brunel Drive
Stretton
Burton-on-Trent
Staffs
DE13 0BY
Tel: 01283 741133
Fax: 01283 741974
Email: sales@italianoptions.com
wholesale to trade

JOHNSON-BAKER & CO LTD
Ivy Cross
Shaftesbury
Dorset
SP7 8PU
Tel: 01747 853445
Fax: 01747 853444
Email: johnsonbaker@btclick.com
Website: www.johnsonbaker.co.uk
wholesale to trade and retail

PACKAGING SUPPLIES
Unit 15, Churchfields Business Park
Clensmore Street
Kidderminster
Worcs
DY10 2JY
Tel: 01562 743621
Fax: 01562 827433
Email: enquiries@printedcarrierbags.co.uk
Website: www.printedcarrierbags.co.uk
Personalised printed carrier bags; no minimum quantity.

ARTSTAT
PO Box 4
621 Liverpool Road
Irlam
Manchester
M44 5BB
Tel: 0161 777 9543
wholesale to trade
WHOLESALE distributor of Artists Materials, Craft and Stationery products. Cash and Carry warehouse and showroom open Monday to Friday, 8am-4pm. Also dispatch by carrier. Family-run business established in 1978.

CHARLOTTES CRAFTY CORNER
2 High Street
Yeadon
Leeds
West Yorks LS19 7PP
Email: helengoodrich@blueyonder.co.uk
Website: www.charlottescc.co.uk
retail premises and mail order

DORRIE DOODLE
44 Union Terrace
Aberdeen AB10 1NP
Tel: 01224 648948
Fax: 01224 649320
Email: dorriedood@aol.com
retail premises and mail order

FANCY THAT!
New Street Centre
27 New Street
The Barbican
Plymouth
Devon PL1 2NB
Tel: 01752 256265
Fax: 01752 405277
Email: pauline@fancythat.fsnet.co.uk
retail premises and mail order

ONCE UPON A TIME
49B High Street
Cricklade
Wilts SN6 6DA
Tel: 01793 759280
Fax: 01285 861302
Email: mail@itsonceuponatime.co.uk
Website: www.itsonceuponatime.co.uk
retail premises and mail order

THE PAPER SHED
March House
Tollerton
York YO61 1QQ
Tel: 01347 838253
Fax: 01347 838096
Email: papershed@papershed.com
Website: www.papershed.com
mail order only; secure internet sales site

PAPERWORKS
40 Manor Road
Dorridge
Solihull
West Midlands B93 8DX
Tel: 01564 771452
Fax: 01564 730257
Email: sales@paperworkscardcraft.co.uk
Website: www.paperworkscardcraft.co.uk
mail order only; secure internet sales site

RACHELLE BLONDEL
Studio 4C, Farfield Mill
Garsdale Road
Sedbergh
Cumbria LA10 5LW
Tel: 078009 979427
Email: rb@rachelleblondel.co.uk
Website: www.lavenderdragon.co.uk
retail premises and mail order for hand-made paper; secure internet sales site

ROSS ART & CRAFT
6 Bow Street
Rugeley
Staffs WS15 2BT
Tel: 01889 579598
Website: www.rossartandcraft.com
retail premises and mail order

PARCHMENT & VELLUM

KINGFISHER CRAFTS
23 Kingfisher Close
West Moors
Ferndown
Dorset BH22 0DX
Tel: 01202 855414
Email: alison.yeates@btinternet.com
Website:
www.kingfishercrafts.btinternet.co.uk
mail order only

WILLIAM COWLEY
97 Caldecote Street
Newport Pagnell
Bucks MK16 0DB
Tel: 01908 610038
Fax: 01908 611071
original manufacturer, direct seller and seller to trade

PATCHWORK & QUILTING

THE CLOTH SHOP
23 Upper Mall, Sundial House
Culceth
Warrington
Cheshire WA3 4EH
Tel: 01925 762691
retail premises and mail order

THE COTTON PATCH
1285 Stratford Road
Hall Green
Birmingham B28 9AJ
Tel: 0121 702 2840
Fax: 0121 778 5924
Email: mailorder@cottonpatch.net
Website: www.cottonpatch.co.uk
retail premises and mail order; secure internet sales site

COUNTRY THREADS
2 Pierrepont Place
Bath
BA1 1JX
Tel/Fax: 01225 480056
retail premises and mail order

CRAFTS & QUILTS
Unit 5 The Barn
Heart of the Shires Shopping Village
A5 Watling Street
nr Weedon
Northants NN7 4LB
Tel: 01327 342317
Website: www.craftsandquilts.co.uk
retail premises and mail order

DIRECT KNITTING & SEWING SUPPLIES LTD
Husqvarna Viking Studio
769-771 Attercliffe Road
Sheffield

South Yorks S9 3RF
Tel: 0114 244 9888
Fax: 0114 261 7299
Email: sew@dkss.solis.co.uk
Website: www.sewandknit.co.uk
retail premises and mail order; secure internet sales site

HOUSE OF PATCHWORK
30/32 Tower Centre
Hoddesdon
Herts EN11 8UD
Tel: 01992 447544
Fax: 01992 446892
Email: sales@houseofpatchwork.co.uk
Website: www.houseofpatchwork.co.uk
retail premises only

HUSQVARNA VIKING STUDIO
4 Savoy Buildings
27 Truro Road
St Austell
Cornwall PL25 5JE
Tel: 01726 72506
Email: studio@staustell27.fsnet.co.uk
Website: www.husqvarnaviking.com
retail premises only

PATCHWORK PLUS
129 Station Road
Cark-in-Cartmel
nr Grange-over-Sands
Cumbria LA11 7NY
Tel/Fax: 01539 559009
Email: sales@patchworkplus.co.uk
Website: www.patchworkplus.co.uk
retail premises and mail order

THE STITCHERS PATCH
47 The Green
Aberdeen
AB11 6NY
Tel: 01224 585878
Email: stitcherspatch@aol.com
Website: www.thestitcherspatch.co.uk
retail premises and mail order

WHITE COTTAGE COUNTRY CRAFTS
24 Post Office Road
Seisdon
Wolverhampton
West Midlands WV5 7HA
Tel: 01902 896917
retail premises and mail order

WOLFIN TEXTILES LTD
359 Uxbridge Road
Hatch End
Middx HA5 4JN
Tel: 020 8428 9911
Fax: 020 8428 9955
Email: cotton@wolfintextiles.co.uk
Website: www.wolfintextiles.co.uk
retail premises and mail order

PATTERNS (PAPER) FOR CLOTHES MAKING

SIMPLICITY LTD
PO Box 367, Coronation Street
South Reddish
Stockport
Cheshire SK5 7WZ
Tel: 0161 480 8734
Fax: 0800 731 0767
Email: simplicityuk@btrim.co.uk
Website: www.simplicity.com
original manufacturer and seller to retail only

PEWTERCRAFT

THE SMITHFIELD COMPANY
Unit 9, Lake Park
Caton Road
Lancaster
Lancs LA1 3NX
Tel: 01524 762883
Email: info@smithfieldgallery.co.uk
Website: www.smithfieldgallery.co.uk
supplier of raw materials such as metals, fabrics and papers via retail premises and mail order; secure internet sales site

POLYMER CLAY

POLYMER CLAY PIT
3 Harts Lane
Wortham
Diss
Norfolk IP22 1PQ
Tel/Fax: 01379 890176
Email: info@polymerclaypit.co.uk
Website: www.polymerclaypit.co.uk
mail order only

PORCELAIN DOLLS/DOLLMAKING

DEAR DOLLY ARAL
Medlar House
Southminster Road
Mayland
Chelmsford
Essex CM3 6EB
Tel: 01621 774773
Fax: 01621 774770
Email: deardollyaral@aol.com
Website: www.deardollyaral.com
wholesale to trade and retail; secure internet sales site

M WANKE UK LTD
468-470 Old London Road
Hastings
East Sussex
TN35 5BG
Tel: 01424 444692
Fax: 01424 420660
Email: debbie@mwanke.com
Website: www.mwanke.com
retail premises and mail order

PRESSED FLOWERS

see under 'Flowers'

PRINTING & REPRO

CREWE COLOUR PRINTERS LTD
Unit 1, Millbuck Way
Springvale Industrial Estate
Sandbach
Cheshire
CW11 3SH
Tel: 01270 761113
Fax: 01270 766386
Email: repro@crewecolourprinters.com

PRINTEC (UK) LTD
Unit 5, Deanfield Court
Link 59 Business Park
Pimlico Link Road
Clitheroe
Lancs BB7 1QS
Tel: 01200 425500
Fax: 01200 425511
Email: info@printec.uk.com
retail premises and mail order

PYROGRAPHY

BURNT OFFERINGS
10 Long Croft
Aston-on-Trent
Derbys DE72 2UH
Tel: 01332 792036
Email: bob@burnerneill.freeserve.co.uk
Website: www.bobneillpyrography.co.uk
mail order only

JACK CHEYETTE
55 Pine Tree Avenue
Leicester
Leics LE5 1AL
Tel/Fax: 0116 276 8056
Email: ncheyette@aol.com
mail order only
Excellent range of leather blanks for Pyrography and Painting. New lines added monthly. Bookmarks, keyrings, purses and handbags, all in high quality natural leather.

RIBBONS

CRAFTY RIBBONS
3 Beechwood
Clump Farm
Tin Pot Lane
Blandford
Dorset DT11 7TD
Tel: 01258 455889
Email: info@craftyribbons.com
Website: www.craftyribbons.com
retail premises and mail order

J.E.M.'S SEWING MACHINE & NEEDLECRAFT CENTRE
19 Sun Street
Canterbury
Kent CT1 2HX
Tel: 01227 457723
Email: canterburysewing@btconnect.com
retail premises and mail order

RIBBON DESIGNS
PO Box 382
Edgware
Middx HA8 7XQ
Tel/Fax: 020 8958 4966
Email: info@ribbondesigns.co.uk
wholesale to trade and retail; mail order

BLADE RUBBER STAMPS LTD
12 Bury Place
London
WC1A 2JL
Tel: 020 7831 4123
Fax: 020 7831 4242
Email: info@bladerubber.co.uk
Website: www.bladerubber.co.uk
retail premises and mail order; secure internet sales site

KATY'S CORNER
77B Standish Street
St Helens
Merseyside WA10 1HY
Tel: 01744 22360
Fax: 0151 431 1835
Email: cath@katyscorner.org.uk
Website: www.katyscorner.org.uk
retail premises and mail order; secure internet sales site

MILLER'S CREATIVITY SHOP
28 Stockwell Street
Glasgow
G1 4RT
Tel: 0141 553 1660
Fax: 0141 553 1583
Email: info@millers-art.co.uk
Website: www.millers-art.co.uk
retail premises and mail order
Scotland's largest and most exciting art and craft supply shop. Established 1834. Excellent on-line website. Workshops available. Regular exhibitor at Hobbycraft and Rubber Stamping shows. Visit us soon!

ONCE UPON A TIME
49B High Street
Cricklade
Wilts SN6 6DA
Tel: 01793 759280
Fax: 01285 861302
Email: mail@itsonceuponatime.co.uk
Website: www.itsonceuponatime.co.uk
retail premises and mail order

SIMPLY STAMPS
Shop 3, Strand Court
Strand Quay
Rye
East Sussex TN31 7DB
Tel/Fax: 01797 229060
Email: info@simplystampsfriends.com
Website: www.simplystampsfriends.com
retail premises and mail order

STAMP ADDICTS
Park Lane Lodge
Park Lane
Gamlingay
Beds SG19 3PD
Tel/Fax: 01767 650329
Email: info@stampaddicts.co.uk
Website: www.stampaddicts.com
mail order only; secure internet sales site

THE STAMP CRAFT STUDIO
11 The Arcade
Letchworth Garden City
Herts SG6 3ET
Tel: 01462 681551
Fax: 01462 686155
Email: info@thestampcraftstudio.com
Website: www.thestampcraftstudio.com
retail premises and mail order

STAMPS UNLIMITED
148 Kings Road
Newbury
Berks
RG14 5RG
Tel: 01635 44717
Fax: 01635 32707
Email: enquiries@stampsunlimited.com
Website: www.stampsunlimited.com
original manufacturer and direct seller
Manufacturers of 'Impressions' and 'Rubber Stamp Craft' designs. Retail premises open 9am-5pm Monday to Friday. Bespoke and manufacturing service available. Organisers of Artstamps England, Scotland and Wales exhibitions.

RUGMAKING

J.E.M.'S SEWING MACHINE & NEEDLECRAFT CENTRE
19 Sun Street
Canterbury
Kent
CT1 2HX
Tel: 01227 457723
Email: canterburysewing@btconnect.com
retail premises and mail order

RAG ART
Unit 2, Tudor Yard
Lawnside Road
Ledbury
Herefordshire
HR8
2BZ
Tel: 01531 637373
Email: ragartmadd@aol.com
Website: www.ragartstudios.com
mail order only

SCRAPBOOKING

MAMELOK PRESS LTD
Northern Way
Bury St Edmunds
Suffolk
IP32 6NJ
Tel: 01284 762291
Fax: 01284 703689
Email: info@mamelok.co.uk
Website: www.mamelok.co.uk
original manufacturer and direct seller; secure internet sales site
Manufacturers of an extensive range of embossed and diecut scrapbook pictures (scraps) for 3D/flat découpage, card making, scrapbooking and all your decorative crafting activities.
Try them, they're special!

PAPERARTS SCRAPBOOKING
3-4 Market Square
Minchinhampton
Stroud
Glos
GL6 9BW
Tel: 01453 886038
Email: enquiries@paperarts.co.uk
Website: www.paperarts.co.uk
retail premises and mail order; secure internet sales site

PLACE OF MY HEART
17 Lawder Place
Dunblane
Perthshire
FK15 0NF
Tel: 01786 823344
Email: sue@bearsofmyheart.com
mail order only

SCULPTURE

ALEC TIRANTI LTD
70 High Street
Theale
Reading
Berks RG7 5AR
Tel: 0118 930 2775
Fax: 0118 932 3487
Email: enquiries@tiranti.co.uk
Website: www.tiranti.co.uk
retail premises and mail order

THE SMITHFIELD COMPANY
Unit 9, Lake Park
Caton Road
Lancaster
Lancs LA1 3NX
Tel: 01524 762883
Email: info@smithfieldgallery.co.uk
Website: www.smithfieldgallery.co.uk
supplier of raw materials such as metals, fabrics and papers via retail premises and mail order; secure internet sales site

SILK CRAFT

SILKCRAFT
14 Morley Close
Dronfield Woodhouse, Dronfield
Sheffield S18 8YQ
Tel/Fax: 01246 290179
Email: beckalison@yahoo.co.uk
Website: www.silkcraft.co.uk
wholesale (mail order only) to trade and retail; secure internet sales site

SILK PAINTING

THE FABRIC COLOUR WORKSHOP
Pride Rock Leisure Park
Leeds Road
Ilkley
West Yorks LS29 8AS
Tel/Fax: 01943 432044
retail premises and mail order
Silk Painting – starter kits, Marabu silk paints and general silk painting supplies. Including: plain silk scarves and the pre-outlined silk products from the Arty's range and silk by the metre.

SLATEWORK

INIGO JONES & CO LTD
Y Groeslon
Caernarfon
Gwynedd LL54 7UE
Tel: 01286 830242
Fax: 01286 831247
Email: slate@inigojones.co.uk
Website: www.inigojones.co.uk
original manufacturer and seller to retail only; secure internet sales site

SUGARCRAFT

SQUIRES KITCHEN SUGARCRAFT LTD
Alfred House
3 Waverley Lane
Farnham
Surrey GU9 8BB
Tel: 0845 225 5671
Fax: 0845 225 5673
Website: www.squires-group.co.uk
retail premises and mail order; secure internet sales site

TOOLS/EQUIPMENT

AVERY KNIGHT & BOWLERS
James Street West
Bath BA1 2BT
Tel: 01225 425894
Fax: 01225 445753
Email: sales@averyknight.co.uk
Website: www.averyknight.co.uk
retail premises and mail order; secure internet sales site

BRISTOL DESIGN
14 Perry Road
Bristol BS1 5BG
Tel: 0117 929 1740
Email: craft@bristol-design.co.uk
retail premises and mail order; woodworking tools

DAVGRO TOOLING
41 Limes Avenue
Aylesbury
Bucks HP21 7HB
Tel/Fax: 01296 481869
Email: davgro1@hotmail.com
Website: www.davgro.co.uk
original manufacturer and direct seller

THE ESSENTIALS COMPANY
April House
Davey Lane
Charsfield
Woodbridge
Suffolk IP13 7QG
Tel/Fax: 01473 737567
Email: info@theessentialscompany.co.uk
Website: www.theessentialscompany.co.uk
mail order only; secure internet sales site

EUROPEAN MACHINERY SALES LTD
Unit 16, Great Northern House
Great Northern Terrace
Lincoln
Lincs LN5 8HJ
Tel/Fax: 01522 575004
Email: sales@ems-ltd.fsnet.co.uk
Website: www.ems-ltd.fsnet.co.uk
wholesale to trade

HINDLEYS LTD
Hillcrest Works
230 Woodbourn Road
Sheffield
South Yorks S9 3LQ
Tel: 0114 278 7828
Fax: 0114 278 8558
Email: sales@hindleys.com
Website: www.hindleys.com
Hindleys stock a comprehensive range of tools, products and materials; mail order (UK and overseas)

H S WALSH & SONS LTD
243 Beckenham Road
Beckenham
Kent BR3 4TS
Tel: 020 8778 7061
Fax: 020 8676 8669
Email: steve@hswalsh.com
Website: www.hswalsh.com
trade premises and mail order
Jewellers', watchmakers' and craft tools, equipment and materials. Jewellery findings, pearl and bead rethreading supplies, clock spares, ultrasonic cleaners, ear piercing equipment and engraving machines. Branches in Kent, London and Birmingham's Jewellery Quarter.
230-page catalogue £4 with a £5 refund voucher. Monthly newsletter on request.

METALCRAFT
66 Clough Road
Hull
East Yorks HU5 1SR
Tel: 01482 345067
Fax: 01482 441141
Email: info@jandcrwood.co.uk
original manufacturer and direct seller

PROOPS BROTHERS LTD
Technology House
24 Saddington Road
Fleckney
Leics LE8 8AW
Tel: 0116 240 3400
Fax: 0116 240 3300
Email: jessica@proopsbrothers.co.uk
Website: www.proopsbrothers.com
original manufacturer, wholesaler, retail premises and mail order; secure internet sales site
The original Proops Brothers supplies everything for the craft and hobby enthusiast. A vast range of specialist hand tools perfect for woodworking, modelmaking, dollshouse making and lots, lots more!

SWANN-MORTON LTD
Owlerton Green
Sheffield S6 2BJ
Tel: 0114 234 4231
Fax: 0114 231 4966
Email: info@swann-morton.com
Website: www.craftknives.com
original manufacturer and seller to retail only

TEMPSFORD STAINED GLASS
The Old School
Tempsford
Beds SG19 2AW
Tel: 01767 641014
Fax: 01767 641124
Email: tsg@dial.pipex.com
Website: http://tempsford.ngt
retail premises and mail order; secure internet sales site
Open to shop callers including mail ordering service. Suppliers of coloured glasses, tools, materials and instructional books for all your stained glass requirements. Experienced, trained staff on hand.

Please tell all suppliers you saw their entry in The Craftworker's Year Book

TOYMAKING

ADMIRAL BEARS SUPPLIES
37 Warren Drive
Ruislip
Middx HA4 9RD
Tel/Fax: 020 8868 9598
Email: info@admiral-bears.com
Website: www.admiral-bears.com
mail order only; secure internet sales site

CHARLIES FURS & FEATURES
Blakemere Craft Centre
Sandiway
Northwich
Cheshire CW8 2EB
Tel/Fax: 01606 888814
Email: charliesfursandfeatures@btopenworld.com
Website: www.charliesfurs.co.uk
retail premises and mail order

PEACOCK FIBRES LTD
Gain Mill
Gain Lane
Bradford
West Yorks BD2 3LW
Tel: 01274 633900
Fax: 01274 633910
Email: info@peacockfibres.co.uk
Website: www.peacockfibres.co.uk
bear supplies and filling materials – original manufacturer and direct seller by mail order; secure internet sales site

WEAVING/SPINNING/DYEING

BOB TAILS
220 Seaside Road
Aldbrough
Hull
East Yorks HU11 4RY
Tel: 01964 527801
original manufacturer and direct seller

CAROLE KEATS
Webbs Green Farm
Soberton
Southampton
Hants SO32 3PY
Tel: 01489 877465
Email: webbsgreenfarm@msn.com

Website:
www.easisites.co.uk/webbsgreenfarmwool
retail premises and mail order; secure internet sales site

FIONA NISBET
Withymoor Cottage
Burleydam
Whitchurch
Shropshire SY13 4BQ
Tel: 01948 871618
Email: fionanisbet@yahoo.co.uk

HALDANES
Gateside
Fife KY14 7ST
Tel: 01337 860767
Fax: 01337 868983
Email: haldanesltd@aol.com
Website: www.haldanes.co.uk
mail order only; secure internet sales site

HANDWEAVERS STUDIO & GALLERY LTD
29 Haroldstone Road
London E17 7AN
Tel: 020 8521 2281
Email: handweaversstudio@msn.com
Website: www.handweaversstudio.co.uk
retail premises and mail order; original manufacturer and direct seller

HILLTOP SPINNING & WEAVING CENTRE
Windmill Cross
Canterbury Road
Lyminge
Folkestone
Kent CT18 8HD
Tel: 01303 862617
Email: sue@handspin.co.uk
Website: www.handspin.co.uk
mail order only

MAUREEN PREEN
Ivy House
Deep Cutting
Pool Quay
Welshpool
Powys SY21 9LJ
Tel: 07816 301682
retail premises and mail order

RAW FIBRES
The Old Signal Box
Station Workshops
Robin Hoods Bay
North Yorks YO22 4RA
Tel: 01947 880632
Fax: 01947 881119
Email: rosemary@beaconhillfarm.fsnet.co.uk
Website: www.brigantia.co.uk
retail premises and mail order

SNAIL TRAIL HANDWEAVERS
Penwenallt Farm
Cilgerran
Cardigan
Pembrokeshire SA43 2TP
Tel/Fax: 01239 841228
Email: martin@snail-trail.co.uk
Website: www.snail-trail.co.uk
original manufacturer and seller to retail only

STUDIO SUPPLIES + DON PORRITT LOOMS
The Studio
Leathley Road
Menston
West Yorks LS29 6DP
Tel: 01943 878329
Fax: 01943 884141
retail premises and mail order

TYNSELL HANDSPINNING SUPPLIES
53 Cross Green Road
Huddersfield
West Yorks
HD5 9XX
Tel: 01484 518328
mail order only

WITHIES (WILLOW) FOR BASKETS & STRUCTURES

JACOBS YOUNG & WESTBURY
Bridge Road
Haywards Heath
West Sussex RH16 1UA
Tel: 01444 412411
Fax: 01444 457662
Email: sales@jyw-uk.com
wholesale to trade and retail
UK's leading importer of cane, bamboo, seagrass, chair rush and willow. The range is complemented with stool frames, picture tray bases, natural and coloured raffia and ready manufactured cane seating.

WOODEN GIFTS/LASER ENGRAVING

WOODEN WONDERS LTD
Farley Farm House
Chiddingly
East Sussex BN8 6HW
Tel: 01825 872856
Fax: 01825 872733
Email: info@woodenwonders.co.uk
Website: www.woodenwonders.co.uk
original manufacturer and direct seller; secure internet sales site

WOOD VENEERS

REIF & SON LTD
Unit 8, Blue Chip Business Park
Atlantic Street
Altrincham
Cheshire WA14 5DD
Tel: 0161 927 9192
Fax: 0161 927 9193
Email: reif@btconnect.com
Website: www.wood-veneer.co.uk
wholesale to trade and retail and mail order

WOODWORKING

BOON & LANE LTD
7-9-11 Taylor Street
Luton
Beds LU2 0EY
Tel: 01582 723224
Fax: 01582 402298
Website: www.blockmaker.com
original manufacturer and direct seller

CHRISTOPHER MILNER WOODWORKING SUPPLIES
Beresford Lane
Woolley Moor
nr Alfreton
Derbys DE55 6FH
Tel/Fax: 01246 590062
Email: milnerwoodwork@aol.com
mail order only

CRAFT DESIGNS
4 Grassfield Way
Knutsford
Cheshire WA16 9AF
Tel/Fax: 01565 651681
Email: david@craftdesigns.co.uk
Website: www.craftdesigns.co.uk
mail order supplier of woodworking plans

CRAFT SUPPLIES LTD
The Mill
Millers Dale
nr Buxton
Derbys SK17 8SN
Tel: 01298 871636
Fax: 01298 872263
Email: sales@craft-supplies.co.uk
Website: www.craft-supplies.co.uk
retail premises and mail order; secure internet sales site

JOHN BODDY'S FINE WOOD & TOOL STORE LTD
Riverside Sawmills
Boroughbridge
North Yorks YO51 9LJ
Tel: 01423 322370
Fax: 01423 323810
Email: info@john-boddys-fwts.co.uk
retail premises and direct mail

M.H.C. INDUSTRIALS LTD
Wetmore Road
Burton-on-Trent
Staffs DE14 1QN
Tel: 01283 564651
Fax: 01283 511526
Email: sales@mhcind.co.uk
Website: www.mhcind.co.uk
wholesale to trade and retail

PROOPS BROTHERS LTD
Technology House
24 Saddington Road
Fleckney
Leics LE8 8AW
Tel: 0116 240 3400
Fax: 0116 240 3300
Email: jessica@proopsbrothers.co.uk
Website: www.proopsbrothers.com
original manufacturer, wholesaler, retail premises and mail order; secure internet sales site
The original Proops Brothers supplies everything for the craft and hobby enthusiast. A vast range of specialist hand tools perfect for woodworking, modelmaking, dollshouse making and lots, lots more!

21st CENTURY YARNS
Unit 18, Langston Priory Workshops
Kingham
Oxon OX7 6UP
Tel: 01608 683762
Email: yarns21stcentury@aol.com
Website: www.21stcenturyyarns.com
mail order only; secure internet sales site

TEXERE YARNS
College Mill
Barkerend Road
Bradford
West Yorks BD14 4AU
Tel: 01274 722191
Fax: 01274 393500
Email: info@texere.co.uk
Website: www.texere.co.uk
retail premises and mail order; secure internet sales site

REPRESENTATIVE BODIES IN CRAFT & ART

The following section is a directory of the multifarious organisations which exist today to represent, assist and promote the crafts and arts. Such bodies tend to be constituted in slightly different ways and this is reflected in the subsections under which they fall. Sometimes you will find an address but no telephone number (or vice versa); this is usually when the contact is at a private address (home of the membership secretary, for instance) and they do not wish this information to be published. The various costs quoted are, as with the rest of the information, as supplied to us and are the annual membership fees (net of VAT) unless otherwise stated.

Where we note that a newsletter or bulletin is published, this is more often than not only distributed to members. Many organisations will, however, be more than happy to let you have a sample copy if you are considering joining.

Where we use the term 'selective', we mean that the organisation undertakes vetting of prospective members' work before allowing an application for membership to proceed.

ASSOCIATIONS AND FEDERATIONS

APPLIED ARTS SCOTLAND
The Lighthouse
11 Mitchell Lane
Glasgow G1 3NU
Tel: 0141 572 1835
Email: office@appliedartsscotland.org.uk
Membership: Non-selective with fee of approx £25. Must live/work in Scotland. Registered Charity status. Publishes newsletter.

ASSOCIATION FOR CONTEMPORARY JEWELLERY
PO Box 37807
London SE23 1XJ
Tel: 020 8291 4201
Email: enquiries@acj.org.uk
Website: www.acj.org.uk
Contact: Sue Hyams
Membership: Non-selective with fee of £40 (full) or £15 (student/new graduates). For makers of contemporary jewellery.
Publishes newsletter.

ASSOCIATION OF BLAIRGOWRIE CRAFTWORKERS
c/o Heathcote
Golf Course Road
Rosemount
Blairgowrie
Perthshire PH10 6LF
Tel: 01250 874533
Email: arthurlo1137@aol.com
Contact: Arthur Logan
Membership: Selective with fee of £20.
Craftmakers of all types from any area eligible.
Publishes newsletter and colour members guide.

ASSOCIATION OF BRITISH DESIGNER SILVERSMITHS
PO Box 42034
London E5 9YB
Tel: 07944 786011
Email: info@theabds.co.uk
Website: www.theabds.co.uk
Contact: Alex Ramsay
Membership: Selective membership with fee of £150. Must live/work in the UK. Also available are Friend (£40) and non-selective Student (£10) and Graduate (£50) grades. Corporate membership costs £250. For those involved in silversmithing.
Publishes newsletter.

ASSOCIATION OF GUILDS OF WEAVERS, SPINNERS & DYERS
3 Gatchell Meadow
Trull
Taunton
Somerset TA3 7HY
Tel: 01823 325345
Email: paddybakker@onetel.net.uk
Website: www.wsd.org
Contact: Paddy Bakker
Membership: An association of the guilds widespread in this craft area. Fees vary from individual guild to guild, many of which have their own listing in the next subsection.
Registered Charity status.
Publishes newsletter.

ASSOCIATION OF HOT FOIL PRINTERS & ALLIED TRADES
15 Hunt Street
Atherton
Manchester M46 9JF

Tel: 0845 166 8395
Fax: 0845 166 8396
Email: association@hotfoilprinting.org
Website: www.hotfoilprinting.org
Contact: Paul Forshaw
Membership: Non-selective with fees of £25 (UK) and £35 (non-UK).
Publishes monthly magazine.

ASSOCIATION OF WOODTURNERS OF GREAT BRITAIN
The Stacks
Sandrock Hill
Crowhurst
Battle
East Sussex
TN33 9AT
Tel/Fax: 01424 830170
Email: lepringle@clara.co.uk
Website: www.woodturners.co.uk
Contact: Lionel Pringle
Membership: Non-selective with a fee of £12.50. For woodturners.
Publishes newsletter.

BASKETMAKERS' ASSOCIATION
Highlanes Farm
Brockton
Eccleshall
Staffs
ST21 6LY
Tel/Fax: 01630 620363
Email: isobeledge@hotmail.com
Website: www.basketassoc.org
Contact: Isobel Edge
Membership: Non-selective with fees of £20 (individual) and £27 (couple). For those involved in basketmaking, chair seating and allied crafts.
Publishes newsletter.

BASKETMAKERS SOUTH WEST
3 Shobrooke Village
Crediton
Devon
EX17 1AT
Tel: 01363 774382
Email: jones@3shob.fsnet.co.uk
Contact: Mandy Jones
Membership: Non-selective with fees of £6 for members of the Basketmakers' Association (see entry above) and £8 for others. For those involved in basketry, chairseating, sculpture in willow or other plant materials.
Publishes newsletter.

BRITISH ARTIST BLACKSMITHS ASSOCIATION
11 Main Street
Ratho
Newbridge
Midlothian EH28 8RS
Tel: 0131 333 1300
Fax: 0131 333 3354
Email: phil@rathobyres.demon.co.uk
Website: www.baba.org.uk
Contact: Phil Johnson
Membership: Non-selective with fees of £60 (full) or £35 (students). World-wide membership for those involved in metal work (with any combination material). Aims are education of apprentices and students and of each other. Collaboration through group projects, forge-ins and exhibitions. Inspiration through the sharing of ideas, techniques and experiences.
Publishes quarterly magazine.

BRITISH ASSOCIATION FOR MODERN MOSAIC
23 Lovelace Crescent
Exmouth
Devon EX8 3PP
Tel: 01395 278648
Email: apunton@bamm.org.uk
Website: www.bamm.org.uk
Contact: Allan Punton
Membership: Non-selective with fee of £12. For mosaic artists.
Publishes newsletter.

BRITISH DOLL ARTISTS ASSOCIATION
49 Cromwell Road
Beckenham
Kent BR3 4LL
Website: www.britishdollartists.org.uk
Contact: Mrs June Rose Gale
Membership: Selective with fee of £35. For professional artists who make and sell all-original dolls (i.e. all sculpture, painting and costume design by artist).

BRITISH HOROLOGICAL INSTITUTE
Upton Hall
Upton
Newark
Notts NG23 5TE
Tel: 01636 813795
Fax: 01636 812258
Email: clocks@bhi.co.uk
Website: www.bhi.co.uk
Contact: Zanna Perry

Membership: Professional membership is selective with a fee of £95. Non-selective grades are Student (£48) and Associate (£58).
Publishes 'Horological Journal' (see last section of book).

BRITISH WOODCARVERS ASSOCIATION
25 Summerfield Drive
Nottage
Porthcawl
Mid Glam CF36 3PB
Tel/Fax: 01656 786937
Email: johnb@sullivanjb.freeserve.co.uk
Website: www.bwa-woodcarving.fsnet.co.uk
Contact: John Sullivan
Membership: Non-selective with an annual fee of £17.
Publishes newsletter.

CLERKENWELL GREEN ASSOCIATION
Pennybank Chambers
33-35 St John's Square
London EC1M 4DS
Tel: 020 7251 0276
Fax: 020 7250 0297
Email: info@cga.org.uk
Website: www.cga.org.uk
Contact: Claire Gutteridge
Membership: Non-selective with fee of £35. For makers of both contemporary and traditional crafts living/working in Greater London.
Registered Charity status.
Publishes newsletter.

CONTEMPORARY APPLIED ARTS
2 Percy Street
London W1T 1DD
Tel: 020 7436 2344
Fax: 020 7436 2446
Website: www.caa.org.uk
Contact: Sonia Collins
Membership: Selective with fee of £75. For UK based craftspeople in ceramics, glass, jewellery, silver, textiles or wood.
Membership by invitation, with selection panel held twice a year.
Registered Charity status.

CORNWALL CRAFTS ASSOCIATION
Trelowarren Gallery
Mawgan
Helston
Cornwall TR6 3AF
Tel/Fax: 01326 221567
Email: help@cornwallcrafts.co.uk
Website: www.cornwallcrafts.co.uk
Contact: Andrea Wilkinson
Membership: Selective with a fee of £50; also associate grade at £15. Must live/work in Cornwall. Annual programme of exhibitions at association's two permanent exhibition spaces; as above and Trelissick Gallery.
Publishes newsletter.

COUNTRY CRAFTS ASSOCIATION
c/o 29 Wallis Avenue
Lincoln
Lincs LN6 8AS
Tel: 01522 687911
Fax: 01522 822189
Website:
www.country-crafts-association.info
Contact: Colin Hornsey
Membership: Selective with fee of £15.
Association of local craftworkers with most members living in the East Midlands (meetings held in Lincoln).

DORSET ARTS & CRAFTS ASSOCIATION
21 St Anthony's Road
Bournemouth
Dorset BH2 6PB
Tel/Fax: 01202 553113
Email: pador@talk21.com
Website: www.dorsetartsandcrafts.org
Contact: Paul Newsome
Membership: Non-selective with fee of £7.
Must live/work in Dorset.
Registered Charity status.
Publishes newsletter.

DRY STONE WALLING ASSOCIATION
Lane Farm
Crooklands
Milnthorpe
Cumbria LA7 7NH
Tel: 01539 567953
Email: information@dswa.org.uk
Website: www.dswa.org.uk
Membership: Non-selective with fees of £20 (open), £50 (professional) and £80 (corporate). For dry stone wallers.
Registered Charity status.

EAST ANGLIAN POTTERS ASSOCIATION
Vine Leigh Cottage
Main Street, Wardy Hill
Coveney

Ely
Cambs CB6 2DF
Tel: 01353 778462
Email: tonypugh@onetel.com
Website: www.the-eapa.org
Contact: Tony Pugh
Membership: Selective and non-selective grades. Fees are £25 (individual), £45 (joint at same address), £5 (student) and £45 (group corporate). For ceramicists in any discipline living or working in East Anglia. Registered Charity status.

FEDERATION OF BRITISH ARTISTS
17 Carlton House Terrace
London SW1Y 5BD
Tel: 020 7930 6844
Fax: 020 7839 7830
Email: info@mallgalleries.com
Website: www.mallgalleries.org.uk
Contact: John Deston
Umbrella organisation for 9 national art societies. Selective membership starts at £100. For working artists producing paintings, prints, drawings, sculpture and mixed media. Registered Charity status.
Publishes newsletter.

FLOWERS & PLANTS ASSOCIATION
266-270 Flower Market
New Covent Garden Market
London SW8 5NB
Tel: 020 7738 8044
Fax: 020 7738 8083
Email: info@flowers.org.uk
Website: www.flowers.org.uk
A not-for-profit trade promotional association; with an information service for both the press and public.

THE GA (GIFTWARE ASSOCIATION)
10 Vyse Street
Birmingham B18 6LT
Tel: 0121 236 2657
Fax: 0121 237 1106
Email: geeta.krishnan@ga-uk.org
Website: www.ga-uk.org
Contact: Geeta Krishnan
Membership: Non-selective with fee of £100+.
Publishes newsletter.

GWYNEDD & CLWYD ASSOCIATION OF CRAFTWORKERS
Groesffordd
Graiglwyd Road
Penmaenmawr
Conwy
LL34 6YG
Tel: 01492 623274
Contact: Biddy Hepper
Membership: Selective with a fee of £27.50. Must live/work in the (former) Gwynedd/Clwyd areas.
Publishes newsletter.

HAMPSHIRE WOODTURNERS ASSOCIATION
c/o Thornton House
Brimpton Common
Reading
RG7 4RF
Email: david.ackroyd@btopenworld.com
Website:
www.hants-woodturners-hwa.co.uk
Contact: Bob Hope (mail) or David Ackroyd (email).
Membership: Non-selective with a fee of £17 plus £5 joining fee.
Publishes newsletter

KENT POTTERS ASSOCIATION
c/o 'Fairview Barn'
Upper Street
Broomfield
nr Maidstone
Kent ME17 1PS
Tel: 01622 863554
Website: www.kentpotters.co.uk
Contact: Janet Jackson
Membership: Non-selective with fees of £18 (full), £14 (associate), £10.50 (full-time student) and £30 (family). Open to anyone interested in ceramics/pottery.
Publishes newsletter.

LOCHABER CRAFTS & FOOD PRODUCERS ASSOCIATION
Toad Hall
Acharacle
Argyll PH36 4JX
Tel: 01967 402279
Email: john.dye@virgin.net
Contact: Anne Dye
Membership: Selective with fee of £30. Must live/work in Lochaber, Highland region of Scotland.
Publishes Craft Trail.

MIDLANDS POTTERS ASSOCIATION
271 Yardley Wood Road
Moseley
Birmingham
B13 9JL
Tel: 0121 449 0850
Email: helenwillismpa@hotmail.com
Website:
www.midlandpotters.pwp.blueyonder.co.uk
Contact: Helen Willis
Membership: Non-selective with fees of £20 (full), £10 (concessions) or £30 (workshop). For ceramicists.
Publishes newsletter.

NATIONAL ASSOCIATION OF DECORATIVE & FINE ARTS SOCIETIES
NADFAS House
8 Guildford Street
London WC1N 1DA
Tel: 020 7430 0730
Fax: 020 7242 0686
Email: ncoke@nadfas.org.uk
Website: www.nadfas.org.uk
Contact: Natalie Coke
Membership: Non-selective with national fee of £15. Comprises local societies with their own membership rates.
Registered Charity status.

NATIONAL ASSOCIATION OF DISABLED CRAFTWORKERS
4 Crosshill Cottages
Mauchline
Ayrshire KA5 5HJ
Tel/Fax: 01290 552174
Email: nadcw@aol.com
Membership: Non-selective with individual fee of £5 and corporate fee of £50.
Registered Help Line status; no charge for advice, which is also freely given to non-members.

NORTHERN POTTERS ASSOCIATION
18 Riley Close
Bracebridge Heath
Lincoln
Lincs LN4 2QS
Tel: 01522 859105
Email: smithsatbbh@ntlworld.com
Website: www.northern-potters.org.uk
Contact: P M Smith
Membership: Non-selective with fees of £25 (full), £22 paid by Standing Order) and £10 (student). Restricted to potters.
Publishes newsletter.

ORIGIN DYFED GALLERY LTD
26 Blue Street
Carmarthen
Dyfed SA31 3LE
Tel: 01267 220377
Contact: Paula Hall
Membership: Selective with fee of £50 for craftworkers and artists; also a cardmaker grade at £25. Must live/work in Dyfed region.
Publishes newsletter.

ORKNEY CRAFT INDUSTRIES ASSOCIATION
c/o Outerdykes
Stenness
Orkney KW16 3HA
Tel: 01856 850207
Fax: 01856 850819
Email: ocia@e-scotland.co.uk
Website: www.orkneydesignercrafts.com
Contact: Andi Ross
Membership: Selective with fee of £100. Must live/work in Orkney.
Publishes informal newsletter.

QUILT ASSOCIATION
Minerva Arts Centre
High Street
Llanidloes
Powys SY16 4LU
Tel: 01686 413467
Email: quilts@ic24.net
Website: www.quilt.org.uk
Contact: Sonia Fox
Membership: Non-selective with fee of £6. For quilters. This permanent quilt centre has a gallery with changing exhibitions through the year, workshops and demonstrations, books and cards on quilting and other crafts, and a sales area with quilts old and new, fabric and threads.
Registered Charity status.
Publishes newsletter

REDESMERE CRAFTS ASSOCIATION
c/o 17 Beechwood Drive
Eaton Village
nr Congleton
Cheshire CW12 2NQ
Tel: 01260 297087
Contact: Wenda Dobson
Membership: Cannot take further members at present (recruitment when member retires). Association organises craft events

(see Organiser section) and invites non-members to participate as guest craftworkers.

RUGBY CRAFT ASSOCIATION
10 Dewar Grove
Hillmorton
Rugby
Warks
CV21 4AT
Tel: 01788 575761
Contact: Mrs Christine Hughes
Membership: Selective with fee of £5.
Makers of hand-made crafts only.

SCOTTISH BORDERS CRAFTS ASSOCIATION
Kalemouth
Kelso
Roxburghshire
TD5 8LE
Tel/Fax: 01835 850266
Email:
mail@scottishborderscraftsassociation.org.uk
Website:
www.scottishborderscraftsassociation.org.uk
Contact: Margaret Jeary
Membership: Non-selective with fee of £18.
Must live/work in the Scottish Borders Council area.
Publishes newsletter.

SCOTTISH LETTERCUTTERS ASSOCIATION
6 Dean Terrace
Edinburgh
EH4 1ND
Email: lettercutting@hotmail.com
Contact: Jane Raven
Membership: Non-selective with a fee of £50. For lettercutters living/working in Scotland.

SCOTTISH POTTERS ASSOCIATION
1 Admiralty Gardens
Old Kilpatrick
Glasgow G60 5HU
Tel: 01389 890991
Email: alund@beantighe.co.uk
Website: www.scottishpotters.org
Contact: Pam Dyson
Membership: Non-selective with fees of £20 (individual), £40 (workshop) and £18 (seniors/apprentices). Open to anyone interested in ceramics.
Publishes newsletter.

WALES CRAFT COUNCIL
Henfaes Lane
Welshpool
Powys SY21 7BE
Tel: 01938 555313
Fax: 01938 556237
Email: info@walescraftcouncil.co.uk
Website: www.walescraftcouncil.co.uk
Contact: Pauline Muggleton
Membership: Non-selective with fee of £50.
Members must live/work in Wales.
Publishes newsletter.

WYE VALLEY CRAFTS ASSOCIATION
6 Forsdene Walk
Coalway
Coleford
Glos GL16 7JZ
Tel: 01594 832428
Email: alc.summer6@fsnet.co.uk
Website: www.wyevalleycrafts.co.uk
Contact: Alison Summers
Membership: Selective with fees of £15 (full) and £10 (associate). All crafts must be hand-made or hand finished. The association has a permanent shop based at Tintern and arranges events throughout the year.

GUILDS, GROUPS AND CLUBS

3 SHIRES CRAFT GUILD
The Old Bakehouse
Harpley Road
Defford
Worcs WR8 9BL
Tel: 01386 750475
Email: joanstrong@defford52.freeserve.co.uk
Website: www.3-shires-craft-guild.ik.com
Contact: Mrs Joan Strong
Membership: By invitation (having first come as a guest). Selective with fees (under review) of £10 (individual) or £15 (joint).
Must live/work within Gloucestershire, Herefordshire, Worcestershire. A non-profit making organisation.

ABINGDON SILVER GROUP
c/o 11 Meadowside
Abingdon
Oxon OX14 5DU
Tel: 01235 522276
Membership: Non-selective with a fee of £35 registration and £2 per evening session. For

those working with silver to produce silver-ware or jewellery.

AINSDALE CROSS STITCH CLUB
30 Mill Road
Ainsdale
Southport
Merseyside PR8 3HY
Tel: 01704 576964
Contact: Mrs Karen Woolley
Membership: Non-selective with fee of £7 plus £2 per meeting. For both beginner and experienced cross stitchers. Social evenings, sales, demonstrations and exhibitions of members' work.

ALSAGER PATCHWORKERS & QUILTERS
c/o 6 Fairview Avenue
Alsager
Stoke-on-Trent ST7 2NW
Tel: 01270 875210
Email: lynsmo@aol.com
Website: www.alsagerpqs.org
Contact: Lyn Smolenska
Membership: Non-selective with no fee. Open meetings held monthly (usually third Thursday) at YPCC in Rode Heath on the Cheshire/Staffs border. Club welcomes everyone interested in patchwork/quilting and it aims to provide a focus for these crafts in the area.

ANGLESEY CRAFTWORKERS GUILD
Bryn Hyfryd
Gwalchmai
Anglesey LL65 4RB
Tel: 01407 720393
Email: pat@daydreams.fsbusiness.co.uk
Contact: Pat Cleever
Membership: Selective with fee of £28. Membership by invitation to those who live/work on Anglesey.
Publishes newsletter.

ARGYLL GREEN WOODWORKERS ASSOCIATION
Old Poltalloch
Kilmartin
Argyll PA31 8RQ
Tel: 01852 500366
Email: gordon.graystephens@scottishnativewoods.org.uk
Contact: Gordon Gray Stephens
Membership: Selective with fees of £15 (family/business), £10 (ordinary/individual) and £5 (low wage).
Registered Charity status.

BATIK GUILD
1 William Terrace
Norton
Stockton-on-Tees
Teesside
TS20 2HF
Email: thelma@1william.freeserve.co.uk
Website: www.batikguild.org.uk
Contact: Thelma Russell
Membership: Non-selective with a fee of £18. For those involved in wax resist textiles.
Publishes newsletter.

BEDFORDSHIRE GUILD OF SPINNERS, WEAVERS & DYERS
13 Sanderson Road
Westoning
Beds
MK45 5JY
Tel: 01525 721266 (evenings)
Contact: C Branscombe
Membership: Non-selective. For those with any connection to these crafts.
Registered Charity status.

BERKSHIRE GUILD OF SPINNERS, WEAVERS & DYERS
7 Plover Close
Wokingham
Berks RG41 3JD
Tel: 0118 901 9946
Email:
info@berks-spinners-weavers-dyers.org.uk
Website:
www.berks-spinners-weavers-dyers.org.uk
Contact: Sue Turnbull
Membership: Non-selective with a fee of £12. For stated crafters and also crocheters.
Publishes newsletter.

BOWLAND GUILD OF SPINNERS, WEAVERS & DYERS
34 Wordsworth Drive
Great Harwood
Blackburn
Lancs BB6 7LA
Tel: 01254 877667
Contact: Margaret Bradley
Membership: Non-selective with fee of £23. For those involved in spinning, weaving, dyeing and related crafts (e.g. feltmaking).
Publishes newsletter.

BRECKNOCK GUILD OF SPINNERS, WEAVERS & DYERS
c/o The Forge
Cantref
Brecon
Powys
LD3 8LR
Tel: 01874 665691
Contact: Carole Webb
Membership: Non-selective with a fee of £12.50 plus £1 per meeting. For spinners, weavers and dyers.

BRITISH POLYMER CLAY GUILD
c/o 2 Shelburne Way
Derry Hill
Calne
Wilts
SN11 9PA
Tel: 01249 813862
Fax: 01249 816673
Email: philippa.todd@btinternet.com
Website: www.polymerclaypit.co.uk/polyclay/guild/britpol.htm
Contact: Philippa Todd
Membership: Non-selective with fee of £10 (UK) and £15 (non-UK). For those involved in anything associated with polymer clay.
Publishes newsletter.

BRITISH STICKMAKERS GUILD
c/o 19 Woodmancote Road
Worthing
West Sussex
BN14 7HT
Tel: 01903 205015
Email: c.hutcheon@lineone.net
Contact: C Hutcheon
Membership: Non-selective with fee of £8. BSG objectives are the cultivation of collecting and the art of making walking sticks, canes, staffs and shepherds' crooks.

BRITISH SUGARCRAFT GUILD
National Office, Wellington House
Messeter Place
Eltham
London SE9 5DP
Tel: 020 8859 6943
Fax: 020 8859 6117
Email: nationaloffice@bsguk.org
Website: www.bsguk.org
Membership: Non-selective with fee of £18 (UK) and £24 (non-UK). For those in sugarcraft, anywhere in world.
Publishes newsletter.

CAMBRIDGESHIRE GUILD OF WEAVERS, SPINNERS & DYERS
c/o 24 School Close
Gamlingay
Sandy
Beds SG19 3JY
Tel: 01767 650904 (evenings only)
Email: chris.tucker@zen.co.uk
Website: under construction; email for update.
Contact: Chris Tucker
Membership: Non-selective with fee of £15. Primarily for weavers, spinners and dyers, but also other textile crafters. The guild runs exhibitions but no firm dates for 2005 were available when we went to press.
Publishes newsletter.

CEREDIGION CRAFT MAKERS
Pwyll-y-Berllan
Llanrhystud
Ceredigion SY23 5ED
Tel: 01974 272026
Email: garthenor@organicpurewool.co.uk
Website: www.ccmcrafts.co.uk
Contact: Chris King
Membership: Non-selective with fee of £10. Must live/work in Ceredigion.

COHESION GLASSMAKERS NETWORK
City of Sunderland
Chief Executive's Division
Business & Investment Team
Sunderland
Tyne & Wear SR2 7DN
Tel: 0191 553 1219
Fax: 0191 553 1180
Email: anne.tye@sunderland.gov.uk
Website: www.cohesionglassnetwork.org
Contact: Anne Tye
Membership: Non-selective with fee of £35. Network is based in the North East of England but is open to glassmakers anywhere.
Publishes newsletter.

COUNTY DOWN CRAFTS
11 Scotch Street
Downpatrick
Co Down BT30 6AQ
Tel: 028 4461 7214
Fax: 028 4461 7133
Email: jan.irwin@virgin.net
Website: www.countydowncrafts.com
Contact: Jan Irwin
Membership: Non-selective with fee of £40.
Publishes newsletter.

CRAFT GUILD OF TRADITIONAL BOWYERS & FLETCHERS
'Yew Corner'
29 Batley Court
Oldland
South Glos BS30 8YZ
Tel/Fax: 0117 932 3276
Website: www.bowyersandfletchersguild.org
Contact: H Hewitt Soar, The Clerk
Membership: Full membership (UK only) is selective with fee of £10. By invitation. For makers of longbows and arrows. Associate membership is available to overseas craftspeople satisfying the guild's criteria of excellence.

CRAFT GUILD OF WEST LANCASHIRE
83 Elmers Green
Skelmersdale
Lancs WN8 6SB
Tel: 01695 733428
Email: info@craftguildwestlancs.co.uk
Website: www.craftguildwestlancs.co.uk
Contact: Pam MacDonald
Membership: Selective with a fee of £42. Must live/work in Lancashire.
Publishes newsletter.

CRAFTMARK
Enterprise House
Partnership Court
The Ramparts
Dundalk
County Louth
Republic of Ireland
Tel: 00 353 42 939 6944
Fax: 00 353 42 932 7101
Email: enquiries@craftmark.ie
Website: www.craftmark.ie
Contact: Sarah Daly
Membership: Non-selective with a fee of €10/£6.75. For those involved in craft, applied art and design and living/working in the North East Border region of Ireland (Northern Ireland and Republic of Ireland). See Markets etc section for background info.

CRAVEN GUILD OF WEAVERS, SPINNERS & DYERS
The Old Schoolhouse
Newchurch-in-Pendle
Burnley
Lancs BB12 9JR
Tel: 01282 612633
Email: marilyn.clarkson@tesco.net
Contact: Marilyn Clarkson
Membership: Non-selective with a fee of £15. For the stated crafters.
Registered Charity status.

CROSS STITCH GUILD
Pinks Barn
London Road
Fairford
Glos GL7 4AR
Tel: 0800 328 9750
Fax: 01285 713779
Email: helen@crossstitchguild.com
Website: www.thecrossstitchguild.com
Contact: Helen King
Membership: Non-selective with fees of £25 (UK) and £30 (non-UK). For counted needleworkers.
Publishes newsletter.

DACORUM & CHILTERN POTTERS GUILD
c/o Broomfield
36 Box Lane
Boxmoor
Herts HP3 0DJ
Tel: 01442 404122
Website: www.thedcpg.org.uk
Contact: Digby Stott
Membership: Non-selective with fees of £17 (individual), £21 (family) and £9 (student).
Open to ceramicists.
Publishes quarterly bulletin.

DANE COPPICE CRAFTS GROUP
c/o 10 Eaton Close
Sandbach
Cheshire CW11 1HS
Tel: 01270 760810
Email: aileen.thompson@btinternet.com
Website: www.spindizzy.net/dccg/
Contact: Aileen Thompson
Membership: Non-selective with fee of £10 for individuals; discount for students and family members. An informal cooperative group concerned with willow and associated crafts. Organises group exhibitions, courses, talks and meetings.

DESIGNER JEWELLERS GROUP
c/o 38 Cornwell House
21 Clerkenwell Green
London SE24 0DX
Tel: 07941 024739
Email: oliviaschlevogt@yahoo.co.uk
Website: www.designerjewellersgroup.co.uk
Contact: Olivia Schlevogt

Membership: Selective with fee of £60. For designer jewellers.

DEVON GUILD OF CRAFTSMEN
Riverside Mill
Bovey Tracey
Devon TQ13 9AF
Tel: 01626 832223
Fax: 01626 834220
Email: jenny@crafts.org.uk
Website: www.crafts.org.uk
Contact: Jenny Plackett
Membership: Selective with a fee of £92.50. Must live/work west of a line from Bristol to Southampton. Riverside Mill centre is now the largest contemporary crafts centre in the South West.
Registered Charity status.

DISS & DISTRICT GUILD OF WEAVERS, SPINNERS & DYERS
c/o Southview
Common Road
Shelfanger
Diss
Norfolk IP22 2DP
Tel: 01379 643563
Contact: Mrs Pam Ross
Membership: Non-selective with fee of £10. For those involved in textiles, weaving, spinning and dyeing.

DORSET GUILD OF WEAVERS, SPINNERS & DYERS
c/o The Old Barns
13 Fordington Dairy
Athelstan Road
Dorchester
Dorset DT1 1FD
Tel: 01305 250456
Contact: Mrs Lynne Davenport on 01258 860089
Membership: Non-selective with a fee of £12. For stated crafters and also knitters.
Publishes newsletter.

EAST SURREY GUILD OF WEAVERS, SPINNERS & DYERS
c/o Foxhollow
Crampshaw Lane
Ashtead
Surrey KT21 2UE
Tel: 01372 272971
Email: eve.hindley@fsmail.net
Contact: Mrs Eve Hindley
Membership: Non-selective with fee of £10. For those involved in the textile crafts.
Publishes newsletter.

EAST SUSSEX GUILD OF CRAFTWORKERS
Woodfield
Pett Road
Guestling
East Sussex TN35 4EX
Tel: 01424 812513
Contact: Mrs M Althorp
Membership: Selective with fees of £15 (exhibiting members) and £7.50 (non-exhibiting). Annual show held midsummer and a joint show in November.

EGG CRAFTERS GUILD OF GREAT BRITAIN
The Studio
7 Hylton Terrace
North Shields
Tyne & Wear NE29 0EE
Tel/Fax: 0191 258 3648
Email: joanccutts@aol.com
Website:
http://uk.geocities.com/eggcraftersguild
Contact: Mrs J C Cutts
Membership: Non-selective with fees of £13 (UK) and £25 (non-UK). For those involved in egg decoration.
Publishes newsletter.

EMBROIDERERS' GUILD
Apartment 41
Hampton Court Palace
Surrey KT8 9AU
Tel: 020 8943 1229
Fax: 020 8977 9882
Email:
administrator@embroiderersguild.com
Website: www.embroiderersguild.com
Membership: Non-selective with various fees. Registered Charity status.
Publishes two magazines.

EMBROIDERERS GUILD – SWANSEA BRANCH
8 Bron-y-Bryn
Killay
Swansea SA2 7NP
Tel: 01792 205935
Email: margodav@simast.freeuk.com
Contact: Jane Riseborough
Membership: Non-selective with annual fee.

For embroiderers.
Registered Charity status.
Publishes newsletter.

EXETER CRAFTS GUILD LTD
Quayside Crafts
42 The Quay
Exeter
Devon EX2 4AL
Tel: 01392 214332
Contact: Mike Shields
Membership: Selective; must live/work in West Country. Quayside Crafts is run and manned by members. The work of over 50 local artists and craftworkers is on display.

FERMANAGH CRAFTS CONSORTIUM
The Buttermarket
Down Street
Enniskillen
Co Fermanagh BT74 7DU
Tel: 028 6632 4499
Email: cdo@fermanaghcraft.com
Website: www.fermanaghcraft.com
Membership: Selective with fee of £25. Must live/work in Co Fermanagh, Northern Ireland.
Publishes newsletter.

GALLOWAY CRAFT GUILD
76 King Street
Castle Douglas
Kirkcudbrightshire DG7 1AD
Contact: Bunty Davies
Membership: Non-selective with fee of £15.
Must live/work in Dumfries and Galloway.
Publishes newsletter.

GLAMORGAN GUILD OF WEAVERS, SPINNERS & DYERS
9 Charlotte Square
Rhiwbina
Cardiff CF14 6ND
Tel: 029 2062 4834
Email: s.nicholls@easynet.co.uk
Contact: Jane Nicholls
Membership: Non-selective with fee of £20.
For anyone interested in all these crafts and living/working in Cardiff and the surrounding area.
Registered Charity status.
Publishes newsletter.

GLOUCESTERSHIRE GUILD OF CRAFTSMEN
The Guild Gallery
The Painswick Centre
Bisley Street
Painswick
Glos GL6 6QQ
Tel: 01452 814745
Email: join@guildcrafts.org.uk
Website: www.guildcrafts.org.uk
Membership: Selective with fee of £80.
Registered Charity status applied for.

GRESFORD CRAFT GROUP
Brora
Springfield Court
Gresford
Wrexham LL12 8HY
Tel/Fax: 01978 852856
Email: valatbrora@aol.com
Contact: Val Shields
Membership: Non-selective with attendance fee of £1 per attendance. For anyone interested in the textile crafts. The group structure is very informal; it is self-funding, runs various events and surplus is given to charity. The annual exhibition in 2005 will be 14-17 June.

GUILD OF BRITISH DÉCOUPEURS
18 Pembridge Close
Charlton Kings
Cheltenham
Glos GL52 6XY
Tel: 01242 235302
Contact: Madeleine Smith
Membership: Non-selective with a fee of £15. For découpeurs.
Publishes newsletter.

GUILD OF ESSEX CRAFTSMEN
c/o 10 The Furlongs
Ingatestone
Essex CM4 0AH
Tel: 01277 356008
Email: reelspin@route56.co.uk
Membership: Selective with a fee of £20.
Must live or exhibit within Essex.
Membership generally by invitation.
Publishes newsletter.

GUILD OF GLASS ENGRAVERS
87 Nether Street
London N12 7NP
Fax: 020 8446 4050

Email: enquiries@gge.org.uk
Website: www.gge.org.uk
Contact: Christine Reyland
Membership: Selective grades with fees of £50-£60 and non-selective at £30. For glass engravers.
Registered Charity status.
Publishes newsletter.

GUILD OF MACHINE KNITTERS
Ty Gwyn
Crow End
Bourn
Cambs CB3 7SY
Tel/Fax: 01954 719359
Email: membership@guild-mach-knit.org.uk
Website: www.guild-mach-knit.org.uk
Membership: Non-selective with a fee of £12.
Publishes newsletter.

GUILD OF NEEDLE LACES
c/o 36 Cleeve
Tamworth
Staffs B77 2QD
Email: trish@hughes655.fsnet.co.uk
Contact: Mrs Trish Hughes
Membership: Non-selective with fees payable (apply). Restricted to those involved in needle lace.

GUILD OF RAILWAY ARTISTS
45 Dickins Road
Warwick
Warks CV34 5NS
Tel: 01926 499246
Email: frank.hodges@tinyworld.co.uk
Website: www.railart.co.uk
Contact: Frank Hodges
Membership: Selective with fees of £20 (full; by election) and £15 (associate; by selection). For fine artists with railway subject matter.

GUILD OF SILK PAINTERS (NORTHERN BRANCH)
1 William Terrace
Norton
Stockton-on-Tees TS20 2HF
Email: thelma@1william.freeserve.co.uk
Contact: Thelma Russell
Membership: Non-selective with fee of £5 plus £3 per meeting attended. For silk painters. Meetings at Shipley Art Gallery in Gateshead.
Publishes newsletter.

GUILD OF TRADITIONAL UPHOLSTERERS
c/o Cherry Garth
The Hamlet
Gallowtree Common
Oxon RG4 9BU
Tel: 0118 972 2921
Contact: Philip Wellesley-Davies
Membership: Selective with annual fee payable. Selection involves a written examination and presentation of a specified piece of upholstery which will be scrutinised to ensure it meets the guild's high standards of skills and workmanship.

GWENT EMBROIDERERS' GUILD
2 Winchester Close
Newport NP20 3BL
Tel: 01633 815018
Membership: Non-selective with fee of £20. For those involved in embroidery and textiles.
Registered Charity status.

HALLAMSHIRE & DISTRICT GUILD OF WEAVERS, SPINNERS & DYERS
18 Crabtree Lane
Sheffield
South Yorks S5 7AY
Tel: 0114 242 5966
Email: hgwsd@yahoo.co.uk
Contact: Karen Graham
Membership: Non-selective with a fee of £21. For the stated crafters.
Registered Charity status.
Publishes newsletter.

HAMPSHIRE & BERKSHIRE GUILD OF CRAFTSMEN
The Cottage
Woodgreen
Fordingbridge
Hants SP6 2AR
Email: nickbarberton@hotmail.com
Website: www.hants.org.uk/hbguild/
Contact: Nick Barberton
Membership: Selective with a fee of £30. Must live/work in Hampshire/Berkshire.

HAMPSHIRE GUILD OF WEAVERS, SPINNERS & DYERS
51 Edgar Road
Winchester
Hants SO23 9SJ
Tel: 01962 820370

Email: anntwizzle@yahoo.co.uk
Website: www.hants.org.uk/hantsguildwsd/
Contact: Ann Lovick
Membership: Non-selective with a fee of £12. Must live/work in Hampshire. For those involved in fibres/textiles.

HIGH PEAK WOODTURNERS
c/o 2 Meadway
Bramhall
Stockport
Cheshire SK7 1LA
Tel: 0161 439 5176
Email: davidl.bagnall@ntlworld.com
Website: www.hpwt.org.uk
Contact: David Bagnall
Membership: Non-selective with fee of £27. For woodturners and woodcarvers.
Publishes newsletter.

ISLE OF WIGHT GUILD OF WEAVERS, SPINNERS & DYERS
'Edelweiss'
Fine Lane
Shorwell
Newport
Isle of Wight PO30 3JY
Tel: 01983 741375
Email: wsd.iow@vespers.demon.co.uk
Contact: Renella Phillips
Membership: Non-selective with fee of £10. For the stated crafters.

JORVIK WOODTURNING GROUP
10 Sargent Avenue
Bishopthorpe
York YO23 2QY
Tel: 01904 704092
Email: revtim@evansacomb.freeserve.co.uk
Contact: Tim Evans
Membership: Non-selective with fees of £25 (adult) and £12.50 (junior). The group serves woodturners in a very wide area centred on York. Plenty of room for more members.
Publishes newsletter.

KENNET VALLEY GUILD OF WEAVERS, SPINNERS & DYERS
71 Maple Crescent
Newbury
Berks RG14 1LP
Tel: 01635 43846
Email: albert.moss@virgin.net
Contact: Albert Moss
Membership: Non-selective with fee of £10.50. Member of National Association.
Publishes 'The Shuttle'.

KENT GUILD OF SPINNERS, DYERS & WEAVERS
25 Pickering Street
Maidstone
Kent ME15 9RS
Tel: 01622 744665
Email: pam@hawkerj.freeserve.co.uk
Contact: Pam Hawker
Membership: Non-selective with fee of £20. Must live/work in Kent and be involved in stated crafts.
Registered Charity status.
Publishes newsletter.

KINGSTON & DISTRICT BRANCH – EMBROIDERERS' GUILD
8 Flanchford Road
London W12 9ND
Tel/Fax: 020 8743 9707
Email: fgsinclair@aol.com
Website: www.embroiderersguild.com
Contact: Frances Sinclair
Membership: Non-selective with fee of £19. For those involved in embroidery and related crafts.
Registered Charity status.
Publishes newsletter.

KNITTING & CROCHET GUILD
108 Park Lane
Kidderminster
Worcs DY11 6TB
Tel: 01562 754367 (after 5pm)
Email: guild@blueyonder.co.uk
Website:
www.knitting-and-crochet-guild.org.uk
Contact: Mrs Anne Budworth
Membership: The organisation for all hand knitters, machine knitters and crocheters. Non-selective with fee of £18 (adults).
Registered Charity status.
Publishes quarterly journal ('SlipKnot').
See also display advertisement.

LACE GUILD
The Hollies
53 Audnam
Stourbridge
West Midlands DY8 4AE
Tel: 01384 390739
Fax: 01384 444415
Email: hollies@laceguild.org

Website: www.laceguild.org
Contact: Maggie Jenkins
Membership: Non-selective with fees of £23 (UK), £27 (Europe) and £31 (rest of world). For those involved in lacemaking (all types).
Registered Charity status.
Publishes newsletter.

LONDON GUILD OF WEAVERS, SPINNERS & DYERS
25 Princes Gardens
Ealing
London
W5 1SD
Tel: 020 8997 0291
Email: daphne@cliffe33.freeserve.co.uk
Website: www.londonguildofweavers.org.uk
Contact: Daphne Ratcliffe
Membership: Non-selective with fee of £14 plus £2 joining fee. Mainly for stated crafters.
Publishes newsletter.

LUDLOW DESIGNER MAKERS
Wills Cottage
64 Britons Lane
Linley Brook
Bridgnorth
Shropshire
WV16 4TA
Tel: 01746 765078
Email: caroline@carolinebennett.co.uk
Contact: Caroline Bennett
Membership: Selective with a fee of £35. Trained and experienced makers with skill, originality and flair in design are encouraged to apply. Based in Ludlow but applicants from nearby parts of Herefordshire and South Shropshire are welcome to apply.

MAKERS GUILD IN WALES
Craft in the Bay
The Flourish
Lloyd George Avenue
Cardiff Bay
Cardiff
CF10 4ES
Tel: 029 2048 4611
Website: www.makersguildinwales.org.uk
Contact: Molly Curley
Membership: Selective with a fee of £40 (2004). Must live/work in Wales. A cooperative company limited by guarantee.
Registered Charity status.
Publishes newsletter.

MERIONETH NEEDLECRAFT GROUP
c/o 1 Church Street
Tywyn
Gwynedd
LL36 9DA
Tel: 01654 710550
Contact: Anne Rees
Membership: Non-selective with fee of £7. For needlecrafters/machine embroiderers (modern and traditional) living/working in Merionnydd/Powys/Gwynedd. Cannot take further members at present.

MERSEYSIDE GUILD OF WEAVERS
6 Castlegrange Close
Moreton
Wirral
Merseyside
CH46 3SX
Tel: 0151 678 1557
Email: chris@cgrange.fsnet.co.uk
Website: www.merseyweaver.org.uk
Contact: Mrs Chris Holmes
Membership: Non-selective with fee of £16.
Registered Charity status.
Publishes newsletter.

MIDDLE ESSEX GUILD OF WEAVERS, SPINNERS & DYERS
6 Crown Street
Castle Hedingham
Halstead
Essex
CO9 3DB
Tel: 01787 462172
Email: megwsd@uk2.net
Website: www.spinandweave.org.uk
Contact: Mrs Chris Applebee
Membership: Non-selective with fee of £17. Visitors £1 per day (max. 3 visits per annum). For all textile crafters. Members also display and demonstrate at craft events and fairs.
Registered Charity status.

MID LANCS GUILD OF SPINNERS, WEAVERS & DYERS
c/o 241 Bolton Road North
Ramsbottom
Bury
Lancs BL0 0SA
Tel: 01706 826154
Contact: Patricia Barrett
Membership: Non-selective with fee of £10. For those involved in weaving, spinning, dyeing and associated textile crafts.

MONTGOMERYSHIRE GUILD OF WEAVERS, SPINNERS & DYERS
Coed y Cwm
Castle Caereinion
Welshpool
Powys SY21 9AR
Tel: 01938 850394
Email: lynnegeldart@btinternet.com
Contact: Mrs Lynne Geldart
Membership: Non-selective with fee of £10. For weavers, spinners, dyers etc.

NEW FOREST GUILD OF WEAVERS, SPINNERS & DYERS
2 Myvern Close
Holbury
Southampton
Hants SO45 2HZ
Tel: 023 8089 3982
Contact: Bettina Beauchamp
Membership: Non-selective with fee of £17.50. For the stated crafters. Registered Charity status. Publishes newsletter.

NORFOLK CRAFTSMEN'S GUILD
3 Northall Green
Dereham
Norfolk NR20 4BA
Tel: 01362 694633
Contact: Mrs J Batey
Membership: Non-selective with fee of £12. Must live/work in East Anglia.

NORTH & MID-WALES LACEMAKERS
c/o Swn-y-Gwynt
Caersws
Powys SY17 5HH
Tel: 01686 689048
Contact: Pat Gibson
Membership: Non-selective with no annual fees. Must live in, or attend classes in, Wales.

NORTHAMPTONSHIRE GUILD OF DESIGNER CRAFTSMEN
28 High Street
Milton Malsor
Northants NN7 3AS
Tel: 01604 858470
Email: bobwalder@compuserve.com
Contact: Bob Walder
Membership: Selective with fee of £25 plus £5 jurying fee. No painters.
Publishes newsletter.

OXFORDSHIRE BASKETMAKERS
2 Frenchay Road
Oxford
Oxon OX2 6TG
Tel: 01865 554281
Fax: 01865 512927
Email: felicity.wood@tesco.net
Contact: Felicity Wood
Membership: Non-selective with fee of £5. For those in Oxfordshire and on its boundaries involved in making all types of basketry and chair seating.
Publishes newsletter.

PARCHMENT CRAFT GUILD
c/o 56 Highmoor Road
Corfe Mullen
Wimborne
Dorset BH21 3PT
Email: parchmentguild@tiscali.co.uk
Membership: Friends pay £12 annually while full members must pass a series of exams (fee also £12).

PEAK DISTRICT PRODUCTS
c/o The Old Post Office
Bradley
Ashbourne
Derbys DE6 1PN
Tel/Fax: 01335 370112
Email: pauline@silkpainter.co.uk
Website: www.peakdistrictproducts.co.uk
Contact: Pauline Townsend
Membership: Selective with a fee of £250. Must live/work in the Peak District. This is a professional, full-time craftworkers group run by the members.

PEMBROKESHIRE CRAFT MAKERS
Waterfront Gallery
The Old Sail Loft
The Docks
Milford Haven
Pembrokeshire SA73 3AF
Tel: 01646 699556
Email: julie.randell@btopenworld.com
Website:
www.pembrokeshirecraftmakers.co.uk
Contact: David Randell
Membership: Selective with fee of £70, reduced to introductory fee of £35 in first year. Craftwork must be of a high standard and is subject to vetting on applying. Members must live/work in Pembrokeshire. The group celebrates its Silver Jubilee in 2005.
Publishes newsletter.

PIPERS' GUILD
Mardle Cottage
Thorrington Road
Great Bentley
Essex CO7 8QD
Tel: 01206 257373
Email: edwarddrk@aol.com
Website: www.pipersguild.org
Contact: Ted Drake
Membership: Non-selective with payment between £10 and £20, at members' discretion. For those making, playing or decorating bamboo pipes.
Registered Charity status.
Publishes newsletter.

RAMPTON SPINNERS
c/o Rose Cottage
23 Church Street
Bourn
Cambs CB3 7SJ
Tel: 01954 718893
Email: heatherdean@onetel.com
Contact: Heather Dean
Membership: Non-selective with fee of £12. Emphasis on weaving, spinning and dyeing.

SHREWSBURY GUILD OF SPINNERS, WEAVERS & DYERS
Westview Cottage
Snailbeach
Minsterley
Shrewsbury
Shropshire SY5 0LW
Tel: 01743 791774
Contact: Diane Norrell
Membership: Non-selective with fee of £15. For those involved in the textile crafts.

SIRHOWY VALLEY LACEMAKERS
6 Julian Heights
Fleur-de-Lys
Blackwood
Gwent NP12 3TT
Tel: 01443 821445
Contact: Mrs Betty Bridge
Membership: Non-selective with fee of £9 plus 50p per meeting. For bobbin lacemakers.

SOMERSET GUILD OF CRAFTSMEN
Cedarwood
Stoke Road
North Curry
Taunton
Somerset TA3 6HN
Tel: 01823 490408
Website: www.somersetguild.co.uk
Contact: David Applegate
Membership: Selective for Craft Members with a fee of £60 and non-selective for Associate Members with a fee of £20. Some members from adjacent counties. Guild has its own craft gallery in Martock and participates in the Bath & West Show. It also organises a bi-annual show at the Bishop's Palace, Wells.

SOUTH WEST TEXTILE GROUP
Highfield Farm House
Woodhill, Stoke St Gregory
Taunton
Somerset TA3 6EW
Tel: 01823 490733
Email: loucottey@lycos.com
Website: http://aphelia.maddoc.net/swtg/
Contact: Louise Cottey
Membership: Non-selective with a fee of £25. Must live/work in South West England.
Publishes newsletter.

SOUTHEND SPINNERS & WEAVERS GUILD
48 Albert Road
Benfleet
Essex SS7 4DJ
Tel: 01268 752158
Contact: Mrs P Everett
Membership: Non-selective with fee of £13.

SOUTHERN CERAMIC GROUP
31 Combe Crescent
Bury
Pulborough
West Sussex RH20 1PH
Tel: 01798 831596
Email: jo_powell@pottery.com
Contact: Jo Powell
Membership: Non-selective with fee of £18. For ceramicists.

STAFFORDSHIRE MARQUETRY GROUP
c/o 15 Newport Road
Eccleshall
Staffs ST21 6BE
Tel: 01785 850614 (eve + weekends)
Email: quentin@staffsmarq.freeserve.co.uk
Website: www.staffsmarq.freeserve.co.uk
Contact: Quentin Smith
Membership: Non-selective with fee of £2

plus £1.50 per meeting attended. Also free e-membership via the website. For those involved in marquetry, parquetry, inlay, veneering and related arts/crafts.
Publishes quarterly newsletter (also posted on website).

SUSSEX GUILD OF DESIGNERS & MAKERS
The Gate House
Flowers Green
Herstmonceux
East Sussex BN27 1RL
Tel: 01323 833239
Email: info@thesussexguild.co.uk
Website: www.thesussexguild.co.uk
Contact: Mrs J Cooper
Membership: Open to those in Sussex and adjoining counties. Selective with a fee of £85. Not open to painters.
Registered Charity status.
Publishes newsletter.

TEXTILES 21
424 Livingstone Road
Wrose
Bradford
West Yorks BD21 1QD
Tel: 01274 597283
Email: sandrainskip@hotmail.com
Contact: Sandra Inskip
Membership: Selective but no annual fee. For those in textiles, with emphasis on knitting and crochet. A group of individuals interested in promoting traditional textile skills.

UK COLOURED PENCIL SOCIETY
c/o White Meadows
Horton
Devizes
Wilts SN10 3NB
Email: secretary@ukcps.co.uk
Website: www.ukcps.co.uk
Contact: Pat Heffer
Membership: Non-selective with fees of £25 (full) and £17.50 (associate). For overseas, add £5 to chosen level. For coloured pencil artists.
Publishes newsletter.

UK FACET CUTTERS GUILD
PO Box 2480
Stoke-on-Trent
Staffs ST7 2WT
Website: www.ukfcg.org
Contact: Mavis Smith
Membership: Non-selective with fees of £21 (individual), £26 (joint) and £5 (young).
Publishes bi-monthly Faceter's StoneChat newsletter.

WEALDEN POTTERS
c/o Longmead
Tunbridge Wells Road
Mayfield
East Sussex TN20 6NU
Tel: 01435 872193
Email: delgirl@onetel.com
Contact: Jan Deller
Membership: Non-selective with fees of £20 (single) and £27 (joint); concessions if paying early for following year or joining late in the year. For ceramic crafters.

WEST ESSEX & EAST HERTS GUILD OF SPINNERS, WEAVERS & DYERS
Bell House
Bell Lane
Widford
Herts SG12 8SH
Tel: 01279 842804
Email: pat@holder.flyer.co.uk
Contact: Mrs P Holder
Membership: Non-selective with a fee of £15.

WEST RIDING WOODTURNERS GROUP
13 Hill Crest
Hebden Bridge
West Yorks HX7 6BQ
Tel: 01422 843774
Email: david.jacksonii@tesco.net
Contact: David Jackson
Membership: Non-selective with fee of £20 (2004). For those involved in woodturning and associated work.

WEST SURREY GUILD OF SPINNERS, WEAVERS & DYERS
c/o Spring Cottage
Tilford
Farnham
Surrey GU10 2BN
Tel: 01252 792916
Website: www.wsd.org.uk
Contact: Josephine Mackenzie
Membership: Non-selective with fee of £13.
For the stated crafters.
Registered Charity status.

WEST SUSSEX GUILD OF WEAVERS, SPINNERS & DYERS
c/o Skippool, Copse Lane
Walberton
Arundel
West Sussex BN18 0QH
Tel: 01243 543462
Contact: Mrs Jean Minter
Membership: Non-selective with fee of £18. For the stated crafters; new members always welcome.

SOCIETIES

BEAD SOCIETY OF GREAT BRITAIN
1 Casburn Lane
Burwell
Cambs CB5 0ED
Email: spangles4beads@ntlworld.com
Website: www.beadsociety.freeserve.co.uk
Contact: Carole Morris
Membership: Non-selective with fees of £10 (UK) or £13 (non-UK). For those with anything related to beads/beadwork.
Publishes newsletter.

BRAID SOCIETY
2 Normanton
Buckland Road
Reigate
Surrey RH2 9RQ
Tel: 01737 242623
Email: sjessett@hotmail.com
Website: www.braidsociety.org
Contact: Mrs Sandy Jessett
Membership: Non-selective with fee of £15. For those involved in braids and woven narrow bands.
Publishes newsletter.

BRITISH SOCIETY OF MASTER GLASS PAINTERS
PO Box 15
Minehead
Somerset TA24 8ZX
Tel: 01643 862807
Email: secretary@bsmgp.org.uk
Website: www.bsmgp.org.uk
Contact: Chris Wyard
Membership: Non-selective with fees of £30 (full), £15 (students) and £18 (seniors). For stained glass craftworkers and artists.
Publishes newsletter.

CALLIGRAPHY & LETTERING ARTS SOCIETY
54 Boileau Road
London SW13 9BL
Tel: 020 8741 7886
Email: info@clas.co.uk
Website: www.clas.co.uk
Contact: Sue Cavendish
Membership: Non-selective with fees of £25 (UK) plus £7 overseas.
Registered Charity status.

CONTEMPORARY GLASS SOCIETY
c/o Broadfield House Glass Museum
Compton Drive
Kingswinford
West Midlands DY6 9NS
Tel/Fax: 01603 507737
Email: admin@cgs.org.uk
Website: www.cgs.org.uk
Contact: Pam Reekie
Membership: Non-selective with fees of £30 (professional) and £20 (concessions).
Publishes newsletter.

DESIGNER BOOKBINDERS
6 Queen Square
London WC1N 3AR
Tel: 01485 529381
Email:
membership@designerbookbinders.org.uk
Website: www.designerbookbinders.org.uk
Contact: Lester Bath
Membership: Non-selective grades are associate (£35), student (£17.50) and overseas (£38) with a fee of £35 for the selective associateship. There are also selective licentiateship and fellowship grades of membership.
Registered Charity status.
Publishes newsletter.

EAST YORKSHIRE LACE SOCIETY
c/o 12 Everthorpe Lane
North Cave
East Yorks HU15 2LF
Tel/Fax: 01430 423204
Email: eyls@2bconsultancy.co.uk
Contact: Mrs Elizabeth Blackledge
Membership: Selective with a fee of £6. For lacemakers of all types.

LACE SOCIETY
Lynwood
Stratford Road
Oversley Green
Alcester
Warks B49 6PG
Tel: 01789 762594
Contact: Mrs Marjory Carter
Membership: Non-selective with fees of £6 or £30 to cover five years. For lacemakers.
Publishes newsletter.

MARQUETRY SOCIETY
c/o 13 Cavendish Road
Felixstowe
Suffolk IP11 2AR
Tel: 01394 278453
Fax: 01473 233974
Email: warrenashley@btopenworld.com
Website: www.marquetry.org
Contact: Ashley Warren
Membership: Non-selective with fee of £16.
Actively seeking new members.
Publishes newsletter.

NATIONAL SOCIETY OF PAINTERS, SCULPTORS & PRINTMAKERS
122 Copse Hill
Wimbledon
London SW20 0NL
Tel: 020 8946 7878
Website: www.nationalsociety.org
Contact: Gwen Spencer
Membership: Selective with fees of £85 (full) or £42.50 (associate). Annual exhibition in London plus occasional regional exhibitions.
For those involved in the stated arts.
Registered Charity status.
Publishes newsletter.

NORFOLK CONTEMPORARY CRAFT SOCIETY
c/o The White House
Town Street
Hickling
Norfolk NR12 0AY
Tel: 01692 598747
Fax: 01692 598403
Email: secretary@norfolkcraft.co.uk
Website: www.norfolkcraft.co.uk
Contact: Jennifer Boland
Membership: Full (maker) membership is selective and there is a fee of £35. Friends grade is £15. Must live/work in Norfolk or have connections with the county.
Publishes newsletter.

PAPERWEIGHT
19 Station Road
Harpenden
Herts AL5 4XA
Website: www.paperweight.demon.co.uk
Membership: Non-selective with fee of £20.
Publishes newsletter.

POOLE PRINTMAKERS
5 Bowling Green Alley
Poole
Dorset BH15 1AG
Tel: 01202 883187
Email: pooleprintmakers@btopenworld.com
Contacts: Elizabeth Cotton (mail) or Penny Austin ('phone).
Membership: Non-selective with fees of £60 (full) and £20 (friend). For printmakers.
Registered Charity status.
Publishes newsletter.

RICHMOND ARTS & CRAFTS SOCIETY
c/o 1 Racecourse Court
Richmond
North Yorks DL10 4SP
Tel: 01748 826268
Email: alan@gilpinsmartarts.fsnet.co.uk
Membership: Non-selective with fee of £15.
Publishes newsletter.

ROYAL BIRMINGHAM SOCIETY OF ARTISTS
4 Brook Street
St Paul's Square
Birmingham B3 1SA
Tel: 0121 236 4353
Fax: 0121 236 4555
Email: secretary@rbsa.org.uk
Website: www.rbsa.org.uk
Contact: Tara Quinn
Membership: Selective with fees of £105 (elected) and £95 (associate). There is a friends grade of membership at £22.
Registered Charity status.
Publishes newsletter.

ROYAL BRITISH SOCIETY OF SCULPTORS
108 Old Brompton Road
London SW7 3RA
Tel: 020 7373 8615
Fax: 020 7370 3721
Email: info@rbs.org.uk
Website: www.rbs.org.uk
Contact: Claire Foster

Membership: Associate membership is selective with a fee of £125 for sculptors.
Registered Charity status.

RUFFORD WOOD FIRING SOCIETY
18 Riley Close
Bracebridge Heath
Lincoln LN4 2QS
Tel: 01522 859105
Email: smithsatbbh@ntlworld.com
Contact: Eric Smith
Membership: Non-selective with fee of £50.
For ceramicists.
Publishes newsletter.

SCOTTISH GLASS SOCIETY
1 The Lade
Balerno
Edinburgh EH14 7LB
Tel: 0131 449 2050
Email: elizabethcull@tiscali.co.uk
Website: www.scottishglasssociety.com
Contact: Liz Cull
Membership: Non-selective with fees of £15 (full), £5 (students) and £35 (corporate).
Registered Charity status.

SOCIETY OF BOOKBINDERS
Binders Cottage
55B High Street
Bridgnorth
Shropshire WV16 5DX
Email:
membership@societyofbookbinders.com
Website: www.societyofbookbinders.com
Contact: Dermot Creece
Membership: Non-selective with fee of £32.
Registered Charity status.
Publishes newsletter.

SOCIETY OF SCRIBES & ILLUMINATORS
The Art Workers' Guild
6 Queen Square
London
WC1N 3AT
Tel/Fax: 01524 251534
Email: scribe@calligraphyonline.org or gillianhazeldine@tiscali.co.uk
Website: www.calligraphyonline.org
Contact: Gillian Hazeldine
Membership: Selective grade for calligraphers, letterers and illuminators with fee of £36. Also non-selective grade of lay member costing £28.
Publishes newsletter.

SOCIETY OF WOOD ENGRAVERS
3 West Street
Oundle
Northants PE8 4EJ
Tel/Fax: 01832 275028
Email: g.waddington@dial.pipex.com
Website: www.woodengravers.co.uk
Contact: Geri Waddington
Membership: Selective with fee of £35. Also non-selective subscriber grade at £25 (UK). For those involved in wood engraving and relief printmaking.
Publishes newsletter.

SOUTH WALES POTTERS
Y Faen Felin Pottery
3 Russell Close
New Inn
Pontypool
Torfaen
NP4 0LZ
Tel: 01495 756775
Email: enquiry@southwalespotters.org.uk
Website: www.southwalespotters.co.uk
Contact: Helen Jones
Membership: Non-selective with fee of £25. For potters; generally those resident in South and West Wales, but not limited to this area.

SUFFOLK CRAFT SOCIETY
Rookery House
Cockfield Road
Felsham
Suffolk
P30 0QJ
Tel: 01284 828273
Email: organiser@suffolkcraftsociety.org
Website: www.suffolkcraftsociety.org
Contact: Monique Gregson (when e-mailing)
Membership: Selective with fee of £45. Must live/work in Suffolk or on its borders.
Publishes newsletter.

TEXTILE SOCIETY
17 Geneva Avenue
Malvern
Worcs WR14 3PX
Website: www.textilesociety.org.uk
Contact: June Morris
Membership: Non-selective with fees of £15 (individual), £20 (household), £8.50 (concessions) and £30 (institutions). For those involved in textiles.
Registered Charity status.
Publishes newsletter.

UNITED SOCIETY OF ARTISTS
Halvergate
27 Castle Mead
King's Stanley
Glos GL10 3LB
Tel: 01453 823571
Membership: Selective with fees of £110 (full) and £90 (associate). The society exhibits all schools of art work at Westminster annual show in London. The society has an international membership.
Publishes newsletter.

WEY CERAMICS SOCIETY
Email: enquiries@weyceramics.co.uk
Website: www.weyceramics.co.uk
Membership: Non-selective with fee of £15. For ceramicists and clayworkers living/working in Surrey and surrounding counties. Send e-mail for new secretary's details as these were changing just as we went to press.
Publishes newsletter. Organises 2 annual exhibitions.

CITY LIVERY COMPANIES & MISCELLANEOUS

APPLIED ARTS SCOTLAND
The Lighthouse
11 Mitchell Lane
Glasgow
G12 0LN
Tel: 0141 572 1835
Email: office@appliedartsscotland.org.uk
Membership: Non-selective with fee of £25. This is a limited company (with charitable status) covering all crafts by those living/working in Scotland or Scots living abroad.
Publishes newsletter.

BLACK MOUNTAINS CIRCLE
Court Cupboard Gallery
New Court Farm
Llantilio Pertholey
Abergavenny NP7 8AU
Tel: 01873 852011
Email: blackmntncircle@btconnect.com
Website: www.courtcupboard.com
Contact: Wilma Allen or Sue Saunders
Membership: Selective with joining fee of £40 and annual fee £40. Must live/work within 50 mile radius. A Craft Cooperative . Commission based on numbers of hours spent manning the gallery per annum.
Publishes newsletter.

CONNECT UK
Unit 7, Navigation Wharf
Carre Street
Sleaford
Lincs NE34 7TW
Tel: 01529 414830 or 01529 414532
Email: info@connect-uk.org
Website: www.connect-uk.org
Contact: Clare Edwards
A Regional Network for artists, makers and designers. Eligibility defined by 20 categories. Must live/work in the East Midlands. Otherwise non-selective and with no annual fee.
Publishes newsletter.

THE CRAFTERS
High Street
Melrose
Roxburghshire TD6 9PA
Tel: 01896 823714
Website:
www.melrose.bordernet.co.uk/traders/crafters/
Contact: Lorraine Harrison
Membership: A cooperative run by its members; open to all types of crafters in the Scottish Borders region. They have guest exhibitors at the shop in Melrose on a monthly basis and these are not necessarily from the region.

CRAFT SALON GROUP
95 St Mary Graces Court
Cartwright Street
London
E1 8NB
Tel/Fax: 020 7702 3394
Email: aandvperry@tiscali.co.uk
Website: www.craftsalon.org.uk (under development)
Affiliated to the Worshipful Company of Painter-Stainers (see below) and effectively the UK arm of the international Salon Group. The aim at present is educational and the group sends a few students/apprentices to the Salon Group's annual event to learn 'at the feet of the masters' so to speak. The intention in 2005 is to hold or support weekend (or longer) masterclasses.
Membership is selective (by invitation) but there is no annual fee; members represent all the decorative arts.

DALGLISH ADVISORY BUREAU
Gurtof House
Boltby
Thirsk
North Yorks YO7 2DY
Tel: 01845 537280
Contact: Alec Dalglish
Advisory function in the crafts (hand knitting and crochet) and education sphere.
Enclose SAE if writing.

THE GOLDSMITHS' COMPANY
Goldsmiths' Hall
Foster Lane
London EC2V 6BN
Tel: 020 7606 7010
Fax: 020 7606 1511
Email: the.clerk@thegoldsmiths.co.uk
Website: www.thegoldsmiths.co.uk
Contact: The Clerk
Membership is by service, patrimony or redemption
Publishes newsletter

THE IRONMONGERS' COMPANY
Ironmongers' Hall
Barbican
London EC2Y 8AA
Tel: 020 7776 2311
Fax: 020 7600 3519
Email: helen@ironhall.co.uk
Website: www.ironhall.co.uk
Contact: Helen Sant
Registered Charity status

NATIONAL NEEDLEWORK ARCHIVE
Boldre House
5 Boldrewood Road
Southampton
Hants SO16 7BW
Tel: 023 8079 1066
Email: nna@boldre.freeserve.co.uk
Website:
www.nationalneedleworkarchive.org.uk
A not-for-profit voluntary organisation, the NNA records all types and ages of needlework in the community for national archives and research. Currently seeking charity status.

POTTERS
Unit 19
Clifton Down Shopping Centre
Whiteladies Road
Clifton
Bristol BS8 2NN
Tel: 0117 973 7380
Email: margcrump@aol.com
Website: www.pottersbristol.com
Contact: Margaret Crump
A marketing cooperative to sell the ceramics and ceramic sculpture of its members and to promote understanding of this craft amongst the general public. Selective membership but no annual fee.

SHISHA
The Department Store
5 Oak Street
Manchester M4 5JD
Tel: 0161 838 5250
Fax: 0161 838 5255
Email: alnoor@shisha.net
Website: www.shisha.net
Contact: Alnoor Mitha
Shisha is a charitable organisation and a limited company by guarantee and is the international agency for contemporary South Asian crafts and visual arts. Alnoor Mitha is Director, Fareda Khan Deputy Director, Angela Harris Coordinator and Pippa Kenyon Projects Administrator.

WORSHIPFUL COMPANY OF CLOCKMAKERS
Fourth Floor, Salters' Hall
4 Fore Street
London EC2Y 5DG
Tel: 020 7638 5500
Fax: 020 7638 5522
Email: clockmakersco@aol.com
Website: www.clockmakers.org
Contact: Peter Gibson, The Clerk
This is the City Livery Company for those involved in the manufacture of clocks and watches. Membership is selective and there is a payment of £100 joining fee and £50 per annum administration charge.

WORSHIPFUL COMPANY OF FRAMEWORK KNITTERS
86 Park Drive
Upminster
Essex RM14 3AS
Tel/Fax: 01708 510439
Email: clerk@frameworkknitters.co.uk
Website: www.frameworkknitters.co.uk
Contact: Alan J Clark
Membership is selective, by formal application and then interview and the annual fee is £100.
Publishes newsletter.

WORSHIPFUL COMPANY OF FURNITURE MAKERS
Painters' Hall
9 Little Trinity Lane
London EC4V 2DB
Tel: 020 7248 1677
Fax: 020 7248 1688
Email: clerk@furnituremkrs.co.uk
Website: www.furnituremkrs.co.uk
Contact: Mrs J A Wright
For those actively engaged in the furniture making industry. Freeman status is selective and costs range from £40 to £190 per annum depending on age.
Registered Charity status.

WORSHIPFUL COMPANY OF GLAZIERS & PAINTERS OF GLASS
Glaziers Hall
9 Montague Close
London SE1 9DD
Tel/Fax: 020 7403 6652
Email: info@worshipfulglaziers.com
Website: www.worshipfulglaziers.com
For stained glass artists and craftsmen. Membership is by invitation and costs £162.50 per annum.

WORSHIPFUL COMPANY OF PAINTER-STAINERS
Painters' Hall
9 Little Trinity Lane
London EC4V 2AD
Tel: 020 7236 7070
Fax: 020 7236 7074
Contact: Hon Maurice Robson
An ancient guild for those involved in decorative painting, graining and guilding.
Registered Charity status.

QUANGOS, REGIONAL & OTHER UK BODIES

ARTS COUNCIL ENGLAND, EAST
48-49 Bateman Street
Cambridge
Cambs CB2 1LR
Tel: 0845 300 6200 (National Contact Centre)
Fax: 0870 242 1271
Email: enquiries@artscouncil.org.uk
Website: www.artscouncil.org.uk
Regional office of Arts Council England, the national funding and advisory body for contemporary crafts and visual arts. Advice, resources/grants, regional promotions, information updates.
Registered Charity status.
Publishes newsletter.

ARTS COUNCIL ENGLAND, EAST MIDLANDS
St Nicholas Court
25-27 Castle Gate
Nottingham
Notts NG1 7AR
Email: louise.rainbow@artscouncil.org.uk
Website: www.artscouncil.org.uk
Contact: Louise Rainbow - Assistant Officer, Craft & Literature
Regional office, as entry above.

ARTS COUNCIL ENGLAND, SOUTH WEST
Bradninch Place
Gandy Street
Exeter
Devon EX4 3LS
Tel: 0845 300 6200
Fax: 01392 229229
Email: erica.steer@artscouncil.org.uk
Website: www.artscouncil.org.uk
Contact: Erica Steer - Crafts Officer
Publishes newsletter.
Regional office, status as above.

ARTS COUNCIL ENGLAND, WEST MIDLANDS
82 Granville Street
Birmingham B1 2LH
Tel: 0845 300 6200
Fax: 0121 643 7239
Email: enquiries@artscouncil.org.uk
Website: www.artscouncil.org.uk
Regional office, status as above.

ARTS COUNCIL ENGLAND, YORKSHIRE
21 Bond Street
Dewsbury
West Yorks WF13 1AX
Tel: 0845 300 6200
Email: anne.brown@artscouncil.org.uk
Website: www.artscouncil.org.uk
Contact: Anne Brown
Publishes newsletter
Regional office, status as above.

ARTS COUNCIL OF NORTHERN IRELAND
MacNeice House
77 Malone Road

Belfast
BT9 6AQ
Tel: 028 9038 5200
Fax: 028 9066 1715
Email: idavidson@artscouncil-ni.org
Website: www.artscouncil-ni.org
Contact: Iain Davidson
The national funding and development body for the arts in Ulster.
Publishes newsletter.

ARTS COUNCIL OF WALES
Mid & West Wales Office
6 Gardd Llydaw
Jacksons Lane
Carmarthen
Carmarthenshire
SA31 1QD
Tel: 01267 234248
Fax: 01267 233084
Email: nathalie.camus@artswales.org.uk
Website: www.artswales.org.uk
Contact: Nathalie Camus
The national funding and development body for the arts in Wales.
Registered Charity status.
Publishes newsletter.

CRAFTS COUNCIL
44a Pentonville Road
Islington
London N1 9BY
Tel: 020 7278 7700
Fax: 020 7806 2506
Email: reference@craftscouncil.org.uk
Website: www.craftscouncil.org.uk
The Crafts Council is the national centre for contemporary crafts in the UK and is core funded by Arts Council England. There are both selective and non-selective grades of membership.
Registered Charity status. Publishes 'Crafts' and 'Makers News' (see Directory of Publications).

MADE IN CUMBRIA
County Offices
Busher Walk
Kendal
Cumbria LA9 4RQ
Tel: 01539 732736
Fax: 01539 729480
Email: office@madeincumbria.co.uk
Website: www.madeincumbria.co.uk
Contact: Sue Andrews
This is an Economic Development Initiative of Cumbria County Council for all Cumbrian craftworkers and artists.

SCOTTISH ARTS COUNCIL
12 Manor Place
Edinburgh EH3 7DD
Tel: 0845 603 6000 (local rate)
Fax: 0131 225 9833
Email: help.desk@scottisharts.org.uk
Website: www.scottisharts.org.uk
The national funding, development and advocacy body for the arts in Scotland.
Publishes newsletter.

NON-UK BASED BODIES

CLEWBAY CRAFT & DESIGN GROUP
Cloonan
Islandeady
Castlebar
Co Mayo
Republic of Ireland
Tel/Fax: 00 353 94 902 5384
Email: thegannons@eircom.net
Contact: Gill Gannon
Membership: Selective with fee of €20. Must live/work in Co Mayo, Republic of Ireland.

CRAFT POTTERS SOCIETY OF IRELAND
c/o 4 Mount Anville Lawn
Goatstown
Dublin 14
Co Dublin
Republic of Ireland
Tel: 00 353 1 298 7067
Email: ceramicsireland@yahoo.com
Website: www.ceramicsireland.org
Contact: Patricia Casey
Membership: Non-selective membership with fees of €35 (single member),€45 (joint members up to 3) and€15 (students and seniors). Voluntary, not-for-proft organisation.
Publishes magazine.

CRAFTS COUNCIL OF IRELAND
Castle Yard
Kilkenny
Co Kilkenny
Republic of Ireland
Tel: 00 353 56 776 1804
Fax: 00 353 56 776 3754

Email: info@ccoi.ie
Website: www.ccoi.ie
Contact: Caroline O'Riordan
The Crafts Council of Ireland is the national design and economic development organisation for the craft industry in Ireland. Its activities are funded by Enterprise Ireland. The Council acts on the craft industry's behalf advising government and state agencies on issues affecting the industry, in assisting the industry in promotion and marketing and in vocational craft and design training.
Publishes newsletter.

NEDERLANDSE VAKGROEP KERAMISTEN
Dutch Ceramists Association
Eendenbrink 3
2492 PE 's-Gravenhage
HOLLAND
Tel: 00 31 70 4444 189
Fax: 00 31 84 2209 778
Email: secretariaat@nvk-keramiek.nl
Website: www.nvk-keramiek.nl
Contact: Frits van der Zweep
There are two grades of membership. Working Membership, for those who are professionally working with clay. The fee is €125 per annum, inc subscription to 'Keramiek' magazine. Non-working Membership is for art students and those in the process of setting themselves as professional ceramic artists, for which the fee is €75 and also includes the magazine.

SCULPTORS SOCIETY OF IRELAND
Corner Halston Street and Mary's Lane
Dublin 7
Co Dublin
Republic of Ireland
Tel: 00 353 1 872 2296
Email: valerie@sculptors-society.ie
Website: www.sculptors-society.ie
Contact: Valerie Early
Membership: The society offers membership to professional visual artists working in all media from all areas.
Registered Charity status.
Publishes newsletter.

WORLD CRAFTS COUNCIL - EUROPE
50 rue Achille Chavée
7100 La Louvière
BELGIUM
Tel: 00 32 64 22 92 85
Fax: 00 32 64 28 52 17
Email: wcceurope@wcc-europe.org
Website: www.wcc-europe.org
International, non-governmental, non-profit organisation recognised by UNESCO; for design-led, contemporary craft. Its general objective is to strengthen the status of crafts as a vital part of cultural and economic life, to promote a sense of fellowship among the craftspeople of the world and to offer them encouragement, help and advice.
Membership subscription is calculated in three different groups according to purchasing power parity multiplied by the population of the member country. E-mail for details on how this works out.
WCC-Europe publishes Directory of Members, promotional leaflet and WCC-Europe Awards for Contemporary Craft leaflet. It also circulates an information exchange newsletter.

Notes ✎

CRAFT COURSE PROVIDERS

This section of our book takes a look at a variety of specialist courses around Britain that are currently being provided to assist those who wish to acquire, and then advance, particular craft and art skills. Some of these course providers offer special discounts to our readers and where this is the case it is noted at the end of their entries.

ALISON VICTORIA SCHOOL OF SEWING
71 Market Street
Ashby-de-la-Zouch
Leics LE65 1AH
Tel: 01530 416300
Fax: 01530 416309
Email: alison@schoolofsewing.co.uk
Website: www.schoolofsewing.co.uk
Contact: Alison Smith
Courses: Workshops on all aspects of Dressmaking, Tailoring and Corsetry.
Course Structure Options: Daytime; Part-Time.

ALSTON HALL COLLEGE
Alston Lane
Longridge
Preston
Lancs PR3 3BP
Tel: 01772 784661
Fax: 01772 785835
Email: alston.hall@ed.lancscc.gov.uk
Website: www.alstonhall.com
Contact: Dorothy Little
Courses: Beadwork; Embroidery & Textile Art; Enamelling; Feltmaking; Floral Craft; Hand-made Cards; Lacemaking; Machine Knitting; Picture Framing; Pottery; Sewing Skills; Silversmithing; Spinning; Stained Glass; Willow Work; and a wide range of Art courses.
Course Structure Options: Daytime; Evenings; Residential.

ASSOCIATION FOR CERAMIC TRAINING & DEVELOPMENT
St James House
Webberley Lane
Longton, Stoke-on-Trent
Staffs ST3 1RJ
Tel: 01782 597016
Fax: 01782 597015
Email: keith@actd.co.uk
Website: www.actd.co.uk
Contact: Keith Marsh
Not providers of training themselves, but responsible for commissioning Craft Pottery NVQ training and similar.

BARNET COLLEGE
Wood Street
Barnet
Herts EN5 4AZ
Tel: 020 8440 6321
Fax: 020 8441 5236
Website: www.barnet.ac.uk
Courses: Calligraphy; Carpentry & Joinery; Ceramics; Design Crafts; Glass; Interior Design; Jewellery/Silversmithing/Enamelling; Soft Furnishings & Upholstery; Stained Glass; and Watercolour, Painting & Drawing.
Course Structure Options: Daytime; Evenings; Full-Time; Part-Time.
Courses accredited by Edexcel and City & Guilds, with appropriate certifications awarded. Interview required for full-time programmes.

THE BEETROOT TREE
South Street
Draycott
Derbys DE72 3PP
Tel/Fax: 01332 873929
Email: info@thebeetroottree.com
Website: www.thebeetroottree.com
Contact: Alysn Midgelow-Marsden
Courses: Art Techniques; Ceramic Techniques; Glass Techniques; Jewellery Techniques; Textile Techniques.
Course Structure Options: On-site; Daytime; Evenings.

BELSTEAD HOUSE EDUCATION & CONFERENCE CENTRE
Sprites Lane
Ipswich
Suffolk IP8 3NA
Tel: 01473 686321
Fax: 01473 686664
Email:
belstead.house@educ.suffolkcc.gov.uk
Contact: Louise Peck
Courses: 3D Textiles; Baltimore Quilting; Bead Needleweaving; Bookbinding; Bucks Point & Floral Torchon Lace; Calligraphy; Découpage; Monoprinting; Patchwork; Painting; and Pottery.
Course Structure Options: Daytime; Residential.

BENNINGTON HOUSE CRAFT COURSES
Bennington House
59 Albany Road
Southtown
Great Yarmouth
Norfolk NR31 0EU
Tel: 01493 602887
Contact: Jennifer Dagger
Courses: Weekend residential Rubber Stamping courses using all the latest techniques. Loads of stamps, inks, embossing powders, pearl ex, foils, liquid appliqué, Stylus tips, shrink plastic, Tamp a tiles, etc.
Course Structure Options: Daytime; Evenings; Residential; Video/CD.

BERYL JARVIS
90 Asfordby Road
Melton Mowbray
Leics LE13 0HR
Tel: 01664 850418
Courses: Machine Knitting - one-to-one or groups as required. Wide range of tuition available, from beginners to individual requests.
Course Structure Options: On-site; Daytime; Evenings; Part-Time; also Remote/Travelling.

BISHOP BURTON COLLEGE
York Road
Bishop Burton
Beverley
East Yorks HU17 8QG
Tel: 01964 553000
Fax: 01964 553101
Email: nequesta@bishopb.ac.uk
Website: www.bishopburton.ac.uk
Contact: Anne Nequest
Courses: Basic Upholstery; Buttoning; Sewing Machine Techniques; Soft Furnishings (inc. appliqué, m/c embroidery, tucks & pleats, quilting etc).
Course Structure Options: On-site; Daytime; Evenings; Part-Time.
Courses accredited by City & Guilds and Levels 1 and 2 awarded. These could lead on to PDC qualifications or HNC.

BLACK MOUNTAINS CIRCLE
Court Cupboard Gallery
New Court Farm
Llantilio Pertholey
Abergavenny NP7 8AU
Tel: 01873 859269
Email: blackmntncircle@btconnect.com
Website: www.courtcupboardgallery.com
Contact: Sue Saunders
Courses: A programme of 150 craft and art based courses through the year.
Course Structure Options: Daytime; Part-Time.

BROADLAND ARTS CENTRE
The Old School
Dilham
North Walsham
Norfolk NR28 9TT
Tel/Fax: 01702 475361
Email: bac@dammery.freeserve.co.uk
Website: www.broadlandart.co.uk
Contact: Angela Dammery
Courses: Creative Embroidery; Painting (acrylic, oil, pastel, watercolour); Oriental Brush Painting; Printmaking; Renaissance Skills (fresco/tempera/sgraffito/gilding); and Silk Painting.
Course Structure Options: On-site; Daytime; Residential; Remote/Travelling.
Foundation Art is a City & Guilds accredited course.
SPECIAL CWYB READER OFFER - 10% discount will be offered on most courses. Quote reference 'BAC 001' when applying.

BROMLEY ADULT EDUCATION
Widmore Centre
Nightingale Lane
Bromley
Kent BR1 2SQ
Tel: 020 8460 0020
Fax: 020 8466 7299
Email: karenstrudwick@bromleyadulteducation.ac.uk
Contact: Karen Strudwick
Courses: Clothesmaking; Doll Making; Embroidery; Enamelling; Jewellery; Lace Making; Patchwork & Quilting; Pattern Cutting; Polymer Clay; Silversmithing; Soft Furnishing; Stained Glass; and Upholstery.
Course Structure Options: Daytime; Evenings; Part-Time.
Some courses are accredited by City & Guilds (7922 and 7923 awarded for Patchwork/Quilting and Embroidery).
Feeder courses offered will lead students on to progression route of accredited courses.

BRUNEL UNIVERSITY ARTS CENTRE
Cleveland Road
Uxbridge
Middx UB8 3PH
Tel/Fax: 01895 273482

Email: artscentre@brunel.ac.uk
Website: www.brunel.ac.uk/depts/artscentre
Contact: Jay Wilkinson
Courses: Calligraphy; Drawing; Ikebana; Painting; Paperclay; Pottery; Sculpture; Stained Glass.
Course Structure Options: Daytime; Evenings; Part-Time.

BUCKINGHAMSHIRE ADULT LEARNING
Missenden Abbey
Great Missenden
Bucks
HP16 0BD
Tel: 0845 045 4040
Fax: 01753 783756
Email: adultlearning@buckscc.gov.uk
Website:
www.aredu.org.uk/missendenabbey
Contact: Ann Howarth
Courses: Wide range of arts and crafts.
Course Structure Options: Part-Time; Residential.
Some courses lead to City & Guilds qualifications and certificates. Minimum age is 16.

BURTON MANOR
The Village
Burton
Neston
Cheshire
CH64 5SJ
Tel: 0151 336 5172
Fax: 0151 336 6586
Email: enquiry@burtonmanor.com
Website: www.burtonmanor.com
Contact: Janet Hooper
Courses: Calligraphy; Ceramics; Découpage; Drawing; Embroidery; Jewellery Making; Painting; Pastels; Portraits; Printing; Textiles; Weaving; Willow Weaving; and Woodcarving.
Course Structure Options: On-site; Residential; Daytime; Part-Time; Weekends.
The 'Painting & Drawing' course is accredited by the Open College Network.

BURY LIFELONG LEARNING SERVICE
Education Department
Athenaeum House
Market Street
Bury
Lancs BL9 0BN
Tel: 0161 253 7593
Fax: 0161 253 7266
Email: g.hughes@bury.gov.uk
Contact: Mrs Gillian Hughes
Courses: Art; Cake Decoration; Calligraphy; Ceramics; Design; Embroidery; Fashion; Garment Making; Jewellery; Patchwork & Quilting; Photography; Pottery; and Soft Furnishing.
Course Structure Options: Daytime; Evenings; Part-Time.
Courses variously accredited by City & Guilds and GMOCN, with certificates awarded for completion of all accredited courses. Courses are used to underpin knowledge.

CALLIGRAPHY, DRAWING & WATERCOLOUR / CORRESPONDENCE COURSES
Scottshandy
St Helen's Avenue
Pocklington
York YO42 2JF
Tel/Fax: 01759 302760
Email: storeyjen@jensign.freeserve.co.uk
Website: www.jennystoreyartcourses.co.uk
Contact: Jenny Storey
Courses: Calligraphy; Drawing; Watercolour.
Course Structure Options: All the above are correspondence courses.
A completion certificate is awarded.
SPECIAL CWYB READER OFFER - 5% discount on Comprehensive Course. Quote reference 'CW2005' when applying.

THE CALLIGRAPHY STUDIO
Yonkin Farm
Kinnerton
Powys LD8 2PF
Tel/Fax: 01547 560330
Email: calligraphy-studio@lineone.net
Website: www.contractshop.co.uk
Contact: Linda Hayter
Courses: Calligraphy, Lettering & Design.
Course Structure Options: On-site; Daytime. Also Correspondence.
Accredited courses include City & Guilds; these courses can lead on to higher qualifications.

CHARLIE'S FURS & FEATURES
PO Box 814
Northwich
Cheshire CW8 2WF
Tel/Fax: 01606 888814
Email: charliesfursandfeatures@btopenworld.com
Website: www.charliesfurs.co.uk
Contact: Richard or Helen Ives

Courses: Teddy Bear Making.
Course Structure Options: Daytime.
SPECIAL CWYB READER OFFER - 10% off bearmaking components purchased during the course.

CITY & GUILDS OF LONDON ART SCHOOL
124 Kennington Park Road
London SE11 4DJ
Tel: 020 7735 2306
Fax: 020 7582 5361
Email: info@cityandguildsartschool.ac.uk
Website: www.cityandguildsartschool.ac.uk
Contact: Nina Hilton
Courses: Life Drawing, Print Making, Stone Carving and Wood Carving.
Course Structure Options: On-site; Daytime; Evenings; Full-Time; Part-Time.
Study can be for Diploma, Postgraduate Diploma or C&G Certificate of Study. Previous experience needed for Diploma and PGDip courses.

CLAIRE NICOL TEXTILES
Bramley Cottage
New Street
King's Stanley
Glos GL10 3JU
Tel: 01453 821593
Contact: Claire Nicol
Courses: Rag Rug Making for all levels - hooking and prodding and braided. Also Felt Rugs. Fun textile experiment sessions on fused fibres.
Course Structure Options: Daytime; Evenings; Part-Time.
SPECIAL CWYB READER OFFER - 10% discount. Quote reference 'Silver Jubilee Craftworker's Yearbook' when applying.

CLEVELAND COLLEGE OF ART & DESIGN
Church Square
Hartlepool
TS24 7EX
Tel: 01429 422000
Fax: 01429 422122
Email: tricia.mckenzie@ccad.ac.uk
Website: www.ccad.ac.uk
Contact: Tricia McKenzie
Courses: Printed, Embroidered, Embellished and Manipulated Textile and Surface Designs for Fashion Fabrics and Accessories, Furnishings and Interior Products, Greetings Cards and Giftware.
Course Structure Options: On-site; Daytime; Full-Time; Part-Time.
Courses accredited by the University of Teesside. Degree course available; BA (Hons) Textiles & Surface Design. There is a portfolio interview and entry qualifications (120 UCAS points) or accreditation for prior experience or learning.

COLLY BROOK FINE FURNISHINGS
Colly Brook House
Knowbury
Ludlow
Shropshire SY8 3LN
Tel/Fax: 01584 890315
Email: courses@collybrook.co.uk
Website: www.collybrook.co.uk
Contact: Pen Harrison
Courses: Soft Furnishing courses, including: Blinds; Curtain Making; Cushions; Headboards; Loose Covers; Pelmets; Swags & Tails; and Valances.
Course Structure Options: Daytime.
SPECIAL CWYB READER OFFER - 5% discount. Quote reference 'CWY' when applying.

CRAFT SUPPLIES LTD
The Mill, Millers Dale
nr Buxton
Derbys SK17 8BN
Tel: 01298 871636
Fax: 01298 872263
Email: sales@craft-supplies.co.uk
Website: www.craft-supplies.co.uk
Contact: Eve Middleton
Courses: Woodturning; Woodcarving; and Woodworking.
Course Structure Options: On-site; Daytime; Residential.

CRAFTSCHOOL.CO.UK
25 Christchurch Street East
Frome
Somerset BA11 1QQ
Tel: 01373 303620
Email: vicky@craftschool.co.uk
Website: www.craftschool.co.uk
Contact: Vicky Crockett
Courses: Enamelling; General Crafts; Jewellery; Precious Metal Clay; Resin Casting; and Tiara Making.
Course Structure Options: On-site; Daytime; Evenings; Residential; Remote/Travelling.
SPECIAL CWYB READER OFFER - 10% discount on Vicky Crockett courses; quote offer reference 'Craftworker's Year Book' when applying.

CRAFTS COUNCIL
44A Pentonville Road
Islington
London N1 9BY
Tel: 020 7806 2534
Fax: 020 7837 6891
Email: edu_assistant@craftscouncil.org.uk
Website: www.craftscouncil.org.uk/education
Contact: Education Assistant
The Crafts Council organises a wide range of events, talks and conferences relating to all forms of craft in association with its national exhibitions programme throughout the year. Make contact for details of specific events.

CREATIVE STITCHES
34 La Grande Pièce
St Peter
Jersey JE3 7AE
Tel/Fax: 01534 482097
Email: creativestitches@yahoo.com
Website: www.creativestitches.co.uk
Contact: Frankie Garrett
Courses: Bargello; Blackwork; Cross-Stitch; Drawn Thread; Embroidery; Hardanger; Tapestry; and Trapunto.
Course Structure Options: On-site; Part-Time; Residential.

CREATIVE STUDY CENTRE
University of Central Lancashire
Penrith
Cumbria CA11 0AH
Tel: 01768 863791
Email: plewington@uclan.ac.uk
Website: www.cumbria.ac.uk/cumbria
Contact: Patricia Lewington
Courses: Design; Floristry; Mixed Media; Painting; Patchwork & Quilting; Stitched Textiles; Soft Furnishings; and Sugarcraft.
Course Structure Options: Daytime; Evenings; Part-Time.
Courses accredited variously by City & Guilds, NCFE, OCNW and ABC. Certificates in Design & Craft and Creative Crafts available. Level 1, 2 and 3 courses are equivalent to National Levels.

CROCHET DESIGN
11 North Street
Morecambe
Lancs LA4 5LR
Tel: 01524 831752
Email: paulineturner@crochet.co.uk
Website: www.crochet.co.uk

Contact: Pauline Turner
Course Structure Options: Daytime; Correspondence.
Certificate for each part of course and Diploma on completion of all three parts. These courses have been accepted for NVQs and teaching qualifications.
SPECIAL CWYB READER OFFER – 10% off materials sold by Crochet Design. Please quote reference 'ICDIP4' when applying.

CUMBRIA INSTITUTE OF THE ARTS
Brampton Road
Carlisle
Cumbria CA3 9AY
Tel: 01228 400300
Fax: 01228 514491
Email: recept@cumbria.ac.uk
Website: www.cumbria.ac.uk
Contact: Maggi Toner-Edgar
Courses: Year '0' and BA (Hons) Contemporary Applied Arts (full-time and part-time); MA Contemporary Applied Arts (part-time). Broad-based programmes which include embroidered and constructed textiles, ceramics, printed textiles etc.
Course Structure Options: Daytime; Evenings; Full-Time; Part-Time.

Courses accredited by the University of Central Lancashire. Entry requirement is completion of BTEC National Diploma, Diploma in Foundation Studies, Access to Higher Education course, Advanced GNVQ or two Grade Cs at A2.

DANE COPPICE CRAFTS GROUP
10 Eaton Close
Sandbach
Cheshire CW11 1HS
Tel: 01270 760810
Email: aileen.thompson@btinternet.com
Website: www.spindizzy.net/dccg/
Contact: Aileen Thompson
Courses: This is a cooperative willow and associated coppice crafts group which maintains a local willowbed and which runs associated meetings and courses. Annual artist in residence.
Course Structure Options: 2-day course over one weekend based at Brereton Heath Country Park. Course could be used as background to City & Guilds Basketry qualification. Discount offered to registered students and family members.

DEAN HERITAGE CENTRE
Camp Mill
Soudley
Cinderford
Glos GL14 2UB
Tel: 01594 822170
Fax: 01594 823711
Email: deanmuse@btinternet.com
Website: www.deanheritagemuseum.com
Contact: Deborah Cook
Courses: Coppicing & Woodland Crafts; Dry Stone Walling; Hedge Laying; Hurdle Making; Pole Lathe Turning; Stool Making. Duration varies from one day to five days. Costs range from £35 to £185. The centre features craft workshops, art exhibitions, and these craft and rural traditional skills courses. The Dean Oak shop sells items hand crafted by local makers from Forest of Dean timber.

DENMAN COLLEGE
Marcham
Abingdon
Oxon OX13 6NW
Tel: 01865 391991
Fax: 01865 391966
Email: info@denman.org.uk
Website:-
www.womens-institute.org.uk/college
Courses: Appliqué; Beading; Bookbinding; Calligraphy; Canvaswork; Cardmaking; Découpage; Design; Drawing; Egg Decorating; Embroidery; Enamelling; Encaustic Art; Feltmaking; Glass Painting; Goldwork; Interior Design; Jewellery; Lacemaking; Loom Weaving; Mosaic; Modelling; Painting; Parchment Craft; Patchwork; Pewterwork; Pyrography; Quilling; Quilting; Rugmaking; Shibori; Silk Painting; Stained Glass; Stumpwork; Sugarcraft; and Wood Finishing.
Course Structure Options; Residential.
Some courses accredited by OCN, City & Guilds and could lead to other qualifications and contribute to NVQs.

DILLINGTON HOUSE
Ilminster
Somerset TA19 9DT
Tel: 01460 258613
Fax: 01460 52433
Email: dillington@somerset.gov.uk
Website: www.dillington.co.uk
Courses: Antique Furniture Restoration; Drawing; Découpage; Embroidery; Lace Making; Paint Effects for Furniture; Papier Mâché; Silk Painting; Upholstery; and Watercolour Painting.
Course Structure Options: Daytime; Residential.

THE EARNLEY CONCOURSE
Earnley
Chichester
West Sussex PO20 7JL
Tel: 01243 670392
Fax: 01243 670832
Email: info@earnley.co.uk
Website: www.earnley.co.uk
Courses: Basket Weaving; Batik; Calligraphy; Carving; China Restoration; Embroidery; Handspinning; Painting; Silk Painting; Stained Glass; Upholstery; Weaving; and Woodwork.
Course Structure Options: Residential.

ELIZABETH SYKES BATIKS
Islay House Square
Bridgend
Isle of Islay
Argyll
PA44 7NZ
Tel/Fax: 01496 810147
Email: ehs@islatran.demon.co.uk

Website: www.islatran.demon.co.uk
Contact: Liz Sykes
Courses: One-day introductory course in Batik.
Course Structure Options: Daytime.
Minimum age 12 years.

ENCAUSTIC ART ONLINE COURSES
Trem ar Daf
Glogue
Pembrokeshire
SA36 0ED
Tel: 01239 831401
Email: mail@encausticteachers.com
Website: www.encausticteachers.com
Contact: Michael Bossom
Courses: A basic teaching skills course in Encaustic Art that requires the student to complete a portfolio of assigned images as proof of skills, all given through an online course.

FEATHER GRAPHICS
Arts & Crafts at Stable Yard
5 Stable Yard
Downs Barn
Milton Keynes
Bucks MK14 7RZ
Tel: 01908 609214 or ans. 01908 607030
Fax: 01908 609214
Email: caseygreen@tesco.net
Website: www.createmk.co.uk
Contact: Helen Casey-Green
Courses: Textiles: Batik/Silk Painting; Devoré Velvet. Printmaking: Intaglio - Drypoint/Engraving using safe techniques; Relief - collographic technique and mono-printing. Figure Drawing.
Course Structure Options: On-site; Daytime; Evenings. Courses also given to larger groups at a venue of their choice.
See Display Advertisement.

THE GALLERY AT BLAKEMERE
Blakemere Craft Centre
Chester Road
Sandiway
Cheshire CW8 2EB
Tel/Fax: 01606 888048
Contact: Jeanette Hyde
Courses: Six-week Watercolour course.
Course Structure Options: On-site; Daytime. Held every Thursday. Hosted by Gordon Wilkinson for beginners and improvers; continuous throughout the year. £150 + free lunch.

GRAFFHAM WEAVERS
Shuttles
Graffham
Petworth
West Sussex
GU28 0PU
Tel: 01798 867348
Email: grafweav@aol.com
Website: www.graffhamweavers.co.uk
Contact: Barbara Mullins
Courses: Rug Weaving and Chemical Dyeing.
Course Structure Options: On-site; Daytime; Part-Time.

GREENWICH COMMUNITY COLLEGE
Greenwich Park Centre
Royal Hill
Greenwich
London
SE10 8PY
Tel: 020 8858 2211
Fax: 020 8293 9883
Email: kimm@gcc.ac.uk
Website: www.gcc.ac.uk
Contact: Kim Miller
Courses: Art & Design; Basketry; Beading; Calligraphy; Clock Repair; Clothes Making; Computer Graphics & DTP; Embroidery; Glass & China Painting; Lacemaking; Leatherwork; Millinery; Mosaic; Patchwork; Pottery; Sculpture; Stained Glass; Toymaking; Upholstery; Weaving; and Woven Textiles.
Course Structure Options: On-site; Daytime; Evenings; Full-Time; Part-Time; also Saturdays.
Accredited variously by LOCW, City & Guilds, NCFE, BTEC, ASDAN. Certification to these and also Access to Art & Design. Entry to some qualifications requires some previous experience.

THE HANDWEAVERS STUDIO & GALLERY LTD
29 Haroldstone Road
London
E17 7AN
Tel: 020 8521 2281
Email: handweaversstudio@msn.com
Website: www.handweaversstudio.co.uk
Courses: Feltmaking (one weekend); Loom Weaving (two weekends); Spinning (one Saturday); and Tapestry Weaving (one weekend).
Course Structure Options: Daytime, as above; On-site.

HEREFORDSHIRE COLLEGE OF ART & DESIGN
Folly Lane
Hereford HR1 1LT
Tel: 01432 845303
Fax: 01432 341099
Email: headmin@hereford-art-col.ac.uk
Website: www.hereford-art-col.ac.uk
Contact: Fiona Watkins
Courses: Blacksmithing; Design Crafts; Digital Media; Fine Art; Graphic Design; Illustration; Photography; and Spatial Design.
Course Structure Options: On-site; Daytime; Evenings; Full-Time; Part-Time. Short courses, accredited by the University of Wales & Gloucestershire. Certification for the FE and HE courses. Portfolio of art required for entry to some art courses.

HIGHAM HALL COLLEGE
Bassenthwaite Lake
Cockermouth
Cumbria CA13 9SH
Tel: 01768 776276
Fax: 01768 776013
Email: admin@highamhall.com
Website: www.highamhall.com
Contact: Alex Alexandre
Courses: Calligraphy; Ceramics; Embroidery; Photography; Painting (all mediums); Sculpture; Silk Painting; Willow and others.
Course Structure Options: On-site; Daytime; Full-Time; Part-Time; Residential.

HOBBY CERAMICRAFT
Odiham Road
Heckfield
Hook
Hants RG27 0LS
Tel/Fax: 0118 932 6153
Email: enquiries@hobbyceramicraft.co.uk
Website: www.hobbyceramicraft.co.uk
Courses: Ceramic Café owners course, Pottery Painting Parties course and Hobby Ceramic courses.
Course Structure Options: Daytime; most courses are held at the weekend.
These courses are aimed at those with the intention or interest in running their own business in this area.

THE HUB
Navigation Wharf
Carre Street
Sleaford
Lincs NG34 7TW
Tel: 01529 308710
Fax: 01529 308711
Email: hub@leisureconnection.co.uk
Website: www.thehubcentre.org
Contact: Bryony Robins
Courses: Courses and workshops covering a wide variety of craft and design disciplines, including: Bronze Casting; Ceramics; Jewellery; Kiln Glass; Metal Working; Stained Glass; Textiles; and Wood Carving.
Course Structure Options: Daytime; On-site.

HUDDERSFIELD TECHNICAL COLLEGE
E Block, New North Road
Huddersfield
West Yorks HD1 5NN
Tel: 01484 437138
Fax: 01484 437101
Contact: Linda Savage
Courses: City & Guilds Design & Craft 7822, 7922, 7923 in Fashion Wear, Interior Decor; Millinery; Soft Furnishings, Stitched Textiles; and Upholstery.
Course Structure Options: On-site; Daytime; Evenings; Full-Time; Part-Time.
Courses accredited by City & Guilds, with certification on completion.

INTUITION
The Woodlands
West Side
North Littleton
Evesham
Worcs WR11 8QP
Tel: 01386 832932
Email: judy.size@firenet.com
Website: www.intuitioncourses.com
Contact: Judi Size
Courses: Weekly classes: Appliqué; Machine Embroidery; Patchwork; Quilting; Soft Furnishings; Upholstery. One-day workshops: 'Know Your Own Sewing Machine'; Tassel Making.
Course Structure Options: Daytime; Evenings; Part-Time.
City & Guilds approved since 1997.

JOHN BODDY'S FINE WOOD & TOOL STORE LTD
Riverside Sawmills
Boroughbridge
North Yorks YO51 9LJ
Tel: 01423 322370
Fax: 01423 323810
Email: info@john-boddys-fwts.co.uk

Courses: Chair Caning; French Polishing; Furniture Restoration; Woodcarving, Finishing, Gilding; Routing and Veneering; Woodturning; and Woodworking.
Course Structure Options: On-site; Daytime. 1, 2 and 3-day courses.
Certificates of Attendance awarded.

JOHN BUCHANAN
St Ives Craft Centre
Halsetown
St Ives
Cornwall TR26 3NB
Tel: 01736 795078
Fax: 01736 799881
Courses: Craft of the Studio Potter; Craft of Painting in Watercolour.
Course Structure Options: On-site; Daytime; Part-Time; Residential. Pottery from the Craft Centre and Painting from riverside, beachside chalet or on location and visits of interest. Credits towards degree study have been gained by some students.
SPECIAL CWYB READER OFFER - 10% discount. Quote reference 'JB05' when applying.

KENT ADULT EDUCATION SERVICE
Monson Road
Tunbridge Wells
Kent TN1 1LS
Tel: 0845 606 5606
Fax: 01892 529743
Website: www.kent.gov.uk/adulted
Courses: Calligraphy; Cookery; Drawing; Dressmaking; Furniture Restoration; Interior Design & Decorative Effects; Lacemaking; Painting; Patchwork & Quilting; Photography; Pottery; Printing; Sculpture; Silversmithing & Jewellery; Soft Furnishings; Upholstery; and Weaving.
Course Structure Options: On-site; Daytime; Evenings; Part-Time.
Some courses accredited by NOCN, City & Guilds, with relevant certification on completion.

KERSBROOK TRAINING
2 Kersbrook Cross
Bray Shop
Callington
Cornwall
PL17 8QW
Tel/Fax: 01566 782907
Email: rose@smith1317.fsnet.co.uk
Website: www.kersbrooktraining.co.uk
Contact: Rosemarie Smith
Courses: Mixed Textiles; Creative Embroidery; City & Guilds 7822, Embroidery, Feltmaking, Tapestry Weaving, Stumpwork; City & Guilds 7922/7923 Certificate/Diploma in Embroidery.
Course Structure Options: On-site; Daytime; Part-Time; Correspondence.
Courses accredited by City & Guilds, with certification to National Vocational Qualification Level 2 or Level 3. Diploma counts towards foundation degree.

LEEDS COLLEGE OF ART & DESIGN
Blenheim Walk
Leeds LS2 9AQ
Tel: 0113 202 8060
Fax: 0113 202 8001
Email: martin.speak@leeds-art.ac.uk
Website: www.leeds-art.ac.uk
Contact: Martin Speak
Courses: Cabinet Making; Drawing & Design; Gilding; Restoration; Upholstery; Veneering; Woodfinishing; Woodturning (all

elements of HND Furniture Making & Restoration); plus ND Design Crafts; BA (Hons) Furniture and many part-time courses. Course Structure Options: Daytime; Evenings; Full-Time; Part-Time.
Courses accredited by Edexcel and City & Guilds, with attendant qualifications awarded. Course completion can lead to study for higher qualifications. Interviews are carried out for entry to the full-time courses.

LETCHWORTH SETTLEMENT
Nevells Road
Letchworth Garden City
Herts
SG6 4UB
Tel: 01462 682828
Contact: Sarah Carrick
Courses: Beadwork; Calligraphy; Creative Stitchery; Embroidery; Lacemaking; Machine Embroidery; Parchment Crafts; Patchwork & Quilting; Rubber Stamping; Sugar Crafts; Upholstery; and Watercolours & Pastels.
Course Structure Options: Daytime; Evenings; Part-Time.
Embroidery and Patchwork & Quilting accredited by City & Guilds. Attendees take membership of Letchworth Settlement, an independent charity.

LIQUID GLASS CENTRE
Stowford Manor Farm
Wingfield
Trowbridge
Wilts
BA14 9LH
Tel: 01225 768888
Email: info@liquidglasscentre.com
Website: www.liquidglasscentre.com
Contact: Helga Watkins-Baker
Courses: Glassblowing; Glass Kiln Casting; Fusing & Slumping; Explore Glass; Summer School.
Course Structure Options: On-site; Daytime.
SPECIAL CWYB READER OFFER – 10% discount. Quote reference 'CYB' when applying.

MALVERN HILLS COLLEGE
Albert Road North
Malvern
Worcs WR14 2YH
Tel: 01684 584559
Email: caroline.park@evesham.ac.uk
Website: www.evesham.ac.uk
Contact: Caroline Park
Courses: Acrylics, Oils & Paint; Bookbinding; Ceramics; China Painting; Dressmaking; Embroidery; Interiors; Jewellery; Painting & Drawing (watercolour, botanical, life); Passementerie; Photography; Sculpture; Soft Furnishings; Stained Glass; and Upholstery.
Course Structure Options: On-site; Daytime; Evenings; Full-Time; Part-Time.
Some courses accredited by OCN, City & Guilds, HNC Edexcel. Some degree modules from University College Worcester. Appropriate certification awarded for accredited, non-recreational courses. Some can lead to further study such as HNC Spatial Design.

NORTH ESSEX ADULT COMMUNITY COLLEGE
The Witham Centre
Spinks Lane, Witham
Essex CM8 1EP
Tel: 01376 516533
Fax: 01376 513099
Email: neacc@essexcc.gov.uk
Website: www.neacc.ac.uk
Contact: Sebastian Chew or Stella Snow
Courses: Bobbin Lace; Calligraphy; Drawing; Dressmaking; Embroidery; Fleece Sewing; Furniture Restoration; Hand-made Cards; Life Drawing; Painting; Pastels; Patchwork; Photography; Pottery; Print Effects & Furniture Painting; Prints & Printmaking; Sculpture; Silk Painting; Tailoring; Tiffany Stained Glass; Upholstery; Watercolours; and Woodworking.
Course Structure Options: Daytime; Evenings; Part-Time; On-site; Remote/Travelling (inc teaching in care homes).
Some courses are accredited by City & Guilds leading to Level 3 (Embroidery) and Level 1 (Photography) certification. The accredited courses could lead to progression to HNC/HND etc.

NORTH LINDSEY COLLEGE
Kingsway, Scunthorpe
North Lincs DN17 1AJ
Tel: 01724 294092
Email: angie.hodgson@northlindsey.ac.uk
Contact: Angie Hodgson
Courses: Drawing & Painting; Fashion Design; Fine Art; Graphic Design; Multi Media; and Textile Design.
Course Structure Options: Daytime; Evenings; Full-Time; Part-Time.
Courses accredited by Edexcel, NCFE and

NOCN. Level 1, 2 and 3 qualifications available. These can lead on to HND, Degree and Foundation Degree. Candidates will be interviewed and there are entry requirements.

NORTH WARWICKSHIRE & HINCKLEY COLLEGE
London Road
Hinckley
Leics
LE10 1HQ
Tel: 024 7624 3044
Fax: 01455 633930
Email: janet.kidner@nwarks-hinckley.ac.uk
Website: www.nwhc.ac.uk
Contact: Janet Kidner
Courses: Constructed Textile Design; Embroidery; Fashion Design; Pattern Cutting; Printed Textile Design; Soft Furnishings; and Upholstery.
Course Structure Options: On-site; Daytime; Evenings; Full-Time; Part-Time.
Courses accredited by Edexcel/OCN, with appropriate certification on completion. There is a progression route offered from all courses. NDs require four GCSEs; for HNDs request leaflet.

OXFORD SUMMER SCHOOL
c/o Gable End
Hatford
nr Faringdon
Oxon SN7 8JF
Tel/Fax: 01367 710593
Email: richard@thespeeds.freeserve.co.uk
Website: www.oxfordsummerschool.com
Contact: Richard Speed
Courses: Beads & Jewellery; Beadwork; Book Structures; Calligraphy; Cane Basketry; Ceramics; Creative Embroidery; Creative Textiles; Decorated Surfaces; Drawing; Dyeing & Weaving; Exotic Chandeliers; Felted Knitwear; Feltwork; Furniture Restoration; Handknitting; Machine Embroidery; Moving Toys; Painting; Photography; Portraits; Printmaking; Silver Jewellery; and Stained Glass.
Course Structure Options: All these take place between 25-30 July 2005 at Oxford Community School. Practical workshops from one to six days, 9.30am to 4.30pm with one tutor to 10 students. Certificates available on request.
SPECIAL CWYB READER OFFER - 10% discount. Quote 'Craftworker's Year Book' when applying.

PIE CHAMBERS TEXTILES
33 Sturford Lane
Temple
Corsley
Wilts BA12 7QR
Tel: 01373 832856
Email: pie@tulsi.freeserve.co.uk
Website: www.tulsi.uk.com
Contact: Pie Chambers
Courses: Full and refresher Kilim Weaving courses - also Shibori resist techniques. Workshops in rural India as an integral part of an Indian journey.
Course Structure Options: Daytime; Evenings; Full-Time; Residential.
Completion of full courses could lead to higher qualifications.
SPECIAL CWYB READER OFFER - 10% discount on accommodation costs. Quote offer reference 'Toby' when applying.

QUEENS PARK ART CENTRE
Queens Park
Aylesbury
Bucks HP21 7RT
Tel: 01296 424332
Fax: 01296 337363
Email: qpc@ukonline.co.uk
Website: www.qpc.org
Contact: Louise Griffiths-Kimber
Courses: Embroidery; Lace Making; Life Drawing; Oil Painting; Patchwork; Pottery; Willow & Cane Craft; and Woodwork (recreational courses).
Course Structure Options: Daytime; Evenings; Part-Time.

REASEHEATH COLLEGE
Reaseheath
Nantwich
Cheshire CW5 6DF
Tel: 01270 613242
Email: enquiries@reaseheath.ac.uk
Website: www.reaseheath.ac.uk
Contact: Sue Bone
Courses: Design & Craft Embroidery; Floristry; and Patchwork & Quilting.
Course Structure Options: Daytime; Evenings.
Courses accredited by City & Guilds and Certificate or Diploma awarded for appropriate levels.

THE ROBERT JAMES STUDIO
14 Trent Close
Sompting, Lancing

West Sussex
BN15 0EJ
Tel/Fax: 01903 751592
Email: info@rjamesstudio.co.uk
Website: www.rjamesstudio.co.uk
Contact: Mary or Bob Kershaw
Courses: Sculpture/Modelling/Handbuilding in Clay. For absolute beginners through to intermediate level. Fully hands-on tuition for individuals or small groups (maximum 4). Flexible content tailored to each student's needs. Imaginative projects available for beginners, with tangible results. Follow-on/development sessions arranged as required. Courses include an opportunity for time on the potter's wheel.
Course Structure Options: Daytime; Full-Time; Part-Time. Weekend and weekday availability of courses of 1-5 days' duration, with flexible start/finish times to suit clients' travel arrangements Non-residential, but assistance freely available with locating local B&B or small hotel. Refreshments, light lunch and other items are included. Children must be accompanied by a responsible adult. Clients should be appropriately dressed for working with clay and especially for the wheel. Generous standard discounts apply when booking for more than 1 person and/or more than 1 day.

SEW CREATIVE
Wroxham Barns
Tunstead Road
Hoveton
Norfolk
NR12 8QU
Tel: 01603 781665
Email:
sewcreative@sylvia79.fsbusiness.co.uk
Contact: Sylvia Graham
Courses: Appliqué; Crochet; Patchwork; Quilting; and Rag Rugs.
Course Structure Options: Daytime.

SHIRLEY STEWART'S POTTERY COURSES
140 Lewisham Way
London
SE14 6PD
Tel: 020 8692 2513
Email: shirley.stewart1@ukgateway.net
Website: www.shirley-stewart.co.uk
Contact: Shirley Stewart
Courses: Weekend Throwing and Glazemaking workshops. Evening Studio Ceramic courses. After-school Clay Workshops for children.

SNAIL TRAIL HANDWEAVERS
Penwenallt Farm
Cilgerran
nr Cardigan
Pembrokeshire SA43 2TP
Tel/Fax: 01239 841228
Email: martin@snail-trail.co.uk
Website: www.snail-trail.co.uk
Contact: Martin Weatherhead
Courses: Weaving, Spinning and Dyeing.
Course Structure Options: Daytime; Residential; and Remote/Travelling.
Courses accredited by SWOCAC. Subject to SWOCAC fees, a credit certificate can be issued.

STANTON GUILDHOUSE TRUST
Stanton
Broadway
Worcs
WR12 7NE
Tel: 01386 584357
Fax: 01386 584078
Email: guildhouse@can-online.org.uk
Website: www.stantonguildhouse.org.uk
Contact: Susan Mawson
Courses: Calligraphy; Creative Writing; Furniture Restoration; Patchwork, Quilting & Appliqué; Pottery; Stained Glass & Kiln-Fired Glass; Stone Carving; Watercolour Art; Woodcarving; Woodturning; and Woodwork.
Course Structure Options: On-site; Daytime; Evenings; Part-Time; Residential.

SWANSEA COLLEGE
Llwyn y Bryn Arts Annexe
77 Walters Road
Swansea
SA1 4QA
Tel: 01792 284021
Fax: 01792 645681
Email: p.rochester@swancoll.ac.uk
Website: www.swancoll.ac.uk
Contact: Petrina Rochester
Courses: Access to Art & Design. AS/A Level - Fine Arts, Graphics, 3D, Photography. National Diploma - Fashion, Fine Art, Graphics, Photography. City & Guilds - Ceramics, Dress Making, Interior Design, Photography, Soft Furnishing.
Course Structure Options: On-site; Daytime; Evenings; Full-Time; Part-Time.
Courses accredited by City & Guilds and EdExcel. College offers a range of levels with nationally recognised bodies. All courses are platforms to gain skills to progress in education or employment. All candidates will be interviewed.

THE THRESHING BARN
Lower Lady Meadows Farm
Bradnop
Leek
Staffs ST13 7EZ
Tel: 01538 304494
Email: janet@threshingbarn.com
Website: www.threshingbarn.com
Contact: Janet Thurman
Courses: Cardmaking; Dyeing (natural and synthetic); Feltmaking; Papermaking; Rag Rugs; Soapmaking; Spinning; Weaving; Willow Baskets and Structures etc.
Course Structure Options: On-site; Daytime.
SPECIAL CWYB READER OFFER - 10% off group booking for 6 people or more. Quote offer reference 'CRAFTWORKER'S YEAR BOOK' when applying.

URCHFONT MANOR COLLEGE
Urchfont
Devizes
Wilts SN10 4RG
Tel: 01380 840495
Fax: 01380 840005
Email: urchfontmanor@wiltshire.gov.uk
Contact: Mandy Dixon
Courses: Many Textile Art/Embroidery courses plus Bookbinding; Calligraphy; Cane and Rush Seating; Chairmaking; Dyeing; Lacemaking; Quilting; Silver Jewellery Making; Stained Glass; Weaving; Willow Work; and Wood Engraving.
Course Structure Options: Daytime; Residential; and weekend and week-long short breaks.
A few courses are accredited by City & Guilds so therefore can lead to these recognised qualifications.

WEST DEAN COLLEGE
West Dean
Chichester
West Sussex PO18 0QZ
Tel: 01243 811301
Fax: 01243 818293
Email: enquiries@westdean.org.uk
Website: www.westdean.org.uk
Courses: Art; Basketmaking, Chairseating & Willow Work; Books & Lettering; Decorative Arts; Glass & Mosaics; Metalworking; Photography & Digital Imaging; Pottery & Ceramics; Sculpture; Textiles; and Woodworking & Furniture Making.
Course Structure Options: Short residential courses from weekend up to 9 days. Also one-day, non-residential courses. Work done here can be included in portfolios for accredited courses. Some require entry qualifications/experience. Short course fees set at 75% of their true cost.

WESTHOPE COLLEGE
Westhope
Craven Arms
Shropshire SY7 9JL
Tel: 01584 861293
Website: www.westhope.org.uk
Contact: Anne Dyer
Courses: Non-vocational short courses in a wide range of crafts, plus City & Guilds courses in various textile and other subjects.
Course Structure Options: Daytime; Residential; Correspondence; also weekends.
Some courses accredited by City & Guilds, leading to various Creative Studies Diplomas.

WOMBOURNE SCHOOL OF MILLINERY
Mill Lane Farmhouse
Mill Lane
Wombourne
Staffs WV5 0LE
Tel/Fax: 01902 893683
Email: mail@hatcourses.co.uk
Website: www.hatcourses.co.uk
Contact: Ann Morse-Brown
Courses: Making hats of all kinds by traditional blocking methods. Open courses cover modern, non-traditional work too, according to each student's individual wishes. Also tiara making.
Course Structure Options: On-site; Daytime; Part-Time; Residential; also e-books (www.how2hats.com) on hat making subjects.
After courses, a certificate is presented, signed by tutor and course director. This may be useful on CV as the school is known in the millinery world.

WOOD-SHOP
Lethenty Mill
Inverurie
Aberdeenshire AB51 0HQ
Tel: 01467 622489
Fax: 01467 629631
Email: info@wood-shop.co.uk
Website: www.wood-shop.co.uk
Contact: Allan Fyfe
Courses: Making Wooden Furniture with hand tools from Wood-Shop's own range of

designs; based on the local vernacular.
Course Structure Options: Evenings.
Attendees must be over 18.

WORLD EMBROIDERY WORKSHOPS
2 Woodlands
Kirbymisperton
Malton
North Yorks YO17 6XW
Tel: 01653 668419
Email:
worldembroidery@kirbymisperton.freeserve.co.uk
Contact: Caroline Crabtree
Courses: Appliqué; Beadwork; Dyeing; Feltmaking; Patchwork; Shisha Embroidery; and Wearable Art.
Course Structure Options: Daytime; Part-Time.

ZANTIUM STUDIOS
Godfrey Hole House
Hopton
Wirksworth
Derbys DE4 4DF
Tel/Fax: 01629 824377
Email: studios@zantium.co.uk
Website: www.zantium.co.uk
Contact: Alison Massey
Courses: Beadmaking; Botanical Illustration; Jewellery; Pebble Mosaic; Stained Glass; Tile Mosaic; Watercolour; and Willow Sculpture.
Course Structure Options: Daytime; Residential.

ON-LINE DIRECTORY

Resource Website: www.artcourses.co.uk

Covered here are all types of practical arts and crafts, such as painting, pastels, drawing, sculpture, pottery, textiles, glass, ironworking, basketmaking etc. Find information on dozens of practical art and craft courses via this web directory which covers part-time classes, workshops and holidays in Britain and Europe.

Course providers wishing to apply for a free trial entry should e-mail:
crafts@artcourses.co.uk
See Display Advertisement

Notes ✎

Make sure you get your copy of The Craftworker's Year Book every year, on publication.
Place a Standing Order today and let us do the rest - if you want to pay by cheque then we'll send you an invoice in advance of going to press or, if you prefer to use your VISA or MasterCard, then we'll call you to take details (don't send these in the post).

Give us an e-mail address as well and we can also keep you up to date with improvements and changes.

Please fill in your details below and mail to us at:

WRITE ANGLE PRESS, Standing Orders, 16 Holm Oak Drive, Madeley, Crewe CW3 9HR

NAME: ______________________________

COMPANY/ORGANISATION: ______________________________

ADDRESS: ______________________________

____

______________________________ POSTCODE: ______________

E-MAIL: ______________________________

VAT NUMBER (NON-UK BUYERS IN EU ONLY) ______________________________

I would like to set up a Standing Order for The Craftworker's Year Book, commencing with the 2006 edition.

I require STANDARD POSTAGE ☐ FIRST CLASS ☐ AIRMAIL ☐

I wish to pay by cheque on invoice ☐

I want you to call me so that I can pay by VISA/MasterCard ☐

Signed: ______________________________

Date: ______________________________

I am interested in stocking this title as a retailer - please send me details ☐

YOU CAN ALSO E-MAIL THE RELEVANT PARTS OF THIS FORM TO US AT:
charles.wallin@btclick.com

PUT 'STANDING ORDERS' IN THE SUBJECT LINE OF YOUR MESSAGE. THANKS.

DIRECTORY OF PUBLICATIONS

Details are given below on a range of specialist publications covering the field of crafts and arts. Please note that in this directory we generally give the subscription address, which in some cases is different from that of the editorial office. If you have an editorial enquiry, therefore, it is best to send an email or fax and direct it clearly to the editorial staff. Quite a few of the publishers listed have very kindly agreed to issue CWYB readers with a free sample copy for appraisal (subject to limited stocks). In addition, some have put together special subscription offers for you; do read all the entries and the adverts and do make sure you always quote the unique reference when writing to take advantage of discounts and offers. Finally, if you find that your favourite craft magazine is not included in this directory, do give us their details or get them to contact us in good time for free listing in the 2006 edition.

12 x 12 SCRAPBOOKING MAGAZINE
Magmaker Ltd
Cromwell Court
New Road
St Ives
Cambs PE27 5BF
Tel: 01480 496130
Fax: 01480 495514
Email: info@magmaker.com
Schedule: Monthly, published in true 12 x 12 square format.
Every edition contains a section of unique lignin/acid-free background/Cutting sheets worth £4.
Sample copies available at £4.95.

A-N MAGAZINE
Subscriptions Dept, First Floor
7-15 Pink Lane
Newcastle upon Tyne
Tyne & Wear NE1 5DW
Tel: 0191 241 8000
Fax: 0191 241 8001
Email: subs@a-n.co.uk
Website: www.a-n.co.uk
Schedule: Monthly
Available by mail order and via a wide range of galleries, bookshops and newsagents.
Price: Single copy £4.25. Annual order £28 for UK Artists (£25 if direct debit), £35 for Europe Artists, £48 for Rest of World Artists and £50 for all other individuals and organisations (£47 if by direct debit).
Free sample copy available to CWYB readers

ARTISTS & ILLUSTRATORS
A&I Subscription Department
Freepost KE8338
Leicester LE87 4AF
Tel: 01858 435307
Email: benl@quarto.com
Schedule: Monthly
Available via newsagent and direct by mail order. Price: Single copy £2.80. Annual order (mailed by A&I) £25. Annual order (newsagent) £33.60.
Free sample copy available to CWYB readers. This is a strictly limited offer
See also display advertisement.

ART OF ENGLAND
Masterclass Publications
Airedale Lodge
Stafford Road
Eccleshall
Staffs ST21 6JP
Tel: 01785 851660
Fax: 01785 850173
Email: info@artofengland.com
Website: www.artofengland.com
Schedule: Bi-monthly
Available from art supply shops, public and private galleries and direct by annual order.
Price: Single copy £2.60. Annual order £15.
Free sample back copy available to CWYB readers. This is a strictly limited offer
See also display advertisement.

BLACK & WHITE PHOTOGRAPHY
GMC Publications
166 High Street
Lewes
East Sussex BN7 1XU
Tel: 01273 488005
Fax: 01273 402866
Email: ailsam@thegmcgroup.com
Website: www.gmcpubs.com
Schedule: Monthly
Available via newsagent and direct by mail order. Price: Single copy £3.45. Annual order (mailed) £37.25 or £31 if paid by direct debit. £41.40 via newsagents.

CAKE CRAFT & DECORATION
Subscriptions Department
Tower House
Sovereign Park
Market Harborough
Leics
LE16 9EF
Tel: 01858 439605
Email: cake@subscription.co.uk
Website: www.cake-craft.com
Schedule: Monthly
Available via newsagent or direct by mail order. Price: Single copy £3.40. Annual order (mailed) £40.80 for UK, £53.50 for Europe (airmail) and £69.50 for Rest of World (airmail).
See also display advertisement.

CAKES & SUGARCRAFT
Squires Kitchen Magazine Publishing Ltd
Squires House
3 Waverley Lane
Farnham
Surrey
GU9 8BB
Tel: 0845 22 55 671/2
Fax: 0845 22 55 673
Email: orderinfo@squires-group.co.uk
Website: www.squires-group.co.uk
Schedule: Quarterly
Available via WH Smith retail chains, supermarkets and independent newsagents, direct by mail order and also from sugarcraft shops. Back copies also available. See website.
Price: Annual order (mailed by Squires) £19.96 for UK, £28 for Europe and £34 for Rest of World.
See also display advertisement.

CARDMAKING & PAPERCRAFT
Origin Publishing Ltd
14th Floor, Tower House
Bristol
BS1 3BN
Tel: 0117 927 9009 or 01858 438822
Fax: 0117 934 9008
Website:
www.cardmakingandpapercraft.co.uk/subscribe_Index.asp
Schedule: Monthly (plus one special)
Available via newsagents, supermarkets, craft shops and subscription.
Price: Single copy £3.35.
See also display advertisement.

CERAMIC REVIEW
Ceramic Review Publishing Ltd
25 Foubert's Place
London W1F 7QF
Tel: 020 7439 3377
Fax: 020 7287 9954
Email: subscriptions@ceramicreview.com
Website: www.ceramicreview.com
Schedule: Bi-monthly
Price: Single copy £7.50 (inc UK p+p). Annual UK order (mailed) £36. With CPA membership, £32 annually. Student discount price £32.
*** SPECIAL OFFER – one free copy for all NEW subscribers ***

CERAMICS IRELAND
Journal of the Craft Potters Society of Ireland
Araglin
Old Connaught Avenue
Bray
Co Wicklow
Republic of Ireland
Tel: 00 353 1 282 0963
Email: ceramicsireland@yahoo.com
Website: www.ceramicsireland.org
Schedule: Bi-annual (Spring/Summer and Autumn/Winter)
Price: Single copy €4.50 or £3.50. Free to Society members (see last part of Representative Bodies section).
See also display advertisement.

CRAFT BUSINESS
Aceville Publications Ltd
Castle House
97 High Street
Colchester
Essex CO1 1TH
Tel: 01206 505940
Fax: 01206 505945
Email: craftbusiness@aceville.co.uk
Website: www.craftbusiness.com
Schedule: Bi-monthly
Free to confirmed businesses.

CRAFT CREATIONS MAGAZINE
Craft Creations Ltd
Ingersoll House
Delamare Road
Cheshunt
Herts EN8 9HD
Tel: 01992 781900
Fax: 01992 634339
Email: enquiries@craftcreations.com
Website: www.craftcreations.com *(cont p.300)*

Schedule: Quarterly (Spring etc)
Available by mail order. Price: Annual order (mailed) £12 for UK, £16 for Europe, £21 for Rest of World. Single back issues priced at £3 for UK, £4 for Europe and £5.25 for Rest of World. All prices subject to occasional revision. Back issues subject to availability. This is a craft magazine dedicated to making greetings cards.

CRAFT GALLERIES GUIDE
BCF Books
Burton Cottage Farm
East Coker
Yeovil
Somerset BA22 9LS
Tel: 01935 862731
Email: cm@craftgalleries.co.uk
Website: www.bcfbooks.co.uk
Schedule: Biennial; 7th edition (December 2003), 8th edition in Dec 2005.
Available via bookshops and direct by mail order. Normal price £16 plus £4 p&p.
SPECIAL CWYB READER OFFER – £15 fully inclusive; cheques payable to 'Craft Galleries'. Quote reference 'CYB'.

CRAFTS BEAUTIFUL
Aceville Publications Ltd
Castle House
97 High Street
Colchester
Essex CO1 1TH
Tel: 01206 505940
Fax: 01206 505945
Email: martin.lack@aceville.co.uk
Website: www.crafts-beautiful.com
Schedule: Monthly
Annual order (mailed) £37.20 for UK, £57.95 for Europe, £59.95 for USA and £69.95 for Rest of World.

CRAFTS MAGAZINE
Crafts Council
44a Pentonville Road
London N1 9BY
Tel: 020 7806 2542
Fax: 020 7837 0858
Email: crafts@craftscouncil.org.uk
Website: www.craftscouncil.org.uk
Schedule: Bi-monthly
Available via newsagent and direct by mail order. Price: Single copy £5.50. Annual order (mailed) UK/Eire £29, Europe £37, USA $59, Rest of World £44 for individual subscribers (higher rates for institutions and businesses). Special Student rates – UK/Eire £25, Europe £34, USA $53, Rest of World £38 (photocopy of student ID required). Subscriber offers and competitions in every issue, plus regular special discounts.
See also display advertisement.

CRAFTSMAN MAGAZINE
PSB Design & Print Consultants Ltd
PO Box 5
Driffield
East Yorks YO25 8JD
Tel: 01377 255213
Fax: 01377 255730
Email: sales@craftsman-magazine.com
Website: www.craftsman-magazine.com
Schedule: Monthly
Available via newsagent, direct by mail order and at selected craft fairs and craft centres. Price: Single copy £2.95. Annual order (mailed) £29.50. Annual order (via newsagent) £35.40. Six month subscription (mailed) also available at £17.70.
Free sample copy available to CWYB readers
See also display advertisement.

CRAFT STAMPER
Traplet Publications Ltd
Traplet House
Pendragon Close
Malvern
Worcs WR14 1GA
Tel: 01684 588500
Fax: 01684 578558
Email: customerservice@traplet.com
Website: www.traplet.com
Schedule: Monthly
Available via newsagent and direct by mail order. Price: Single copy £3.50. Annual order (mailed) £37.80 (correct at time of going to press but may be subject to change).
See also display advertisement.

CREATIVE CARDMAKING IDEAS
Quarto Subscription Department
Freepost KE8338
Leicester LE87 4AF
Tel: 01858 435307
Email: benl@quarto.com
Schedule: Monthly
Available via newsagent and direct by mail order. Price: Single copy £2.99. Annual

order (mailed by Quarto) £30. Annual order (newsagent) £35.88.
Free sample copy available to CWYB readers. This is a strictly limited offer
See also display advertisement.

CREATIVE SCRAPBOOKING
Quarto Subscription Department
Freepost KE8338
Leicester LE87 4AF
Tel: 01858 435307
Email: benl@quarto.com
Schedule: Monthly
Available via newsagent and direct by mail order. Price: Single copy £2.95. Annual order (mailed by Quarto) £30. Annual order (newsagent) £35.40.
Free sample copy available to CWYB readers. This is a strictly limited offer

CROSS STITCH COLLECTION
Freepost BS4900
Somerton
Somerset TA11 6BR
Tel: 0870 444 8670
Email: living.subs@futurenet.co.uk
Website: www.futurenet.com
Schedule: 13 issues per year
Available via newsagent and by subscription. Price: Single copy £4.99. Annual order (mailed) £41.50.
SPECIAL CWYB READER OFFER – 20% discount on shop price. Quote reference 'CW2005'.

CROSS STITCHER
Freepost BS4900
Somerton
Somerset TA11 6BR
Tel: 0870 444 8459
Email: living.subs@futurenet.co.uk
Website: www.futurenet.com
Schedule: 13 issues per year
Available via newsagent and by subscription. Price: Single copy £3.35. Annual order (mailed) £32.
SPECIAL CWYB READER OFFER – 27% discount on shop price. Quote reference 'CW2005'.

CROSS STITCH GALLERY
Creative Crafts Publishing Ltd
Well Oast
Brenley Lane
Faversham
Kent ME13 9LY
Tel: 01227 750215
Fax: 01227 750813
Email: enquiries@ccpuk.co.uk
Schedule: Bi-monthly
Available via newsagent and direct by mail order. Price: Single copy £3.99. Annual order (mailed) £23.94 with free gift. Annual order (via newsagent) £23.94.
Free sample copy available to CWYB readers
See also display advertisement.

DOLLS HOUSE MAGAZINE
GMC Publications
166 High Street
Lewes
East Sussex BN7 1XU
Tel: 01273 488005
Fax: 01273 402866
Email: christianeb@thegmcgroup.com
Website: www.gmcpubs.com
Schedule: Monthly
Available via newsagent and direct by mail order. Price: Single copy £3.45. Annual order (mailed) £37.25 or £31 if paid by direct debit. £41.40 via newsagents.

EMBROIDERY
EG Enterprises Ltd
PO Box 42B
East Molesey
Surrey KT8 9BB
Tel: 020 8943 1229 Extn 28
Fax: 020 8977 9882
Email: jjardine@embroiderersguild.com
Website: www.embroiderersguild.com/embroidery/
Schedule: Bi-monthly
Available mainly direct by mail order. Price: Single copy £4.90. Annual subscription (mailed) UK £29.40, Europe £36, The Americas £42.30, Rest of World £43.50.
See also display advertisement

ENGINEERING IN MINIATURE
EIM Publishing
The Fosse, Fosse Way
Leamington Spa
Warks CV31 1XN
Tel: 01926 614101
Fax: 01926 614293
Email: info@engineeringinminiature.co.uk
Website: www.engineeringinminiature.co.uk
Schedule: Monthly
Available via newsagent and direct by mail

(cont p.304)

order. Price: Single copy £2.45. Annual order (mailed) £29.40 for UK, £39.60 for Europe, £39 for Canada/USA Airspeed, £41.40 for Rest of World Airspeed.

FURNITURE & CABINETMAKING
GMC Publications
166 High Street
Lewes
East Sussex BN7 1XU
Tel: 01273 488005
Fax: 01273 402866
Email: coline@thegmcgroup.com
Website: www.gmcpubs.com
Schedule: Monthly
Available via newsagent and direct by mail order. Price: Single copy £3.45. Annual order (mailed) £37.25 or £31 if paid by direct debit. £41.40 via newsagents.

GOOD WOODWORKING
Freepost BS4900
Somerton
Somerset
TA11 6BR
Tel: 0870 444 8472
Email: living.subs@futurenet.co.uk
Website: www.futurenet.com
Schedule: 13 issues per year
Available via newsagent and by subscription. Price: Single copy £3.20. Annual order (mailed) £28.99.
SPECIAL CWYB READER OFFER – 30% discount on shop price. Quote reference 'CW2005'.

HOROLOGICAL JOURNAL
British Horological Institute
Upton Hall, Upton
Newark
Notts NG23 5TE
Tel: 01636 817603
Fax: 01636 812258
Email: clocks@bhi.co.uk
Website: www.bhi.co.uk
Schedule: Monthly
Available by mail order only. Priced at between £48 and £95 (annual order mailed).
Some limited free sample copies available to CWYB readers

IMAGE MAGAZINE
Association of Photographers
81 Leonard Street
London
EC2A 4QS
Tel: 020 7739 6669
Fax: 020 7739 8707
Email: image@aophoto.co.uk
Website: www.the-aop.org
Schedule: Monthly
Free to all AOP members. Otherwise available from AOP at annual price of £24 (UK) or £36 (non-UK).

JANE GREENOFF'S CROSS STITCH
Freepost BS4900
Somerton
Somerset
TA11 6BR
Tel: 0870 444 8479
Email: living.subs@futurenet.co.uk
Website: www.futurenet.com
Schedule: 7 issues per year
Available via newsagent and by subscription. Price: Single copy £3.99. Annual order (mailed) £19.99.
SPECIAL CWYB READER OFFER – 28% discount on shop price. Quote reference 'CW2005'.

KNITTING
GMC Publications
166 High Street
Lewes
East Sussex
BN7 1XU
Tel: 01273 488005
Fax: 01273 402866
Email: katet@thegmcgroup.com
Website: www.gmcpubs.com
Schedule: Monthly
Available via newsagent and direct by mail order. Price: Single copy £3.45. Annual order (mailed) £37.25 or £31 if paid by direct debit. £41.40 via newsagents.

MACHINE KNITTING MONTHLY
RPA Publishing Ltd
PO Box 1479
Maidenhead
Berks
SL6 8YX
Tel: 01628 783080
Fax: 01628 633250
Email: rpa@surf3.net
Website: www.machineknittingmonthly.co.uk
Schedule: Monthly
Available via newsagent and direct by mail order. Price: Single copy £2.75. Annual order (mailed or via newsagent) £33. Six issues available for £17.00. Annual sub-

scription Europe £42 and for Rest of World £55.
Free sample copy available to CWYB readers
SPECIAL CWYB READER OFFER – £4 off annual subscription price. Quote reference 'Craftworker's Year Book'.
See also display advertisement.

MAKERS NEWS
Resource Centre
Crafts Council
44a Pentonville Road
London N1 9BY
Tel: 020 7806 2501
Fax: 020 7833 4479
Email: reference@craftscouncil.org.uk
Website: www.craftscouncil.org.uk
Schedule: Bi-annual (April/October)
Available direct from Crafts Council only. This is the Crafts Council's business and professional development newsletter for contemporary crafts people. It is distributed free to all the 4,500 makers who are on the National Register of Makers as well as to craft guilds and societies, all Arts Council England offices and other relevant organisations.

MAKING CARDS
Magmaker Ltd
Cromwell Court
New Road
St Ives
Cambs PE27 5BF
Tel: 01480 496130
Fax: 01480 495514
Email: info@makingcardsmagazine.com
Schedule: Monthly
Available by direct subscription and from selected craft shops. Price: Single copy £3.25. Annual order (mailed) £39. Half-year available at £19.50.
*** SPECIAL OFFER SUB – 12 issues for £36 – save £3 ***

NEEDLE & HOBBY CRAFTS
Bates Business Centre
Church Road
Harold Wood
Romford
Essex
RM3 0JF
Tel: 01708 379897
Fax: 01708 379804
Email: editorial@hobbycrafts.net
Website: www.hobbycrafts.net
Schedule: Bi-monthly
Available direct by mail order only. Price: Annual order (mailed) £20.
Free sample copy available to CWYB readers

NEW STITCHES
Creative Crafts Publishing Ltd
Well Oast
Brenley Lane
Faversham
Kent ME13 9LY
Tel: 01227 750215
Fax: 01227 750813
Email: enquiries@ccpuk.co.uk
Website: www.newstitches.com
Schedule: Monthly
Available via newsagent and direct by mail order. Price: Single copy £3.75. Annual order (mailed) £39.95 with free gift. Annual order (via newsagent) £45.
Free sample copy available to CWYB readers. Offer while stocks last
See also display advertisement.

NEW WOODWORKING
GMC Publications
166 High Street
Lewes
East Sussex
BN7 1XU
Tel: 01273 488005
Fax: 01273 402866
Email: markc@thegmcgroup.com
Website: www.gmcpubs.com
Schedule: Monthly
Available via newsagent and direct by mail order. Price: Single copy £2.75. Annual order (mailed) £29.65 or £24.75 if paid by direct debit. £33 via newsagents.

OUTDOOR PHOTOGRAPHY
GMC Publications
166 High Street
Lewes
East Sussex
BN7 1XU
Tel: 01273 488005
Fax: 01273 402866
Email: keithw@thegmcgroup.com
Website: www.gmcpubs.com
Schedule: Monthly
Available via newsagent and direct by mail order. Price: Single copy £3.25. Annual

order (mailed) £35 or £29.25 if paid by direct debit. £39 via newsagents.

PAPERCRAFT INSPIRATIONS
Freepost BS4900
Somerton
Somerset TA11 6BR
Tel: 0870 220 6165
Email: living.subs@futurenet.co.uk
Website: www.futurenet.com
Schedule: 13 issues per year
Available via newsagent and by subscription. Price: Single copy £3.35. Annual order (mailed) £32.
SPECIAL CWYB READER OFFER – 27% discount on shop price. Quote reference 'CW2005'.

PARCHMENT CRAFT
Magmaker Ltd
Cromwell Court
New Road
St Ives
Cambs PE27 5BF
Tel: 01480 496130
Fax: 01480 495514
Email: info@parchmentcraftmagazine.com
Schedule: Monthly
Available by direct subscription and from selected craft shops. Price: Single copy £2.95. Annual order (mailed) £35.40. Half-year available for £17.70.
*** SPECIAL OFFER SUB – 12 issues for £33 – save £2.40 ***

PATCHWORK & QUILTING
Traplet Publications Ltd
Traplet House
Pendragon Close
Malvern
Worcs WR14 1GA
Tel: 01684 588500
Fax: 01684 578558
Email: customerservice@traplet.com
Website: www.traplet.com
Schedule: Monthly
Available via newsagent and direct by mail order. Price: Single copy £3.20. Annual order (mailed) £34.20 (correct at time of going to press but may be subject to change).
See also display advertisement.

PRACTICAL CRAFTS
Traplet Publications Ltd
Traplet House
Pendragon Close
Malvern
Worcs WR14 1GA
Tel: 01684 588500
Fax: 01684 578558
Email: customerservice@traplet.com
Website: www.traplet.com
Schedule: Monthly
Available via newsagent and direct by mail order. Price: Single copy £2.95. Annual order (mailed) £31.85 (correct at time of going to press but may be subject to change).
See also display advertisement.

PRACTICAL WOODWORKING
Highbury Leisure
Berwick House
8-10 Knoll Rise
Orpington
Kent BR6 0PS
Tel: 01689 899200
Credit Card Hotline: 01353 654429
Email:
practicalwoodworking@getwoodworking.com
Website: www.hhc.co.uk/practicalwood
Schedule: Monthly
Annual subscription available on www.nexusonline.com/pages/nexusdirect.cgi for £30.70.

QUICK & EASY CRAFTS
Aceville Publications Ltd
Castle House
97 High Street
Colchester
Essex CO1 1TH
Tel: 01206 505940
Fax: 01206 505945
Email: martin.lack@aceville.co.uk
Website: www.quickandeasycrafts.co.uk
Schedule: 13 issues per year
Annual order (mailed) £38.50 for UK, £59.95 for Europe, £65.95 for USA and £69.95 for Rest of World.

QUICK & EASY CROSS STITCH
Freepost BS4900
Somerton
Somerset TA11 6BR
Tel: 0870 444 8670
Email: living.subs@futurenet.co.uk
Website: www.futurenet.com
Schedule: 13 issues per year
Available via newsagent and by subscription.

Price: Single copy £3.35. Annual order (mailed) £32.
SPECIAL CWYB READER OFFER – 27% discount on shop price. Quote reference 'CW2005'.

QUICK CARDS MADE EASY
Origin Publishing Ltd
14th Floor, Tower House
Bristol
BS1 3BN
Tel: 0117 927 9009 or 01858 438822
Fax: 0117 934 9008
Website:
www.cardmakingandpapercraft.co.uk/subscribe_Index.asp
Schedule: Monthly (plus one special)
Available via newsagents, supermarkets, craft shops and subscription.
Price: Single copy £3.35.
See also display advertisement.s

THE ROUTER
GMC Publications
166 High Street
Lewes
East Sussex BN7 1XU
Tel: 01273 488005
Fax: 01273 402866
Email: slawson@thegmcgroup.com
Website: www.gmcpubs.com
Schedule: Bi-monthly
Available via newsagent and direct by mail order. Price: Single copy £3.25. Annual order (mailed) £17.50 or £14.60 if paid by direct debit. £19.50 via newsagents.

ROUTING
Highbury Leisure
Berwick House, 8-10 Knoll Rise
Orpington
Kent BR6 0PS
Tel: 01689 899200
Credit Card Hotline: 01353 654429
Email: routing@getwoodworking.com
Website: www.hhc.co.uk/routing
Schedule: Bi-monthly
Annual subscription available on www.nexusonline.com/pages/nexusdirect.cgi for £15.80.

SCRAPBOOK CRAFT
Dalesway Print & Promotions
The Royal Oak Yard
Raikes Road
Skipton
North Yorks BD23 1NP
Tel: 0845 456 1631
Fax: 01756 797003
Email: editor@scrapbookcraft.co.uk
Website: www.scrapbookcraft.co.uk
Schedule: Bi-monthly
Available by mail order and from selected craft outlets. Single copy £2.95. Annual order (mailed) £18.
Subscribe for one year and get free extra copy.
See also display advertisement.

SECOND STEPS
BCF Books
Burton Cottage Farm
East Coker
Yeovil
Somerset BA22 9LS
Tel: 01935 862731
Email: cm@craftgalleries.co.uk
Website: www.bcfbooks.co.uk
Schedule: Biennial; 3rd edition (March 2003) is current edition.
A one-stop resource book for new makers in the craft world, covering CVs to business plans. Illustrated with case studies by gallery owners, makers and tutors. Includes a comprehensive list of addresses, contacts and book titles for reference. Normal price £8 (inc p&p).
SPECIAL CWYB READER OFFER – £6.50 fully inclusive; cheques payable to 'Craft Galleries'. Quote reference 'CYB'.
See also display advertisement.

SECOND STEPS PORTFOLIO 2
A new publication from BCF Books (details as previous entry) promoting the work of new makers not yet showing regularly with galleries. They each get a minimum of a page to promote themselves with photo and text plus contact details. The book is given free to gallery owners. Otherwise the cost is £5 (inclusive). NOTE: Makers interested in an entry will receive 5% off entry fee by quoting 'CYB'.
See also display advertisement.

SEW BRIDAL
Butterick Company Ltd
New Lane
Havant
Hants PO9 2ND
Tel: 0870 777 9966

Fax: 023 9249 2769
Email: retail@butterick-vogue.co.uk
Website: www.sewbridal.com
Schedule: Annual
Available via newsagent, by direct subscription and from fabric shops. Price: £3.95.

SEWING WORLD
Traplet Publications Ltd
Traplet House, Pendragon Close
Malvern
Worcs
WR14 1GA
Tel: 01684 588500
Fax: 01684 578558
Email: customerservice@traplet.com
Website: www.traplet.com
Schedule: Monthly
Available via newsagent and direct by mail order. Price: Single copy £3.25. Annual order (mailed) £35.10 (correct at time of going to press but may be subject to change).
See also display advertisement.

SEW TODAY
Butterick Company Ltd
New Lane
Havant
Hants PO9 2ND
Tel: 0870 777 9966
Fax: 023 9249 2769
Email: retail@butterick-vogue.co.uk
Website: www.sewdirect.com
Schedule: 10 issues per year
Available via newsagent, by direct subscription and from fabric shops. Price: Single copy £3.25. Subscription promotion rates shown in magazine.
See also display advertisement.

THE SHOWMAN'S DIRECTORY
Lance Publications
Park House
Park Road
Petersfield
Hants GU32 3DL
Tel: 01730 266624
Fax: 01730 260117
Email: info@showmans-directory.co.uk
Website: www.showmans-directory.co.uk
Price: £24.50. The professional outdoor event services directory. An annual definitive guide to town, county, country, agricultural, air, steam and horse shows. Over 1,300 organisers of outdoor events listed. Also directory of breeds and other societies.
See also display advertisement.

THE SHUTTLE
Kennet Valley Guild of WS&D
71 Maple Crescent
Newbury
Berks RG14 1LP
Tel: 01635 43846
Email: albert.moss@virgin.net
Schedule: Quarterly
Available by mail order only. Free to guild members.
Free sample copy available to CWYB readers (send 1st class stamp)

SLIPKNOT
Knitting & Crochet Guild
108 Park Lane
Kidderminster
Worcs DY11 6TB
Tel: 01562 754367 (after 5pm)
Email: guild@blueyonder.co.uk
Website:
www.knitting-and-crochet-guild.org.uk
Schedule: Quarterly
Normally just distributed free to members of the Guild (only), the organisation for all hand knitters, machine knitters and crocheters.
Free sample copy available to CWYB readers

STEAM HERITAGE GUIDE
TEE Publishing Ltd
The Fosse
Fosse Way
Leamington Spa
Warks CV31 1XN
Tel: 01926 614101
Fax: 01926 614293
Email: info@teepublishing.com
Website: www.teepublishing.com
Schedule: Annual
Available via newsagent and direct by mail order. Price: £3.95.

STITCH WITH THE EMBROIDERERS' GUILD
EG Enterprises Ltd
PO Box 42B
East Molesey
Surrey KT8 9BB
Tel: 020 8943 1229 Extn 35
Fax: 020 8977 9882
Email: jjardine@embroiderersguild.com

Website:
www.embroiderersguild.com/embroidery/
Schedule: Bi-monthly
Available mainly direct by mail order. Price: Single copy £3.85. Annual subscription (mailed) UK £23.10, Europe £27.60, The Americas £34.20, Rest of World £36.
See also display advertisement

THE TEXTILE DIRECTORY
The Textile Directory Ltd
107 High Street
Evesham
Worcs WR11 4EB
Tel: 0870 220 2820
Fax: 01386 760401
Email: sales@thetextiledirectory.com
Website: www.thetextiledirectory.com
Schedule: Annual
Available by mail order, from www.amazon.co.uk or from good bookshops. Cover price £9.99. The fully searchable and frequently updated website is now a free to access service. The book has over 1,500 listings. A very useful directory.
See also display advertisement.

TRADITIONAL WOODWORKING
Waterways World Ltd
151 Station Street
Burton-on-Trent
Staffs
DE14 1BG
Tel: 01283 742950
Fax: 01283 742958
Email: subscriptions@twonline.co.uk
Schedule: Monthly
Available direct by mail order and via newsagents. Price: Single copy £2.95. Annual order (mailed) £34.20.
See also display advertisement.

WOODCARVING
GMC Publications
166 High Street
Lewes
East Sussex
BN7 1XU
Tel: 01273 488005
Fax: 01273 402866
Email: slawson@thegmcgroup.com
Website: www.gmcpubs.com
Schedule: Bi-monthly
Available via newsagent and direct by mail order. Price: Single copy £3.45. Annual order (mailed) £18.50 or £15.50 if paid by direct debit. £20.70 via newsagents.

WOODTURNING
GMC Publications
166 High Street
Lewes
East Sussex
BN7 1XU
Tel: 01273 488005
Fax: 01273 402866
Email: gmcwt@aol.com
Website: www.gmcpubs.com
Schedule: Monthly
Available via newsagent and direct by mail order. Price: Single copy £3.45. Annual order (mailed) £37.25 or £31 if paid by direct debit. £41.40 via newsagents.

THE WOODWORKER
Highbury Leisure
Berwick House
8-10 Knoll Rise
Orpington
Kent
BR6 0PS
Tel: 01689 899200
Credit Card Hotline: 01353 654429
Email: woodworker@getwoodworking.com
Website: www.hhc.co.uk/woodworker
Schedule: Monthly
Annual subscription available on www.nexusonline.com/pages/nexusdirect.cgi for £30.70.

WORKBOX NEEDLECRAFTS MAGAZINE
Ebony Media Ltd
PO Box 25
Liskeard
Cornwall
PL14 6XX
Tel: 01579 340100
Fax: 01579 340400
Email: workbox@ebony.co.uk
Website: www.ebony.co.uk/workbox/
Schedule: Bi-monthly
Available direct by mail order. Price: Single copy £2.75. Annual order (mailed) £14. Two years (mailed) £27.

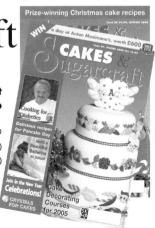